A POETICS OF
POSTMODERNISM

A POETICS OF POSTMODERNISM

HISTORY, THEORY
FICTION

LINDA HUTCHEON

New York and London

First published 1988
by Routledge
11 New Fetter Lane, London EC4P 4EE

Simultaneously published in the USA and Canada
by Routledge
29 West 35th Street, New York, NY 10001

Reprinted 1989, 1990, 1991, 1992, 1995, 1996, 1999

Routledge is an imprint of the Taylor & Francis Group

© 1988 Linda Hutcheon

Printed and bound in Great Britain by the University Printing House, Cambridge

British Library Cataloguing in Publication Data
A catalogue record for this book is available from the British Library

Library of Congress Cataloguing in Publication Data
A catalogue record for this book is available from the Library of Congress

ISBN 0-415-00705-4 (hbk)   ISBN 0-415-00706-2 (pbk)

CONTENTS

Acknowledgements   vii

Preface   ix

PART I

1 Theorizing the postmodern: toward a poetics   3

2 Modelling the postmodern: parody and politics   22

3 Limiting the postmodern: the paradoxical aftermath of modernism   37

4 Decentering the postmodern: the ex-centric   57

5 Contextualizing the postmodern: enunciation and the revenge
  of "parole"   74

6 Historicizing the postmodern: the problematizing of history   87

PART II

7 Historiographic metafiction: "the pastime of past time"   105

8 Intertextuality, parody, and the discourses of history   124

9 The problem of reference   141

10 Subject in/of/to history and his story   158

11 Discourse, power, ideology: humanism and postmodernism   178

12 Political double-talk   201

13 Conclusion: a poetics or a problematics?   222

   Bibliography   232

   Index   259

ACKNOWLEDGEMENTS

No text is without its intertexts, we have been taught. This one is no exception. The finely honed readings of postmodern texts by two colleagues in particular deserve mention right at the start: those of Alison Lee and Janet Paterson. Not only have they offered worthy examples to follow but also both have been provocative critics of various parts of this book. So too has been Graham Knight, the most critical and acute reader one could ever wish for. For listening to or reading parts of this study, or for just tossing ideas around with me, I would particularly like to thank Catherine Belsey, Aruna Srivastava, Susan Bennett, Magdalene Redekop, and Pamela McCallum. I owe much as well to the members of three graduate classes at McMaster University and the University of Toronto, for they were the guinea pigs upon which these ideas were tested – and the stimulus for their (sometimes total) rethinking.

Over the last few years, a number of university audiences have heard parts of the research that went into this study. I would like to thank those institutions for inviting me to speak and for giving me the chance to work out my ideas in a public forum: Columbia University, Queen's University, University of Toronto, University of Calgary, University of Alberta, Catholic University of America, University of Saskatchewan, University of Ottawa, Concordia University, York University, McGill University, Université de Montréal, University of Western Ontario. Similarly I would like to thank the professional associations whose conferences also gave an occasion for trying out new ideas on new audiences: the Modern Language Association (and Northeastern MLA), Royal Society of Canada, Association of Canadian University Teachers of English, Association for Canadian and Quebec Literatures, Canadian Comparative Literature Association, American Comparative Literature Association, Canadian Philosophy Association (Society for Hermeneutics and Postmodern Thought), and the International Association for Philosophy and Literature.

Similarly parts of this book have appeared in shorter and earlier versions (often with quite different foci) in various journals (*Textual Practice, Cultural Critique, Diacritics, Genre, English Studies in Canada*) and in essay collections (*Gender and Theory: A Dialogue between the Sexes* [ed. L. Kauffman], *Intertextuality and Contemporary American Fiction* [ed. P. O'Donnell and R. Con Davis], *Future Indicative: Canadian Literature and Literary Theory* [ed. J. Moss]). To the editors' interest in and support of work in progress I am greatly indebted.

Perhaps the greatest intertextual framework of this study, though, is that of all the current debates on the nature and definition of the postmodern. Though this book would have been finished a lot earlier without them, I can only be grateful that I had such wonderful minds to think both with and against. My particular debts to each will be clear from references in the text, but I would like to single out the ones who most stimulated me and helped me formulate my own notions: Andreas Huyssen, Teresa de Lauretis, Arthur Kroker, Alan Wilde, Charles Russell, Charles Newman, Brian McHale, Fredric Jameson, Terry Eagleton, and especially those theorist-practitioners: Martha Rosler, Paolo Portoghesi, Charles Jencks, and Victor Burgin, to mention only a few.

Three particular thanks must end this list. One is to an institution – the Canada Council – whose Killam Research Fellowship gave me the time and the financial support needed to write this book. The second is to Methuen and especially to Janice Price, for having confidence in my work and being so supportive of it. And the last is, as always, to my spouse, Michael, for his constant encouragement, unfailing good humor, fine critical sense, and amazing patience in putting up with my postmodern obsessions.

Linda Hutcheon
Toronto 1987

PREFACE

What will no longer do is either to eulogize or to ridicule
postmodernism *en bloc*. The postmodern must be salvaged from its
champions and from its detractors.   *Andreas Huyssen*

This study is neither a defense nor yet another denigration of the cultural
enterprise we seem determined to call postmodernism. You will not find
here any claims of radical revolutionary change or any apocalyptic wailing
about the decline of the west under late capitalism. Rather than either
eulogize or ridicule, what I have tried to do is study a current cultural
phenomenon that exists, has attracted much public debate, and so deserves
critical attention. Based on the notion that any theorizing must derive from
that which it purports to study, my focus here is on those points of
significant overlap of theory with aesthetic practice which might guide us to
articulate what I want to call a "poetics" of postmodernism, a flexible
conceptual structure which could at once constitute and contain postmodern culture and our discourses both about it and adjacent to it. The
points of overlap that seem most evident to me are those of the paradoxes set
up when modernist aesthetic autonomy and self-reflexivity come up against
a counterforce in the form of a grounding in the historical, social, and
political world. The model I have used is that of postmodern architecture, as
theorized by Paolo Portoghesi and Charles Jencks and as actualized by
Ricardo Bofill, Aldo Rossi, Robert Stern, Charles Moore, and others. By
analogy, what would characterize postmodernism in fiction would be what I
here call "historiographic metafiction," those popular paradoxical works
like García Márquez's *One Hundred Years of Solitude*, Grass's *The Tin Drum*,
Fowles's *A Maggot*, Doctorow's *Loon Lake*, Reed's *The Terrible Twos*,
Kingston's *The Woman Warrior*, Findley's *Famous Last Words*, Rushdie's
Shame, and the list could go on. There are also parallel paradoxical

manifestations of the postmodern in film, video, photography, painting, dance, music, and other literary genres, and these form part of the sample from which this poetics will be derived.

In *Narcissistic Narrative*, my interest had been in the "metafictional paradox" of self-conscious narratives which demanded of the reader both detachment and involvement. In *A Theory of Parody*, my interest shifted to the more general issue of the paradoxes of parody – as signaling ironic difference at the heart of similarity and as an authorized transgression of convention. Given this definition, parody appeared to require investigation by a doubled model that combined the semiotic (pragmatics) with the formally intertextual. But it was in moving to an even more general consideration of postmodern art (which is both intensively self-reflexive and parodic, yet it also attempts to root itself in that which both reflexivity and parody appear to short-circuit: the historical world) that I realized that the formalist and pragmatic approaches I had used in the other two studies would need expanding to include historical and ideological considerations demanded by these unresolved postmodern contradictions that worked to challenge our entire concept of both historical and literary knowledge, as well as our awareness of our ideological implication in our dominant culture. This is where my personal interests have coincided with what Frank Lentricchia has called a crisis in literary studies today, caught as it is between the urge to essentialize literature and its language into a unique, vast, closed textual preserve and the contrasting urge to make literature "relevant" by locating it in larger discursive contexts (1980, xiii). Postmodern art and theory both incarnate this very crisis, not by choosing sides, but by living out the contradiction of giving in to both urges.

Paradoxes, in general, can delight or trouble. Depending on temperamental make-up, we shall be either seduced by their stimulating teasing or upset with their frustrating lack of resolution. There is no dialectic in the postmodern: the self-reflexive remains distinct from its traditionally accepted contrary – the historico-political context in which it is embedded. The result of this deliberate refusal to resolve contradictions is a contesting of what Lyotard (1984a) calls the totalizing master narratives of our culture, those systems by which we usually unify and order (and smooth over) any contradictions in order to make them fit. This challenge foregrounds the process of meaning-making in the production and reception of art, but also in broader discursive terms: it foregrounds, for instance, how we make historical "facts" out of brute "events" of the past, or, more generally, how our various sign systems grant meaning to our experience.

None of this is new to postmodernism. As Umberto Eco showed with such bravado in *The Name of the Rose*, the encoding and decoding of signs and their interrelations was also an interest of the medieval period. And the contradictions of the self-reflexive and the historical can be found in Shakespeare's history plays, not to mention *Don Quixote*. What is newer is the constant attendant irony of the context of the postmodern version of these contradictions and also their obsessively recurring presence as well. This explains, perhaps, why so many of our finest cultural critics have felt the need to address the topic of postmodernism. What their debates have shown is that the postmodern is, if it is anything, a problematizing force in our culture today: it raises questions about (or renders problematic) the common-sensical and the "natural." But it never offers answers that are anything but provisional and contextually determined (and limited). In Foucault's (1985, 14–22) sense of the notion of problematizing – as generating discourses – postmodernism has certainly created its own problematic, its own set of problems or issues (which were once taken for granted) and possible approaches to them.

I admit that "problematize" is an awkward term – as are others I have deliberately and unavoidably used in this study: theorize, contextualize, totalize, particularize, textualize, and so on. My reason for choosing what to some readers will seem linguistic barbarisms is that they are all now already part of the discourse of postmodernism. Just as new objects require new names, so new theoretical concepts require new designations. For example "to totalize" does not just mean to unify, but rather means to unify with an eye to power and control, and as such, this term points to the hidden power relations behind our humanist and positivist systems of unifying disparate materials, be they aesthetic or scientific. My second reason for using the "-ize" form of each of these terms is to underline the concept of *process* that is at the heart of postmodernism: whether it be in fiction like Swift's *Waterland* or in films like Schell's *Marlene*, it is the process of negotiating the postmodern contradictions that is brought to the fore, not any satisfactorily completed and closed product that results from their resolution.

The six chapters of Part I constitute a presentation, from as broad a sample base as possible, of a framework in which to discuss the postmodern: its history in relation to modernism and the 1960s; its structural model derived from the architecture that first gave it its name; its relation to the "ex-centric" minoritarian discourses that shaped it; its challenges to those theories and practices that suppress the "situating" of discourse (production, reception, historical/social/political/aesthetic contexts). In using examples from many art forms and a variety of theoretical perspectives what I want to avoid is the very common kind of vagueness about just what is being called postmodern, as well as the radical simplifications that lead to misreadings of the complexity of postmodern cultural practices. Often the theory is just based on too partial a sampling of the various discourses available to it. In addition to outlining the model and historical background of postmodernism, this section presents what I see as the major points of overlap between theory and practice. In investigating these points, however, I have become very aware of the danger of recuperating the specificity of each manifestation and have tried to avoid any such "totalizing" in the name of the postmodern. For example, although feminism has had a major impact on the direction and focus of postmodernism, I would not want to equate the feminist with the postmodern for two reasons. First, this would obscure the many different kinds of feminisms that exist, ranging from liberal humanist to radical poststructuralist. But even more important, to co-opt the feminist project into the unresolved and contradictory postmodern one would be to simplify and undo the important political agenda of feminism. I have tried to retain the tension between discrete independence from and influence upon post-modernism in my discussion of not only feminist, but also black, Asian, native, ethnic, gay, and other important (oppositional) minoritarian perspectives.

Part I ends with a detailed consideration of what is, in fact, the guiding concern of the entire book: the problematizing of history by postmodernism. Despite its detractors, the postmodern is not ahistorical or dehistoricized, though it does question our (perhaps unacknowledged) assumptions about what constitutes historical knowledge. Neither is it nostalgic or antiquarian in its critical revisiting of history. The recent work of Hayden White, Paul Veyne, Michel de Certeau, Dominick LaCapra, Louis O. Mink, Fredric Jameson, Lionel Gossman, and Edward Said, among others, has raised the same issues about historical discourse and its relation to the literary as has historiographic metafiction: issues such as those of narrative form, of intertextuality, of strategies of representation, of the role of language, of the relation between historical fact and experiential event, and, in general, of the epistemological and ontological consequences of the act of rendering problematic that which was once taken for granted by historiography – and literature.

The seven chapters of Part II are more specifically focused on historio-graphic metafiction. Chapter 7 acts as an introduction to the ones that follow in presenting the major implications of that problematic confrontation of history with metafiction. Works like E. L. Doctorow's *The Book of Daniel* or Christa Wolf's *Cassandra* mark the "return" of plot and questions of reference which had been bracketed by late modernist attempts to explode realist narrative conventions: the French New New Novel or the texts of *Tel Quel*, the Italian *neoavanguardia*, American surfiction. These are all more radical in form than postmodern novels, which are more compromised, if you like, in their paradoxical inscribing *and* contesting of these same conventions. Historiographic metafiction's somewhat different strategy subverts, but only through irony, not through rejection. Problematizing replaces exploding. Novels like Thomas's *The White Hotel* or Rushdie's *Midnight's Children* do the same with notions of subject-formation: they challenge the humanist assumption of a unified self and an integrated consciousness by both installing coherent subjectivity and subverting it. The tenets of our dominant ideology (to which we, perhaps somewhat simplistically, give the label "liberal humanist") are what is being contested by postmodernism: from the notion of authorial originality and authority to the separation of the aesthetic from the political. Postmodernism teaches that all cultural practices have an ideological subtext which determines the conditions of the very possibility of their production of meaning. And, in art, it does so by leaving overt the contradictions between its self-reflexivity and its historical grounding. In theory, be it poststructuralist (a term we now seem to use to cover everything from deconstruction to discourse analysis), Marxist, feminist, or New Historicist, the contradictions are not always this overt, but are often implied – as in the Barthesian anti-authorizing authority or the Lyotardian master-narrativizing of our suspicion of master narratives. These paradoxes are, I believe, what has led to the political ambidexterity of postmodernism in general, for it has been celebrated and decried by both ends of the political spectrum. If you ignore half of the contradiction, however, it becomes quite easy to see the postmodern as either neoconservatively nostalgic/ reactionary or radically disruptive/revolutionary. I would argue that we must beware of this suppression of the full complexity of postmodernist paradoxes.

Wilfully contradictory, then, postmodern culture uses and abuses the conventions of discourse. It knows it cannot escape implication in the economic (late capitalist) and ideological (liberal humanist) dominants of its time. There is no outside. All it can do is question from within. It can only problematize what Barthes (1973) has called the "given" or "what goes without saying" in our culture. History, the individual self, the relation of language to its referents and of texts to other texts – these are some of the notions which, at various moments, have appeared as "natural" or unproblematically common-sensical. And these are what get interrogated. Despite the apocalyptic rhetoric that often accompanies it, the postmodern marks neither a radical Utopian change nor a lamentable decline to hyperreal simulacra. There is not a break – or not yet, at any rate. This study is an attempt to see what happens when culture is challenged from within: challenged or questioned or contested, but not imploded.

PART I

1

THEORIZING THE POSTMODERN: TOWARD A POETICS

I

Clearly, then, the time has come to theorize the term [postmodernism], if not to define it, before it fades from awkward neologism to derelict cliché without ever attaining to the dignity of a cultural concept. *Ihab Hassan*

Of all the terms bandied about in both current cultural theory and contemporary writing on the arts, postmodernism must be the most over- and under-defined. It is usually accompanied by a grand flourish of negativized rhetoric: we hear of discontinuity, disruption, dislocation, decentring, indeterminacy, and antitotalization. What all of these words literally do (precisely by their disavowing prefixes – *dis, de, in, anti*) is incorporate that which they aim to contest – as does, I suppose, the term *post*modernism itself. I point to this simple verbal fact in order to begin "theorizing" the cultural enterprise to which we seem to have given such a provocative label. Given all the confusion and vagueness associated with the term itself (see Paterson 1986), I would like to begin by arguing that, for me, postmodernism is a contradictory phenomenon, one that uses and abuses, installs and then subverts, the very concepts it challenges – be it in architecture, literature, painting, sculpture, film, video, dance, TV, music, philosophy, aesthetic theory, psychoanalysis, linguistics, or historiography. These are some of the realms from which my "theorizing" will proceed, and my examples will always be specific, because what I want to avoid are those polemical generalizations – often by those inimical to postmodernism: Jameson (1984a), Eagleton (1985), Newman (1985) – that leave us guessing about just what it is that is being called postmodernist, though never in doubt as to its undesirability. Some assume a generally accepted "tacit definition" (Caramello 1983); others locate the beast by temporal (after 1945? 1968? 1970? 1980?) or economic signposting (late capitalism). But in as pluralist and fragmented a culture as that of the western world today, such designations are not terribly useful if they intend to generalize about all the vagaries of our culture. After all, what does television's "Dallas" have in common with the architecture of Ricardo Bofill? What does John Cage's music share with a play (or film) like *Amadeus*?

In other words, postmodernism cannot simply be used as a synonym for the contemporary (cf. Kroker and Cook 1986). And it does not really describe an international cultural phenomenon, for it is primarily European and American (North and South). Although the concept of *modernism* is largely an Anglo-American one (Suleiman 1986), this should not limit the poetics of *postmodernism* to that culture, especially since those who would argue that very stand are usually the ones to find room to sneak in the French *nouveau roman* (A. Wilde 1981; Brooke-Rose 1981; Lodge 1977). And almost everyone (e.g. Barth 1980) wants to be sure to include what Severo Sarduy (1974) has labelled – not postmodern – but "neo-baroque" in a Spanish culture where "modernism" has a rather different meaning.

I offer instead, then, a specific, if polemical, start from which to operate: as a cultural activity that can be discerned in most art forms and many currents of thought today, what I want to call postmodernism is fundamentally contradictory, resolutely historical, and inescapably political. Its contradictions may well be those of late capitalist society, but whatever the cause, these contradictions are certainly manifest in the important postmodern concept of "the presence of the past." This was the title given to the 1980 Venice Biennale which marked the institutional recognition of postmodernism in architecture. Italian architect Paolo Portoghesi's (1983) analysis of the twenty facades of the "Strada Novissima" – whose very newness lay paradoxically in its historical parody – shows how architecture has been rethinking modernism's purist break with history. This is not a nostalgic return; it is a critical revisiting, an ironic dialogue with the past of both art and society, a recalling of a critically shared vocabulary of architectural forms. "The past whose presence we claim is not a golden age to be recuperated," argues Portoghesi (1983, 26). Its aesthetic forms and its social formations are problematized by critical reflection. The same is true of the postmodernist rethinking of figurative painting in art and historical narrative in fiction and poetry (see Perloff 1985, 155–71): it is always a critical reworking, never a nostalgic "return." Herein lies the governing role of irony in postmodernism. Stanley Tigerman's dialogue with history in his projects for family houses modelled on Raphael's palatial Villa Madama is an ironic one: his miniaturization of the monumental forces a rethinking of the social function of architecture – both then and now (see Chapter 2).

Because it is contradictory and works within the very systems it attempts to subvert, postmodernism can probably not be considered a new paradigm (even in some extension of the Kuhnian sense of the term). It has not replaced liberal humanism, even if it has seriously challenged it. It may mark, however, the site of the struggle of the emergence of something new. The manifestations in art of this struggle may be those almost undefinable and certainly bizarre works like Terry Gilliam's film, *Brazil*. The postmodern ironic rethinking of history is here textualized in the many general parodic references to other movies: *A Clockwork Orange, 1984*, Gilliam's own *Time Bandits* and Monty Python sketches, and Japanese epics, to name but a few. The more specific parodic recalls range from *Star Wars'* Darth Vadar to the Odessa Steps sequence of Eisenstein's *Battleship Potemkin*. In *Brazil*, however, the famous shot of the baby carriage on the steps is replaced by one of a floor cleaner, and the result is to reduce epic tragedy to the bathos of the mechanical and debased. Along with this ironic reworking of the history of film comes a temporal historical warp: the movie is set, we are told, at 8:49 am, sometime in the twentieth century. The decor does not help us identify the time more precisely. The fashions mix the absurdly futuristic with 1930s styling; an oddly old-fashioned and dingy setting belies the omnipresence of computers – though even they are not the sleekly designed creatures of today. Among the other typically postmodern contradictions in this movie is the co-existence of heterogenous filmic genres: fantasy Utopia and grim dystopia; absurd slapstick comedy and tragedy (the Tuttle/Buttle mix-up); the romantic adventure tale and the political documentary.

While all forms of contemporary art and thought offer examples of this kind of postmodernist contradiction, this book (like most others on the subject) will be privileging the novel genre, and one form in particular, a form that I want to call "historiographic metafiction." By this I mean those well-known and popular novels which are both intensely self-reflexive and yet paradoxically also lay claim to historical events and personages: *The French Lieutenant's Woman, Midnight's Children, Ragtime, Legs, G., Famous Last Words*. In most of the critical work on postmodernism, it is narrative – be it in literature, history, or theory – that has usually been the major focus of attention. Historiographic metafiction incorporates all three of these domains: that is, its theoretical self-awareness of history and fiction as human constructs (historio*graphic meta*fiction) is made the grounds for its rethinking and reworking of the forms and contents of the past. This kind of fiction has often been noticed by critics, but its paradigmatic quality has been passed by: it is commonly labelled in terms of something else – for example as "midfiction" (A. Wilde 1981) or "paramodernist" (Malmgren 1985). Such labeling is another mark of the inherent contradictoriness of historiographic metafiction, for it always works *within* conventions in order to subvert them. It is not just metafictional; nor is it just another version of the historical novel or the non-fictional novel. Gabriel García Márquez's *One Hundred Years of Solitude* has often been discussed in exactly the contradictory terms that I think define postmodernism. For example Larry McCaffery sees it as both metafictionally self-reflexive and yet speaking to us powerfully about real political and historical realities: "It has thus become a kind of model for the contemporary writer, being self-conscious about its literary heritage and about the limits of mimesis . . . but yet managing to reconnect its readers to the world outside the page" (1982, 264). What McCaffery here adds as almost an afterthought at the end of his book, *The Metafictional Muse*, is in many ways my starting point.

Most theorists of postmodernism who see it as a "cultural dominant" (Jameson 1984a, 56) agree that it is characterized by the results of late capitalist dissolution of bourgeois hegemony and the development of mass culture (see Jameson 1984a [via Lefebvre 1968]; Russell 1980a; Egbert 1970; Calinescu 1977). I would agree and, in fact, argue that the increasing uniformization of mass culture is one of the totalizing forces that post-modernism exists to challenge. Challenge, but not deny. But it does seek to assert difference, not homogeneous identity. Of course, the very concept of difference could be said to entail a typically postmodern contradiction: "difference," unlike "otherness," has no exact opposite against which to define itself. Thomas Pynchon allegorizes otherness in *Gravity's Rainbow* through the single, if anarchic, "we-system" that exists as the counterforce of the totalizing "They-system" (though also implicated in it). Postmodern difference or rather differences, in the plural, are always multiple and provisional.

Postmodern culture, then, has a contradictory relationship to what we usually label our dominant, liberal humanist culture. It does not deny it, as some have asserted (Newman 1985, 42; Palmer 1977, 364). Instead, it contests it from within its own assumptions. Modernists like Eliot and Joyce have usually been seen as profoundly humanistic (e.g. Stern 1971, 26) in their paradoxical desire for stable aesthetic and moral values, even in the face of their realization of the inevitable absence of such universals. Postmodernism differs from this, not in its humanistic contradictions, but in the provisionality of its response to them: it refuses to posit any structure or, what Lyotard (1984a) calls, master narrative – such as art or myth – which, for such modernists, would have been consolatory. It argues that such systems are indeed attractive, perhaps even necessary; but this does not make them any the less illusory. For Lyotard, postmodernism is char-acterized by exactly this kind of incredulity toward master or meta-narratives: those who lament the "loss of meaning" in the world or in art are really mourning the fact that knowledge is no longer primarily narrative knowledge of this kind (1984a, 26). This does not mean that knowledge somehow disappears. There is no radically new paradigm here, even if there is change.

It is no longer big news that the master narratives of bourgeois liberalism are under attack. There is a long history of many such skeptical sieges to positivism and humanism, and today's footsoldiers of theory – Foucault, Derrida, Habermas, Vattimo, Baudrillard – follow in the footsteps of Nietzsche, Heidegger, Marx, and Freud, to name but a few, in their attempts to challenge the empiricist, rationalist, humanist assumptions of our cultural systems, including those of science (Graham, 1982, 148; Toulmin 1972). Foucault's early rethinking of the history of ideas in terms of an "archaeology" (in *The Order of Things*, 1970; *The Archaeology of Knowledge*,

1972) that might stand outside the universalizing assumptions of humanism is one such attempt, whatever its obvious weaknesses. So is Derrida's more radical contesting of Cartesian and Platonic views of the mind as a system of closed meanings (see B. Harrison 1985, 6). Like Gianni Vattimo's *pensiero debole* (weak thought) (1983; 1985), these challenges characteristically operate in clearly paradoxical terms, knowing that to claim epistemological authority is to be caught up in what they seek to displace. The same applies to Habermas's work, though it often appears somewhat less radical in its determined desire to work from within the system of "Enlightenment" rationality and yet manage to critique it at the same time. This is what Lyotard has attacked as just another totalizing narrative (1984b). And Jameson (1984b) has argued that both Lyotard and Habermas are resting their arguments on different but equally strong legitimizing "narrative archetypes."

This game of meta-narrative one-upmanship could go on and on, since arguably Jameson's Marxism leaves him vulnerable too (see Chapter 12). But this is not the point. What is important in all these internalized challenges to humanism is the interrogating of the notion of consensus. Whatever narratives or systems that once allowed us to think we could unproblematically and universally define public agreement have now been questioned by the acknowledgement of differences – in theory and in artistic practice. In its most extreme formulation, the result is that consensus becomes the illusion of consensus, whether it be defined in terms of minority (educated, sensitive, élitist) or mass (commercial, popular, conventional) culture, for *both* are manifestations of late capitalist, bourgeois, informational, postindustrial society, a society in which social reality is structured by discourses (in the plural) – or so postmodernism endeavors to teach.

What this means is that the familiar humanist separation of art and life (or human imagination and order *versus* chaos and disorder) no longer holds. Postmodernist contradictory art still installs that order, but it then uses it to demystify our everyday processes of structuring chaos, of imparting or assigning meaning (D'Haen 1986, 225). For example, within a positivistic frame of reference, photographs could be accepted as neutral representations, as technological windows on the world. In the postmodern photos of Heribert Berkert or Ger Dekkers, they still represent (for they cannot avoid reference) but what they represent is self-consciously shown to be highly filtered by the discursive and aesthetic assumptions of the camera-holder (D. Davis 1977). While not wanting to go as far as Morse Peckham (1965) and argue that the arts are somehow "biologically" necessary for social change, I would like to suggest that, in its very contradictions, postmodernist art (like Brecht's epic theater) might be able to dramatize and even provoke change from within. It is not that the modernist world was "a world in need of mending" and the postmodernist one "beyond repair" (A. Wilde 1981, 131). Postmodernism works to show that all repairs are human constructs, but that, from that very fact, they derive their value as well as their limitation. All repairs are both comforting and illusory. Postmodernist interrogations of humanist certainties live within this kind of contradiction.

Perhaps it is another inheritance from the 1960s to believe that challenging and questioning are positive values (even if solutions to problems are not offered), for the knowledge derived from such inquiry may be the only possible condition of change. In the late 1950s in *Mythologies* (1973), Roland Barthes had prefigured this kind of thinking in his Brechtian challenges to all that is "natural" or "goes without saying" in our culture – that is, all that is considered universal and eternal, and therefore unchangeable. He suggested the need to question and demystify first, and then work for change. The 1960s were the time of ideological formation for many of the postmodernist thinkers and artists of the 1980s and it is now that we can see the results of that formation (see Chapter 12).

Perhaps, as some have argued, the 1960s themselves (that is, at the time) produced no enduring innovation in aesthetics, but I would argue that they did provide the background, though not the definition, of the postmodern (cf. Bertens 1986, 17), for they were crucial in developing a different concept of the possible function of art, one that would contest the "Arnoldian" or humanist moral view with its potentially élitist class bias (see R. Williams 1960, xiii). One of the functions of art in mass culture, argued Susan Sontag, would be to "modify consciousness" (1967, 304). And many cultural commentators since have argued that the energies of the 1960s have changed the framework and structure of how we consider art (e.g. Wasson 1974). The conservatism of the late 1970s and 1980s may have their impact when the thinkers and artists being formed now begin to produce their work (cf. McCaffery 1982), but to call Foucault or Lyotard a neoconservative – as did Habermas (1983, 14) – is historically and ideologically inaccurate (see too Calinescu 1986, 246; Giddens 1981, 17).

The political, social, and intellectual experience of the 1960s helped make it possible for postmodernism to be seen as what Kristeva calls "writing-as-experience-of-limits" (1980a, 137): limits of language, of subjectivity, of sexual identity, and we might also add: of systematization and uniformization. This interrogating (and even pushing) of limits has contributed to the "crisis in legitimation" that Lyotard and Habermas see (differently) as part of the postmodern condition. It has certainly meant a rethinking and putting into question of the bases of our western modes of thinking that we usually label, perhaps rather too generally, as liberal humanism.

II

What is the postmodern scene? Baudrillard's excremental culture? Or a final homecoming to a technoscape where a "body without organs" (Artaud), a "negative space" (Rosalind Krauss), a "pure implosion" (Lyotard), a "looking away" (Barthes) or an "aleatory mechanism"

(Serres) is now first nature and thus the terrain of a new political
refusal?   *Arthur Kroker and David Cook*

What precisely, though, is being challenged by postmodernism? First of all,
institutions have come under scrutiny: from the media to the university,
from museums to theaters. Much postmodern dance, for instance, contests
theatrical space by moving out into the street. Sometimes it is overtly
measured by the clock, thereby foregrounding the unspoken conventions of
theatrical time (see Pops 1984, 59). Make-believe or illusionist conventions
of art are often bared in order to challenge the institutions in which they find
a home – and a meaning. Similarly Michael Asher sandblasted a wall of the
Toselli Gallery in Milan in 1973 to reveal the plaster beneath. This was his
"work of art," one that collapsed together the "work" and the gallery so as to
reveal at once their collusion and the strong but usually unacknowledged
power of the gallery's invisibility as a dominant (and dominating) cultural
institution (see Kibbins 1983).

The important contemporary debate about the margins and the boundaries of social and artistic conventions (see Culler 1983, 1984) is also the result
of a typically postmodern transgressing of previously accepted limits: those
of particular arts, of genres, of art itself. Rauschenberg's narrative (or
discursive) work, *Rebus*, or Cy Twombly's series on Spenserian texts, or
Shosaku Arakawa's poster-like pages of *The Mechanism of Meaning* are
indicative of the fruitful straddling of the borderline between the literary and
visual arts. As early as 1969, Theodore Ziolkowski had noted that the

> new arts are so closely related that we cannot hide complacently behind the
> arbitrary walls of self-contained disciplines: poetics inevitably gives way to general
> aesthetics, considerations of the novel move easily to the film, while the new
> poetry often has more in common with contemporary music and art than with the
> poetry of the past.
>
> (1969, 113)

The years since have only verified and intensified this perception. The
borders between literary genres have become fluid: who can tell anymore
what the limits are between the novel and the short story collection (Alice
Munro's *Lives of Girls and Women*), the novel and the long poem (Michael
Ondaatje's *Coming Through Slaughter*), the novel and autobiography (Maxine
Hong Kingston's *China Men*), the novel and history (Salman Rushdie's
Shame), the novel and biography (John Banville's *Kepler*)? But, in any of these
examples, the conventions of the two genres are played off against each
other; there is no simple, unproblematic merging.

In Carlos Fuentes's *The Death of Artemio Cruz*, the title already points to the
ironic inversion of biographical conventions: it is the death, not the life, that
will be the focus. The subsequent narrative complications of three voices
(first-, second-, and third-person) and three tenses (present, future, past)
disseminate but also reassert (in a typically postmodernist way) the

enunciative situation or discursive context of the work (see Chapter 5). The traditional verifying third-person past tense voice of history and realism is both installed and undercut by the others. In other works, like Italian writer Giorgio Manganelli's *Amore*, the genres of theoretical treatise, literary dialogue, and novel are played off against one another (see Lucente 1986, 317). Eco's *The Name of the Rose* contains at least three major registers of discourse: the literary-historical, the theological-philosophical, and the popular-cultural (de Lauretis 1985, 16), thereby paralleling Eco's own three areas of critical activity.

The most radical boundaries crossed, however, have been those between fiction and non-fiction and – by extension – between art and life. In the March 1986 issue of *Esquire* magazine, Jerzy Kosinski published a piece in the "Documentary" section called "Death in Cannes," a narrative of the last days and subsequent death of French biologist, Jacques Monod. Typically postmodern, the text refuses the omniscience and omnipresence of the third person and engages instead in a dialogue between a narrative voice (which both is and is not Kosinski's) and a projected reader. Its viewpoint is avowedly limited, provisional, personal. However, it also works (and plays) with the conventions of both literary realism and journalistic facticity: the text is accompanied by photographs of the author and the subject. The commentary uses these photos to make us, as readers, aware of our expectations of both narrative and pictorial interpretation, including our naive but common trust in the representational veracity of photography. One set of photos is introduced with: "I bet the smiling picture was taken last, I always bet on a happy ending" (1986, 82), but the subsequent prose section ends with: "look at the pictures if you must but . . . don't bet on them. Bet on the worth of a word" (82). But we come to learn later that there are events – like Monod's death – that are beyond both words and pictures.

Kosinski calls this postmodern form of writing "autofiction": "fiction" because all memory is fictionalizing; "auto" because it is, for him, "a literary genre, generous enough to let the author adopt the nature of his fictional protagonist – not the other way around" (1986, 82). When he "quotes" Monod, he tells the fictive and questioning reader that it is in his own "*autolingua* – the inner language of the storyteller" (86). In his earlier novel, *Blind Date*, Kosinski had used Monod's death and the text of his *Chance and Necessity* as structuring concepts in the novel: from both, he learned of our need to rid ourselves of illusions of totalizing explanations and systems of ethics. But it is not just this kind of historiographic metafiction that challenges the life/art borders or that plays on the margins of genre. Painting and sculpture, for instance, come together with similar impact in some of the three-dimensional canvases of Robert Rauschenberg and Tom Wesselman (see D'Haen 1986 and Owens 1980b). And, of course, much has been made of the blurring of the distinctions between the discourses of theory and literature in the works of Jacques Derrida and Roland Barthes – or somewhat less fashionably, if no less provocatively, in some of the writing of Ihab

Hassan (1975; 1980a) and Zulfikar Ghose (1983). Rosalind Krauss has called this sort of work "paraliterary" and sees it as challenging both the concept of the "work of art" and the separation of that concept from the domain of the academic critical establishment: "The paraliterary space is the space of debate, quotation, partisanship, betrayal, reconciliation; but it is not the space of unity, coherence, or resolution that we think of as constituting the work of art" (1980, 37). This is the space of the postmodern.

In addition to being "borderline" inquiries, most of these postmodernist contradictory texts are also specifically parodic in their intertextual relation to the traditions and conventions of the genres involved. When Eliot recalled Dante or Virgil in *The Waste Land*, one sensed a kind of wishful call to continuity beneath the fragmented echoing. It is precisely this that is contested in postmodern parody where it is often ironic discontinuity that is revealed at the heart of continuity, difference at the heart of similarity (Hutcheon 1985). Parody is a perfect postmodern form, in some senses, for it paradoxically both incorporates and challenges that which it parodies. It also forces a reconsideration of the idea of origin or originality that is compatible with other postmodern interrogations of liberal humanist assumptions (see Chapter 8). While *theorists* like Jameson (1983, 114–19) see this loss of the modernist unique, individual style as a negative, as an imprisoning of the text in the past through pastiche, it has been seen by postmodern *artists* as a liberating challenge to a definition of subjectivity and creativity that has for too long ignored the role of history in art and thought. On Rauschenberg's use of reproduction and parody in his work, Douglas Crimp writes: "The fiction of the creating subject gives way to the frank confiscation, quotation, excerptation, accumulation and repetition of already existing images. Notions of originality, authenticity and presence . . . are undermined" (1983, 53). The same is true of the fiction of John Fowles or the music of George Rochberg. As Foucault noted, the concepts of subjective consciousness and continuity that are now being questioned are tied up with an entire set of ideas that have been dominant in our culture until now: "the point of creation, the unity of a work, of a period, of a theme . . . the mark of originality and the infinite wealth of hidden meanings" (1972, 230).

Another consequence of this far-reaching postmodern inquiry into the very nature of subjectivity is the frequent challenge to traditional notions of perspective, especially in narrative and painting. The perceiving subject is no longer assumed to a coherent, meaning-generating entity. Narrators in fiction become either disconcertingly multiple and hard to locate (as in D. M. Thomas's *The White Hotel*) or resolutely provisional and limited – often undermining their own seeming omniscience (as in Salman Rushdie's *Midnight's Children*). (See Chapter 10.) In Charles Russell's terms, with postmodernism we start to encounter and are challenged by "an art of shifting perspective, of double self-consciousness, of local and extended meaning" (1980a, 192).

As Foucault and others have suggested, linked to this contesting of the unified and coherent subject is a more general questioning of *any* totalizing or homogenizing system. Provisionality and heterogeneity contaminate any neat attempts at unifying coherence (formal or thematic). Historical and narrative continuity and closure are contested, but again, from within. The teleology of art forms – from fiction to music – is both suggested and transformed. The centre no longer completely holds. And, from the decentered perspective, the "marginal" and what I will be calling (Chapter 4) the "ex-centric" (be it in class, race, gender, sexual orientation, or ethnicity) take on new significance in the light of the implied recognition that our culture is not really the homogeneous monolith (that is middle-class, male, heterosexual, white, western) we might have assumed. The concept of alienated otherness (based on binary oppositions that conceal hierarchies) gives way, as I have argued, to that of differences, that is to the assertion, not of centralized sameness, but of decentralized community – another postmodern paradox. The local and the regional are stressed in the face of mass culture and a kind of vast global informational village that McLuhan could only have dreamed of. Culture (with a capital C and in the singular) has become cultures (uncapitalized and plural), as documented at length by our social scientists. And this appears to be happening in spite of – and, I would argue, maybe even because of – the homogenizing impulse of the consumer society of late capitalism: yet another postmodern contradiction.

In attempting to define what he called the "trans-avant-garde," Italian art critic Achille Bonito Oliva found he had to talk of differences as much as similarities from country to country (1984, 71–3): it would seem that the "presence of the past" depends on the local and culture-specific nature of each past. The questioning of the universal and totalizing in the name of the local and particular does not automatically entail the end of all consensus. As Victor Burgin reminds us: "*Of course* moralities and histories are 'relative', but this does not mean they do not *exist*" (1986, 198). Postmodernism is careful not to make the marginal into a new center, for it knows, in Burgin's words, that "[what] have expired are the absolute guarantees issued by over-riding metaphysical systems" (198). Any certainties we do have are what he calls "positional," that is, derived from complex networks of local and contingent conditions.

In this sort of context, different kinds of texts will take on value – the ones that operate what Derrida calls "breaches or infractions" – for it is they that can lead us to suspect the very concept of "art" (1981a, 69). In Derrida's words, such artistic practices seem "to mark and to organize a structure of resistance to the philosophical conceptuality that allegedly dominated and comprehended them, whether directly, or whether through categories derived from this philosophical fund, the categories of esthetics, rhetoric, or traditional criticism" (69). Of course, Derrida's own texts belong solely to neither philosophical nor literary discourse, though they partake of both in a deliberately self-reflexive and contradictory (postmodern) manner.

Derrida's constant self-consciousness about the status of his own discourse raises another question that must be faced by anyone – like myself – writing on postmodernism. From what position can one "theorize" (even self-consciously) a disparate, contradictory, multivalent, current cultural phenomenon? Stanley Fish (1986) has wittily pointed out the "anti-foundationalist" paradox that I too find myself in when I comment on the importance of Derrida's critical self-consciousness. In Fish's ironic terms: "Ye shall know that truth is not what it seems and *that* truth shall set you free." Barthes, of course, had seen the same danger earlier as he watched (and helped) demystification become part of the *doxa* (1977, 166). Similarly Christopher Norris has noted that in textualizing all forms of knowledge, deconstruction theory often, in its very unmasking of rhetorical strategies, itself still lays claim to the status of "theoretical knowledge" (1985, 22). Most postmodern theory, however, realizes this paradox or contradiction. Rorty, Baudrillard, Foucault, Lyotard, and others seem to imply that any knowledge cannot escape complicity with some meta-narrative, with the fictions that render possible any claim to "truth," however provisional. What they add, however, is that *no* narrative can be a natural "master" narrative: there are no natural hierarchies; there are only those we construct. It is this kind of self-implicating questioning that should allow postmodernist theorizing to challenge narratives that do presume to "master" status, without necessarily assuming that status for itself.

Postmodern art similarly asserts and then deliberately undermines such principles as value, order, meaning, control, and identity (Russell 1985, 247) that have been the basic premises of bourgeois liberalism. Those humanistic principles are still operative in our culture, but for many they are no longer seen as eternal and unchallengeable. The contradictions of both postmodern theory and practice are positioned within the system and yet work to allow its premises to be seen as fictions or as ideological structures. This does not necessarily destroy their "truth" value, but it does define the conditions of that "truth." Such a process reveals rather than conceals the tracks of the signifying systems that constitute our world – that is, systems constructed by us in answer to our needs. However important these systems are, they are not natural, given, or universal (see Chapter 11). The very limitations imposed by the postmodern view are also perhaps ways of opening new doors: perhaps now we can better study the interrelations of social, aesthetic, philosophical, and ideological constructs. In order to do so, postmodernist critique must acknowledge its own position as an ideological one (Newman 1985, 60). I think the formal and thematic contradictions of postmodern art and theory work to do just that: to call attention to both what is being contested and what is being offered as a critical response to that, and to do so in a self-aware way that admits its own provisionality. In Barthesian terms (1972, 256), it is criticism which would include in its own discourse an implicit (or explicit) reflection upon itself.

In writing about these postmodern contradictions, then, I clearly would not want to fall into the trap of suggesting any "transcendental identity" (Radhakrishnan 1983, 33) or essence for postmodernism. Instead, I see it as an ongoing cultural process or activity, and I think that what we need, more than a fixed and fixing definition, is a "poetics," an open, ever-changing theoretical structure by which to order both our cultural knowledge and our critical procedures. This would not be a poetics in the structuralist sense of the word, but would go beyond the study of literary discourse to the study of cultural practice and theory. As Tzvetan Todorov realized, in a later expanding and translating of his 1968 *Introduction to Poetics*: "Literature is inconceivable outside a typology of discourses" (1981a, 71). Art and theory about art (and culture) should both be part of a poetics of postmodernism. Richard Rorty has posited the existence of "poetic" moments "as occurring periodically in many different areas of culture – science, philosophy, painting and politics, as well as the lyric and the drama" (1984b, 4). But this is no coincidental moment; it is made, not found. As Rorty explains (23n):

> it is a mistake to think that Derrida, or anybody else, "recognized" problems about the nature of textuality or writing which had been ignored by the tradition. What he did was to think up ways of speaking which made old ways of speaking optional, and thus more or less dubious.

It is both a way of speaking – a discourse – and a cultural process involving the expressions of thought (Lyotard 1986, 125) that a poetics would seek to articulate.

A poetics of postmodernism would not posit any relation of causality or identity either among the arts or between art and theory. It would merely offer, as provisional hypotheses, perceived overlappings of concern, here specifically with regard to the contradictions that I see as characterizing postmodernism. It would be a matter of reading literature through its surrounding theoretical discourses (Cox 1985, 57), rather than as continuous with theory. It would not mean seeing literary theory as a particularly imperialistic intellectual practice that has overrun art (H. White 1978b, 261); nor would it mean blaming self-reflexive art for having created an "ingrown" theory wherein "specific critical and literary trends [have] buttressed each other into a hegemonic network" (Chénetier 1985, 654). The interaction of theory and practice in postmodernism is a complex one of shared responses to common provocations. There are also, of course, many postmodern artists who double as theorists – Eco, Lodge, Bradbury, Barth, Rosler, Burgin – though they have rarely become the major theorists or apologists of their own work, as the *nouveaux romanciers* (from Robbe-Grillet to Ricardou) and surfictionists (Federman and Sukenick especially) have tended to do. What a poetics of postmodernism would articulate is less the theories of Eco in relation to *The Name of the Rose* than the overlappings of concern between, for instance, the contradictory form of the writing of theory in Lyotard's *Le Différend* (1983) and that of a novel like Peter Ackroyd's *Hawksmoor*. Their sequentially ordered sections are equally

disrupted by a particularly dense network of interconnections and intertexts, and each enacts or performs, as well as theorizes, the paradoxes of
continuity and disconnection, of totalizing interpretation and the impossibility of final meaning. In Lyotard's own words:

> A postmodern artist or writer is in the position of a philosopher: the text he writes,
> the work he produces are not in principle governed by preestablished rules, and
> they cannot be judged according to a determining judgement, by applying familiar
> categories to the text or to the work. Those rules and categories are what the work
> of art itself is looking for.
>
> (1984b, 81)

III

> To analyze discourses is to hide and reveal contradictions; it is to show
> the play that they set up within it; it is to manifest how it can express
> them, embody them, or give them a temporary appearance.
> *Michel Foucault*

Jameson has listed "theoretical discourse" among the manifestations of
postmodernism (1983, 112) and this would include, not only the obvious
Marxist, feminist, and poststructuralist philosophical and literary theory,
but also analytic philosophy, psychoanalysis, linguistics, historiography,
sociology, and other areas. Recently critics have begun to notice the
similarities of concern between various kinds of theory and current literary
discourse, sometimes to condemn (Newman 1985, 118), sometimes merely
to describe (Hassan 1986). With novels like Ian Watson's *The Embedding*
around, it is not surprising that the link would be made. I do not at all think,
however, that this has contributed to any "inflation of discourse" at the
expense of historical contextualization (Newman 1985, 10), primarily because historiography is itself taking part in what LaCapra has called a
"reconceptualization of culture in terms of collective discourses"
(1985a, 46). By this, he does not mean to imply that historians no longer
concern themselves with "archivally based documentary realism", but only
that, within the discipline of history, there is also a growing concern with
redefining intellectual history as "the study of social meaning as historically
constituted" (46) (see too H. White 1973; 1980; 1981; 1984). This is exactly
what historiographic metafiction is doing: Graham Swift's *Waterland*, Rudy
Wiebe's *The Temptations of Big Bear*, Ian Watson's *Chekhov's Journey*.

In the past, of course, history has often been used in novel criticism,
though usually as a model of the realistic pole of representation. Postmodern fiction problematizes this model to query the relation of both history
to reality and reality to language. In Lionel Gossman's terms:

> Modern history and modern literature [I would say *post*modern in both cases] have
> both rejected the ideal of representation that dominated them for so long. Both
> now conceive of their work as exploration, testing, creation of new meanings,

rather than as disclosure or revelation of meanings already in some sense "there," but not immediately perceptible.

(1978, 38–9)

The view that postmodernism relegates history to "the dustbin of an obsolete episteme, arguing gleefully that history does not exist except as text" (Huyssen 1981, 35) is simply wrong. History is not made obsolete: it is, however, being rethought – as a human construct. And in arguing that *history* does not exist except as text, it does not stupidly and "gleefully" deny that the *past* existed, but only that its accessibility to us now is entirely conditioned by textuality. We cannot know the past except through its texts: its documents, its evidence, even its eye-witness accounts are *texts*. Even the institutions of the past, its social structures and practices, could be seen, in one sense, as social texts. And postmodern novels – *The Scorched-Wood People, Flaubert's Parrot, Antichthon, The White Hotel* – teach us about both this fact and its consequences.

Along with the obvious and much publicized case of postmodern architecture (Jencks 1977; 1980a; 1980b), it has been (American) black and (general) feminist theory and practice that have been particularly important in this postmodernist refocusing on historicity, both formally (largely through parodic intertextuality) and thematically. Works like Ishmael Reed's *Mumbo Jumbo*, Maxine Hong Kingston's *China Men*, and Gayl Jones's *Corregidora* have gone far to expose – very self-reflexively – the myth- or illusion-making tendencies of historiography. They have also linked racial and/or gender difference to questions of discourse and of authority and power that are at the heart of the postmodernist enterprise in general and, in particular, of both black theory and feminism. All are theoretical discourses that have their roots in a reflection on actual praxis and continue to derive their critical force from their conjunction with that social and aesthetic practice (on feminism, see de Lauretis 1984, 184). It is true that, as Susan Suleiman (1986, 268, n. 12) acutely noted, literary discussions of post-modernism often appear to exclude the work of women (and, one might add, often of blacks as well), even though female (and black) explorations of narrative and linguistic form have been among the most contesting and radical. Certainly women and Afro-American artists' use of parody to challenge the male white tradition from within, to use irony to implicate and yet to critique, is distinctly paradoxical and postmodernist. Both black and feminist thought have shown how it is possible to move theory out of the ivory tower and into the larger world of social praxis, as theorists like Said (1983) have been advocating. Women have helped develop the postmodern valuing of the margins and the ex-centric as a way out of the power problematic of centers and of male/female oppositions (Kamuf 1982). Certainly Susan Swan's *The Biggest Modern Woman of the World*, a biographical metafiction about a real (and, by definition, ex-centric) giantess, would suggest precisely this in its opposition to what the protagonist sees as "emblem fatigue": "an affliction peculiar to giants [or women or blacks or ethnics] who are always having to shoulder giant expectations from normal folk" (1983, 139). (See Chapter 4.)

Lately there have been other critical works which have come close to articulating the kind of poetics I think we need, though all offer a somewhat more limited version. But they too have investigated the overlappings of concern between current philosophical and literary theory and practice. Evan Watkins's *The Critical Act: Criticism and Community* aims to derive a theory of literature that can "elicit from recent poetry in particular the means of talking about and talking back to developments in theory" (1978, x). His model, however, is one of "dialectical reciprocity" that often implies a causal relationship (12) that the sort of poetics I envisage would avoid.

David Carroll's fine study, *The Subject in Question: The Languages of Theory and the Strategies of Fiction* (1982), is somewhat more limited than a general poetics of postmodernism would be, for it focuses on the aporias and contradictions specifically in the work of Jacques Derrida and Claude Simon in order to study the limitations of both theory and fiction in examining the problem of history, limitations that are made evident by the revealing confrontation of theory with practice. As I see it, however, a poetics would not seek to place itself in a position *between* theory and practice (1982, 2) on the question of history, but rather would seek a position *within* both. A work like Peter Uwe Hohendahl's *The Institution of Criticism* (1982), while limited to the German context, is useful here in showing the kind of question that a poetics positioned within both theory and practice must ask, especially regarding the norms and standards of *criticism* – the autonomous institution that mediates theory and practice in the field of literary studies.

Allen Thiher's *Words in Reflection: Modern Language Theory and Postmodern Fiction* comes closest to defining a poetics in that it studies some current theories together with contemporary literary practice in order to show what he feels to be a major "displacement in the way we think and, perhaps more important, write the past" (1984, 189). However, this lucid and thorough study limits itself to modern language theory and linguistically self-reflexive metafiction and posits a kind of influence model (of theory over fiction) that a poetics of postmodernism would not be willing to do. Rather than separating theory from practice, it would seek to integrate them and would organize itself around issues (narrative, representation, textuality, subjectivity, ideology, and so on) that both theory and art problematize and continually reformulate in paradoxical terms. (See all of Part II.)

First, however, any poetics of postmodernism should come to terms with the immense amount of material that has already been written on the subject of postmodernism in all fields. The debate invariably begins over the meaning of the prefix, "post" – a four-letter word if ever there was one. Does it have as negative a ring of supersession and rejection as many contend (Barth 1980; Moser 1984)? I would argue that, as is most clear perhaps in postmodern architecture, the "Post Position" (Culler 1982a, 81) signals its

contradictory dependence on and independence from that which temporally preceded it and which literally made it possible. Postmodernism's
relation to modernism is, therefore, typically contradictory, as we shall see
in Chapter 3. It marks neither a simple and radical break from it nor a
straightforward continuity with it: it is both and neither. And this would be
the case in aesthetic, philosophical, or ideological terms.

Of the many arguments mounted on either side of the modernist/
postmodernist debate, let me here consider only one in detail, a recent and
influential one, that of Terry Eagleton in his 1985 article, "Capitalism,
Modernism and Postmodernism." In fact, much of what is offered here is
repeated in other theorizing on postmodernism. Like many before him
(both defenders and detractors), Eagleton separates practice and theory,
choosing to argue primarily in abstract theoretical terms and almost seeming
deliberately to avoid mention of exactly what kind of aesthetic practice is
actually being talked about. This strategy, however clever and certainly
convenient, leads only to endless confusion. My first response to his article,
for instance, was that, from the descriptive theorizing alone, Eagleton, like
Jameson (1983; 1984a), must mean something quite different from what I do
by postmodernism in art. Yet they both make passing references to architecture, and so I suppose I must presume, though I cannot prove from their
texts, that we are all indeed talking of the same kind of artistic manifestation.
And so, I will proceed on that assumption.

I want to look at each of Eagleton's eight major points in the light of the
specific postmodern artistic practice I have been discussing, for I think that
his absolutist binary thinking – that makes postmodernism into the negative
and opposite of modernism – negates much of the complexity of that art. His
theory is neat, but maybe too neat. For example can the historical and
discursive contextualizing of Doctorow's *Ragtime* really be considered dehistoricized and devoid of historical memory? It may alter received historical
opinion but it does not evade the notions of historicity or historical determination (see Chapter 6). Is the highly individualized and problematic voice
of Saleem Sinai in *Midnight's Children* really to be dubbed "depthless" and
"without style"? Is that novel (or are Coover's *The Public Burning* or
Doctorow's *The Book of Daniel*) to be seriously labelled as empty of political
content? Yet Eagleton asserts all of this – minus the examples – as defining
what he calls postmodernism (1985, 61).

He continues. And I would again ask: in Findley's *Famous Last Words*, does
the obvious "performativity" of the text really "replace truth" (Eagleton
1985, 63) or does it, rather, question *whose* notion of truth gains power and
authority over others and then examine the process of how it does so? The
Brechtian involvement of the reader – both textualized (Quinn) and extra-
textual (us) – is something Eagleton appears to approve of in the modernist
"revolutionary" avant-garde. But it is also a very postmodern strategy, and
here leads to the acknowledgement, not of truth, but of truths in the plural,
truths that are socially, ideologically, and historically conditioned (see

Chapter 12). Eagleton sees that postmodernism dissolves modernist boundaries, but sees this as a negative, an act of becoming "coextensive with commodified life itself" (68). But historiographic metafiction like Puig's *Kiss of the Spider Woman* works precisely to combat any aestheticist fetishing of art by *refusing* to bracket exactly what Eagleton wants to see put *back* into art: "the referent or real historical world" (67). What such fiction also does, however, is problematize both the nature of the referent and its relation to the real, historical world by its paradoxical combination of metafictional self-reflexivity with historical subject matter (see Chapter 9). How, then, could Cortázar's *A Manual for Manuel* be reduced to celebrating "kitsch" (68)? Is all art that introduces non-high art forms (here, those of journalism and the spy story) by definition kitsch? What Eagleton (like Jameson – 1984a – before him) seems to ignore is the subversive potential of irony, parody, and humor in contesting the universalizing pretensions of "serious" art (see Chapters 2 and 8).

Eagleton broadens the scope of his attack on postmodernism by describing it as "confidently post-metaphysical" (70). The one thing which the provisional, contradictory postmodernist enterprise is *not* is "confidently" anything. A novel like Banville's *Doctor Copernicus* does not confidently accept that things are things, as Eagleton asserts. Its entire formal and thematic energy is founded in its philosophical problematizing of the nature of reference, of the relation of word to thing, of discourse to experience. Postmodern texts like *The White Hotel* or *Kepler* do not confidently disintegrate and banish the humanist subject either, though Eagleton says postmodernism (in his theoretical terms) does. They *do* disturb humanist certainties about the nature of the self and of the role of consciousness and Cartesian reason (or positivistic science), but they do so by inscribing that subjectivity and only then contesting it (see Chapter 10).

I have deliberately discussed each of Eagleton's eight points in terms of specific examples in order to illustrate the dangers of separating neat theory from messy practice. A poetics of postmodernism must deal with *both* and can theorize only on the basis of all the forms of postmodern discourse available to it. As Nicholas Zurbrugg (1986, 71) has argued, too many of the theorists of postmodernism have simplified and misread the complexities and creative potential of postmodern cultural practices by predicating their theories on a very partial sampling. For example the constant complaint that postmodernism is either ahistorical or, if it uses history, that it does so in a naive and nostalgic way, just will not stand up in the light of actual novels such as those listed above or films like *Crossroads* or *Zelig*. What starts to look naive, by contrast, is the reductive belief that any recall of the past must, by definition, be sentimental nostalgia or antiquarianism. What postmodernism does, as its very name suggests, is confront and contest any modernist discarding *or* recuperating of the past in the name of the future. It suggests no search for transcendent timeless meaning, but rather a re-evaluation of and a dialogue with the past in the light of the present. We could call this, once again, "the presence of the past" or perhaps its "present-ification" (Hassan 1983). It does not deny the *existence* of the past; it does question whether we can ever *know* that past other than through its textualized remains.

However, the binary oppositions that are usually set up in the writing on postmodernism – between past and present, modern and postmodern, and so on – should probably be called into question, if only because, like the rhetoric of rupture (*dis*continuity, *de*centering, and so on), *post*modernism literally names and constitutes its own paradoxical identity, and does so in an uneasy contradictory relationship of constant slippage. So much that has been written on this subject has physically taken the form of opposing columns, usually labelled modernist versus postmodernist (see Hassan 1975, 1980b; cf. Lethen 1986, 235–6). But this is a structure that implicitly denies the mixed, plural, and contradictory nature of the postmodern enterprise.

Whether this complexity is a result of our particularly contradictory age, caught between "myths of totality" and "ideologies of fracture" (Hassan 1980a, 191) is another question. Surely many ages could be so described. Whatever the cause, a poetics of postmodernism should try to come to grips with some of the obvious paradoxes in both theory and practice. Let me offer just a few more examples: one would be the contradiction or irony of Lyotard's (1984a) obviously meta-narrative theory of postmodernism's incredulity to meta-narrative (see Lacoue-Labarthe 1984) or of Foucault's early anti-totalizing epistemic totalizations. These are typically paradoxical: they are the masterful denials of mastery, the cohesive attacks on cohesion, the essentializing challenges to essences, that characterize postmodern theory. Similarly historiographic metafiction – like postmodern painting, sculpture, and photography – inscribes and only then subverts its mimetic engagement with the world. It does not reject it (cf. Graff 1979); nor does it merely accept it (cf. Butler 1980, 93; A. Wilde 1981, 170). But it does change irrevocably any simple notions of realism or reference by directly confronting the discourse of art with the discourse of history.

A further postmodern paradox that this particular kind of fiction enacts is to be found in its bridging of the gap between élite and popular art, a gap which mass culture has no doubt broadened. Many have noted postmodernism's attraction to popular art forms (Fiedler 1975; Tani 1984) such as the detective story (Fowles's *A Maggot*) or the western (Doctorow's *Welcome to Hard Times* or Thomas Berger's *Little Big Man*). But what has not been dealt with is the paradox of novels like *The French Lieutenant's Woman* or *The Name of the Rose* themselves being at once popular best-sellers and objects of intense academic study. I would argue that, as typically postmodernist contradictory texts, novels like these parodically use and abuse the conventions of both popular and élite literature, and do so in such a way that they can actually *use* the invasive culture industry to challenge its own commodification processes from within. And, in addition, if élitist culture has indeed been fragmented into specialist disciplines, as many have argued, then hybrid novels like these work both to address and to subvert that fragmentation through their pluralizing recourse to the discourses of history, sociology, theology, political science, economics, philosophy, semiotics, literature, literary criticism, and so on. Historiographic metafiction clearly acknowledges that it is a complex institutional and discursive network of élite, official, mass, popular cultures that postmodernism operates in.

What we seem to need, then, is some way of talking about our culture which is neither "unificatory" nor "contradictionist" in a Marxist dialectical sense (Ruthven 1984, 32). The visible paradoxes of the postmodern do not mask any hidden unity which analysis can reveal. Its irreconcilable incompatibilities are the very bases upon which the problematized discourses of postmodernism emerge (see Foucault 1977, 151). The differences that these contradictions foreground should not be dissipated. While unresolved paradoxes may be unsatisfying to those in need of absolute and final answers, to postmodernist thinkers and artists they have been the source of intellectual energy that has provoked new articulations of the postmodern condition. Despite the obvious danger, they do not appear to have brought on what LaCapra has called a "lemming-like fascination for discursive impasses" (1985a, 141) that might threaten to undermine *any* working concept of "theorizing." The model of contradictions offered here – while admittedly only another model – would hope to open up any poetics of postmodernism to plural, contestatory elements without necessarily reducing or recuperating them. In order to try to avoid the tempting trap of co-option, what is necessary is the acknowledging of the fact that such a position is itself an ideology, one that is profoundly implicated in that which it seeks to theorize. Criticism, as Barthes reminded us, is "essentially an activity, i.e., a series of intellectual acts profoundly committed to the historical and subjective existence (they are the same) of the man [sic] who performs them" (1972, 257).

In other words, we cannot exempt our own "discriminating scholarly discourse" as Douwe Fokkema would like (1986a, 2), for it too is as institutionalized as the fiction or the painting or the philosophy or the history it would pretend to scrutinize. Within such a "postmodernist" ideology, all a poetics of postmodernism would do would be self-consciously to enact the metalinguistic contradiction of being inside and outside, complicitous and distanced, inscribing and contesting its own provisional formulations. Such an enterprise would obviously not yield any universal truths but, then again, that would not be what it sought to do. To move from the desire and expectation of sure and single meaning to a recognition of the value of differences and even contradictions might be a tentative first step to accepting responsibility for both art and theory *as signifying processes*. In other words, maybe we could begin to study the implications of both our *making* and our *making sense* of our culture.

2

MODELLING THE POSTMODERN: PARODY AND POLITICS

I

That postmodern theses have deep roots in the present human
condition is confirmed today in the document on architecture issued
by the Polish union Solidarity. This text accuses the modern city of
being the product of an alliance between bureaucracy and
totalitarianism, and singles out the great error of modern architecture
in the break of historical continuity. Solidarity's words should be
meditated upon, especially by those who have confused a great
movement of collective consciousness [postmodernism] with a
passing fashion. *Paolo Portoghesi*

We have seen that what both its supporters and its detractors seem to want to
call "postmodernism" in art today – be it in video, dance, literature, painting,
music, architecture, or any other form – seems to be art marked paradoxically
by both history and an internalized, self-reflexive investigation of the nature,
the limits, and the possibilities of the discourse of art. On the surface,
postmodernism's main interest might seem to be in the processes of its own
production and reception, as well as in its own parodic relation to the art of the
past. But I want to argue that it is precisely parody – that seemingly
introverted formalism – that paradoxically brings about a direct confrontation
with the problem of the relation of the aesthetic to a world of significance
external to itself, to a discursive world of socially defined meaning systems
(past and present) – in other words, to the political and the historical.

My focus in this chapter will be on what I think offers the best model for a
poetics of postmodernism: postmodern architecture, the one art form in
which the label seems to refer, uncontested, to a generally agreed upon
corpus of works. Throughout, my (non-specialist) discussion will be clearly
indebted to the work of architect/theorists like Charles Jencks and Paolo
Portoghesi, the major voices in the postmodern debates. This will be my
model, because the characteristics of this architecture are also those of
postmodernism at large – from historiographic metafictions like Christa

Wolf's *Cassandra* or E. L. Doctorow's *The Book of Daniel* to metafilmic historical movies like Peter Greenaway's *The Draughtsman's Contract*, from the video art of Douglas Davis to the photography of Vincent Leo. And all of these art works share one major contradictory characteristic: they are all overtly historical and unavoidably political, precisely because they are formally parodic. I will argue throughout this study that postmodernism is a fundamentally contradictory enterprise: its art forms (and its theory) at once use and abuse, install and then destabilize convention in parodic ways, self-consciously pointing both to their own inherent paradoxes and provisionality and, of course, to their critical or ironic re-reading of the art of the past. In implicitly contesting in this way such concepts as aesthetic originality and textual closure, postmodernist art offers a new model for mapping the borderland between art and the world, a model that works from a position within both and yet not totally within either, a model that is profoundly implicated in, yet still capable of criticizing, that which it seeks to describe.

As we have seen, such a paradoxical model of postmodernism is consistent with the very name of the label for *post*modernism signals its contradictory dependence upon and independence from the modernism that both historically preceded it and literally made it possible. Philip Johnson probably could not have built the postmodern Transco Tower in Houston if he had not first designed the modernist purist form of Pennzoil Place – and if he had not begun his career as an architectural historian. All architects know that, by their art's very nature as the shaper of public space, the act of designing a building is an unavoidably social act. Parodic references to the history of architecture textually reinstate a dialogue with the past and – perhaps inescapably – with the social and ideological context in which architecture is (and has been) both produced and lived. In using parody in this way, postmodernist forms want to work toward a public discourse that would overtly eschew modernist aestheticism and hermeticism and its attendant political self-marginalization.

I am fully aware that my last sentence constitutes a kind of "red flag" in the light of the debate on postmodernism being argued out on the pages of the *New Left Review*. We saw in the last chapter that, in reply to Fredric Jameson's "Postmodernism, Or The Cultural Logic of Late Capitalism" (1984a), Terry Eagleton found himself in an oddly inverted Lukácian position, championing that same hermetic modernism (which Lukács had denigrated) in his rush to join the now fashionable attack on postmodernism. Without ever really giving an example of what to him would be an actual postmodernist work of art (as if there were not considerable disagreement on this topic in both theory and practice), Eagleton simply states that postmodernism will not do, that the only way to develop an "authentically political art in our own time" (1985, 72) would be to combine somehow the revolutionary avant-garde with modernism:

An art today which, having learnt from the openly committed character of avant-garde culture, might cast the contradictions of modernism in a more explicitly political light, could do so effectively only if it had also learnt its lesson from modernism too – learnt, that is to say, that the "political" itself is a question of the emergence of a transformed rationality, and if it is not presented as such will still seem part of the very tradition from which the adventurously modern is still striving to free itself.

(1985, 73)

But, were Eagleton to look at actual postmodernist art today – and at architecture, in particular – he would see that the art for which he calls already exists. Postmodernist art is precisely that which casts "the contradictions of modernism in an explicitly political light." In fact, as architect Paolo Portoghesi reminds us, it has arisen from the very conjunction of modernist and avant-garde politics and forms (1983, 35). But it also suggests that we must be critically conscious of the myths of both the modernists and the late-romantic avant-garde. The "élitism" of Dada and of Eliot's verse is exactly what postmodernism paradoxically seeks to exploit and to undercut. But the theorist/practitioners of postmodernism in all the arts – from Umberto Eco to Karlheinz Stockhausen – are emphatic in their commitment to the formation (or recollection) of a more generally shared collective aesthetic code. They insist: "It is not just the cry of rage of a minority of intellectuals who want to teach others how to live, and who celebrate their own solitude and separateness" (Portoghesi 1983, 81).

Furthermore, Edward Said has argued that we must realize that all art is discourse-specific, that it is to some degree "worldly," even when it appears to deny any such connection (1983,4). The paradox of postmodernist parody is that it is *not* essentially depthless, trivial kitsch, as Eagleton (1985, 61; 68) and Jameson (1984a, 85) both believe, but rather that it can and does lead to a vision of interconnectedness: "illuminating itself, the artwork simultaneously casts light on the workings of aesthetic conceptualization and on art's sociological situation" (Russell 1980a, 189). Postmodernist ironic recall of history is neither nostalgia nor aesthetic cannibalization (cf. Jameson 1984a, 67). Nor can it be reduced to the glibly decorative (cf. Frampton 1983).

It is true, however, as we shall see at length in Part II, that postmodern art does not offer what Jameson desires – "genuine historicity" – that is, in his terms, "our social, historical and existential present and the past as 'referent'" or as "ultimate objects" (1984a, 67). But its deliberate refusal to do so is not a naïve one: what postmodernism does is to contest the very possibility of our ever being able to *know* the "ultimate objects" of the past. It teaches and enacts the recognition of the fact that the social, historical, and existential "reality" of the past is *discursive* reality when it is used as the referent of art, and so the only "genuine historicity" becomes that which would openly acknowledge its own discursive, contingent identity. The past as referent is not bracketed or effaced, as Jameson would like to believe: it is incorporated and modified, given new and different life and meaning. This is the lesson taught by postmodernist art today. In other words, even the most self-conscious and parodic of contemporary works do not try to escape, but indeed foreground, the historical, social, ideological contexts in which they have existed and continue to exist. This is as true of music as of painting; it is as valid for literature as it is for architecture.

It is not surprising that a post-Saussurian kind of pragmatics or semiotics has had a strong appeal for those studying this kind of parodic art. Postmodernism self-consciously demands that the "justifying premises and structural bases" of its modes of "speaking" be investigated to see what permits, shapes, and generates what is "spoken" (Russell 1980a, 186). According to one important, but often neglected aspect of the Saussurian model, language is a social contract: everything that is presented and thus received through language is already loaded with meaning inherent in the conceptual patterns of the speaker's culture. In an extension of the meaning of "language," we could say that the *langue* of architecture is in some ways no different from that of ordinary language: no single individual can alter it at his or her own will; it embodies certain culturally accepted values and meanings; it has to be learned in some detail by users before it can be employed effectively (Broadbent 1969, 51). The architecture of the 1970s and 1980s has been marked by a deliberate challenge to the conventions and underlying assumptions of that *langue*, but it is a typically postmodern and self-conscious challenge offered from *within* those very conventions and assumptions.

Whatever modernism's historical and social ideals at its inception, by the end of the Second World War its innovatory promises had become symbols – and causes – of alienation and dehumanization. Modernism in architecture had begun as a "heroic attempt after the Great War and the Russian Revolution to rebuild a war-ravaged Europe in the image of the new, and to make building a vital part of the envisioned renewal of society" (Huyssen 1986, 186). In reaction against what modernist ahistoricism then led to, however, postmodern parodic revisitations of the history of architecture interrogate the modernist totalizing ideal of progress through rationality and purist form (Lyotard 1986, 120).

As a way of textually incorporating the history of art, parody is the formal analogue to the dialogue of past and present that silently but unavoidably goes on at a social level in architecture, because the relation of form to function, shape to use of space, is not a new problem for architects. It is in this way that parodic postmodern buildings can be said to parallel, in their form and their explicitly social contextualizing, contemporary challenges on the level of theory. Any study of the actual aesthetic *practice* of postmodernism quickly makes clear its role in the crises of *theoretical* legitimation that have come to our attention in the now infamous Lyotard (1984a)–Habermas (1983)–Rorty (1984a) debate. Perhaps it is at this level that the ideological status of postmodernist art should be argued out, instead of at that of an understandable, if knee-jerk, reaction against its implication in the mass culture of late capitalism.

To rage, as so many do, following Adorno, against mass culture as only a

negative force may be, as one architect/critic has remarked, "simply continuing to use an aristocratic viewpoint and not knowing how to grasp the
liberating result and the egalitarian charge of this [postmodernist] profa-
nation of the myth" of élitist romantic/modernist originality and unique
genius (Portoghesi 1983, 28). In fact the architecture of the 1970s from the start
signalled a conscious move away from the modern movement or the
International Style as much for overtly ideological as for aesthetic reasons.
The social failure of the great modernist housing projects and the inevitable
economic association of "heroic" modernism with large corporations combined to create a demand for new architectural forms that would reflect a
changed and changing social awareness. These new forms were not, by any
means, monolithic. They did, however, mark a shared return to such rejected
forms as the vernacular (that is, to local needs and local architectural
traditions), to decoration and a certain individualism in design, and, most
importantly, to the past, to history. Modernism's great purist monuments to
the corporate élite and to the cultural seats of power (museums, theatres) gave
way, for example, to the Centre Pompidou's (at least stated) desire to make
culture part of the business of everyday living.

What soon became labelled as *post*modernism challenged the survival of
modernism by contesting its claims to universality: its transhistorical
assertions of value were no longer seen as based – as claimed – on reason or
logic, but rather on a solid alliance with power, with what Portoghesi calls its
"identification with the productive logic of the industrial system" (1982, 3). In
addition, any feeling of "inevitability" (Hubbard 1980, 78) of form was shown
to be historically and culturally determined. The "inevitable" was not eternal,
but learned. Peter Eisenman's houses deliberately undercut our "natural"
reactions to space in order to reveal to us that these reactions are, in fact,
cultural. And, just as modernism (oedipally) had to reject historicism and to
pretend to a parthenogenetic birth fit for the new machine age, so postmodernism, in reaction, returned to history, to what I have been calling
"parody," to give architecture back its traditional social and historical
dimension, though with a new twist this time.

What I mean by "parody" here – as elsewhere in this study – is *not* the
ridiculing imitation of the standard theories and definitions that are rooted in
eighteenth-century theories of wit. The collective weight of parodic *practice*
suggests a redefinition of parody as repetition with critical distance that
allows ironic signalling of difference at the very heart of similarity. In
historiographic metafiction, in film, in painting, in music, and in architecture,
this parody paradoxically enacts both change and cultural continuity: the
Greek prefix *para* can mean both 'counter' or 'against' and 'near' or 'beside.'
Jameson argues that in postmodernism "parody finds itself without a
vocation" (1984a, 65), replaced by pastiche, which he (bound by a definition
of parody as ridiculing imitation) sees as neutral or blank parody. But the
looking to both the aesthetic and historical past in postmodernist architecture
is anything but what Jameson describes as pastiche, that is "the random

cannibalization of all the styles of the past, the play of random stylistic allusion" (65–6). There is absolutely nothing random or "without principle" in the parodic recall and re-examination of the past by architects like Charles Moore or Ricardo Bofill. To include irony and play is *never* necessarily to exclude seriousness and purpose in postmodernist art. To misunderstand this is to misunderstand the nature of much contemporary aesthetic production – even if it does make for neater theorizing.

II

> O beautiful, for spacious skies, for amber waves of grain, has there ever
> been another place on earth where so many people of wealth and power
> have paid for and put up with so much architecture they detested as
> within thy blessed borders today? *Tom Wolfe*

In order to understand why ironic parody should, seemingly paradoxically, become such an important form of postmodernist architecture's desire to reinstate a "worldly" connection for its discourse, we should remind ourselves of what the tyranny of "heroic" or high modernism has meant in the twentieth century. There have been two kinds of reactions to this modernist hegemony: those from architects themselves and those from the public at large. Perhaps the most eloquent and polemical of the recent public responses has been that of Tom Wolfe in his *From Bauhaus to Our House*, which opens with the wonderfully parodic American lament with which I began this section. Wolfe's is a negative aesthetic response to what he amusingly calls "the whiteness & lightness & leanness & cleanness & bareness & spareness of it all" (1981, 4). But it is also an ideological rejection of what can only be called the modernist architects' "policing" of the impulses of both the clients and the tenants of their buildings. This is the tyranny of the European theorists working in their "compounds" (be they the Bauhaus or, later, the American universities). This is a tyranny – both moral and aesthetic – over American clients. In Wolfe's terms: "No alterations, special orders, or loud talk from the client permitted. We know best. We have exclusive possession of the true vision of the future of architecture" (1981, 17). The clients – even if they did foot the bill – were still considered the "bourgeois" to be despised and, if possible, confounded by the architectural clerisy's élitist esoteric theories.

The *users* of the buildings were also to be controlled. Although Gropius and Le Corbusier both designed workers' housing, neither seems to have felt the need to consult those who would live there: it must have been tacitly assumed that the intellectually underdeveloped would allow the architects to arrange their lives for them. Not surprisingly, many of the worker housing projects of high modernism, like the infamous Pruitt-lgoe one in St Louis, degenerated into shabby welfare housing and were finally and literally blown up, when their social failure was acknowledged. Similarly those so-called non-bourgeois concrete and glass skyscraper apartment buildings and hotels became the housing of the bourgeois – the only ones who could afford to live there. But the control of the architect was often even more extreme: in the Seagram Building, Mies allowed only white blinds on the plate glass windows and demanded that these be left in only one of three positions, open, shut, or half-way.

Modernist architects seemed to set themselves up in one of two privileged positions with regard to the groups that were actually to occupy their designs. One position is what George Baird (1969) has called that of the *Gesamtkünstler* who took for granted an ability to enhance the lives of the future tenants by dramatically heightening their experience of their environment. This position is one over and above them; the attitude is a paternalistic one toward the tenant/child. On the other hand, some modernists saw themselves as, in Baird's terms, the "life-conditioners." Not above, but now outside the experience of the tenant, the scientistic architect regarded the tenant as object and the building as an experiment. Be the stance one of indifference or arrogance, it is certainly not hard to see how it could come to be labelled as élitist. And one need only recall Le Corbusier's oddly Platonic Nietzschean view of society controlled by the enlightened businessman and the architect, both the products of an impersonal, universal, transhistorical force symbolized by the machine. The lessons of the past were rejected in the name of this new brand of liberal élitism or idealistic paternalism (see Jencks 1973, 51–4; 72). Although Le Corbusier saw himself as the apolitical technocrat, the ideological assumptions behind his aesthetic theories of purist rationality might be seen to have played a role in his collaboration with the Vichy government and the failure, in practical terms, of his rather simplistic theory of social good through pure form. We must, of course, beware of making our own simplistic associations of architectural style and single ideologies. Portoghesi reminds us that "History proves that forms and models survive the type of power that produced them, and that their meaning changes in time according to the social use that is made of them" (1983, 140). And such was indeed the case with the modernist premises which postmodernism used – but transformed.

What we should not forget is that the act of designing and building is always a gesture in a social context (Baird 1969, 81), and this is one of the ways in which formal parody meets social history. Architecture has both an aesthetic (form) and social (use) dimension. The odd combination of the empirical and the rational in modernist theory was meant to suggest a scientific determinism that was to combat the cumulative power and weight of all that had been inherited from the past. Faith in the rational, scientific mastery of reality implicitly – then explicitly – denied the inherited, evolved cultural continuity of history. It is perhaps a loss of faith in these modernist values that has led to *post*modernist architecture today. The practitioners of this new mode form an eclectic grouping, sharing only a sense of the past (though not a "random" one) and a desire to return to the idea of architecture as both communication and community (despite the fact that both of these concepts, from a postmodern perspective, now have a distinctly problematic and decentralized ring to them). The two major theoretical spokesmen of this mixed group have been Paolo Portoghesi and Charles Jencks – both practicing architects.

As early as 1974, in *Le inibizioni dell'architettura moderna*, Portoghesi argued for the return of architecture to its roots in practical needs and in the (now problematized) aesthetic and social sense of continuity and community. Memory is central to this linking of the *past* with the *lived*. As an architect working in Rome, Portoghesi cannot avoid direct confrontation with the layers of history in his city and with the example of the baroque architects before him. History is not, however, a repository of models: he is not interested in copying or in straight revivalism. Like all the post*modernists* (and this is the reason for the label) he knows he cannot totally reject modernism, especially its material and technological advances, but he wants to integrate with these positive aspects of the immediate past the equally positive aspects of the more remote and repressed history of forms. All must be used; all must also be put into question, as architecture "writes" history through its modern re-contextualizing of the forms of the past. Surely this is exactly what Jameson (1984a, 85) and Eagleton (1985, 73) are calling for, but failing to see in postmodernist architecture, where the collective architectural language of postmodernism is put into ironic contact with "the entire historical series of its past experiences" in order to create an art that is "paradoxical and ambiguous but vital" (Portoghesi 1983, 10–11). (Portoghesi refuses to limit this historical borrowing to post-industrial periods and has been accused of being reactionary for it – Frampton 1983, 20.)

An example might make clearer the form taken by this kind of historical interrogation or ironic contamination of the present by the past. Portoghesi's early (1959–60) Casa Baldi is a direct parody (in the sense of repetition with ironic distance) of Michelangelo's Capella Sforza in S. Maria Maggiore. The exact structural echoing is made parodic – that is ironically different – by the use of new materials: vertically placed bricks and stones, instead of plaster. In addition, the church's interior shaping of corners has become the house's exterior form. Another kind of formal echoing occurs in the relation of this building to its environment. Portoghesi inverts the eighteenth-century taste for inserting ruins into the garden: the nearby (real) Roman ruins, overrun with vegetation, are echoed in his allowing nature to overrun the house as well. In his other designs, Portoghesi re-contextualizes and (literally) inverts the forms of the past in an even more radical way: a baroque church ceiling (in Borgo d'Ale) can become the basis of a Portoghesi floor plan – ironically that of the Royal Palace of Amman.

The implication of this kind of relationship to the historical forms of the past is perhaps best expressed by architect Aldo van Eyck:

Man, after all, has been accommodating himself physically in this world for thousands of years. His natural genius has neither increased nor decreased during that time. It is obvious that the full scope of this enormous environmental experience cannot be contained in the present unless we telescope the past, i.e. the entire human effort, into it. This is not historical indulgence in a limited sense, not a question of travelling back, but merely of being aware of what 'exists' in the present – what has travelled into it.

(1969, 171)

The naïveté of modernism's ideologically and aesthetically motivated rejection of the past (in the name of the future) is not countered here by an equally naïve antiquarianism, as Jameson and Eagleton assert. On the contrary, what does start to look naive, as I suggested in the last chapter, is this reductive notion that any recall of the past must, by definition, be sentimental nostalgia.

By its doubly parodic, double coding (that is, as parodic of both modernism and something else), postmodernist architecture also allows for that which was rejected as uncontrollable and deceitful by both modernism's *Gesamtkünstler* and its "life-conditioner": that is, ambiguity and irony. Architects see themselves as no longer above or outside the experience of the users of their buildings; they are now in it, subject to its echoing history and its multivalent meanings – both the results of the "recycling and creative transformation of any number of prototypes which [have] survived in the western world for centuries" (Portoghesi 1982, 5). In Portoghesi's words: "It is the loss of memory, not the cult of memory, that will make us prisoners of the past" (111). To disregard the collective memory of architecture is to risk making the mistakes of modernism and its ideology of the myth of social reform through purity of structure. Jane Jacobs has clearly documented the failure of this myth in her *Death and Life of Great American Cities* (1961), and even the opponents of postmodernism agree on the social and aesthetic effects of modernism on major urban centers.

Yet postmodernism does not entirely negate modernism. It cannot. What it does do is interpret it freely; it "critically reviews it for its glories and its errors" (Portoghesi 1982, 28). Thus modernism's dogmatic reductionism, its inability to deal with ambiguity and irony, and its denial of the validity of the past were all issues that were seriously examined and found wanting. Postmodernism attempts to be historically aware, hybrid, and inclusive. Seemingly inexhaustible historical and social curiosity and a provisional and paradoxical stance (somewhat ironic, yet involved) replace the prophetic, prescriptive posture of the great masters of modernism. An example of this new collaborative position would be Robert Pirzio Biroli's rebuilding of the Town Hall in Venzone, Italy following a recent earthquake. An elegant re-reading of the local structural models (mostly Palladian) of the Veneto region is here filtered through both the modernist technology best suited to a structure built in a seismic area and the particular needs of a modern administrative center. Even more significantly, perhaps, this building was designed with the help of a co-operative formed by the inhabitants of the destroyed village – who also literally worked at the rebuilding themselves. Here memory played a central role: both the material and cultural memory of the users of the site and the collective architectural memory of the place (and architect).

This is not to deny that there is also kitsch, kitsch that is being labelled as postmodernism: the tacking of classical arches onto the front of modernist skyscrapers, for instance. This trendy attempt to capitalize on the popularity of postmodern historicism is not the same as postmodernism itself, but is a sign of its (perhaps inevitable) commodification. Just as modernist techniques and forms became debased by dilution and commercialization, so the same has happened to the postmodern. This does not, however, undermine the positive potential value of postmodernist architecture as a whole and its salutary and necessary critique of some of the "unexamined cant" of modernism (Hubbard 1980, 8). A young Toronto architect, Bruce Kuwabara (1987), recently pointed to the importance of the postmodern breaking up of modernist dogma and its reconsideration of the urban heritage of the city. Another architect, Eberhardt Zeidler (1987), has compared this postmodern shattering of the doxa to that of mannerism's challenge to the classical order of architecture. Neither is in itself radically new, but both open things up to the possibility of the new.

There are always two ways of reading the contradictions of postmodernism, though. What Tom Wolfe (1981, 103–9; 127–9) sees as postmodernism's failure to break completely with modernism is interpreted by Portoghesi as a necessary and often even affectionate "dialogue with a father" (1982, 80). What Wolfe sees as Robert Venturi's empty ironic references, Portoghesi sees as a way of involving the decoding observer in the process of meaning-generating through ambiguity and multivalence (1982, 86). It is also a way to mark an ideological stance: the Venturis, in their work on Las Vegas, for instance, can be seen – as Jencks (1977, 70) notes – to

express, in a gentle way, a mixed appreciation for the American Way of Life. Grudging respect, not total acceptance. They don't share all the values of a consumer society, but they want to speak to this society, even if partially in dissent.

What to Wolfe is just camp historical reference in the work of Charles Moore is seen by Portoghesi as revealing the nearly limitless possibilities for recycling historic forms (1982, 86). Moore's famous Piazza d'Italia in New Orleans is perhaps the best example of what novelist John Fowles (1974, 18) once called both a homage and a kind of ironic thumbed nose to the past. With none of modernism's iconoclasm, this parodic project shows both its critical awareness and its love of history by giving new meaning to old forms, though often not without irony. We are clearly dealing here with classical forms and ornamentation, but with a new and different twist: there is no hand-crafted decoration at all (this is not a celebration of romantic individuality or even gothic craftsmanship). The ornamentation is here, but it is of a new kind, one that partakes, in fact, of the machine-tooled impersonality and standardization of modernism.

Because this is a public area for the Italian community of the city, Moore encodes signs of local Italian ethnic identity – from Latin inscriptions to a parody of the Trevi fountain. That particular corner of Rome is a complex mix of theatrical stage, palace, sculpture, and nature (rocks and water). In Moore's parodic rendition, the same elements are retained, but are now executed in new media. Sometimes even structures are refashioned and "re-functioned": a Tuscan column becomes a fountain, with water running down it. Despite the use of modernist materials like neon, concrete, and stainless steel, there is still a challenge to modernism. This appears not just in the eclectic (but never random) classical echoing, but also in the use of color and ornament in general. The same challenge is also to be seen in the deliberate contextualizing of the piazza into the local architecture. From a nearby skyscraper, Moore took the black and white coloring of the concentric rings, themselves reminiscent of the Place des Victoires in Paris. But what he did with these rings is new: the bull's-eye form draws the eye toward the center, leading us to expect symmetry. But this symmetry is denied by the incompletion of the circles. As in much postmodernist art, the eye is invited to complete the form for itself; such counter-expectation urges us to be active, not passive, viewers.

In another implicitly anti-modernist gesture, Moore takes the actual social use of the square into account. The shape that interrupts the concentric circles is a familiar boot-shaped map of Italy, with Sicily at the point of the bull's eye. Such a focus is apt because most of the Italians in New Orleans are, in fact, Sicilian. On that spot there is a podium for speeches on St Joseph's day. Piazza d'Italia is meant as a return to the idea of architecture as intimately related to the *res publica*, and the awareness of this social and political function is reflected in its echoing of classical forms – that is, an echoing of a familiar and accessible public idiom. In an implied attack on the earnest seriousness of high modernism, such relevance and function here go together with irony: the boot-shape is constructed as a new Trevi fountain, a cascade of broken forms in which (when it works properly) water flows from the highest point (the Alps) to the lowest, along the Po, Arno, and Tiber rivers. This celebration of ethnic public identity is brought about by a formal reworking of the structures and functions of both classical and modernist architecture. The dialogue of past and present, of old and new, is what gives formal expression to a belief in change within continuity. The obscurity and hermeticism of modernism are abandoned for a direct engagement of the viewer in the processes of signification through re-contextualized social and historical references.

III

Those who fear a wave of permissiveness would do well to remember
that the ironic use of quotation and the archaeological artifact as an
objet trouvé are discoveries of the figurative avant-garde of the twenties
that have landed on the island of architecture sixty years late.
Paolo Portoghesi

The other major theorist of postmodernism has been Charles Jencks, upon whose descriptions of Moore's work I have just been drawing. Influenced by modern semiotics, Jencks sees architecture as conveying meaning through language and convention. It is in this context that he situates the parodic recall of the past, the context of the need to look to history to enlarge the available vocabulary of forms. His description of Robert Stern's design for the Chicago Tribune Tower is typical in revealing his interest in the language and rhetoric of architecture:

> The skycolumn, one of the oldest metaphors for the tall building, is used very effectively here to accentuate the vertical dimension and emphasise the top. Unlike the [Adolf] Loos [1922] entry, from which Stern's tower derives, it ends with a flourish. . . . Unlike the Michelangelo pilasters [from the Palazzo Farnese in Rome], to which it also relates, it sets horizontal and vertical faces into extreme opposition by changing the colour and texture. . . . the building seems to ripple and then burst upwards towards its "shower" of grey, gold, white and red – its entablature and advertisement. Since the building is to be made from coloured glass, one would experience an odd oxymoronic contradiction – "glass/masonry" – that, in a way, is as odd as the basic conceit: the skycolumn which supports the sky.
>
> (1980a, 35)

The pun on newspaper columns is deliberate; the black and white of the building are meant to suggest print lines and, of course, the *Chicago Tribune* is red/read all over. The same punning occurs in Thomas Vreeland's World Savings and Loan Association building in California. The formal echoing of the black and white marble stripes of the campanile of the Cathedral in Sienna gives an ironic religious edge to the bank building's large and simple sign: "World Savings."

That such a complex combination of verbal and architectural languages also has direct social implications goes without saying to Jencks. Even without the verbal connection, the ideological dimension is clear. For instance, in his discussion of late-modern architecture (which Jameson confuses with postmodernism – 1984a, 80–3), Jencks points out how the "Slick-Tech" forms of "Corporate Efficiency" imply effortless mechanical control of the users of the buildings (1982, 50). But this industrial aesthetic of utility, exchange, and efficiency has been challenged by a postmodernist return to the historical and semantic awareness of architecture's relationship to the *res publica*, for example, with its very different associations of communal power, political process, and social vision (1982, 92). In other words, the self-reflexive parodic introversion suggested by a turning to the aesthetic past is itself what makes possible an ideological and social intervention. Philip Johnson returned the city street to its users in the plaza of his AT & T Building in New York precisely through his parodic historical recalling of the *loggia* as shared public space.

There are obviously borderline cases, however, where the contradictions of the postmodern use and abuse of conventions may, in fact, be rather problematic. Jencks has trouble dealing with Michael Graves's Fargo/ Moorhead Cultural Bridge with its admitted echoes of Ledoux, Castle Howard, Serliana, Wilson's architecture at Kew, Asplund, Borromini, and others. He adds other parodic reworkings which Graves does not mention, but which he himself notices: of modernist concrete construction, of mannerist broken pediments, and of cubist colors. Jencks acknowledges that the meaning of these historical references would likely be lost on the average citizen of the American mid-west. He seems to want to call this esotoric, private game-playing, but then stops and claims, after all, that "there is a general penumbra of historical meaning which would, I believe, be perceived" (1980b, 19). Like all parody, postmodernist architecture *can* certainly be élitist, if the codes necessary for its comprehension are not shared by both encoder and decoder. But the frequent use of a very common and easily recognized idiom – often that of classical architecture – works to combat such exclusiveness.

In "Post-Modern Classicism," to use Jencks's phrase, such explicit clues as columns and arches should be obvious enough to counteract any tendency to privacy of meaning. Like the "misprision" of Harold Bloom's (1973) poets, burdened by the "anxiety of influence," postmodern classicists "try hard to misread their classicism in a way which is still functional, appropriate and understandable" (Jencks 1980a, 12). It is this concern for "being understood" that replaces the modernist concern for purism of form. The search is now for a public discourse that will articulate the present in terms of the "presentness" of the past and of the social placement of art in cultural discourse – then and now. Parody of the classical tradition offers a set of references that not only remain meaningful to the public but also continue to be compositionally useful to architects.

Parody of this kind, then, is one way of making the link between art and what Said calls the "world," though it appears on the surface to be distinctly introverted, to be only a form of inter-art traffic. It is significant that postmodernist architects do not often use the term parody to describe their ironically recontextualized echoing of the forms of the past. I think this is because of the negative connotations of trivialization caused by the retention of an historically limited definition of parody as ridiculing imitation. It is to this limitation of the meaning of parody that Jameson falls prey. But there appear to be many possible pragmatic positions and strategies open to parody today – at least if we examine actual contemporary works of art: from reverence to mockery. And it is this very range that postmodernist architecture illustrates so well. The mockery is something we always associate with parody; but the deference is another story. Nevertheless, deference is exactly what architects like Thomas Gordon Smith suggest in their loving, if ironic, refunctioning of previous architectural conventions.

Smith's Matthews Street House project in San Francisco incorporates into an unremarkable stucco bungalow the front of a quite remarkable asymmetrical temple, with a Michelangelesque broken pediment. The single column in the middle of the garden is a parody of a historically previous habit of setting classical ruins in the garden or grounds of grand homes. (It is also, therefore, an ironic comment on the modern vulgarization of this habit: the presence of flamingos, dwarves, and lawn jockeys.) What is interesting, though, is that this column is precisely the one that is missing from the portico of the house. This is clearly not straight nostalgic revivalism (like Quinlan Terry's upper-class English country houses). It is closer to Martin Johnson's more extreme Ovenden House, with its definitely ironic echoes of the Victorian polychromatic church, of flying buttresses, and of medieval gunslits in its thick masonry. Parodic echoing of the past, even with this kind of irony, can still be deferential. It is in this way that postmodern parody marks its paradoxical doubleness of both continuity and change, both authority and transgression. Postmodernist parody, be it in architecture, literature, painting, film, or music, uses its historical memory, its aesthetic introversion, to signal that this kind of self-reflexive discourse is always inextricably bound to social discourse. In Charles Russell's words, the greatest contribution of postmodernism has been a recognition of the fact that "any particular meaning system in society takes its place amongst – and receives social validation from – the total pattern of semiotic systems that structure society" (1980a, 197). If the self-conscious formalism of modernism in many of the arts led to the isolation of art from the social context, then postmodernism's even more self-reflexive parodic formalism reveals that it is art as discourse that is what is intimately connected to the political and the social.

Parody has perhaps come to be a privileged mode of postmodern formal self-reflexivity because its paradoxical incorporation of the past into its very structures often points to these ideological contexts somewhat more obviously, more didactically, than other forms. Parody seems to offer a perspective on the present and the past which allows an artist to speak *to* a discourse from *within* it, but without being totally recuperated by it. Parody appears to have become, for this reason, the mode of what I have called the "ex-centric," of those who are marginalized by a dominant ideology. This is clearly true of contemporary architects trying to combat the hegemony of modernism in our century. But parody has also been a favorite postmodern literary form of writers in places like Ireland and Canada, working as they do from both inside and outside a culturally different and dominant context. And parody has certainly become a most popular and effective strategy of the other ex-centrics – of black, ethnic, gay, and feminist artists – trying to come to terms with and to respond, critically and creatively, to the still predominantly white, heterosexual, male culture in which they find themselves. For both artists and their audiences, parody sets up a dialogical relation between identification and distance. Like Brecht's *Verfremdungseffekt*, parody works to distance and, at the same time, to involve both artist and audience in a participatory hermeneutic activity. *Pace* Eagleton and Jameson, only on a very abstract level of theoretical analysis – one which ignores actual works of art – can it be dismissed as a trivial and depthless mode.

David Caute (1972) has argued that if art wants to make us question the "world," it must question and expose *itself* first, and it must do so in the name of public action. Like it or not, contemporary architecture cannot evade its representative social function. As Jencks explains: "Not only does it express the values (and land values) of a society, but also its ideologies, hopes, fears, religion, social structure, and metaphysics" (1982, 178; see too Jameson 1984a, 56). Because architecture both is and represents this state of affairs, it may be the most overt and easily studied example of postmodernist discourse, a discourse which may, in Charles Russell's words, perhaps at first

> appear to be merely the next logical step in accepted art history, but which subsequently must be seen as revealing the fatal limitations of current patterns of seeing or reading, and as having, in fact, effected a fundamental transformation of the practices of art.
>
> (1980a, 182)

Postmodern architecture seems to me to be paradigmatic of our seeming urgent need, in both artistic theory *and* practice, to investigate the relation of ideology and power to all of our present discursive structures, and it is for this reason that I will be using it as my model throughout this study.

3

LIMITING THE POSTMODERN:
THE PARADOXICAL
AFTERMATH OF MODERNISM

I

It is simplistic to make generalities about art, label these generalities,
and then go on to assume that a unified movement (or its demise)
exists because there is now a label.   *Jonathan D. Kramer*

The epigraph's warning is certainly one that must be heeded, but there are
also dangers in refusing to consider a contemporary aesthetic and intellectual phenomenon because you do not like its label. I think the term
"post-modern," as it is sometimes written, means something more than "a
dash surrounded by a contradiction," in Charles Newman's memorable
terms (1985, 17). The dash or hyphen marks more than "a stutter step; a
tenuous graft; the bobbed tale of the hybrid." Of course, there are always
those who worry about what we will label whatever comes after postmodernism. But their worry confuses the postmodern with something like
Jerome Klinkowitz's (1980) "post-contemporary." Postmodernism has a
direct link with what most people seem to have decided to call modernism.
Whatever the disagreements about what precisely characterizes modernism, we appear to have agreed upon recognizing its existence. And the
same is gradually becoming the case with postmodernism. Even Fredric
Jameson, one of its most vociferous antagonists, calls postmodernism a
periodizing concept "whose function is to correlate the emergence of new
formal features in culture with the emergence of a new type of social life and
a new economic order" (1983, 113).

That said, however, Jameson does not so much proceed to define
postmodernism as to assail it for its lacks. Both the enemies of the
postmodern (including Eagleton 1985 and Newman 1985) and its supporters
(Caramello 1983) have refused to define precisely what they mean by their
usage of the term, some (as we have seen) because they admit to assuming a
tacit definition, others because they find too many annoying contradictions
in its use. Somehow neither seems an acceptable excuse for the vagueness

and confusion that result. Clearly for these theorists and critics, among others (see, earlier, Spanos 1972; Graff 1973; Fiedler 1975), postmodernism is an evaluative designation to be used in relation to modernism. Whichever of the two is deemed the positive, the other is made into a "straw-man" adversary; in other words, necessary and important distinctions are reduced and flattened out. However, there has also been other work on postmodernism, as Susan Suleiman (1986) has pointed out, that has been either diagnostic or classificatory/analytic, and I would hope that this chapter falls into the latter category.

There already exist detailed histories of the term "postmodern" that trace its usage over the last century (see Köhler 1977; Bertens 1986; McHale 1987). My interest here is in its present use. I do not want to consider postmodernism in evaluative terms (the decline or the salvation of contemporary art), but as a definable cultural phenomenon worthy of an articulated poetics. The term exists and, if it is to have any function in cultural discourse, its usage should betray some consistency. The model I offered in the last chapter is that of the first more or less uncontested use of the term: that of postmodern architecture. As is the case there, in all the cultural practices I shall be discussing in what follows, the modern is ineluctably embedded in the postmodern (see Hassan 1975, 39–59), but the relationship is a complex one of consequence, difference, and dependence.

If my main emphasis is on the postmodernist novel, it is because it seems to be a preferential forum for *discussion* of the postmodern. Ortega y Gasset has suggested that each epoch prefers a particular genre (1963, 113), and the novel (along with architecture) appears to be the postmodern genre most discussed lately (see Russell 1985, 252). But this does not mean that postmodernism is limited to this one form in actual aesthetic practice (see Mazzaro 1980 and Altieri 1984 for poetry; Schmid 1986 for drama; Foster 1985, Krauss 1985, Burgin 1986, and D. Davis 1977 for visual and video arts). In fact I would like to argue that we must take into account not only other art forms but also theoretical discourse, if we are to define a poetics of the paradoxical creature of our age that we have labelled, for better or worse, as postmodernism. As Rosalind Krauss has pointed out:

> If one of the tenets of modernist literature had been the creation of a work that would force reflection on the conditions of its own construction, that would insist on reading as a much more consciously *critical* act, then it is not surprising that the medium of a *post*modernist literature should be the critical text wrought into a paraliterary form. And what is clear is that Barthes and Derrida are the *writers*, not the critics, that students now read.
>
> (1980, 40)

II

One of the fundamental postmodern acts is the opening up once again
of the question of where the domain of the arts should be, how they
abut on the social and even natural sciences. *David Antin*

The interrogations and contradictions of what I want to call the postmodern begin with the relationship of present art to past art and of present culture to past history. It is symptomatic of this relation of recall that a postmodernist architect like Philip Johnson should begin as both an architectural historian and also a modernist architect, for the postmodern grows out of precisely this conjuncture. In his book, *Form Follows Fiasco* (1977), Peter Blake sees postmodernism arising out of the rethinking of modernism by the modernists themselves, in the face of the social and aesthetic failure of the International Style. Seeing the need for a new direction that would return architecture to the human and material resources of the social landscape, they turned from pure form to function and to the *history* of function. But one never returns to the past without distance, and in postmodern architecture that distance has been signalled by irony.

Many of the foes of postmodernism see irony as fundamentally antiserious, but this is to mistake and misconstrue the critical power of doublevoicing. As Umberto Eco has said, about both his own historiographic metafiction and his semiotic theorizing, the "game of irony" is intricately involved in seriousness of purpose and theme. In fact irony may be the only way we *can* be serious today. There is no innocence in our world, he suggests. We cannot ignore the discourses that precede and contextualize everything we say and do, and it is through ironic parody that we signal our awareness of this inescapable fact. The "already-said" must be reconsidered and can be reconsidered only in an ironic way (in Rosso 1983, 2–5).

This is as far from "nostalgia" as anyone could wish. Yet we have seen that Jameson and Eagleton, in their recent writings on postmodernism, attack it for being nostalgic in its relation to the past. But if nostalgia connotes evasion of the present, idealization of a (fantasy) past, or a recovery of that past as edenic, then the postmodernist ironic rethinking of history is definitely not nostalgic. It critically confronts the past with the present, and vice versa. In a direct reaction against the tendency of our times to value only the new and novel, it returns us to a re-thought past to see what, if anything, is of value in that past experience. But the critique of its irony is doubleedged: the past and the present are judged in each other's light.

For its enemies, however, such a critical use of irony is conveniently overlooked. Postmodernism is deemed reactionary in its impulse to return to the forms of the past (Frampton 1983). But to say this is to ignore the actual historical forms to which artists return. It also overlooks everything that return is in reaction against. In Portoghesi's words (1983, 7):

> This recovery of memory, after the forced amnesia of a half century, is manifest in customs, dress . . . , in the mass diffusion of an interest in history and its products, in the ever vaster need for contemplative experiences and contact with nature that seemed antithetical to the civilizations of machines

that has characterized modernism in the twentieth century. This is not a monolithic nostalgia that bankrupts the present; it is the postmodern's search for "its own 'difference' in the removed repetition and utilization of the entire past" (13). To the enemies of postmodernism this kind of recall provides only a façade to cover up the harsh realities of contemporary high tech consumerism. But to say this is to ignore what modernism in architecture was, and what it has done to the social fabric of our urban centers.

While postmodern architecture has been the art form to come most under attack for its parodic intertextuality and its avowed relation to history (both aesthetic and social), postmodernist fiction has also been called the death of the novel by so many critics that a list would run on for pages. It is important to note, however, that what is usually meant by the use of the term "postmodern" in this case is metafiction, often of the most extreme variety – American surfiction or the French New or New New Novel. Theorists of metafiction themselves argue that this fiction no longer attempts to mirror reality or tell any truth about it (McCaffery 1982, 5; Sukenick 1985, 3). This is certainly one of the consequences of what I see, not as postmodernism, but as an extreme of *modernist* autotelic self-reflexion in contemporary metafiction. It is for this reason that I would like to argue – on the model of postmodern architecture – that the term postmodernism in fiction be reserved to describe the more paradoxical and historically complex form that I have been calling "historiographic metafiction." Surfiction and the New Novel are like abstract art: they do not so much transgress codes of representation as leave them alone (Burgin 1986; 23). Postmodern novels problematize narrative representation, even as they invoke it.

Like the architecture of Charles Moore and Riccardo Bofill, this kind of fiction (*Star Turn, A Maggot, The Old Gringo, Ragtime*, and so on) not only is self-reflexively metafictional and parodic, but also makes a claim to some kind of (newly problematized) historical reference. It does not so much deny as contest the "truths" of reality and fiction – the human constructs by which we manage to live in our world. Fiction does not mirror reality; nor does it reproduce it. It cannot. There is no pretense of simplistic mimesis in historiographic metafiction. Instead, fiction is offered as another of the discourses by which we construct our versions of reality, and both the construction and the need for it are what are foregrounded in the post-modernist novel.

One of the ways that this foregrounding is carried out is by stressing the contexts in which the fiction is being produced – by both writer and reader. In other words, the questions of history and ironic intertextuality necessitate a consideration of the entire "enunciative" or discursive situation of fiction. Postmodernism does not just move the emphasis from the producer or the text to the receiver (cf. Hoffmann, Hornung, and Kunow 1977, 40; Bertens 1986, 46). As we shall see in Chapter 5, it re-contextualizes both the production and reception processes and the text itself within an entire communication situation which includes the social, ideological, historical, and aesthetic contexts in which those processes and that product exist. And in no way are these "inertly 'contextual'" (Batsleer *et al.* 1985, 3). The modernist privileging of the alienated artist's perspective and language gives way to the postmodernist "re-evaluation of the individual's response to his society, and in particular, to society's semiotic codes of behavior, value and discourse" (Russell 1980b, 29), as can be seen in this address to (very specific) readers by the Chinese-American narrator of Maxine Hong Kingston's *The Woman Warrior* (1976, 5–6):

> Chinese Americans, when you try to understand what things in you are Chinese, how do you separate what is peculiar to childhood, to poverty, insanities, one family, your mother who marked your growing with stories, from what is Chinese? What is Chinese tradition and what is the movies?

Specificity of context is part of the "situating" of postmodernism.

In other words, postmodernism goes beyond self-reflexivity to situate discourse in a broader context. Self-conscious metafiction has been with us for a long time, probably since Homer and certainly since *Don Quixote* and *Tristram Shandy* (see Hutcheon 1980; Alter 1975). In film, self-reflexivity has been a common technique of modernist narrative, used to undercut representation and viewer identification (Siska 1979, 286). The more complex and more overt discursive contextualizing of postmodernism goes one step beyond this auto-representation and its demystifying intent, for it is fundamentally critical in its ironic relation to the past and the *present*. This is true of postmodern fiction and architecture, as it is of much contemporary historical, philosophical, and literary theoretical discourse today.

Postmodernism's relationship with contemporary mass culture is not, then, just one of implication; it is also one of critique. Artists *and theorists* alike are implicated in our particular form of industrial capitalism that "organizes production for profit rather than for use" (Eagleton 1983, 34). Critics teach, write, and publish within the same strictures as do postmodern artists. It is self-defeating, as Dominick LaCapra argues, to indulge in "an indiscriminate attack on the 'one-dimensionality' of mass culture and to ignore countercurrents or forces of resistance in it" (1985a, 79). It is not only the Jamesons and Eagletons who represent such "countercurrents," though they certainly do; like the historical avant-garde (Huyssen 1986, viii), postmodernism in general is such a force of resistance, and I would agree with LaCapra that it is futile "to convert literary criticism and intellectual history into negatively critical sociologies of the 'culture industry,' for this would help extirpate modes of interpretation sensitive to countercurrents both in the artefacts of the past and in one's own discourse about them" (1985a, 79). Postmodern art is a particularly didactic art: it teaches us about those countercurrents, if we are willing to listen.

One of the things we must be open to listening to is what I have called the ex-centric, the off-center. Postmodernism questions centralized, totalized, hierarchized, closed systems: questions, but does not destroy (cf. Bertens 1986, 46–7). It acknowledges the human urge to make order, while pointing out that the orders we create are just that: human constructs, not natural or given entities. As we shall see in the next chapter, part of its questioning involves an energizing rethinking of margins and edges, of what does not fit in the humanly constructed notion of center. Such interrogations of the impulse to sameness (or single otherness) and homogeneity, unity and certainty, make room for a consideration of the different and the hetero-geneous, the hybrid and the provisional. This is not a rejection of the former values in favor of the latter; it is a rethinking of each in the light of the others. It is not a move to art as unpremeditated, as composition in a completely open field (cf. Sukenick 1985, 8), nor is it a denial of "the age of the moralized and individual self" (Zavarzadeh 1976, 82). It is more a question-ing of commonly accepted values of our culture (closure, teleology, and subjectivity), a questioning that is totally dependent upon that which it interrogates. This is perhaps the most basic formulation possible of the paradox of the postmodern.

III

> Unfortunately, 'postmodern' is a term *bon à tout faire*. I have the impression that it is applied today to anything the user happens to like. Further, there seems to be an attempt to make it increasingly retroactive: first it was apparently applied to certain writers or artists active in the last twenty years, then gradually it reached the beginning of the century, then still further back. And this reverse procedure continues; soon the postmodern category will include Homer.
> *Umberto Eco*

When Charles Newman attempts to denigrate the "essence" of the postmodern strategy by characterizing it as one of assimilating "voraciously (though rarely systematically) while simultaneously repudiating assimi-lation" (1985, 28), he has, in fact, put his finger on precisely what characterizes postmodernism: contradiction and a move toward anti-totalization. The same is true when Charles Russell calls postmodernism "an art of criticism, with no message other than the need for continuous questioning. It is an art of unrest, with no clearly defined audience other than those predisposed to doubt and to search" (in Russell 1981, 58). Russell intends this as a criticism of the postmodern, for (at this early stage in his theorizing) he would prefer to see in it a new romantic individualism and originality as mediated through modernist transcendence, a move "beyond doubt and distrust toward inspired vision" (5). But this kind of move is not part of the postmodernist enterprise, as he saw later. As the very label of "historiographic metafiction" is intended to suggest, postmodernism remains fundamentally contradictory, offering only questions, never final answers. In fiction, it combines what Malcolm Bradbury (1973, 15) has called "argument by poetics" (metafiction) with "argument by historicism" (historiographic) in such a way as to inscribe a mutual interrogation within the texts themselves.

We have seen that the contradictions that characterize postmodernism reject any neat binary opposition that might conceal a secret hierarchy of values. The elements of these contradictions are usually multiple; the focus is on differences, not single otherness; and their roots are most likely to be found in the very modernism from which postmodernism derives its name (or rather, from the "ideal type notion" of modernism that has resulted from successive canonizations – Huyssen 1986, 53). Many critics have pointed out the glaring contradictions of modernism: its élitist, classical need for order and its revolutionary formal innovations (Kermode 1971, 91); its "Janus-faced" anarchistic urge to destroy existing systems combined with a reactionary political vision of ideal order (Daiches 1971, 197); its compulsion to write mixed with a realization of the meaninglessness of writing (in the work of Beckett or Kafka); its melancholy regret for the loss of presence and its experimental energy and power of conception (Lyotard 1986, 30–1). In fact, Terry Eagleton sees as a positive characteristic of modernism the fact that it retains its contradictions: "between a still ineluctable bourgeois humanism and the pressures of a quite different rationality, which, still newly emergent, is not even able to name itself" (1985, 70). Postmodernism challenges some aspects of modernist dogma: its view of the autonomy of art and its deliberate separation from life; its expression of individual subjectivity; its adversarial status *vis-à-vis* mass culture and bourgeois life (Huyssen 1986, 53). But, on the other hand, the postmodern clearly also developed out of other modernist strategies: its self-reflexive experimentation, its ironic ambiguities, and its contestations of classic realist representation.

However, I would argue not only that postmodernism, like modernism, also retains its own contradictions, but also that it foregrounds them to such an extent that they become the very defining characteristics of the entire cultural phenomenon we label with that name. The postmodern is in no way absolutist; it does not say that "it is both impossible and useless to try and establish some hierarchical order, some system of priorities in life" (Fokkema 1986b, 82). What it does say is that there are all kinds of orders and systems in our world – *and* that we create them all. That is their justification and their limitation. They do not exist "out there", fixed, given, universal, eternal; they are human constructs in history. This does not make them any the less necessary or desirable. It does, however, as we have seen, condition their "truth" value. The local, the limited, the temporary, the provisional are what define postmodern "truth" in novels like John Banville's *Kepler* or Christa Wolfe's *Cassandra*. The point is not exactly that the world is meaningless (A. Wilde 1981, 148), but that any meaning that exists is of our own creation.

In fiction, it is self-reflexivity that works to make the paradoxes of postmodernism overt and even defining. Many have argued that all art possesses some of these devices of self-reference and that they function in much the same way:

Even the most "realistic" of works use such conventions because, rather than trying to "take us in" (that is, to delude us), they prefer to show us how close they have come to doing so, how marvellously verisimilar their illusion is: one cannot appreciate the verisimilar without being aware that it is not the thing itself.

(Krieger 1982, 101; see too 1976, 182–3)

No language, in other words, is really "self-effacing"; all is to some degree "self-apparent," to use Jerome Klinkowitz's terms (1984, 14). Postmodernism, in this perspective, would just be a more self-conscious and overt manifestation of the basic paradox of aesthetic form.

But there are other postmodern contradictions that are less generalizable. While much art uses irony and parody to inscribe and yet critique the discourses of its past, of the "already-said," postmodernism is almost always double-voiced in its attempts to historicize and contextualize the enunciative situation of its art. Black American culture has been defined as one of "double consciousness" (W. E. B. DuBois 1973, 3) in which black and white, slave and master cultures are never reconciled, but held in a doubled suspension. Some types of feminism have argued much the same sort of relationship between female and male culture. The next chapter will investigate how both of these social forces have had their impact on postmodernism, and how its contradictory double- or multiple-voicing is one of the manifestations of this impact.

There are many forms that this paradoxical identity of the postmodern can take. One of the most interesting involves the actual reception of postmodernism. Douwe Fokkema has argued that it is "sociologically limited to mostly academic readers interested in complicated texts" (1986b, 81). (For a similar argument re modernism, see Todd 1986, 79.) But if that is true, how do we account for the fact that *The Name of the Rose, The French Lieutenant's Woman, Ragtime, Midnight's Children, Flaubert's Parrot*, and so many other historiographic metafictions have been prominent on the best-sellers' lists in both Europe and North America? One of the contradictions of postmodernism, I would argue, is that it does indeed "close the gap" that Leslie Fiedler (1975) saw between high and low art forms, and it does so through the ironizing of both. Think of the ironic mixtures of religious history and the detective story in *The Name of the Rose* or of war documentary and science fiction in *Slaughterhouse-Five*. Woody Allen's films (see D'Haen 1986; 226) also close this gap by paradoxically using both familiar movie staples (love, anxiety, sex) and also sophisticated parodic and metafictional forms (for example in *Play it Again, Sam* or *The Purple Rose of Cairo*). Postmodernism is both academic and popular, élitist and accessible.

One of the ways in which it achieves this paradoxical popular-academic identity is through its technique of installing and then subverting familiar conventions of both kinds of art. E. L. Doctorow has claimed that he had to give up trying to write *The Book of Daniel* with the usual realist narrative concern for transition that is characteristic of the nineteenth-century novel (and popular fiction) (in Trenner 1983, 40), yet he self-consciously has his narrating character both exploit and undercut that very structural concern for continuity. In its contradictions, postmodernist fiction tries to offer what Stanley Fish (1972, xiii) once called a "dialectical" literary presentation, one that disturbs readers, forcing them to scrutinize their own values and beliefs, rather than pandering to or satisfying them. But as Umberto Eco has reminded us, postmodern fiction may seem more open in form, but constraint is always needed in order to feel free (in Rosso 1983, 6). This kind of novel self-consciously uses the trappings of what Fish calls "rhetorical" literary presentation (omniscient narrators, coherent characterization, plot closure) in order to point to the humanly constructed character of these trappings – their arbitrariness and conventionality. This is what I mean by the typically contradictory postmodern exploitation and subversion of the familiar staples of both realist and modernist fiction.

We have seen that when postmodern architects showed the world their wares at that Venice Biennale in 1980, they chose as their banner the motto: "the presence of the past." This obvious paradox offers a conjoining of performance in the present and recording of the past. In fiction, this contradiction is played out in terms of parody and metafiction versus the conventions of realism. The metafictionally present modern narrator of Fowles's *The French Lieutenant's Woman* jars with and parodies the conventions of the nineteenth-century novelistic tale of Charles, Sarah, and Ernestina. The various Chinese boxes of narrators and fiction-makers (Fowles, the narrator, his persona, Charles, and finally Sarah) enact the novel's themes of freedom and power, of creation and control. The multiple parodies of specific Victorian novels (by Thackeray, George Eliot, Dickens, Froude, Hardy) are matched by more generic ironic play on nineteenth-century authoritative narrating voices, reader address, and narrative closure.

This complex and extended parody is not, however, just a game for the academic reader. It is overtly intended to prevent any reader from ignoring both the modern and the specifically Victorian social, as well as aesthetic, contexts. We are not allowed to say either that this is "only a story" or that it is "only about the Victorian period." The past is always placed critically – and not nostalgically – in relation with the present. The questions of sexuality, of social inequality and responsiblity, of science and religion, and of the relation of art to the world are all raised and directed both at the modern reader and the social and literary conventions of the last century. The plot structure of *The French Lieutenant's Woman* enacts the dialectic of freedom and power that is the modern existentialist and even Marxist answer to Victorian or Darwinian determinism. But it requires that historical context in order to interrogate the present (as well as the past) through its critical irony. Parodic self-reflexiveness paradoxically leads here to the possibility of a literature which, while asserting its modernist autonomy as art, also manages simultaneously to investigate its intricate and intimate relations with the social world in which it is written and read.

This kind of contradiction is what characterizes postmodern art, which works to subvert dominant discourses, but is dependent upon those same discourses for its very physical existence: the "already-said." Yet, I think it is wrong to see postmodernism as defined in any way by an "either/or" structure. As we shall see in more detail in Chapter 12, it is not a case of its being either nostalgically neoconservative or radically antihumanist in its politics (Foster 1985, 121). It is, actually, both and neither. Certainly it is marked by a return to history, and it does indeed problematize the entire notion of historical knowledge. But the reinstalling of memory is not uncritical or reactionary, and the problematization of humanist certainties does not mean their denial or death. Postmodernism does not so much erode our "sense of history" and reference (Foster 1985, 132), as erode our old sure sense of what both history and reference meant. It asks us to rethink and critique our notions of both.

Both theorists and artists have recognized that paradox can often reek of compromise. Witness video artist Douglas Davis's view:

> If I want to address my art to the world, I must address it through the system, as must everyone else. It this sounds suspiciously like liberalism and compromise, so be it: liberalism and compromise is the only way any true revolutionary has ever worked, save through the sword.
>
> (1977, 22)

Certainly *The French Lieutenant's Woman* would corroborate such a view of contradiction as compromise, but not compromise in the sense of avoidance of questioning or of creating a new and alternate unifying interpretative totality. Postmodernism exploits, but also undermines, such staples of our humanist tradition as the coherent subject and the accessible historical referent, and this may well be what is so irritating about it for Eagleton and Jameson. The contested concepts of artistic originality and "authenticity" and of any stable historical entity (such as "the worker") would appear to be central to their Marxist master narrative. The postmodern blurring of firm distinctions is probably, by definition, anathema to Marxist dialectical reasoning, as it is to any Habermasian position of Enlightenment rationality. Both of these influential positions of opposition to postmodernism are founded on the kind of totalizing meta-narratives (Lyotard 1984a) that postmodernism challenges – that is, at once uses and abuses. I would argue, along with Nannie Doyle and others, that what is positive, not negative, about postmodernism is that it does not attempt to hide its relationship to consumer society, but rather exploits it to new critical and politicized ends, acknowledging openly the "indissoluble relation between cultural production and its political and social affiliations" (Doyle 1985, 169).

Postmodern discourses assert both autonomy and worldliness. Likewise, they participate in both theory and praxis. They offer a collective, historicized context for individual action. In other words, they do not deny the individual, but they do "situate" her/him. And they do not deny that collectivity can be perceived as manipulation as well as activism: witness Pynchon's and Rushdie's novels of paranoia. The postmodern is not quite an avant-garde. It is not as radical or as adversarial. In Charles Russell's view (1985), the avant-garde is self-consciously modern and subject to socio-cultural change. The same is true of the postmodern, but this valuing (fetishizing?) of innovation is conditioned by a re-evaluation of the past which puts newness and novelty into perspective. The avant-garde is also seen as critical of the dominant culture and alienated from it in a way that the postmodern is not, largely because of its acknowledgement of its unavoid-able implication in that dominant culture. At the same time, of course, it both exploits and critically undermines that dominance. In short, the post-modern is not as negating (of the past) or as Utopic (about the future) as is, at least, the historical or modernist avant-garde. It incorporates its past within its very name and parodically seeks to inscribe its criticism of that past.

These contradictions of postmodernism are not really meant to be resolved, but rather are to be held in an ironic tension. For example in John Fowles's *A Maggot*, there are an amazing number of such unresolved and unresolvable paradoxes. On a formal level, the novel holds in tension the conventions of history and fiction (specifically, of romance and science fiction). One of its main narrative structures is that of question and answer (a lawyer's questioning of witnesses), a structure that foregrounds the conflicts between truth and lies, differing perceptions of truth, facts and beliefs, and truth and illusion. The transcribing clerk believes there are two truths: "one that a person believes is truth; and one that is truth incontestible" (1985, 345), but the entire novel works to problematize such binary certainty. The contradictory tensions recur in the twentieth-century narrator/historian's emphasizing of his distance from the 1736 action of his plot. The two major antagonists, the male lawyer Ayscough and the prostitute-turned-Dissenter Rebecca Lee are established as each other's opposite: in gender, class, education, religion. They come to represent reason versus instinct, male versus female, even left versus right hemis-pheres of the brain.

In this novel there are still other unresolved thematic contradictions: the absent "hero," known as His Lordship, is both a scientist and a believer in theories of the physical world that are "more phantasies than probable or experimental truths" (188). Christianity and paganism are also played off against each other constantly in the novel, and the narrator's interest in Dissenters, especially the Shakers, comes from the fact that they too have been perceived in contradictory ways: "Orthodox theologians have always despised the sect's doctrinal naïvety; orthodox priests, its fanaticism; orthodox capitalists, its communism; orthodox communists, its super-stition; orthodox sensualists, its abhorrence of the carnal; and orthodox males, its striking feminism" (450). The different and the paradoxical fascinate the postmodern.

So too do the multiple and the provisional. In the course of the novel, the titular "maggot" is defined as "the larval stage of a winged creature; as is the written text, at least in the writer's hope" (unpaginated prologue, signed by Fowles). We are also told from the start that the word signifies a whim or quirk. Within the plot, maggots are associated with death (260) and with fancy (277). The title's full contradictory force comes from Rebecca's description of the large white object in the cave as a "great swollen maggot . . . tho' not" (355). The challenging of certainty, the asking of questions, the revealing of fiction-making where we might have once accepted the existence of some absolute "truth" – this is the project of postmodernism.

Ihab Hassan sees the oppositional paradox of postmodernism as lying in "its fanatic will to unmaking," on the one hand, and, on the other, "the need to discover a 'unitary' sensibility" (1982, 265). I see this paradox as less oppositional than provisional; I see it, instead, as an inscribing and undercutting of *both* any unitary sensibility *and* any disruptive will to unmake, for these are equally absolutist and totalizing concepts. Post-modernism is characterized by energy derived from the rethinking of the value of multiplicity and provisionality; in actual practice, it does not seem to be defined by any potentially paralyzing opposition between making and unmaking. This is the energy (if also logical inconsistency) we get from those cohesive challenges to coherence in the work of Foucault or Lyotard (see Roth 1985, 107). Postmodernist discourses – both theoretical and practical – need the very myths and conventions they contest and reduce (Watkins 1978, 222); they do not necessarily come to terms with either order or disorder (cf. A. Wilde 1981, 10), but question both in terms of each other. The myths and conventions exist for a reason, and postmodernism investigates that reason. The postmodern impulse is not to seek any total vision. It merely questions. If it *finds* such a vision, it questions how, in fact, it *made* it.

IV

> The great modern achievements were wagers which made gestures, invented methods, but laid no foundations for a future literature. They led in the direction of an immensity from which there was bound to be a turning back because to go further would lead to a new and completer fragmentation, utter obscurity, formlessness without end.
> *Stephen Spender*

History has proved Spender wrong, for in postmodernism we see the results of those wagers and they have not taken the form he imagined. The debate over the definition of both modernism and postmodernism has now been going on for years (see Fokkema 1984, 12–36). There is little firm agreement on their limiting dates, their defining characteristics, even the players in the game. Instead of trying to delimit either, I would like to look at the configuration of concerns in each that could help us define a poetics of postmodernism in its relation to modernism. In other words, I do not want to enter into the arguments of evaluation; nor do I want to set the one enterprise against the other. The entire issue of binary oppositions like this one needs rethinking. What inevitably happens is that one – either modernism or postmodernism – gets privileged over the other.

One of the most influential of postmodern theorists, Ihab Hassan, is fond of creating parallel columns that place characteristics of the one next to their opposite characteristics in the other, usually making clear his preference for the postmodern. But this "either/or" thinking suggests a resolution of what I see as the unresolvable contradictions within postmodernism. For example I would see it less as a case of postmodern play versus modernist purpose, as Hassan claims (1982, 267–8), than as a case of play with purpose. The same is true of all his oppositions: postmodernism is the *process* of making the *product*; it is *absence* within *presence*, it is *dispersal* that needs *centering* in order to *be* dispersal; it is the *ideolect* that wants to be, but knows it cannot be, the *master code*; it is *immanence* denying yet yearning for *transcendence*. In other words, the postmodern partakes of a logic of "both/and," not one of "either/or." And, not surprisingly, those who privilege the modernist over the postmodernist also work in similar oppositional binary terms (Graff 1979; Eagleton 1985; Newman 1985).

As I have already mentioned, the major danger in setting up this kind of structure is that of creating "straw men" in order to make one's point more clearly. For instance when we read that modernism's concept of time is "inescapably linear" and "ideally controllable" (Calinescu 1983, 284), we wonder what happened to those experimental works of Woolf, Joyce, Eliot, and others we think of as modernists. Did modernism really abandon *"intracultural dialogue"* (Calinescu 1983, 275, his italics)? What about *The Waste Land* or *Finnegans Wake*? No matter which "ism" is preferred, both it and its antagonist run the risk of this kind of reduction. And no two critics seem to agree on which reductions to make. Jameson (1984c) sees modernism as oppositional and marginal – what I take as important defining characteristics of the *post*modern. He offers no proof why modernism is somehow exempt from implication in mass culture. (Andreas Huyssen – 1986, viii – suggests that it is because of its élitism that attempted to transcend that mass culture.) Nor does he offer any reason why he sees postmodernism in particular as the dominant aesthetic of consumer society (Jameson 1984c, 197). In this book, I will be arguing that such reasons must be given and that, in defining postmodernism, it is necessary to be as specific and explanatory as possible.

It is all too easy to reject, as does John Barth, all notions of postmodernism based on its being an extension, intensification, subversion, or repudiation of modernism (1980, 69). But modernism literally and physically haunts postmodernism, and their interrelations should not be ignored. Indeed there appear to be two dominant schools of thought about the nature of the interaction of the two enterprises: the first sees postmodernism as a total break from modernism and the language of this school is the radical rhetoric

of rupture; the second sees the postmodern as an extension and intensification of certain characteristics of modernism.

The radical break theory depends upon firm binary oppositions that operate on the formal, philosophical, and ideological levels. On the formal level,
postmodern surface is opposed to modernist depth (A. Wilde 1981, 43;
Sontag 1967), and the ironic and parodic tone of postmodernism contrasts
with the seriousness of modernism (Graff 1979, 55; Zurbrugg 1986, 78). It is
easy to see which half is being privileged here, though it usually is not quite
as clear when the oppositions are between chaos and order or contingency
and coherence (Bradbury 1983, 160; 185). This last point is often made in
terms of the difference between the modernist use of myth as a structuring
device in the work of, for instance, Mann, Pavese, or Joyce (see Begnal 1973;
Beebe 1972, 175; 1974, 1,076) and the postmodern ironic contesting of myth
as master narrative in the novels of Barth, Reed, or Morrison, where there is
no consolation of form or consensual belief (Lyotard 1986, 32–3). Modernism has been seen as creating its own form of aesthetic authority in the face
of a center that was not holding (Hassan 1975, 59; Josipovici 1977, 109), but
if that point is made, it usually entails claiming that postmodernism is to be
defined as anarchic, in complicity with chaos, accepting of uncertainty and
confusion (A. Wilde 1981, 44). Postmodern skepticism is presented as the
refutation and rejection of modernism's heroism (A. Wilde 1981, 132–3). Instead of this kind of opposition, I would argue that what postmodernism
does is use and abuse these characteristics of modernism in order to install a
questioning of *both* of the listed extremes.

Related to these formal and tonal distinctions between the two are
differences in philosophical intent. But even here there is little agreement.
One group (McHale 1987; A. Wilde 1981) sees modernism as epistemological
in its focus, while postmodernism is ontological. The other group just
reverses the adjectives (Krysinski 1981; McCaffery 1982; Russell 1974).
Again, I would argue that the contradictions of postmodernism cannot be
described in "either/or" terms (especially if they are going to be reversible!).
Historiographic metafiction asks both epistemological and ontological
questions. How do we know the past (or the present)? What is the
ontological status of that past? Of its documents? Of our narratives?

For some critics, this philosophical issue is also an ideological one. The
postmodern's epistemological break from modernism is seen by some as
linked to an important new role it is to play in "worldly practices"
(Radhakrishnan 1983, 34). This is precisely what Jameson accuses postmodernism of in a *negative* sense: he sees it as too involved in the economic
system of late capitalism, too institutionalized (1984a, 56). It does not share,
he says, modernism's repudiation of the Victorian bourgeoisie. But perhaps
it questions any such easy repudiation, and does so in the light of its
acknowledgements of its own inescapable ideological implication in precisely the contemporary situation of late capitalism.

It is worth recalling that this same modernism has also been accused of cultural élitism and hermeticism, political conservatism, alienating theories of the autonomy of art, and a search for transcendent, ahistorical dimensions of human experience (Russell 1981, 8). It would not be difficult to figure out what postmodernism challenges and what attempts at change it offers in the stead of such a list: cultural democratizing of high/low art distinctions and a new didacticism, potentially radical political questioning, contextualizing theories of the discursive complexity of art, and a contesting of all ahistorical and totalizing visions. In fact Charles Russell argues precisely this:

> postmodern literature recognizes that all perception, cognition, action, and articulation are shaped, if not determined, by the social domain. There can be no simple opposition to culture, no transcendent perspective or language, no secure singular self-definition, for all find their meaning only within a social framework.
>
> (1985, 246)

Clearly it all depends on who is valorizing what in this kind of theory of an epistemic break between the modern and the postmodern.

The other school of thought argues a relationship of continuity or extension between the two. For David Lodge, they share a commitment to innovation and to a critique of tradition, even if the manifestations of these shared values differ (1977, 220–45). On a formal level, modernism and postmodernism are said to share self-reflexivity (Fokkema 1984, 17), fragmentation (Newman 1985, 113), and a concern for history (literary and social) (Thiher 1984, 216–19). Certainly postmodern works have turned to modernist texts – often in different media – in their parodic play with convention and history. Peter Maxwell Davies has used Joyce's Cyclops episode in *Ulysses* as the model for his *Missa super L'Homme Armé* and Gordon Crosse's Second Violin Concerto uses Nabokov's *Pale Fire* for structural inspiration. Saura's flamenco film of *Carmen* invokes and comments upon both Bizet's opera and Mérimée's story.

On a more theoretical level, some critics see postmodernism as raising the same kinds of issues as modernism: investigating the cultural assumptions underlying our models of history (Josipovici 1977, 145) or challenging the entire western humanistic tradition (Spanos 1972, 147). Others argue that the ironic distance that modernism sets up between art and audience is, in fact, intensified in postmodernism's "double-distancing" (Hayman 1978, 34–6). For others, postmodern fiction completes modernism's break with traditional realism and bourgeois rationalism (Graff 1975), just as postmodern poetry is seen as continuing the modernist challenge to romantic self-transcendence, though its stress on the local and topical does contest modernist impersonality (Altieri 1973, 629).

As this last example suggests, the continuity model is not without its necessary alterations and exceptions. My own response is probably typically postmodernist in its acceptance of both models, for I see as one of the many contradictions of postmodernism that it can both self-consciously incor-porate and equally self-consciously challenge that modernism from which it derives and to which it owes even its verbal existence. There has been a certain move in criticism (see Pütz 1973, 228; Butler 1980, 138; Bertens 1986, 47–8; Todd 1986, 105–6) to distinguish between two types of post-modernism: one that is non-mimetic, ultra-autonomous, anti-referential, and another that is historically *engagé*, problematically referential. I would argue that only the latter properly defines postmodernism, according to the model developed here (based on postmodern architecture). The former presents many difficulties, not the least of which are logical ones. *Can* language and literature *ever* be totally non-mimetic, non-referential, and still remain understandable as literature? This is a theoretical problem that the radical rhetoric of antirepresentation usually ignores. Can there ever really be a total "loss of meaning" in art (Graff 1973, 391)? Would we still call it art? Is there anything to which we cannot grant meaning?

The attempt to make the label "postmodernist" describe these extremes of modernist aestheticism is, I believe, a mistaken one. Much contemporary metafiction is indeed almost solely concerned with its own artifice, its own aesthetic workings. But self-reflexivity has a long history in art, and, in fact, the label of "self-begetting novel" has been used to describe both modernist fiction and the New Novel (Kellman 1980). The postmodernist art I have been and will be describing in this book is historical and political in a way that much metafiction is not. It cannot be described as removing represen-tation and replacing it with textual materiality (Klinkowitz 1985, 192). Nor does it unquestioningly accept the act of fiction-making as a humanist stay against chaos (Alter 1975; Hutcheon 1980; Christensen 1981).

It is the French New and also the New New Novel, along with American surfiction, that are most often cited by critics as examples of postmodernist fiction. But by my model, they would, instead, be examples of late modernist extremism. Others have taken this stand as well: Spanos (1972, 165); Mellard (1980); A. Wilde (1981, 144); Butler (1980, 132). Moder-nist hermeticism and autotelic reflexivity characterize much surfiction and its theorizing. Raymond Federman (as both surfictionist and theorist) claims that his extreme metafiction represents an effort to reinstate things and the world in their proper places, but somehow in a purer state. The way he speaks of surfiction betrays his modernist and almost romantic bias: it is "the kind of fiction that constantly renews our faith in man's imagination and not in man's distorted vision of reality" (1981b, 7). Fiction is "an autonomous art form in its own right" (9). No contradictory and interrogating postmodernist discourse could speak with such authority and certainty.

Postmodern fiction challenges both structuralist/modernist formalism and any simple mimeticist/realist notions of referentiality. It took the modernist novel a long time to win back its artistic autonomy from the dogma of realist theories of representation; it has taken the postmodernist novel just as long to win back its historicizing and contextualizing from the dogma of modernist aestheticism (which would include the hermeticism and ultra-formalism of the "textes" of *Tel Quel*, for example). What I want to call postmodernism in fiction paradoxically uses and abuses the conventions of both realism and modernism, and does so in order to challenge their transparency, in order to prevent glossing over the contradictions that make the postmodern what it is: historical and metafictional, contextual and self-reflexive, ever aware of its status as discourse, as a human construct.

V

> Assumptions about literature involve assumptions about language and about meaning, and these in turn involve assumptions about human society. The independent universe of literature and the autonomy of criticism are illusory.   *Catherine Belsey*

What postmodern aesthetic practice shares with much contemporary theory (psychoanalytic, linguistic, analytic philosophical, hermeneutic, poststructuralist, historiographical, discourse analytic, semiotic) is an interest in interpretative strategies and in the situating of verbal utterances in social action. Although the names of Lacan, Lyotard, Barthes, Baudrillard, and Derrida tend to be the most cited in discussions of postmodernism, the other perspectives listed are just as important to any consideration of contemporary theoretical discourse and its intersection with art. We can not ignore Marxist, neo-pragmatist, and feminist theory, to add only three more important ones to the list. All of these forms of theory will be discussed in the following chapters, at those points where their interests coincide with those of postmodernist artistic practice. What most of these theoretical points of view share today is a desire to question what Christopher Norris calls "the kinds of wholesale explanatory theory which would seek to transcend their own special context or localized conditions of cultural production" (1985, 21). They also tend not to become paralyzed by their very postmodern realization that their own discourses have no absolute claim to any ultimate foundation in "truth." If we accept that all is provisional and historically conditioned, we will not stop thinking, as some fear; in fact, that acceptance will guarantee that we never stop thinking – and rethinking.

A poetics of postmodernism would not set up a hierarchy that might privilege either theory or practice. It would not make theory either autonomous or parasitic. And one of the justifications for keeping the focus on both theory and aesthetic practice would be the didactic and self-consciously theoretical nature of postmodern art itself. Mary Kelly's infamous art work, *Post-Partum Document*, interposes theoretical texts with art objects and artifacts. Similarly the final panel of Marie Yates's *The Missing Woman* is a Lacanian essay on theory that breaks the spell of image and narrative and makes us intensely aware of the power of seduction exercised by both (P. Smith 1985, 191). But it is not only art that crosses the boundary between practice and theory: think of the ecstatic feminist writing of Hélène Cixous or of Lyotard's mixing of literary criticism and literary experimentation in *Le Mur du Pacifique* (1979), or the combining of art criticism and philosophy in his work with artists like Adami (1983), Francken (1983), and Arakawa (1984). All of these examples work to question both traditional critical and creative strategies and their artificial separation.

Edward Said has argued in favor of such border crossing or what he calls "the supervening actuality of 'mixing,' of crossing over, of stepping beyond boundaries, which are more creative human activities than staying inside rigidly policed borders" (1985, 43). And Richard Rorty has defended the overlapping of literary, philosophical, and critical discourses as being culturally healthy (1985, 14–15). I would merely add to these arguments the point that this pluralizing is a distinctly postmodern phenomenon. The sense of uniqueness, closure, and authority once demanded of theory (as well as art) gives way to intertextual play and the admission of intellectual contingency. Philip Lewis (1982) once called Derrida's *Glas* an exemplary text of postmodernism, and certainly all of Derrida's enacting of theory in language is "art." Certainly it is hard not to consider Barthes and Derrida, for example, as writers, rather than as theorists, pure and simple. But what do we call their work? Literary, paraliterary (Krauss 1980, 40), "verbal gestures, *action writing*" (Todorov 1981b, 451)? Maybe we just call them postmodern – contradictory, plural, self-defining. They share with the more specifically "literary" texts of postmodernism a desire to interrogate the nature of language, of narrative closure, of representation, and of the context and conditions of both their production and reception.

Out of the discontent with the systematization and ahistoricism of various critical formalisms has arisen a new interest in "discourse" that has begun to alter how we see meaning as being made (see Chapter 11). What postmodernist art and theory share is an awareness of the social practices and institutions that shape them. Context is all. Pragmatic semiotics and discourse analysis (as developed by feminists, blacks, poststructuralist historiographers, and others) are intended to make us uneasy, to make us question our assumptions about how we make meaning, how we know, how we can know (MacCannell and MacCannell 1982, 9). Like postmodern art, they end up being political and engaged, because they do not and cannot masquerade as modes of neutral analysis. Perhaps the recent popularity of the theories of Mikhail Bakhtin owes much to the fact that they at once offer a framework in which to deal with those parodic, ironic, paradoxical forms of postmodernist practice and also make overt the connection between the aesthetic and the social, historical, and institutional. In postmodernist discourses, as Catherine Belsey has argued in a related context:

> Any attempt to locate a guarantee of meaning in concepts of human experience or human hopes and fears which are outside history and outside discourse is as

inadequate as the formalist belief that the guarantee of meaning is eternally inscribed in the discourse of the text itself.

(1980, 52)

What historiographic metafiction explicitly does, though, is to cast doubt on the very possibility of *any* firm "guarantee of meaning," however situated in discourse. This questioning overlaps with Foucault's challenging of the possibility of knowledge ever allowing any final, authoritative truth. Like Derrida, Foucault knew that he must include his own discourse in this radical doubting, for it is ineradicably dependent upon the very assumptions it seeks to uncover. This kind of theorizing is usually labelled as poststructuralist, because it was made possible by Saussurian insights into the contractual nature of signification and also because it seeks to overcome the limitations of structuralism's synchronic systematizing. Poststructuralist discourse paradoxically contests, yet unavoidably inscribes, the very preconceptions it seeks to challenge. This does not mean it is characterized by any antifoundationalist despair or by some sort of "intellectual disarray" (P. Lewis 1982, 22). Along with postmodernist art, such theory is energized by the need to rethink and problematize everything, even its own identity.

Recently historiography, like much postmodern theory and fiction, has concentrated its efforts on rendering problematic the nature of narrative in particular. There are many reasons for this focus, but Lyotard's (1983; 1984a) postmodern questioning of the legitimacy and legitimating power of narrative as a totalizing scheme of explanation is certainly one of them. Supported by Rorty's (1984a) pragmatist sense of the non-availability of absolute truths and of the futility of meta-systems, and attacked by Habermas's (1983) arguments in favor of a higher rationality that would transcend the cultural consensus upon which Lyotard's position depends, this kind of questioning finds its echoes in many discourses today, from historiographic metafiction like Swift's *Waterland* to feminist films like those of Lizzie Borden.

But there is at least one difference between postmodernist aesthetic practice and Lyotard's later theorizing that his avowed topic – the postmodern condition – should not camouflage. The final manifesto-like tone of "Answering the Question: What is Postmodernism?", his reply to Habermas, is absolutist in a most un-postmodern, if oppositional and avant-garde, way: "Let us wage a war on totality; let us be witnesses to the unpresentable; let us activate the differences and save the honor of the name" (1984b, 82). What I think the art of postmodernism would say, instead, is something like this: "Let us inscribe and then challenge totality; let us (re)present the un(re)presentable; let us activate differences and admit that we thus create the honor of the name and the name itself."

In his earlier writing on the topic of postmodernism, however, Lyotard retains somewhat more of his provisional questioning of unitary concepts (that is, narratives) of history or subjectivity. In his attack on this position,

Jameson (1984b, xvi) appears to mistake a challenge to the "master" status of narrative history for a denial of history itself (or of histories, in Lyotard's terms). As we shall see, contemporary historiographers – Hayden White, Michel de Certeau, Paul Veyne, Louis O. Mink, and others – have, for quite a while now, been questioning the nature of narrative knowledge in the discipline of history. In a similar way, so has historiographic metafiction. Both Robert Coover's *The Public Burning* and E. L. Doctorow's *The Book of Daniel*, in fictionalizing the historical execution of the Rosenbergs, argue that the victims are victims partly because they are traditional (if Marxist) humanists and have unquestioning faith in both history and reason. For them, the recording texts of history (newspapers) must tell the truth. In later chapters, we shall see that the documentary sources as well as the narrative form of history come under as serious scrutiny in this kind of fiction as they do in the philosophy of history today. And this is directly the result of the mutual critical impact of the historiographic and metafictional aspects of the texts themselves. This conjunction manages to ironize both metafiction's (modernist) trust in the imaginative power and the closed, reflexive structures of art and also its opposite, history's assumed correspondence between narration and event, between word and thing. This mutual critical irony functions as a mode of internalized self-conscious theorization that is as paradoxical as any postmodern theory today: it inscribes and then undercuts both the autonomy of art and the referentiality of history in such a way that a new mode of questioning/compromise comes into being. And this contradictory mode, in both theory and practice (or in theory as practice and practice as theory), is what I want to call postmodernist.

4

DECENTERING THE POSTMODERN: THE EX-CENTRIC

I

*Anyone writing a novel . . . must have a clear and firm idea as to what
is good and bad in life.   John Bayley*

Like much contemporary literary theory, the postmodernist novel puts into
question that entire series of interconnected concepts that have come to be
associated with what we conveniently label as liberal humanism: autonomy,
transcendence, certainty, authority, unity, totalization, system, universalization, center, continuity, teleology, closure, hierarchy, homogeneity,
uniqueness, origin. As I have tried to argue, however, to put these concepts
into question is not to deny them – only to interrogate their relation to
experience, without the kind of foreclosing assurance that the epigraph
suggests. The process by which this is done is a process of installing and
then withdrawing (or of using and abusing) those very contested notions.
Criticism does not necessarily imply destruction, and postmodern critique,
in particular, is a paradoxical and questioning beast. Charles Newman has
stated, rather polemically, that "Post-Modernism reflects not a radical
uncertainty so much as an unconsidered suspension of judgment"
(1985, 201), but in being so very categorical, he misses the point of the
postmodern enterprise. It is neither uncertain nor suspending of judgment:
it questions the very bases of any certainty (history, subjectivity, reference)
and of any standards of judgment. Who sets them? When? Where? Why?
Postmodernism marks less a negative "disintegration" of or "decline" in
order and coherence (Kahler 1968), than a challenging of the very concept
upon which we judge order and coherence.

No doubt, this interrogative stance, this contesting of authority is partly,
at least, a result of the decentered revolt, the "molecular politics" ("Introduction" to Sayres *et al.* 1984, 4), of the 1960s. I think it would be hard to argue
that this challenge to models of unity and order is directly caused by the fact
that life today is more fragmented and chaotic; yet many have done so,

claiming that our fiction is bizarre (and even outdated and irrelevant) because life is more bizarre than ever before (Zavarzadeh 1976, 9; Federman 1981b, 6; Hollowell 1977, 4–5; Scholes 1968, 37; Levine 1966). This view has been called simplistic and even lunatic (Newman 1985, 57) in the light of history (both social and literary). But whatever the cause, there have been serious interrogations of those once accepted certainties of liberal humanism.

These challenges have become the truisms of contemporary theoretical discourse. One of the major ones – one that has come from both theory and aesthetic practice – has been to the notion of center, in all its forms. In Chris Scott's postmodern historiographic metafiction *Antichthon*, the historical character, Giordano Bruno, lives out the dramatic consequences of the Copernican displacing of the world and of humankind. From a decentered perspective, as the title suggests, if one world exists, then all possible worlds exist: historical plurality replaces atemporal eternal essence. In postmodern psychoanalytic, philosophical and literary theory, the further decentering of the subject and its pursuit of individuality and authenticity has had significant repercussions on everything from our concept of rationality (Derrida 1970, 1972) to our view of the possibilities of genre (Hoffmann 1986, 186).

If the center will not hold, then, as one of the Merry Pranksters (in Tom Wolfe's *The Electric Kool-Aid Acid Test*) put it, "Hail to the Edges!" The move to rethink margins and borders is clearly a move away from centralization with its associated concerns of origin, oneness (Said 1975a; Rajchman 1985) and monumentality (Nietzsche 1957, 10) that work to link the concept of center to those of the eternal and universal. The local, the regional, the non-totalizing (Foucault 1977, 208) are reasserted as the center becomes a fiction – necessary, desired, but a fiction nonetheless.

Much of the debate over the definition of the term "postmodernism" has revolved around what some see as a loss of faith in this centralizing and totalizing impulse of humanist thought (Lyotard 1984a). Offered as alternatives to system-building are theories which privilege the dialogized or hybrid (Bakhtin 1968; 1981) or which contextualize the urge to totalize as only a momentary aspiration in the history of philosophy (Rorty, according to Schaffer 1985, xiv–xv). Both Marxism and Freudian psychoanalysis have been attacked as totalizing "meta-narratives," yet one could argue that they have been fruitful in analyses of postmodernism precisely because their "split" model (both dialectic and the class struggle or manifest/latent and conscious/unconscious) allows a very postmodern – or contradictory – anti-totalizing kind of totalization or decentered kind of centering. And, while much of the actual criticism of postmodern fiction is still premised on a humanist belief in the universal human urge to generate systems to order experience (e.g. McCaffery 1982; Kawin 1982), the fiction itself challenges such critical assumptions. Pynchon's *Gravity's Rainbow* inscribes and then undercuts – in a typically postmodern way – the certainties of the ordering impulse of positivistic science as well as of humanist history and literature, and it does so by over-totalization, by parodies of systematization.

When the center starts to give way to the margins, when totalizing universalization begins to self-deconstruct, the complexity of the contradictions within conventions – such as those of genre, for instance – begin to be apparent (Derrida 1980; Hassan 1986). Cultural homogenization too reveals its fissures, but the heterogeneity that is asserted in the face of that totalizing (yet pluralizing) culture does not take the form of many fixed individual subjects (cf. Russell 1985, 239), but instead is conceived of as a flux of contextualized identities: contextualized by gender, class, race, ethnicity, sexual preference, education, social role, and so on. As we shall see shortly, this assertion of identity through difference and specificity is a constant in postmodern thought.

To move from difference and heterogeneity to discontinuity is a link that at least the *rhetoric* of rupture has readily made in the light of the contradictions and challenges of postmodernism. Narrative continuity is threatened, is both used and abused, inscribed and subverted (see Sukenick 1985, 14; Tanner 1971, 141–52). The nineteenth-century structures of narrative closure (death, marriage; neat conclusions) are undermined by those postmodern epilogues that foreground how, as writers and readers, we *make* closure: Fowles's *A Maggot,* Thomas's *The White Hotel,* Atwood's *The Handmaid's Tale.* Banville's *Doctor Copernicus* ends with "DC" – both the protagonist's initials and the (initiating/reiterating) *da capo* which refuses closure. Similarly the modernist tradition of the more "open" ending is both used and abused by postmodern self-consciously multiple endings (Fowles's *The French Lieutenant's Woman*) or resolutely arbitrary closure (Rushdie's *Midnight's Children*). From the point of view of theory, Derrida has argued that closure is not only not desirable, but also not even possible, and he has done so in a language of supplement, margin, and deferral. But the particularly contradictory postmodern aspect of what may appear, on the surface, radical here is underlined by Richard Rorty (1984b) when he points out the paradoxical *reliance* of deconstruction (like realism, of course) upon a historically determined concept of metaphysics that it wants to deny: the one that attempts to create "unique, total, closed vocabularies" (19).

This contradiction is typical of postmodernist theory. The decentering of our categories of thought always relies on the centers it contests for its very definition (and often its verbal form). The adjectives may vary: hybrid, heterogeneous, discontinuous, antitotalizing, uncertain. So may the metaphors: the image of the labyrinth without center or periphery might replace the conventionally ordered notion we usually have of a library (Eco's *The Name of the Rose*) or the spreading rhizome might be a less repressively structuring concept than the hierarchical tree (Deleuze and Guattari 1980). But the power of these new expressions is always paradoxically derived from that which they challenge. It may indeed be true, as Craig Owens argues, "when the postmodernist work speaks of itself, it is no longer to proclaim its autonomy, its self-sufficiency, its transcendence; rather, it is to narrate its own contingency, insufficiency, a lack of transcendence" (1980b, 80). But it is also clear that this definition relies on its inverting of a set of values which it contests.

The contradictory nature of postmodernism involves its offering of multiple, provisional alternatives to traditional, fixed unitary concepts in full knowledge of (and even exploiting) the continuing appeal of those very concepts. Postmodern architecture, for example, does not reject the technological and material advances of high modernism of the International Style: it cannot. But it can subvert its uniformity, its ahistoricity, its ideological and social aims – and consequences. As Portoghesi writes:

> In place of faith in the great centered designs, and the anxious pursuits of salvation, the postmodern condition is gradually substituting the concreteness of small circumstantiated struggles with its precise objectives capable of having a great effect because they change systems of relations.
>
> (1983, 12)

This is not a claim to homogenization or totalization, but to heterogeneity and provisionality that goes beyond any simply formal play with types of non-selection (Lodge 1977) to suggest political and social intent.

The center may not hold, but it is still an attractive fiction of order and unity that postmodern art and theory continue to exploit and subvert. That fiction takes many forms in the institutions of culture and, in many of them, its limitations are becoming the focus of attention. The very walls of the traditional museum and the very definition of a work of art come under fire in the performances of Albert Vidal, for instance. His "The Urban Man" is a kind of anthropological performance ritual in which Vidal spends five hours a day in a major public place in a city (Miami's Metro Zoo or the Place d'Youville in Quebec City) offering to passers-by an "exhibit" of post-modern man about his daily business. Similarly the notion of the physical book is challenged in formally hybrid "intermedia" (Caramello 1983, 4), and, of course, the categories of genre are regularly challenged these days. Fiction looks like biography (Banville's *Kepler*), autobiography (Ondaatje's *Running in the Family*), history (Rushdie's *Shame*). Theoretical discourse joins forces with autobiographical memoir and Proustian reminiscence in Barthes's *Camera Lucida* (1981a), where a theory of photography grows out of personal emotion with no pretense to objectivity, finality, authority.

II

> I didn't say that there was no center, that we could get along without the center. I believe that the center is a function, not a being – a reality, but a function. And this function is absolutely indispensable.
> *Jacques Derrida*

The ex-centric, the off-center: ineluctably identified with the center it desires but is denied. This is the paradox of the postmodern and its images are often as deviant as this language of decentering might suggest: the freak is one common example: in films like *Carney* or novels like E. L. Doctorow's *Loon Lake* and Paul Quarrington's *Home Game*. The multi-ringed circus becomes the pluralized and paradoxical metaphor for a decentered world where there is only ex-centricity. Angela Carter's *Nights at the Circus* combines this freak-circus framework with contestings of narrative centering: it straddles the border between the imaginary/fantastic (with her winged woman protagonist) and the realistic/historical, between a unified biographically structured plot, and a decentered narration, with its wandering point of view and extensive digressions.

Another form of this same move off-center is to be found in the contesting of centralization of culture through the valuing of the local and peripheral: not New York or London or Toronto, but William Kennedy's Albany, Graham Swift's fens country, Robert Kroetsch's Canadian West. Postmodern architects similarly look to the local idiom and ethos for their forms. In addition, postmodern painters, sculptors, video artists, novelists, poets, and film-makers join with these architects in collapsing the high/low art hierarchy of earlier times, in an attack on high art centralization of academic interest, on the one hand, and, on the other, on the homogeneity of consumer culture which adapts, includes, and makes all seem accessible by neutralizing and popularizing. To collapse hierarchies is not to collapse distinctions, however. Postmodernism retains, and indeed celebrates, differences against what has been called the "racist logic of the exclusive" (Bois 1981, 45). The modernist concept of single and alienated otherness is challenged by the postmodern questioning of binaries that conceal hierarchies (self/other). When Edward Said calls for theory today to have an "awareness of the differences between situations" (1983, 242) in its "critical consciousness" of its position in the world, he is going beyond the early Foucaldian (1970) definition of modernity in terms of otherness alone. Difference suggests multiplicity, heterogeneity, plurality, rather than binary opposition and exclusion.

It is again to the 1960s that we must turn to see the roots of this change, for it is those years that saw the inscribing into history (Gutman 1981, 554) of previously "silent" groups defined by differences of race, gender, sexual preferences, ethnicity, native status, class. The 1970s and 1980s have seen the increasingly rapid and complete inscribing of these same ex-centrics into both theoretical discourse and artistic practice as andro- (phallo-), hetero-, Euro-, ethno-centrisms have been vigorously challenged. Think of Doctorow's *Ragtime* with its three paralleled families: the Anglo-American establishment one and the marginal immigrant European and American black ones. The novel's action disperses the center of the first and moves the margins into the multiple "centers" of the narrative, in a formal allegory of the social demographics of urban America. In addition, there is an extended critique of American democratic ideals through the presentation of class conflict rooted in capitalist property and moneyed power. The black

Coalhouse, the white Houdini, the immigrant Tateh are all working class, and because of this – not in spite of it – all can therefore work to create new aesthetic forms (ragtime, vaudeville, movies).

The 1960s brought many of these issues explosively into the foreground, as the political and the aesthetic merged in the so-called counter-culture. Therefore, for example, to assert the cultural importance of the 1960s' civil rights movement in the United States is not to deny its political significance. Indeed the rise of militant black protest in literature in the 1960s had direct political consequences. Since then, black literature has also forced reconsiderations of cultural specificity, the canon, and methods of analysis that have had repercussions well beyond the borders of the United States, for it is possible to argue that it literally enabled feminist and other forms of protest. What Henry Louis Gates, Jr, calls "signifying black difference" (1984b) challenged the ethnocentrism that had made the black into a figure of negation or absence – just as androcentrism absented women. What is always important to recall, however, is that difference operates *within* each of these challenging cultures, as well as against the dominant. Blacks and feminists, ethnics and gays, native and "Third World" cultures, do not form monolithic movements, but constitute a multiplicity of responses to a commonly perceived situation of marginality and ex-centricity. And there have been liberating effects of moving from the language of alienation (otherness) to that of decentering (difference), because the center used to function as the pivot between binary opposites which always privileged one half: white/black, male/female, self/other, intellect/body, west/east, objectivity/subjectivity – the list is now well known. But if the center is seen as a construct, a fiction, not a fixed and unchangeable reality, the "old either–or begins to break down," as Susan Griffin put it (1981, 1982, 291) and the new and-also of multiplicity and difference opens up new possibilities.

The autobiographical novels of black American men in the 1960s have given way to a more structurally and ideologically complex form of narrative in the years since, likely partly because of the new voice of black women writers. There is postmodern desire to "make and unmake meaning, effect a simultaneous creative surge and destructive will" (Clarke 1980, 206). But black women have been aided in their particular "voicing" by the rise of the women's movement. There seems to be a general agreement that – like the Québécois separatist and black civil rights movements and the French intellectual Left activists of May 1968 – the American New Left was both male and sexist (see Aronowitz 1984, 38; Robin Morgan 1970; Moi 1985a, 22; 95). The reaction of women against this took a very "sixties" form: a challenging of authority (male, institutional), an acknowledgement of power as the basis of sexual politics, a belief in the role of socio-cultural context in the production and reception of art. All of these contestations would be visible again as the bases of the paradoxes of postmodernism in the immediate future, as feminists and others recognized that, in Ellen Willis's words, "sexism, heterosexism, racism, capitalism and imperialism intersect in complex, often contradictory ways" (1984, 116).

Postmodern feminist fiction like Susan Daitch's *L.C.* foregrounds these contradictions most clearly. Here the position of women in France in 1848 is the initial focus: "Women were considered part of their husbands' accumulated property; they were denied citizenship, had the same legal rights as lunatics and the mentally deficient" (1986, 3). But the protagonist soon learns that this bourgeois concept extends even to the leftist revolutionaries: during a political meeting, Proudhon orders women to the back of the room, provoking her to note the contradiction of "the authoritarian order from one who only a few minutes earlier had spoken of the tyranny of proprietor and legislator" (111). Reduced to an observer of male action, Lucienne sees that

> Without the right to vote, own property or be educated, wives, mothers, mistresses, daughters play the role of sweeps to history, as much a part of an anonymous support system to men of the left as to men of the right.
>
> (1986, 150)

The irony of her words becomes clear within the Berkeley 1968 framing tale where, even with citizenship, the vote, and education, women have not escaped the patriarchal "tyranny of gender," not even women of the New Left. "You're the one who's always talking about rectifying history's erasures," the narrator accuses the male head of her protest group, trying to make him see his own guilty erasure of women, both past and present (248). He is no better than the police, who do not believe her rape-story. The polarized right and left of both centuries are shown to share misogyny and sexism. Women must create and assert their own community, based on their own values.

Black women in particular, though, brought to the general ex-centric re-ordering of culture not just a very precise sense of the social context and community in which they work, but what Barbara Christian has called an awareness of their own personal and historical past as the "foundation for a genuine revolutionary process" (1985, 116). As women in a black (as well as white), male-dominated, heterosexual society, writers like Alice Walker and Toni Morrison have offered alternatives to the alienated other, the individual subject of late capitalism that has been the subject of bourgeois fiction (S. Willis 1985, 214): collective history and a newly problematized sense of female community. The black male world of Morrison's *Song of Solomon* is literally a "Dead" world (in more than name), one that denies life to the women who take on its name (Ruth). The ex-centric community of Pilate, Hagar, and Reba is outside normal society (white or black), outside the town, and infinitely attractive because of its position.

Women operate differently from men here, even in the forms of their revenge. Male revenge – Guitar's – is both as abstract and totalizing ("White people are unnatural. As a race they are unnatural" – Morrison 1977, 157) as that which it avenges in white culture. On the other hand, female revenge –

Circe's – is concrete and specific: it is wreaked on the white family she served and outlived. Her personal historical context validates her vengeance against their property and their heritage. The issue of class joins that of race and gender here, as it does in the juxtaposing of middle-class bourgeois Ruth and the ex-centric Pilate who is beyond materialism, beyond the structures and strictures of society. In this way she is almost beyond class, and even beyond gender: her wisdom comes from the paternal line, her name is male, yet she does not live up to its male connotations of washing her hands of responsibility. Her subversions of these gendered associations are partly because she is really her own construction. In the face of society's marginalization of her (she is demonic, unnatural, with no navel), "she threw away every assumption she had learned and began at zero" (149), setting her own values and goals. What is important is that her ex-centric position gives her an "alien's compassion for troubled people" (150) that allows her to give up "all interest in table manners or hygiene" in exchange for "a deep concern for and about human relationships" (150). The powerful conflating of class, gender, and racial issues can be seen if we compare Pilate to the novel's other masculine-named woman – the white poet Michael-Mary Graham. Heavy irony points to this *parody* of the ex-centric: "Marriage, children – all had been sacrificed to the Great Agony and her home was a tribute to the fastidiousness of her dedication (and the generosity of her father's will)" (192).

This kind of exposition of the complicitous dovetailing of race, class, gender, and ideology has its impact beyond just women writers or blacks or even Americans in general. Let me offer just one example of the postmodern self-consciousness about the complex interconnection of the various -centrisms that has been made possible by these ex-centrics: in John Fowles's *A Maggot*, the major confrontation of the novel (set in eighteenth-century England) is between a male, middle-class lawyer, Ayscough, and a female, lower-class whore-turned-prophet, Rebecca Lee: "these two were set apart from each other not only by countless barriers of age, sex, class, education, native province and the rest, but by something far deeper still: by belonging to two very different halves of the human spirit" (1985, 425). Rebecca's image for Ayscough's inability to understand her is that they have different alphabets and what she says will not fit his (313; 379). Fowles puts gender at the heart of difference here, as Rebecca chides her inquisitor about unearned male power over women – social, physical, and moral. It is a power and authority that blame woman for the sins of man in order to maintain the fiction of "man's superior status vis-à-vis womankind" (318). She rejects his constant attempts to make her a "mirror of thy sex" (357, 422), that is, a sinful image projected from himself onto her. Rebecca's heretical religious beliefs in Holy Mother Wisdom (and her divine female trinity) and in the likelihood of Christ's being a woman are blasphemy to Ayscough. Not content to accept her "natural place as help-meet to man, in house and home alone" (436), she has other plans: "Most of this world is unjust by act of man, not of Our Lord Jesus Christ. Change that is my purpose" (424). In this she joins with the absent male "hero", known as His Lordship (and Our Lord – the connection is made textually – 418), who "would doubt all: birth, society, government, justice" (441) in disobeying the laws of man and God (the Father) as incarnated in his own father. The challenges to patriarchy (Christian, familial, societal) are directly linked with the protests of class and gender, and here they come from men as well as women, but it is a woman who is given the voice in this novel.

Fowles does not really address the issue of race, but almost every other kind of centered structure is called into question. In the introduction to the special issue of *Critical Inquiry* called "'Race,' Writing, and Difference" (12, 1, 1985), Gates calls race "the ultimate trope of difference" (5). From a male black perspective, that may seem the case. Of course, for feminists, gender has taken on that metaphoric role. In both cases, however, it is a difference that defines; it is difference that is valued in and for itself. Most theoretical discussions of difference owe much to the work on the differential system of language and its signifying processes by Saussure, Derrida, Lacan, and others. Meaning can be created only by differences and sustained only by reference to other meaning. Difference is therefore the very basis of the Lacanian definition of the split subject as a meaning-producing entity, itself constructed from a system of differences (Coward and Ellis 1977, 100). The single concept of "otherness" has associations of binarity, hierarchy, and supplementarity that postmodern theory and practice seem to want to reject in favor of a more plural and deprivileging concept of difference and the ex-centric. Postmodernist discourses – either those by women, Afro-Americans, natives, ethnics, gays, and so on, or those provoked by their stands – try to avoid the trap of reversing and valorizing the other, of making the margin into a center, a move that many have seen as a danger for deconstruction's privileging of writing and absence over speech and presence or for some feminisms' gynocentralizing of a monolithic concept of Woman as other than Man. Postmodern difference is always plural and provisional.

III

> We are difference . . . our reason is the difference of discourses, our history the difference of times, our selves the difference of masks. That difference, far from being the forgotten and recoverable origin, is this dispersion that we are and make.   *Michel Foucault*

It has frequently been pointed out that, despite what I have just asserted about differences, postmodern theory and practice have been resolutely white male phenomena and that feminism, in particular, has stayed away from the debates, as if they were not pertinent to feminist concerns (Huyssen 1986, 198). Others have argued that even feminism has been influenced largely by male models of thought (Suleiman 1986, 268, n. 12; Jardine 1982, 55; Ruthven 1984, 11): Mill, Engels, Heidegger, Nietzsche, Marx, Foucault, Barthes, Derrida, Lacan. There are a number of ways of explaining (or recuperating) this fact. One could, as does Alice Jardine, admit the maleness, but argue that its reconceptualization of difference "will be gendered as female" (1982, 60). The potential essentialism of her assertion of "supplementary jouissance" as defining Woman is as problematic as the assertion itself. Her conflation of the female with modernity (male modernity) in the mode of Kristeva, Irigaray, and Montrelay, presents difficulties because it reinforces a gendered duality (and hierarchy) as it allows male modernist artists to appropriate the feminine insofar as they see themselves as marginalized. Thus they are able to ground their oppositional stance toward bourgeois society's values in the feminine, while conveniently ignoring their own misogyny and excluding of women from the literary enterprise (Huyssen 1986, 45–9). As Christa Wolf has remarked in protest: "Flaubert was *not* Madame Bovary" (1984, 300–1). The historical and material reality of the masculinism of much modernist practice must not be papered over with radical rhetoric.

Another way of dealing with the maleness of potentially useful postmodern models like that of deterritorialization (Deleuze and Guattari 1980), is to argue that, were we to accept that male/female are merely illusions within a system of power, we could deploy the model without fear of its maleness interfering with feminist analysis (Massumi 1985, 17–20). But postmodern thought would reject this glossing over of both the differences among the "minoritarian" groups' members and also those differences from the dominant culture. In Derrida's terms: "Masculine and feminine are not even the adverse and possibly contracting parts, but rather the parts of a pseudo-whole" (1984, 89), a pseudo-whole which postmodernism contests through its valorization of the ex-centric and its implication of difference as what Mary Jacobus has called "a multiplicity, joyousness, and heterogeneity which is that of textuality itself" (1979a, 12).

The multiple, the heterogeneous, the different: this is the pluralizing rhetoric of postmodernism that rejects both the abstract category of single otherness created by "coercive separation and unequal privileges" (Said 1985, 43) as well as by the more concrete relegation of the other to the role of "object for enthusiastic information-retrieval" (Spivak 1985, 245). The language of margins and borders marks a position of paradox: both inside and outside. Given this position, it is not surprising that the form that heterogeneity and difference often take in postmodern art is that of parody – the intertextual mode that is paradoxically an authorized transgression, for its ironic difference is set at the very heart of similarity (see Hutcheon 1985). For example, feminist artists like Silvia Kolbowski and Barbara Kruger use ads and commercial fashion plates in new parodic contexts in order to attack the capitalist production of homogeneous images of women. In Kolbowski's "Model Pleasure," for instance, she parodically works to appropriate both these images and the pleasure they produce for both male and female viewers (P. Smith 1985, 192). Similarly black writers (both male and female) parody or repeat with difference the many traditions within which they work: European/American, black/white, oral/written, standard language/ black vernacular: "Canonical Western texts are to be digested rather than regurgitated, but digested along with canonical black formal and vernacular texts" (Gates 1984b, 6). The figure of repetition has been claimed as a tradition in black culture generally (Snead 1984), and perhaps the particularly postmodern variant of this repetition may well be parody: Morrison's Utopian three-woman household in *Song of Solomon* inverting and challenging the dystopic one in Faulkner's *Absalom! Absalom!* (S. Willis 1984, 278–9).

However, parodic double-voicing or heterogeneity is not just a device which allows contesting assertions of difference. It also paradoxically offers a textual model of collectivity and community of discourses which has proved useful to both feminism and postmodernism. The text, but even the title alone, of Yolande Villemaire's *La Vie en prose* points both to the parodic contesting of the clichéd romantic vision of "la vie en rose" and also to the name of an important women's journal in Quebec, *La Vie en rose*. Such assertion – both intertextual and ideological – of community is never, though, intended as a move towards homogenization. Postmodern art is always aware of difference, difference *within* any grouping too, difference defined by contextualization or positioning in relation to plural others. This is one of the lessons of its ex-centric forebears, as Barbara Johnson has shown in her discussion of Zora Neale Hurston's "way of dealing with multiple agendas and heterogeneous implied readers" (1985, 278). As we shall see in the next chapter, postmodern art inherits this concern for context and for the enunciative situation of discourse: that is, the contextualized production and reception of the text. It also inherits the ironic strategy of black "signifying" (Mitchell-Kernan 1973; Gates 1984c) with its urge to contextualize, not to deny or reduce, difference.

To be ex-centric, on the border or margin, inside yet outside is to have a different perspective, one that Virginia Woolf (1945, 96) once called "alien and critical," one that is "always altering its focus," since it has no centering force. This same shifting of perspective, this same concern for respecting difference, can also be seen both in and within postmodern theoretical discourse today. Feminist theory offers perhaps the clearest example of the importance of an awareness of the diversity of history and culture of women: their differences of race, ethnic group, class, sexual preference. It would be more accurate, of course, to speak of feminisms, in the plural, for there are many different orientations that are subsumed under the general label of feminism: images of women criticism (Cornillon 1972); canon-challenging and women's literary history (Showalter 1977); separatist or women-centered gynocriticism (Spacks 1976); feminist "critique" of patriarchal ideology in male texts (Showalter 1979; Ellmann 1968; Munich 1985); psychoanalytic studies of female subjectivity (J. Mitchell 1974; Gallop 1982;

Silverman 1983; de Lauretis 1984); theories of *écriture féminine* or *parler femme* (A. R. Jones 1985; Marks and de Courtivron 1980); lesbian attacks on heterosexism (Zimmerman 1985; Kennard 1986); Marxist-socialist contextualizing (Newton 1981; Moi 1985a; MacKinnon 1981, 1982; Marxist-Feminist Literature Collective 1978); deconstructive interrogations of cultural constructs (Spivak 1978; Kamuf 1982; Belsey 1980); women's perspectives on Afro-American (S. Willis 1985; Christian 1980 and 1985; Pullin 1980; B. Smith 1979), and postcolonial (Spivak 1985; Alloula 1986) experience and identity as women of color. And the list could go on (see Eisenstein 1983). These different feminisms range from liberal humanist to radical poststructuralist in orientation. They consider women as both writers and readers (Flynn and Schweickart 1986; Culler 1982b; Batsleer *et al.* 1985). Like black theory, these kinds of feminism all integrate theory and practice (or experience) in a way that has had a profound effect on the nature of postmodernism where theoretical and artistic discourse can no longer be neatly separated.

When Gloria Hull polemically stated that "Black women poets are not 'Shakespeare's sisters'" in response to writing for a volume with that title (Gilbert and Gubar 1979b), she forcefully illustrated the position of the ex-centric towards one particular and dominant center: liberal humanist discourse and its assumption that subjectivity is produced by or based in somehow eternal values. The ex-centrics have tended to argue, with Teresa de Lauretis, that subjectivity is constituted by "one's personal, subjective, engagement in the practices, discourses, and institutions that lend significance (value, meaning, and affect) to the events of the world" (1984, 159). Unlike the male, white, Eurocentered poststructuralist discourse that has most forcefully challenged humanism's whole, integrated ideal of subjectivity, however, these more ex-centric positionalities know that they cannot reject the subject wholesale, mainly because they have never really been allowed it (N. K. Miller 1982). Their ex-centricity and difference have often denied them access to Cartesian rationality and relegated them to the realms of the irrational, the mad, or at the very least, the alien. They participate in two contradictory discourses: the liberal humanist one of freedom, self-determination, rationality for all and also one of submission, relative inadequacy and irrational intuition for some (Belsey 1980).

The danger is that women will either privilege this second discourse or, in some way, fix an essence of Woman to counter that of Man. Seen in this light, Toni Morrison's *Tar Baby* (1981) can be read as parodically inverting that dangerous feminist centrism that would privilege an essentialized "female," and it does so by making the male, Son, the creature of sexual not rational power, of fluid identity, of unclear origins (despite his generic name). Jadine, on the other hand, chooses to accept the model and roles of white, European, male culture that, as a black woman, she might question: "she chooses in effect to be a creation rather than a creator, an art historian rather than artist, a model rather than designer, a wife rather than woman"

(Byerman 1985, 213). This novel self-consciously evades the danger that postmodern discourse also must constantly attempt to skirt: that it will essentialize its ex-centricity or render itself complicit in the liberal humanist notions of universality (speaking for all ex-centrics) and eternality (forever).

Postmodernism does not move the marginal to the center. It does not invert the valuing of centers into that of peripheries and borders, as much as *use* that paradoxical doubled positioning to critique the inside from both the outside and the inside. Just as Padma, the listening, textualized female narratee of Rushdie's *Midnight's Children*, pushes the narration in directions its male narrator had no intention of taking, so the ex-centric have not only overlapped in some of their concerns with postmodernism, but also pushed it in new directions. Though I would insist that the ex-centrics' agendas only partially overlap and do not coincide with that of the postmodern, it still seems to me that the perspective of these inside-outsiders has added race, ethnicity, sexual orientation and gender to the class analysis of ideology of Althusserian Marxists. The never fully articulated, but always present, system of preconceptions which govern a society includes these differences that go beyond class; differences that challenge from within the possibility of mastery, objectivity, impersonality; differences that do not allow us to forget the role of power, of those "social arrangements of patterned disparity" (MacKinnon 1981, 1982, 2). They have not allowed theory or criticism or art to pose as apolitical (Fetterley 1978, xi; Moi 1985a, 175n vs Ruthven 1984; Moi 1985, 95 vs Foucault 1980). This kind of general political motivation within postmodern theory and practice (though not all the details) owes much to specifically feminist and Marxist challenges to the relations both with modes of representation and with expectations in consumption (Mulvey 1979, 179), without being identical to either. Feminism, like Marxism, is more than just another approach to culture. To reduce either in this way would be to dismantle it as a set of political beliefs with a particular program of cultural politics (Nead 1986, 120–1). As we shall see in Chapter 12, the political "double-talk" of postmodernist contradictory encoding is alien to the specific political orientation of either, though indebted to both.

Edward Said has urged theory to base itself in experience: "Criticism cannot assume that its province is merely the text, not even the great literary text. It must see itself, with other discourse, inhabiting a much contested cultural space" (1983, 225). He seems to ignore the fact that feminism, among other ex-centrics, has been doing just this for some time now: taking a position within the historical and political world outside the ivory tower. Terry Eagleton, however, has noticed:

> It is in the nature of feminist politics that signs and images, written and dramatized experience, should be of especial significance. Discourse in all its forms is an obvious concern for feminists, either as places where women's oppression can be deciphered, or as places where it can be challenged. In any politics which puts

identity and relationship centrally at stake, renewing attention to lived experience and the discourse of the body, culture does not need to argue its way to political relevance.

(1983, 215)

Indeed there are many who have claimed the radical political potential of feminist theory, especially in conjunction with Marxism and/or deconstruction (Culler 1982b, 63; Belsey 1980, 129). But we should not forget that the thematization of writing and difference as anti-patriarchal subversions of oppression is also clear in women's writing, from Audrey Thomas's *Intertidal Life* to Alice Walker's *The Color Purple*. And the political power of the creative process has been claimed not only by women but also by black male writers such as Ishmael Reed and Leon Forrest. The right of expression (however unavoidably implicated in liberal humanist assumptions) is not something that can be taken for granted by the ex-centric. And the *problematizing* of expression – through contextualization in the enunciative situation – is what makes the ex-centric into the postmodern. Many theorists have argued that the major modes of feminist thought are contextual: social, historical, cultural (Gilligan 1982; B. DuBois 1983; Donovan 1984). And post-Saussurian or poststructuralist theory has been one of the strongest forces in moving the emphasis from linguistic and textual system to discursive process, to semiosis or the mutual overdetermination of meaning, perception, and experience in the act of signifying (de Lauretis 1984, 184). And this is the theory most often associated with postmodernism. The reasons for the association are fairly obvious. Both share a concern for power – its manifestations, its appropriations, its positioning, its consequences, its languages. So too do most forms of feminism, of course. All work to challenge our traditional essentialized anchors in God, father, state, and Man through acknowledgement of the particular and the different.

In postmodern fiction, self-reflexivity cannot be separated from the notion of difference. In her fiction/autobiography/biography, *The Woman Warrior*, Maxine Hong Kingston links the postmodern metafictional concerns of narration and language directly to her race and her gender: "story-talking" (the Chinese expression for narrating) is what women do. (As the next book, *China Men*, shows, the men are powerful, however, in their silence.) Language is inescapably gendered for the Chinese: "There is a Chinese word for the female *I* – which is 'slave.' Break the women with their own tongues!" (1976, 47). And it is in terms of language that the young Chinese American girl attempts to construct her subjectivity: "I could not understand 'I.' The Chinese 'I' has seven strokes, intricacies. How could the American 'I' . . . have only three strokes . . . ?" (166). Like her mother, the female narrator story-talks, twisting tales "into designs" (163), and trying to unite the Chinese and "barbarian" tongues like her model, the Chinese woman poet, Ts'ai Yen (209). Her rethinking of personal, familial, and racial history is similar to that of feminist historians in its study of the exclusions that inevitably result from attempts to form totalizing unities or neat evolutions (see B. A. Carroll 1976 and Lerner 1979). Theory and practice once again come together in the postmodern articulation of difference.

IV

> The ways in which we now raise questions of gender and sexuality, reading and writing, subjectivity and enunciation, voice and perform-ance are unthinkable without the impact of feminism, even though many of these activities may take place on the margin of or even outside the movement proper.　*Andreas Huyssen*

While I would not argue a relationship of identity (or antagonism) between postmodern theory and practice or between postmodernism and the ex-centric, there clearly are common concerns. Thanks to the ex-centric, both postmodern theory and art have managed to break down the barrier between academic discourse and contemporary art (which is often marginal-ized, not to say ignored, in the academy). Even more than black theory, perhaps, it has been feminism that has shown the impossibility of separating the theoretical and the aesthetic, the political and the epistemo-logical. As Stephen Heath has proclaimed: "Any discourse which fails to take account of the problem of sexual difference in its own enunciation and address will be, within a patriarchal order, precisely indifferent, a reflection of male domination" (1978, 53). What has been added most recently to this list of "enabling" differences is that of ethnicity. The ethnic revival of the 1960s in the United States has been well documented (Greer 1984; Boelhower 1984; Sukenick 1985, 51–2 and 64–5; see too the volumes of the *Yardbird Readers*). Studies like Sollors's *Beyond Ethnicity* (1986) are made possible by postmodern rethinking of difference in the face of modern, urban, industrial society that was expected to efface ethnicity. Instead, ethnic identity has changed from being a "heathenish liability" to being a "sacred asset" (33) through a very postmodern, contradictory divided allegiance: what Sollors calls consent and descent.

In Angela Carter's novel, *The Infernal Desire Machines of Doctor Hoffman*, the portrait of the "River People" reveals the extreme of this ex-centric ethnicity. These people represent the ultimate and archetypal amalgam of all colonized societies: a people living on a land discovered by the Portuguese; left to the Dutch who then lost it in some peace treaty; resettled by Ukrainians and Scots-Irish with the help of slaves and convicts; resettled once over by "a mixed breed of Middle Europeans, Germans and Scandi-navians" (1972, 67). Here everyone is an expatriate (68); everyone is ex-centric. Carter uses this society to ironic and satiric ends. The language the River people speak is one which both reflects and creates a different process of socialization: "man" means "all men" and so the issue of the particular versus the universal (though not the male versus the female) never arises;

and the only tenses in the language are past and present, enabling them to live "with a complex, hesitant but absolute immediacy" (71) available only to the marginal.

Outside of North America too, then, there are texts which overtly challenge cutlural notions of the centrality of the metropolis, for both France and Britain had former colonial empires, with strong centralized cultures that are now being upset by their own history, as Arab, African, East and West Indian voices demand to be heard. In their postmodern forms these voices are particularly contradictory and contesting. Salman Rushdie's novels are not just about India or Pakistan. The very form of the texts themselves constantly reminds the reader of his/her own ethnocentric biases because these are encoded in the very words being read. In *Midnight's Children*, Saleem says he speaks in Urdu; yet we read his speech in English. In *Shame*, Omar Khayam wants to learn to read English, but the Shakil sisters feel "Angrey double-dutch" will make him mad. And all this, including the sisters' dialogue, we read in English and, in our unconscious and deeply embedded ethnocentrism, assume to be spoken in English (at least until passages like this trip us up). Omar calls himself "a creature of the edge: a peripheral man" (1983, 24), who is alien to both paternal and patriarchal roots. This state is one which the narrator later likens to that of women: his tale begins as "almost excessively masculine" but "the women seem to have taken over; they marched in from the peripheries of the story to demand the inclusion of their own tragedies, histories and comedies, obliging me to couch my narrative in all manner of sinuous complexities, to see my 'male' plot refracted, so to speak, through the prisms of its reverse and 'female' side" (173). The female stories "explain, and even subsume" the male one because social and sexual repression in an authoritarian society mirrors national repression, both past and present. The relation of the center to the ex-centric is never an innocent one.

It is this kind of postmodern contradiction that can also be seen in works like those of Gayl Jones (*Corregidora*) or Joy Kogawa (*Obasan*), works that point to the paradoxical kind of differences that are entailed in being Afro-American or Japanese-Canadian women. This inside-outside position is also, as we have seen, the situation of the Chinese-American woman writer in Maxine Hong Kingston's work. In *The Woman Warrior*, the young American-born Chinese girl lives in a world that is doubly split: "Normal Chinese women's voices are strong and bossy. We American-Chinese girls had to whisper to make ourselves American-feminine" (1976, 172). Not allowed to be fully Chinese (and not wanting to be), yet never fully Americanized, she also grows up in a Chinese patriarchal ethos that does not welcome daughters, one that has an oft-repeated saying: "It is more profitable to raise geese than daughters," one that leaves women behind in villages in China while men remarry in the new world and never return. In response to her mother's statement that "A husband may kill a wife who disobeys him. Confucius said that," the narrator adds bitterly "Confucius, the rational man" (195), putting the ironic emphasis on gender as well as reason. In *China Men*, the intersection of feminine and national identity is even more powerfully revealed. As a child, hearing her father's Chinese obscenities and curses against women, the narrator tries to come to terms with what she sees as his hatred of her: "What I want is for you to tell me that those curses are only common Chinese sayings. That you did not mean to make me sicken at being female" (1980, 9).

In such postmodern historiographic metafiction as this, language – nationalist, sexist, racialist – is made the basis of the narrator's search to define her different (female Chinese-American) subjectivity. And language is also the basis on which the exclusive center rejects: her father was labelled as illiterate by American immigration officials because he could not read English, but only Chinese. It is through language that the status of difference as ex-centricity is thematized. In his laundry, the girl's father marks all the items to be cleaned with "Center" and thus provokes her to ask "how we landed in a country where we are eccentric people" (9). While it is always a fact that the ex-centric relies on the center for its definition, that all forms of radical thought cannot help but be "mortgaged to the very historical categories they seek to transcend" (Moi 1985a, 88), this very postmodern paradox should not lead to despair or complacency. The theory and practice of postmodern art has shown ways of making the different, the off-center, into the vehicle for aesthetic and even political consciousness-raising – perhaps the first and necessary step to any radical change. As I mentioned early in this study, I do not think that postmodernism is that change, but it may presage it. It may be an enabling first stage in its enacting of the contradictions inherent in any transitional moment: inside yet outside, complicitous yet critical. Perhaps the postmodern motto should be that "Hail to the Edges!"

5

CONTEXTUALIZING THE POSTMODERN: ENUNCIATION AND THE REVENGE OF "PAROLE"

I

To reject the validity of the question Who is writing? or Who is
speaking? is simply no longer a radical position in 1984.
Andreas Huyssen

In a precision and elaboration of certain key Foucaldian notions, Timothy J. Reiss has argued, in *The Discourse of Modernism*, that at any given time or in any given place, one discursive model or theory prevails and thus "provides the conceptual tools that make the majority of human practices meaningful" (1982, 11). However, this dominant theoretical model at the same time represses or suppresses an equally potent discursive practice, a practice which gradually works to subvert the theory by revealing its inherent contradictions. At that point, certain forms of the practice itself begin to become tools of analysis. Since the seventeenth century the prevailing theoretical model has been the one variously labelled as "positivist," "capitalist," "experimentalist," "historicist," or simply "modern." Reiss calls it by another name: analytico-referential discourse. His reason for choosing this label is that he sees in this model the coincidence of the order of language (and other signifying systems) with

> the logical ordering of "reason" and with the structural organization of a world given as exterior to both these orders. Its relation is not taken to be simply one of analogy, but one of identity. Its exemplary statement is *cogito-ergo-sum* (reason-semiotic-mediating system-world).
>
> (1982, 31)

Its suppressed practice is that of "the enunciating subject *as discursive activity*" (42).

Science, philosophy, and art (having all functioned in such a way as to suppress the act and responsibility of the enunciation) are now themselves becoming the sites of the surfacing of that very repressed practice. And it is in the various discourses of postmodernism that we are seeing both the inscribing and subverting of the notions of objectivity and linguistic transparency that deny "the enunciating subject." That we seem on the verge of a crisis not unlike that of the seventeenth century will not be surprising news, of course, to readers of both contemporary theory and literature, because the advent of the postmodern condition has been characterized by nothing if not by self-consciousness and by metadiscursive pondering on catastrophe and change. For at least the last twenty years, literary theorists of all persuasions have been hypothesizing, as did Hans Robert Jauss as early as 1969, that the old (in this case, formalist) aesthetic paradigm was exhausted and that the consolidation of a new one was imminent. But without the help of the hindsight that Reiss can use to such good advantage, we would seem to have few means of studying the state of crisis of our present discursive system – that is, unless we are willing to allow the self-reflective quality of both contemporary art and theory to lead us to what may indeed turn out to be those very paradoxes or moments of internal contradiction that mark both change and a provisional kind of (discontinuous) continuity in the emergence of a repressed practice into the position of a new theoretical mode.

In other words, postmodernism might be seen to operate as an internalized challenge to analytico-referential discourse by pointing to the way in which its model of infinite expansion is, in fact, as Reiss shows, underpinned by a drive toward totalization and finite and closed knowledge. The self-conscious theorizing and historicizing of theory by writers such as Edward Said, Terry Eagleton, Teresa de Lauretis, Frank Lentricchia, and, of course, Michel Foucault, have been working in much the same manner as have contemporary art forms such as historiographic metafiction: both have foregrounded the need to break out of the still prevailing paradigms – formalist and humanist – and to "situate" both art and theory in two important contexts. They must be situated, first, within the enunciative act itself, and second, within the broader historical, social, and political (as well as intertextual) context implied by that act and in which both theory and practice take root.

At least since Jakobson's famous formulation of his model of communication (1960), if not before, both literature and literary theory have been self-conscious about the context-dependent nature of linguistic meaning, about the importance to signification of the circumstances surrounding any utterance. An obvious point should be made here: the art of enunciation always includes an enunciating producer as well as a receiver of the utterance, and thus their interrelations are a relevant part of the discursive context. This point needs making only because, in the collective name of scientific universality (and objectivity), novelistic realism, and various critical formalisms, that enunciating entity is what has been suppressed – both as an individual humanist subject and even as the postulated producer of a "situated" discourse. It is the latter that has become the focus of attention in theory lately, from Said's arguments for critical *engagement* to the speech act theorists' views of the utterance as always produced both in a situation (within a set of contextual circumstances), and by and for intentional beings.

In fiction this attention has taken the form of overt textual emphasis on the narrating "I" and the reading "you." In John Berger's historiographic metafiction, *G*, the narrator works to make us aware of the usual conventions of third-person narrative which, in fact, condition the context of our understanding as readers. For example: "The look in her eyes is an expression of freedom which he receives as such, but which we, in order to locate it in our world of third persons, must call a look of simultaneous appeal and gratitude" (1972, 115). We are forced to see that language is given meaning by context, by who is speaking (and listening/reading), where, when, and why: "The same words [sexual nouns] written in reported speech – either swearing or describing – acquire a different character and lose their italics, because they then refer to the speaker speaking and not directly to the acts of sex" (112). The narrator's discourse is paradoxically postmodern, however, for it both inscribes context and then contests its boundaries: "Then why do I want to describe her experience exhaustively, definitively, when I fully recognize the impossibility of doing so? Because I love her. I love you Leonie. . . . It was *he* who said *this*" (135). This slippage from first to third person (and between different first persons) reappears whenever the narrator writes of love or sex – the participatory activities from which he cannot seem to exclude himself (e.g. 162, 201).

Despite the overt foregrounding of the act of production and enunciation in this novel, there is also a paradoxical assertion that the discursive act is also somehow "empty outside of the very enunciation which defines it." These, however, are Roland Barthes's words to define what happens when the concepts of the author and authorial authority are called into question. He continues:

> The author is a modern figure, a product of our society insofar as, emerging from the Middle Ages with English empiricism, French rationalism and the personal faith of the Reformation, it discovered the prestige of the individual, of, as it is more nobly put, the "human person". It is thus logical that in literature it should be this positivism, the epitome and culmination of capitalist ideology, which has attached the greatest importance to the "person" of the author.
>
> (1977, 142–3)

Barthes contests this notion of original and originating author, the source of fixed meaning in the past, and substitutes for it the idea of a textual Scriptor or what I would prefer to call a "producer" who exists only in the time of the text and its reading: "there is no other time than that of the enunciation and every text is eternally written *here and now*" (145). The metaphor for creation changes from one of expression to one of performative inscription, and the discursive context of the text's inscribing is that of a network of "multiple writings, drawn from many cultures and entering into mutual relations of dialogue, parody, contestation" (148). And it is the reader whom Barthes sees as the activator of this contextual network.

Certainly many postmodern novels would support such a view of the importance of the act of reading. Julian Barnes's *Flaubert's Parrot* thematizes the quality and mode of different kinds of readers (such as, lay and professional – 1984, 75–6) and their demands upon a narrator: "You expect something from me too, don't you?" he asks (86). It is not accidental that a line like this might remind us of Camus's *The Fall* with its silent, but inscribed listener; in fact the narrator invokes that novel directly in his text. This textual and thematic attention paid to the process of reading is meant, we learn, as an allegory of the process of interpreting life as well as art:

> life, in this respect, is a bit like reading. And as I said before: if all your responses to a book have already been duplicated and expanded upon by a professional critic, then what point is there to your reading? Only that it's *yours*.
>
> (Barnes 1984, 166)

In emphasizing the receiver's role, postmodern works never, however, repress the process of production. The concept of the artist as unique and originating source of final and authoritative meaning may well be dead, as Barthes claimed. Certainly postmodern works like Sherrie Levine's "After Walker Evans" series of photographs of famous photographs suggest it is. Nevertheless, it is possible to argue that this *position* of discursive authority still lives on, because it is encoded into the enunciative act itself. Increasingly this paradox has itself become the focus of much postmodern art and theory: simultaneous with a general dethroning of suspect authority and of centered and totalized thought, we are witnessing a renewed aesthetic and theoretical interest in the interactive powers involved in the production and reception of texts. The most extreme example I can think of in art is, perhaps, "interactive fiction" or computerized, participatory "compunovels." Here process is all; there is no fixed product or text, just the reader's activity as producer as well as receiver (Niesz and Holland 1984).

This, however, is an extreme. Normally we are merely presented with a self-reflexive exposition of the power relations involved in the interaction of producers and receivers. Michael Coetzee's recent novel *Foe* opens with an enunciative signal of speech: quotation marks. Who is speaking, though? It takes the reader a while to piece together that the speaker is female, British, of another century, and a castaway. But to whom is she speaking? This is harder to ascertain. Later she tells her story to "Robinson Cruso" [sic] (for it is his island on which she has been washed up), but at that point she repeats information she had already given to her initial unidentified interlocutor and, of course, to the reader. It takes almost a third of the novel to discover that the addressee is Daniel Foe (later Defoe) whom she wishes to convince to tell her story of the female castaway to the world. The second part of the novel is specifically and overtly addressed to him, at least until he disappears, and then the narrator, Susan Barton, must write in journal form to herself, though still for Foe's eyes. The third section lacks the quotation marks but is in the first person and is clearly in Susan's voice. But, here we are again unsure as to whom she is addressing, and we thus mirror her own uncertainty: "(but to whom do I confess this?)" (134). The first-person narrator of the fourth and final section is not, however, Susan, for the narrative begins with her death. This voice repeats, in quotation marks, Susan's opening narrative to Foe, but then moves outside those discursive markings, and from there, outside time and narrative logic. The reader is made very aware of the enunciative context in this novel, but is asked to question its customary security of meaning in a typically postmodern way. Enunciation is at once underlined and undermined. Just as Susan Barton is finally at the mercy of both Foe and Coetzee, so too the receiver of any text could be seen to be at the mercy of an *agent provocateur/manipulateur*, the producer. This is the postmodern ironic and problematizing play of enunciation and context.

II

> I was interested to test, to *bend* close to breaking, the very curious relationship which exists between a reader and his author. I wished to challenge the reader to go on suspending his disbelief in my fiction in the face of an emphatic admission on my part that what I was presenting *was* fiction and nothing more – and everything more.
> John Banville

If we were to think in terms of discursive practices rather than in terms of genres and separate discourses, it would not be at all surprising that the art of a given period might share the preoccupations of the theory. It is not in the least accidental, as Terry Eagleton comes to see (1983, 139), that Saussure and Husserl are writing "at about the same time" (110) as Joyce, Eliot, and Pound, with their concern for closed symbolic systems. Eagleton offers a rough three-stage periodization of the history of modern theory, one that, in fact, also corresponds *grosso modo* to the literary changes of the last hundred and fifty years: beginning with "a preoccupation with the author (Romanticism and the nineteenth century); an exclusive concern with the text (New Criticism); a marked shift of attention to the reader over recent years" (74). I would only stress that it was artistic as well as critical romanticism and modernism that did much to bring about that alteration of focus from author to text to reader, and that postmodern art, as well as theory, is perhaps now in a position to show us the next stage. Indeed it may already have done so in its challenge to analytico-referential discourse's repression of the entirety of the enunciating act and its agents.

Take, for example, William Kennedy's historiographic metafiction, *Legs*, the tale of the historical gangster, Jack "Legs" Diamond, as told by his fictional lawyer forty-five years "after the facts," so to speak. This "somewhat unorthodox memoir" (1975, 13) is partly self-justifying, partly didactic, and for both reasons, its narrator is always aware of his productive act of meaning-making in relation to both reader and context: "I say to you, my reader, that here was a singular being in a singular land, a fusion of the individual life with the clear and violent light of American reality, with the fundamental Columbian brilliance that illuminates this bloody republic" (14). Because of such contextualizing, this fictionalizing biography manages to teach us much, not only about Diamond, but also about his times, about bootlegging, and about the Catskill area and its history.

Typical of postmodern fiction, though, the full context in which the enunciation operates here is an intertextual as much as a social one. It is the prohibited reading of Rabelais (his work is on the Index) that makes the staid lawyer decide to get involved with the prohibition-era gangster, that teaches him that his life is a "stupendous bore," and in dire need of "a little Gargantuan dimension" (16). Of course, the Rabelais text resurfaces: Jack, himself larger than life, also (however improbably) reads it. In order to make sense of the hero of his story to both himself and us, the narrator has recourse to intertexts ranging from *The Great Gatsby* to the later Cagney film, *Public Enemy*, based on Diamond's life. But the purpose of these allusions goes beyond the textual to the social, since one of the impulses behind the narration is an attempt to rescue "Legs" Diamond (which is only the papers' name for him) from the version of him offered by American culture – from films to gossip to police files to the press – and in so doing, to foreground how (as receivers) we inevitably, if unthinkingly, approach subjects primarily through cultural representations of them.

The same kind of self-consciousness about the social and textual contexts in which discourse operates can be found in theory as well: for example in Derrida's constant awareness of the contextual status of his own discourse, which he calls "a limited work, but with its own field and framework, a work possible only in a historical, political, theoretical, etc., situation that is highly determined" (1981a, 63). There is hardly a discipline today that has not been touched by this awareness of context and discursive process. For instance Dominick LaCapra has argued for a view of historiography as the process of dialogue with the past carried on through a performative use of language which would "involve both historian and addressee in a process of significant change by moving them to respond to the proffered account and its implications for the existing context of interpretation" (1985a, 37). For history to focus on how texts (such as documents) are read would perforce open it up to a consideration of the political and socio-cultural processes in which they are bound and in which they are given meaning by the historian. Here – as in postmodern fiction – the context is both discursive and institutional (43). As Tony Bennett has argued, texts (be they historical or fictive)

exist only as always-already organized or activated to be read in certain ways just as readers exist as always-already activated to read in certain ways: neither can be

granted a virtual identity that is separable from the determinate ways in which
they are gridded onto one another within the different reading formations.

(1984, 12)

Nevertheless, the lesson of postmodern art is that we must not limit our
investigations to just readers and texts; the process of production too cannot
be ignored. In discussing freedom and constraint in the reading process,
Jonathan Culler has asserted that there "must always be dualisms: an
interpreter and something to interpret" (1982b, 75; see too Josipovici
1982, 33). But postmodernism suggests that there is more to it than this. The
enunciation requires more than just text and receiver in order to activate the
dynamic process of meaning-generating (Metscher 1972 and 1975). The text
has a context, and form is given sense perhaps as much through the
receiver's inference of an act of production as by the actual act of perception.
This would be especially true of ironic postmodern texts where the receiver
does indeed posit or infer an intent to be ironic. If art is seen as historical
production and as social practice, then the position of the producer cannot
be ignored, for there exists a set of social relations between producer
(inferred and real) and audience that can potentially be revolutionized by a
change in the forces of production that might turn the reader into a
collaborator instead of a consumer (Eagleton 1976b, 61). Feminist criticism,
of course, has been aware of these relations (Fetterly 1978), as has the
politically engaged theory that has offered us the "dialectical novel" (Caute
1972) and the "interrogative text" (Belsey 1980). For many theorists, this has
meant a return to, or rather a rethinking of, the ideas of Brecht and the
Frankfurt School. There are constant echoes of Benjamin's idea that "the
rigid, isolated object (work, novel, book) is of no use whatsoever. It must be
reinserted into the context of living social relations" (1973, 87). This has
meant a renewed interest both in the materiality of art and also in the
material conditions of its uses and its users (Kress 1985, 29). In both theory
and practice, this emphasis on specific usage and on the mapping of a
particular pragmatic context is what works to undercut any (conscious or
unconscious) assumption of universal or transhistorical status for postmodern discourses (Lyotard 1977, 39). The "eternal man" (Veyne 1971, 169)
inscribed on the pages on history and theory (and literature) is revealed as
an ideological construct, the creation of a specific historical, social, and
ideological situation.

In *Marxism and the Philosophy of Language*, Mikhail Bakhtin (Voloshinov)
wrote: "The sign cannot be separated from the social situation without
relinquishing its nature as sign. Verbal communication can never be
understood and explained outside of this connection with a concrete
situation" (1973, 95). In addition, he argued that language is not a neutral
medium which is the private property of the user; it is "overpopulated" with
the intentions of others (Bakhtin 1981, 293). Hence the concept of single,
closed "work" shifts to one of plural, open "text" – to use Barthes's

distinction (1977, 158). For Barthes the "text" is "that *social* space which leaves no language safe, outside, nor any subject of the enunciation in position as judge, master, analyst, confessor, decoder" (164). The idea of "text" in this sense, as that which stresses process, context, and enunciative situation, is important to postmodernist discourses, both theoretical and practical. For instance historiographic metafictions like *Legs* or *G.* combine the effects of two important tendencies in poststructuralist theory, tendencies which are often deemed incompatible: as metafiction, they incarnate the Derridean network of traces in their own self-reflexive textuality; but, as "historiographic" metafiction, they present their texts as part of a larger set of Foucaldian discursive practices (defined as bodies of "anonymous, historical rules, always determined in the time and space that have defined a given period, and for a given social, economic, geographical, or linguistic area, the conditions of operation of the enunciative function" – Foucault 1972, 119). Textuality is reinserted into history and into the social and political conditions of the discursive act itself.

No longer to believe in the "author" as a person may be another way to restore the wholeness of the act of enunciation. The producer would be known as a position (like that of the receiver) to be filled within the text. To speak (as I have been) of producers and receivers of texts, then, would be to speak less of individual subjects than of what Eagleton calls "subject positions" (1983, 119) that are not extratextual, but are instead essential constitutive factors of the text. By calling attention to the authority structures of these positions within the text itself, a postmodern text might be able to subvert (even as it installs) the ideology of originality which subtends them. According to Said, the writer then "thinks less of writing originally, and more of rewriting. The image for writing changes from original *inscription* to parallel script" (1983, 135), a change attested to by the proliferation of forms of postmodern parody. In other words, the position of the producer of the text (which modernism and formalism banished in their reaction against nineteenth-century intentionalism) is being rethought. After all, readers – however free and in final control of the act of reading – are also always constrained by what they read, by the text. And in postmodern texts, it is often the process of the production of constraints that is foregrounded: we need only think of the manipulative narrator of a novel like Rushdie's *Midnight's Children*.

However, as I have been suggesting, the producer of the text (at least from the reader's point of view) is never, strictly speaking, a real or even an *implied* one, but is rather one *inferred* by the reader from her/his positioning as enunciating entity. The change from the concept of "author" and authority to this one of production and inference can be seen in Eagleton's reader-focused and contextual definition of intentionality:

> To ask in such a situation, "What do you mean?" is really to ask what effects my language is trying to bring about: it is a way of understanding the situation itself, not an attempt to tune into ghostly impulses within my skull. Understanding my

intention is grasping my speech and behaviour in relation to a significant context. When we understand the "intentions" of a piece of language, we interpret it as being in some sense *oriented*, structured to achieve certain effects; and none of these can be grasped apart from the practical conditions in which the language operates.

(1983, 114)

What is unavoidable and unignorable for any attempt to trace a postmodern poetics of the parodic self-reflexive art (as well as theory) of today is this concept of meaning existing only "in relation to a significant context": that is, the context of the once suppressed enunciative act as a whole, and that of "situated" discourse which does not ignore the social, historical or ideological dimensions of understanding, the "genuine Unconscious" that Jameson sees as having been repressed with History (1981a, 280). As we shall see in more detail in Chapter 11, postmodern "texts" move us to consider discourse or language "in use," and thus what discourse analysts call "the cognitive and especially the social processes, strategies, and contextualization of discourse taken as a mode of interaction in highly complex sociocultural situation" (van Dijk 1985b, 1)

Barbara Herrnstein Smith has suggested that, in narrative theory, we ought to see language as "*verbal responses* – that is, as *acts* which, like any acts, are *performed in response to various sets of conditions*" (1980, 225). As historio-graphic metafiction illustrates in actual narrative practice, to do so would be to change the focus away from individual authorial expression and mimetic representation toward a consideration of shared enunciative context and particular (though not unique) usage. In the light of the structuralist focus on *langue* and on the arbitrary but stable relationship between signifier and signified, postmodernism might be called the "revenge of *parole*" (or at least of the relationship between the subject, as generator of *parole*, and the act or process of generation). Postmodernism highlights discourse or "language put into action" (Benveniste 1971, 223), language operating as communi-cation between two agents. This concern for the production process, rather than the product, is actually inherent in Saussurian theory, but has been suppressed in the more mechanical formalist model of structuralism (Coward and Ellis 1977, 6) – clearly another form of analytico-referential discourse.

Benveniste has suggested that the enunciation, the communicative act, is, in fact, the moment of the construction of the subject in language (by the system of language). The specifically political implications of this moment form the topic of Chapter 10, but what is evident in both postmodern theory and art is an impulse to open up prevailing semiotic models to pragmatics, that is, to the situation of discourse, to what Jameson wrongly reduces to

language itself as an unstable exchange between its speakers, whose utterances are now seen less as a process of the transmission of information or messages, or in terms of some network of signs or even signifying systems, than as . . . an essentially conflictual relationship between tricksters.

(1984b, xi)

In the work of theorists like Reiss and Foucault, the enunciation is also seen as an act conditioned by the operation of certain modalities or laws – including those of the context in which the act takes place and the status or position of its enunciator, "a particular, vacant place that may in fact be filled by different individuals" (Foucault 1972, 96). While this does not entail a destruction of the notion of a coherent subject (producer or receiver or – by extension – fictional character), it does challenge it. It was Foucault who insisted that the subject had to be rethought as a discursive construct (1977, 137), and novels like Thomas's *The White Hotel* or Kennedy's *Legs* overtly do precisely that.

III

> The theory of the subject (in the double sense of the word) is at the heart of humanism and this is why our culture has tenaciously rejected anything that could weaken its hold upon us. *Michel Foucault*

In a postmodern poetics adequate to the art of today, an art that (like advertising) often addresses the collective "you" which is then, perhaps unavoidably, perceived as singular (in English), the issue of subjectivity and the interactive power of, and even collusion between, the subject positions of producer and receiver must be taken into account. In other words, what we witness is the transformation of a suppressed discursive practice (the entirety of the enunciation) into one of the very tools of theoretical analysis. This involves a rethinking of the relation of receiver to both text and inferred producer:

> We have to see ourselves neither as inventively fooling around with texts nor as "decoding" complex ciphers, but as generating a reading of the text by a process which, because it involves an intercourse between our concerns and those of the text of a kind whose outcome we cannot altogether control (we may indeed find ourselves "read" by the text), has more in common with a relationship between persons than with the scientific scrutiny of a natural object. (B. Harrison 1985, 22–3)

The postmodern way of defining the self (an internalized challenge to the humanist notion of integrity and seamless wholeness) has much to do with this mutual influencing of textuality and subjectivity. What Thomas's *The White Hotel* or Wiebe's *The Temptations of Big Bear* overtly enact and teach about this process recalls, not surprisingly, Lyotard's typically postmodern lesson:

> A *self* does not amount to much, but no self is an island; each exists in a fabric of relations that is now more complex and mobile than ever before. Young or old, man or woman, rich or poor, a person is always located at "nodal points" of specific communication circuits, however tiny these may be.
>
> (1984a, 15)

Theory and literature today share the same problematics of the subject; they echo each other's concerns.

What both historiographic metafiction and much theory today also foreground, though, are the implied consequences of such a definition of subjectivity. These novels ask (along with Foucault 1972, 50–5): who is speaking? Who is accorded the right to use language in a particular way? From what institutional sites do we construct our discourses? From what does discourse derive its legitimating authority? From what position do we speak – as producers or interpreters? For Foucault, because of the complexity of the answers to these problematic questions, the subject of discourse is always the dispersed, discontinuous network of distinct sites of action; it is never the controlling transcendental knower. Like other theorists, even those of quite different persuasions, Foucault always insisted on the specific spatio-temporal co-ordinates of the enunciative act and, at the same time, the discursive context of signifying practices within which that act finds its meaning. So too does historiographic metafiction, usually through allegories of textual production and reception within the narrative plot. As Charles Russell explains:

> Like the fictional character who reveals that personality is only the locus of individual and social determinants, the author and text disclose that they are spoken by the language which they give speech to. And even though the writer gives speech its reality by speaking, he or she in turn only exists as the speaker because of the patterns of existent discourse.
>
> (1985, 263)

Postmodern novels like Findley's *Famous Last Words* allegorize precisely this same problematizing of the notions of enunciation and subjectivity.

Others, like Doctorow's *Ragtime*, also work to make these issues problematic, but they do so less by allegory than by textualized questioning of the entire notion of narrative focalization: what is a center of consciousness? What are its implications in terms of totalization of perspective? *Ragtime's* fragmented, iterative structure challenges the traditional realist narrative conventions of the inscription of the subject as coherent and continuous, suggesting perhaps that fragmentation and replication are also, in fact, conditions of subjectivity. The meeting of fictional characters and historical personages in the novel may also have a function in the problematizing of the nature of the subject in the sense that it foregrounds the inescapable contextualizing of the self in both history and society. All of Doctorow's fiction works to this end.

In *The Book of Daniel* the narrator comes to see his subjectivity not in terms of any humanist notion of uniqueness and individuality, but as the result of processes which appear to be outside him (politics). He rejects the "David Copperfield kind of crap" – the realist novel's conventions of ordered and meaningful identity. What Doctorow once called the "novel as private I" is what he cannot write: that I is social and political, as well as fragmented and discontinuous. *Loon Lake's* even more dispersed narrative (shifting voice, tense, and person) paradoxically calls attention to the "novel as public I." The same is true of the problematizing complexity of enunciation in novels like Puig's *Kiss of the Spider Woman* or Scott's *Antichthon*. The frequent switching between first and third person complicates the rooting of subjectivity in language, in that it both inscribes and destabilizes it at the same time.

But historiographic metafiction enacts a concern, not just for the general notion of subjectivity, but for the specific pragmatics of the conditions of production and reception of the text itself, and these two problematizing strategies of enactment work together to suggest "a theory of meaning as a continual cultural production that is not only susceptible of ideological transformation, but materially based in historical change." But what I have just cited is Teresa de Lauretis's description of the pragmatic semiotics of Umberto Eco (1984, 172). Again, the coincidence of theory and practice in postmodernism is not accidental. As we saw in the last chapter, the decentering of the subject effected by the ex-centrics of our culture has resulted from both theory and art, from (for instance) feminist and black critical discourses, but also from their corresponding fiction. As Toni Morrison's *Sula* puts it: "She had no center, no speck around which to grow" (1974, 119). And this is a productive problem both for narrative and for the formation of the subject.

Similarly Christa Wolf's *Cassandra* challenges, from within the tradition, the centered and centering discourse which is not, in fact, usually granted woman in our male western tradition. The fictionalized yet historical Cassandra at first appears to tell her story from both the third-person ("It was here. This is where she stood" – 1984, 3) and first-person perspectives ("Keeping step with the story, I make my way into death" – 3). But we become gradually aware of a modern, female, narrating historian-novelist figure retracing Cassandra's last steps at Mycenae, putting herself almost literally into her predecessor's shoes and footsteps. Her Cassandra is made aware of her future observer: "Whoever is standing there now looks out on the coast" (72). At the end, the tenses shift along with the point of view: "Here is the place. These stone lions looked at her. They seem to move in the shifting light" (138). In the shifting light of the narrative, the past, present, and future merge – as is fitting for the story of Cassandra, the seer (and female artist figure).

In contemporary theory today, what is often invoked when discussing enunciative strategies is Althusser's famous ideological extension of Benveniste's insights into the relation of subjectivity to language:

> you and I are *always already* subjects, and as such constantly practice rituals of ideological recognition, which guarantee for us that we are indeed concrete, individual, distinguishable and (naturally) irreplaceable subjects. The writing I am currently executing and the reading you are currently performing are also in this respect rituals of ideological recognition, including the "obviousness" with which the "truth" or "error" of my reflections may impose itself on you.
>
> (1971, 172–3)

Teresa de Lauretis further elaborates on the kinds of subjects that are constituted in and by ideology: class subjects, race subjects, sexed subjects, and "any other differential category that may have political use-value for particular situations of practice at particular historical moments" (1984, 32). This emphasis on the particular and historical is what undermines the concept of "eternal *man*," in more than one sense.

Many postmodern installations, films, and video art attempt to make the receiver into a Brechtian, aware participant, self-consciously part of the meaning-making process. In *The Austrian Tapes*, Douglas Davis asks the viewer of the video to put her/his hands on his (on the screen). This is not just a game; it is a way of forcing the usually private and passive experience of art into the public space of action. But it does in a typically contradictory postmodern way: Davis wants video art to be on the home TV screen, not in the art gallery. As such it would be able to distinguish itself from film, from the darkness and large screen, and especially from the economic exchange, and so might become a potentially revolutionary form of address: both a form of mass communication (broadcasting) and a mode that takes place in small, private space, continuous with the daily life of the viewer (D. Davis 1977, 20).

Umberto Eco has suggested that postmodernism is born at the moment when we discover that the world has no fixed center and that, as Foucault taught, power is not something unitary that exists outside of us (in Rosso 1983, 3–4). These two insights are echoed constantly in the arts today, from architecture to fiction. As we shall see in more detail in Chapter 11, the relation of power to knowledge and to historical, social, and ideological discursive contexts is an obsession of postmodernism. The recent focus on this relation marks a move away from the formalist assumption that texts are only objects to be analyzed and deciphered. When the locus of meaning shifts from author to text to reader, and finally, to the entire act of enunciation, then we have perhaps moved beyond formalism and even beyond reader-response theory *per se*. We may be on the road to articulating a new theoretical model adequate not only to the self-reflexive art of today but also to our seemingly intense need to counteract our own critical marginalization. If we let the self-reflexivity of postmodern art and theory guide us, we may find ourselves in a position to argue that the discursive practice suppressed by analytico-referential discourse is already on the way to becoming the new model, the new set of analytical tools or ordering principles that mark the postmodern. To examine the conditions, act, and nature of enunciation, to look at the "kinds of *effects* which discourses produce, and how they produce them" (Eagleton 1983, 205), and to do so by examining the institutional, historical, political and social constraints upon production and also the "discursive and cultural (that is, internal) systems that provoke and assimilate literary production" (Said 1983, 152), would certainly be an important step in formulating a poetics of postmodernism.

6

HISTORICIZING THE POSTMODERN: THE PROBLEMATIZING OF HISTORY

I

Every culture cannot sustain and absorb the shock of modern
civilization. There is the paradox: how to become a modern and to
return to sources. *Paul Ricoeur*

One of the few common denominators among the detractors of postmodernism is the surprising, but general, agreement that the postmodern is
ahistorical. It is a familiar line of attack, launched by Marxists and
traditionalists alike, against not only contemporary fiction, but also today's
theory – from semiotics to deconstruction. What interests me here,
however, is not the detail of the debate, but the very fact that history is now,
once again, an issue – and a rather problematic one at that. It seems to be
inevitably tied up with that set of challenged cultural and social assumptions
that also condition our notions of both theory and art today: our beliefs in
origins and ends, unity, and totalization, logic and reason, consciousness
and human nature, progress and fate, representation and truth, not to
mention the notions of causality and temporal homogeneity, linearity, and
continuity (see J. H. Miller 1974, 460–1).

In some ways, these problematizing challenges are not new ones: their
intellectual roots have been firm for centuries, though it is their actual
concentration in a great many discourses today that forces us to take notice
anew. It was only in 1970 that a noted historian could write:

Novelists and playwrights, natural scientists and social scientists, poets, prophets,
pundits, and philosophers of many persuasions have manifested an intense
hostility to historical thought. Many of our contemporaries are extraordinarily
reluctant to acknowledge the reality of past time and prior events, and stubbornly
resistant to all arguments for the possibility or utility of historical knowledge.

(Fischer 1970, 307)

Only a few years later, Hayden White proclaimed that

> one of the distinctive characteristics of contemporary literature is its underlying conviction that the historical consciousness must be obliterated if the writer is to examine with proper seriousness those strata of human experience which is *modern* art's peculiar purpose to disclose.
>
> (1978b, 31)

But his examples are telling: Joyce, Pound, Eliot, Mann – the great modernists, not postmodernists. Today we would certainly have to modify radically this kind of claim in the wake of the postmodern architecture of Michael Graves and Paolo Portoghesi, or films like *The Return of Martin Guerre* or historiographic metafiction like Skvorecky's *Dvorak in Love* or Fuentes's *The Old Gringo*. There seems to be a new desire to think historically, and to think historically these days is to think critically and contextually.

Part of this problematizing return to history is no doubt a response to the hermetic ahistoric formalism and aestheticism that characterized much of the art and theory of the so-called modernist period. If the past were invoked, it was to deploy its "presentness" or to enable its transcendence in the search for a more secure and universal value system (be it myth, religion, or psychology) (Spanos 1972, 158). Some writers seemed caught between skepticism and a mystical-aesthetic ideal of historical understanding (Longenbach 1987). In the perspective of cultural history, of course, it is now easy to see these as reactions against the burden of tradition (in the visual arts and music, as well – Rochberg 1984, 327), often taking the form of an ironic enlisting of the aesthetic past in the overhauling of western civilization (Joyce, Eliot). However, modernism's "nightmare of history" is precisely what postmodernism has chosen to face straight on. Artist, audience, critic – none is allowed to stand outside history, or even to wish to do so (Robinson and Vogel 1971, 198). The reader of Fowles's *The French Lieutenant's Woman* is never allowed to ignore the lessons of the past about the past or the implications of those lessons for the historical present. But surely, one could object, Brecht and Dos Passos were modernists who taught us the same things. And was history not already overtly problematized in what Barbara Foley has called the "metahistorical novel" – *Absalom! Absalom!*, *Orlando*, and so on (1986a, 195)? Well, yes and no: paradoxical postmodernism is both oedipally oppositional and filially faithful to modernism. The provisional, indeterminate nature of historical knowledge is certainly not a discovery of postmodernism. Nor is the questioning of the ontological and epistemological status of historical "fact" or the distrust of seeming neutrality and objectivity of recounting. But the concentration of these problematizations in postmodern art is not something we can ignore.

To speak of provisionality and indeterminacy is not to *deny* historical knowledge, however. This is the misunderstanding suggested by Gerald Graff when he laments: "For if history is seen as an unintelligible flux of phenomena, lacking in inherent significance and structure, then no exertions of the shaping, ordering imagination can be anything but a dishonest refuge from truth" (1973, 403). What the postmodern writing of both history and literature has taught us is that both history and fiction are discourses, that both constitute systems of signification by which we make sense of the past ("exertions of the shaping, ordering imagination"). In other words, the meaning and shape are not *in the events*, but *in the systems* which make those past "events" into present historical "facts." This is not a "dishonest refuge from truth" but an acknowledgement of the meaning-making function of human constructs.

The postmodern, then, effects two simultaneous moves. It reinstalls historical contexts as significant and even determining, but in so doing, it problematizes the entire notion of historical knowledge. This is another of the paradoxes that characterize all postmodern discourses today. And the implication is that there can be no single, essentialized, transcendent concept of "genuine historicity" (as Fredric Jameson desires: 1984a), no matter what the nostalgia (Marxist or traditionalist) for such an entity. Postmodern historicism is wilfully unencumbered by nostalgia in its critical, dialogical reviewing of the forms, contexts, and values of the past. An example might make this point clearer. Jameson has asserted that Doctorow's *Ragtime* is "the most peculiar and stunning monument to the aesthetic situation engendered by the disappearance of the historical referent" (1984a, 70). But it is just as easy to argue that, in that very novel, the historical referent is very present – and in spades. Not only is there an accurate evocation of a particular period of early-twentieth-century American capitalism, with due representation from all classes involved, but historical personages also appear within the fiction. Of course, it is this mixing of the historical and the fictive and this tampering with the "facts" of received history that Jameson objects to. Yet that is the major means to making the reader aware of the particular nature of the historical referent. There is also no conflict between this historical reconstruction/construction and the politics of the novel, as has been claimed (Green 1975–6, 842); indeed they are mutually supportive. If Doctorow does use nostalgia, it is always ironically turned against itself – and us.

The opening of the novel sets the pattern. Describing the year 1902, the narrating voice introduces a potential nostalgia, but surely it is one already tinted with irony: "Everyone wore white in summer. Tennis racquets were hefty and the racquet faces elliptical. There was a lot of sexual fainting. There were no Negroes. There were no immigrants" (1975, 4). Only a page later, we learn that Emma Goldman teaches a quite different view of America: "Apparently there *were* Negroes. There *were* immigrants" (5). And, of course, much of the novel is about precisely those ex-centric parts of society, traditionally excluded from fiction and history. Jameson is right, I think, to see this novel as inscribing a crisis in historicity, but it is his negative judgment that is surprising. The irony that allows critical distancing is what here refuses nostalgia: *Ragtime's* volunteer firemen are anything but sentimental figures, and many American social "ideals" – such as justice – are called into question by their inapplicability to (black) Americans like Coalhouse Walker. There is no generalizing and sentimentalizing away of racism, ethno-centric bias, or class hatred in this novel.

Postmodern works like this one contest art's right to claim to inscribe timeless universal values, and they do so by thematizing and even formally enacting the context-dependent nature of all values. They also challenge narrative singularity and unity in the name of multiplicity and disparity. Through narrative, they offer fictive corporality instead of abstractions, but at the same time, they do tend to fragment or at least to render unstable the traditional unified identity or subjectivity of character. It is not by accident that I have been using here the language of Michel Foucault, for his description of the challenges offered by a Nietzschean "genealogy" to standard notions of history (1977, 142–54) corresponds to what postmodern fiction also suggests in its contesting of the conventions of both historiography and the novel form. As I have been arguing throughout the first part of this study, the postmodern enterprise is one that traverses the boundaries of theory and practice, often implicating one in and by the other, and history is often the site of this problematization.

Of course, this has also been true of other periods, for the novel and history have frequently revealed their natural affinities through their narrative common denominators: teleology, causality, continuity. Leo Braudy (1970) has shown how the problematizing of that continuity and coherence in eighteenth-century history writing found its parallel in the fiction of those years. Today, though, it is less the problem of how to narrate time than the issue of the nature and status of our information about the past that makes postmodern history, theory, and art share certain concerns. In the work of Hayden White, Michel de Certeau, Paul Veyne, Louis O. Mink, Lionel Gossman, and others, a kind of radical suspicion of the act of historiography can be seen. However, *pace* the opponents of postmodernism, there is no lack of concern for history or any radical relativism or subjectivism (Lentricchia 1980, xiv). Instead there is a view of the past, both recent and remote, that takes the present powers and limitations of the writing of that past into account. And the result is often a certain avowed provisionality and irony.

In Umberto Eco's terms: "The postmodern reply to the modern consists of recognizing that the past, since it cannot really be destroyed, because its destruction leads to silence [the discovery of modernism], must be revisited: but with irony, not innocently" (1983, 1984, 67). The semiotic awareness that all signs change meaning with time (MacCannell and MacCannell 1982, 10) prevents both nostalgia and antiquarianism. The loss of innocence is less to be lamented than celebrated: "We can, indeed, no longer assume that we have the capacity to make value-free statements about history, or suppose that there is some special dispensation whereby the signs that constitute an historical text have reference to events in the world" (Kermode 1979, 108). This is the skepticism that has brought us, not just changes in the discipline of history, but the "New Historicism," as it is now labelled, in literary studies.

II

> The new history we are beginning to see these days has little in common with the old – and for an interesting historical reason: its practitioners were nurtured in the theoretical climate of the 1970s, a time during which the individual literary work came to lose its organic unity; when literature as an organized body of knowledge abandoned the boundaries that had hitherto enclosed it, to an extent even abandoned its claims to knowledge; and when history began to seem discontinuous, sometimes in fact no more than just another fiction. It is no wonder that the scholarship we now pursue cannot take the form or speak the language of the older literary history.
> *Herbert Lindenberger*

This new literary history is not an attempt to preserve and transmit a canon or a tradition of thought; it bears a problematic and questioning relation to both history and literary criticism. A recent advertisement for the University of California Press's series on "The New Historicism: Studies in Cultural Poetics," talks of a critical "return to the historical embeddedness of literary production" that is coeval with "innovative explorations of the symbolic construction of reality" in the study of history. There is an exact parallel here with the "New Art History" (Rees and Borzello 1986) of T. J. Clark and *Block* magazine (Bird 1986). Thanks to the pioneering work of Marxists, feminists, gays, black and ethnic theorists, there is a new awareness in these fields that history cannot be written without ideological and institutional analysis, including analysis of the act of writing itself. It is no longer enough to be suspicious or playful as a writer about art or literature (or history, though there it never really was); the theorist and the critic are inevitably implicated in both ideologies and institutions.

Historians such as Le Roy Ladurie have shocked their "establishment" colleagues by refusing to hide their interpretative and narrating acts behind the third-person voice of objectivity that is so common to both historical and literary critical writing. In his *Carnival in Romans* (1979), the historian presents himself, not as metaphorical witness or imaginary participant of the 1580 events, but as a scholar, reporting from outside the story he tells, but from an explicitly and intensely partisan perspective that lays out its value system for the readers to judge for themselves (Carrard 1985). This flaunting of the transgression of the conventions of historiography is a very postmodern conflating of two enunciative systems, those defined by Benveniste as historical and discursive. Historical statements, be they in historiography or realist fiction, tend to suppress grammatical reference to the discursive situation of the utterance (producer, receiver, context, intent) in their attempt to narrate past events in such a way that the events seem to narrate themselves (1971, 206–8). In the postmodern writing of history – and fiction (*Midnight's Children, The White Hotel, Slaughterhouse-Five*) – there is a deliberate contamination of the historical with didactic and situational discursive elements, thereby challenging the implied assumptions of historical statements: objectivity, neutrality, impersonality, and transparency of representation.

What fades away with this kind of contesting is any sure ground upon which to base representation and narration, in either historiography or fiction. In most postmodern work, however, that ground is first inscribed and subsequently subverted: Le Roy Ladurie's work has its impact because of an implied intertextual dialogue with traditional third-person narrative history; *Ragtime* derives its power as much from how it *recalls* as from how it *inverts* Dos Passos's work. As David Carroll has noted, the new and critical "return to history" is one which confronts "the conflictual interpenetration of various series, contexts, and grounds constituting any ground or process of grounding" (1983, 66), but I would add that, in the postmodernist writing of history and literature, it does so by first installing and then critically confronting both that grounding process and those grounds themselves. This is the paradox of the postmodern.

It is a paradox which underlines the separation between "history" as what Murray Krieger calls "the unimpeded sequence of raw empirical realities" (1974, 339) and "history" as either method or writing: "The process of critically examining and analyzing the records and survivals of the past is . . . *historical method*. The imaginative reconstruction of that process is called *historiography*" (Gottschalk 1969, 48). "Imaginative reconstruction" or intellectual systematizing – whichever model suits you best – is the focus of the postmodern rethinking of the problems of how we can and do come to have knowledge of the past. It is the writing of history that, as Paul Ricoeur has shown us, is actually "*constitutive* of the historical mode of understanding" (1984a, 162). It is historiography's explanatory and narrative emplotments of past *events* that construct what we consider historical *facts*. This is the context in which the postmodern historical sense situates itself: outside associations of Enlightenment progress or development, idealist/Hegelian world-historical process, or essentialized Marxist notions of history. Postmodernism returns to confront the problematic nature of the past as an object of knowledge for us in the present. There is no abyssal infinite regress to absence or utter groundlessness in the fiction of Salman Rushdie or Ian Watson, or in the films of Peter Greenaway. The past really did exist. The question is: *how* can we know that past today – and *what* can we know of it? The overt metafictionality of novels like *Shame* or *Star Turn* acknowledges their own constructing, ordering, and selecting processes, but these are always shown to be historically determined acts. It puts into question, at the same time as it exploits, the grounding of historical knowledge in the past real. This is why I have been calling this historiographic metafiction. It can often enact the problematic nature of the relation of writing history to narrativization and, thus, to fictionalization, thereby raising the same questions about the cognitive status of historical knowledge with which current philosophers of history are also grappling. What is the ontological nature of historical documents? Are they the stand-in for the past? What is meant – in ideological terms – by our "natural" understanding of historical explanation?

Historiographic metafiction refutes the natural or common-sense methods of distinguishing between historical fact and fiction. It refuses the view that only history has a truth claim, both by questioning the ground of that claim in historiography and by asserting that both history and fiction are discourses, human constructs, signifying systems, and both derive their major claim to truth from that identity. This kind of postmodern fiction also refuses the relegation of the extratextual past to the domain of historiography in the name of the autonomy of art. Novels like *The Public Burning* and *Legs* assert that the past did indeed exist prior to its "entextualization" into either fiction or history. They also show that both genres unavoidably construct as they textualize that past. The "real" referent of their language once existed; but it is only accessible to us today in textualized form: documents, eye-witness accounts, archives. The past is "archaeologized" (Lemaire 1981, xiv), but its reservoir of available materials is always acknowledged as a textualized one.

This postmodern "return to history", then, is not recuperation or nostalgia or revivalism (J. D. Kramer 1984, 352). From a non-Marxist perspective, at least, Ihab Hassan is right to castigate Jameson for missing the point about history and postmodernism (1986, 507) in the light of architecture like that of Paolo Portoghesi (517, 18n) (and, I would add, in the light of music like that of Stockhausen, Berio, and Rochberg, or novels like those of Fowles, Wolf, Grass, and Banville). Cultural commentators say that Americans turned to history in the 1970s because of their bicentennial. But what would explain the contemporaneous historical investigations in Canada, Latin America, and Europe? Ironically perhaps, it is Jameson who may have put his finger on one of the most important explanations: the members of the 1960s generation (who have, indeed, been the creators of postmodernism) might, for obvious reasons, tend to "think more histori-cally than their predecessors" (1984c, 178). The 1960s saw a move "out of the frame" (Sukenick 1985, 43) into the world of contemporary history (as seen in everything from peace marches to the New Journalism) and materiality (in art, we had George Segal's plaster casts of "reality"). Our recent (and even remote) past is something we share and the abundance of historical fiction and non-fiction being written and read today is perhaps a sign of a desire for what Doctorow once called reading as "an act of community" (in Trenner 1983, 59). To say, as one critic of the postmodern does, that "history, whether as public collective awareness of the past, or as private revisions of public experience, or even as the elevation of private experience to public consciousness, forms the epicenter of the eruptions of contemporary fictional activity" (R. Martin 1980, 24) is not, however, to say that postmodern fiction "decreates" history (14). It may problematize the conventions of teleological closure or developmental continuity, for instance, but that is not to "banish" them from the scene. Indeed it logically could not, for it depends upon them.

To elevate "private experience to public consciousness" in postmodern historiographic metafiction is not really to expand the subjective; it is to render inextricable the public and historical and the private and biographical. What are we to understand when Saleem Sinai, in *Midnight's Children*, tells us that he personally caused things like the death of Nehru or the language riots in India, or when little Oskar tells us that, on his tin drum, he "beat out the rapid, erratic rhythm which commanded everybody's movements for quite some time after August,1914"? Is there a lesson to be learned from the postmodern paradox here: from both the ironically undercut megalomania and the refusal to abnegate personal responsibility for public history? Works like these speculate openly about historical displacement and its ideological consequences, about the way one writes about the past "real," about what constitute "the known facts" of any given event. These are among the problematizations of history by postmodern art today. But, of course, theoretical discourse has not been reticent in addressing these issues either.

III

> With an ever increasing urgency we hear the cry today from various quarters that we must get back to history, and indeed we must. The problem is of course how to get back and what form of history one is proposing to get back to. Too often the cry is made simply out of frustration and in reaction to the various types of formalism that still seem to dominate the intellectual marketplace, to the fact that formalism just won't go away no matter how often and how forcefully history is evoked to chase it away or at least to put it in its place (in the place history assigns to it).   *David Carroll*

Historiographic metafiction explicitly contests the presumptive power of history to abolish formalism. Its metafictional impulse prevents any suppression of its formal and fictive identity. But it also reinstates the historical, in direct opposition to most arguments for the absolute autonomy of art, such as Ronald Sukenick's: "Unless a line is drawn [between art and "real life"], the horde of Factists blunder in waving their banner on which it is written: 'It really happened'" (1985, 44). But it is not as if "it really happened" were an unproblematic statement in itself. Just as definitions of what constitutes literature have changed over the years, so definitions of what makes history writing historical have changed from Livy to Ranke to Hayden White (see Fitzsimmons, Pundt, and Nowell 1954 for a full survey).

There are continuing debates over the definition of the historical field and about the strategies deployed to collect, record, and narrate evidence. As Derrida (1976), among others, has noted, many of these debates assume that the past can be accurately captured; it is just a question of how best to do so. As the record of past reality, history, according to this view, is usually seen as radically alien to literature, whose way to "truth" (be that seen as provisional and limited or as privileged and superior) is based on its autonomous status. This is the view that has institutionalized the separation of historical and literary studies in the academy.

The twentieth-century discipline of history has traditionally been structured by positivist and empiricist assumptions that have worked to separate it from anything that smacks of the "merely literary". In its usual setting up of the "real" as unproblematic presence to be reproduced or reconstructed, history is begging for deconstruction (Parker 1981, 58) to question the function of the writing of history itself. In Hayden White's deliberately provocative terms:

> [historians] must be prepared to entertain the notion that history, as currently conceived, is a kind of historical accident, a product of a specific historical situation, and that, with the passing of the misunderstandings that produced that situation, history itself may lose its status as an autonomous and self-authenticating mode of thought. It may well be that the most difficult task which the current generation of historians will be called upon to perform is to expose the historically conditioned character of the historical discipline, to preside over the dissolution of history's claim to autonomy among the disciplines.
>
> (1978b, 29)

At a less general level, the *way* in which history is written has, of course, come under considerable scrutiny in recent years. History as the politics of the past (the stories of kings, wars, and ministerial intrigues) has been challenged by the French Annales School's rethinking of the frames of reference and the methodological tools of the discipline (see Le Goff and Nora 1974). The resulting refocusing of historiography (Logan 1980, 3) on previously neglected objects of study – social, cultural, economic – in the work of Jacques Le Goff, Marcel Detienne, Jean Paul Aron, and others has coincided with feminism's reorientation of historical method to highlight the past of the formerly excluded ex-centric (women – but also the working class, gays, ethnic and racial minorities and so on). Of course, the same impulse can be seen in historiographic metafiction: Christa Wolf's *Cassandra* retells Homer's historical epic of men and their politics and wars in terms of the untold story of women and everyday life. In historiography, the very concept of time has been made even more problematic than before (Braudy 1970). The work of Fernand Braudel called into question the "history of events," the short time span of traditional narrative historiography of individuals and isolated events in the name of a history of "longue durée" and the "mentalité collective." And the volumes of Paul Ricoeur's *Temps et récit* study in painstaking detail the configurations and refigurations of time by narrative, both historical and fictive.

The analytic philosophy of history as practiced by Arthur Danto and Morton White has raised different, mostly epistemological, questions for modern historiography. But most historians of history feel that the discipline is still largely empirical and practical (Adler 1980, 243), with a radical distrust of the abstract and the theoretical. However, like the poststructuralist, Marxist, and feminist challenges to the similar assumptions still underpinning much literary study today, the provocations of the theorists of history are starting to work to counteract the increasing threat of marginalization of historical study brought about by historians' unwillingness to justify their methods even to themselves (see Fischer 1970; LaCapra 1985a). There have been three major foci of recent theorizations of historiography: narrative, rhetoric, and argument (Struever 1985, 261–4), and of these, it is narrative that most clearly overlaps with the concerns of postmodern fiction and theory.

IV

The one duty we owe to history is to rewrite it.   *Oscar Wilde*

Hayden White feels that the dominant view of historians today has gradually come to be that the writing of history in the form of narrative representations of the past is a highly conventional and indeed literary endeavor – which is not to say that they believe that events never occurred in the past:

> a specifically *historical* inquiry is born less of the necessity to establish *that* certain events occurred than of the desire to determine what certain events might *mean* for a given group, society, or culture's conception of its present tasks and future prospects.
>
> (1986, 487).

The shift from validation to signification, to the way systems of discourse make sense of the past, is one that implies a pluralist (and perhaps troubling) view of historiography as consisting of different but equally meaningful constructions of past reality – or rather, of the textualized remains (documents, archival evidence, witnesses' testimony) of that past. Often this shift is voiced in terms that recall the language of literary poststructualism: "How did [a given historical] phenomenon enter the system entitled history and how has the system of historical writing acquired effective discursive power?" (Cohen 1978, 206). The linking of power and knowledge here suggests the importance of the impact of the work of Michel Foucault and, to some extent, that of Jacques Derrida in our postmodern rethinking of the relation between the past and our writing of it, be it in fiction or historiography. In both domains, there are overt attempts to point to the past as already "semioticized" or encoded, that is, already inscribed in discourse and therefore "always already" interpreted (if only by the selection of what was recorded and by its insertion into a narrative). Historiographic metafiction self-consciously reminds us that, while events did occur in the real empirical past, we name and constitute those events as historical facts by selection and narrative positioning. And, even more basically, we only know of those past events through their discursive inscription, through their traces in the present.

I realize that merely to invoke the word "trace" is to recall the Derridian contesting of what he calls the metaphysical foundations of historiography. Derrida's challenge to the notion of linear historical temporality (1981a, 56ff.) is more radical than the Foucaldian model of discontinuity: it offers a complex notion of repetition and change, iteration and alteration, operating together (LaCapra 1985a, 106), a conceptual "chain" of history: "a 'monumental, stratified, contradictory' history; a history that also implies a new logic of *repetition* and the trace, for it is difficult to see how there could be history without it" (Derrida 1981a, 57). This is set in opposition to any attempt to reflect or reconstruct the "present-in-the-past" (D. Carroll 1978b, 446) as unproblematic presence. Historiography, according to Derrida, is always teleological: it imposes a meaning on the past and does so by postulating an end (and/or origin). So too does fiction. The difference in postmodern fiction is in its challenging self-consciousness of that imposition that renders it provisional. As Michel de Certeau has argued, history writing is a displacing operation upon the real past, a limited and limiting attempt to understand the relations between a place, a discipline, and the construction of a text (1975, 55; 64).

Like Derrida, Michel Foucault has asked us to look at things differently, to shift the level of our analysis out of our traditional disciplinary divisions and into that of discourse. We are no longer to deal, therefore, with either "tradition" or "the individual talent," as Eliot would have us do. The study of anonymous forces of dissipation replaces that of individual "signed" events and accomplishments made coherent by retrospective narrative; contradictions displace totalities; discontinuities, gaps, and ruptures are favored in opposition to continuity, development, evolution; the particular and the local take on the value once held by the universal and the transcendent. For Foucault it is irregularities that define discourse and its many possible interdiscursive networks in culture. For postmodern history, theory, and art, this has meant a new consideration of context, of textuality, of the power of totalization and of models of continuous history.

Foucault's work has joined that of Marxists and feminists in insisting on the pressure of historical contexts that have usually been ignored in formalistic literary studies (Lentricchia 1980, 191), as they have in historical interpretation as well. Historians are now being urged to take the contexts of their own inevitably interpretative act into account: the writing, reception, and "critical reading" of narratives about the past are not unrelated to issues of power, both intellectual and institutional (LaCapra 1985a, 127). Foucault has argued that "the social" is a field of forces, of practices – discourses and their anchoring institutions – in which we adopt various (constantly shifting) positions of power and resistance. The social is thus inscribed within the signifying practices of a culture. In Teresa de Lauretis's terms: "social formations and representations appeal to and position the individual as subject in the process to which we give the name of ideology" (1984, 121).

The focus on discourse in Foucault's work was enabled by more than just the textualized Derridean mode of thought (as Lentricchia claims in 1980, 191); there is Nietzsche and Marx well before Derrida. Foucault is not a simplistic "pan-textualist" (H. White 1986, 485) who reduces the historical real to the textual. In Foucault's own words, discourse is "not an ideal, timeless form that also possesses a history" but is

> from beginning to end, historical – a fragment of history, a unity and discontinuity in history itself, posing the problem of its own limits, its divisions, its trans- formations, the specific modes of its temporality rather than its sudden irruption in the midst of the complicities of time.
>
> (1972, 117)

To speak of discursive practices is not to reduce everything to a global essentialized textuality, but to reassert the specific and the plural, the particular and the dispersed. Foucault's assault on all the centralizing forces of unity and continuity in theory and practice (influence, tradition, evolution, development, spirit, oeuvre, book, voice, origin, *langue*, disci- plines) challenges all forms of totalizing thought (1972, 21–30) that do not acknowledge their role in the very constitution of their objects of study and in the reduction of the heterogeneous and problematic to the homogeneous and transcendental. Critics have not been slow to note in Flaubert's Bouvard and Pécuchet the parodic exemplars of the attempt to totalize the particular and the dispersed (see Gaillard 1980) and to give meaning by the act of centering and universalizing. And Salman Rushdie's narrators are their postmodern heirs.

Theory and practice also intersect in another area of challenge: this time, in the challenge to notions of continuity and tradition. Historiographic metafiction shares the Foucaldian urge to unmask the continuities that are taken for granted in the western narrative tradition, and it does so by first using and then abusing those very continuities. Edward Said has argued that underlying Foucault's notion of the discontinuous is a "supposition that rational knowledge is possible, regardless of how very complex – and even unattractive – the conditions of its production and acquisition" (1975a, 283). The result is a very postmodern paradox, for in Foucault's theory of discontinuous systematization, "the discourse of modern knowledge always hungers for what it cannot fully grasp or totally represent" (285). Be it historical, theoretical, or literary, discourse is always discontinuous yet held together by rules, albeit not transcendent rules (Foucault 1972, 229). All continuity is recognized as "pretended" (Foucault 1977, 154). The particular, the local, and the specific replace the general, the universal, and the eternal. Hayden White has remarked that such a conception applied to historiography

> has profound implications for the assessment of the humanistic belief in a "human nature" that is everywhere and always the same, however different its manifestations at different times and places. It brings under question the very notion of a universal *humanitas* on which the historian's wager on his ability ultimately to "understand" anything human is based.
>
> (1978b, 257)

Foucault was by no means the first to make us aware of any of this. He himself has always pointed to Nietzsche as his predecessor. Rejecting both antiquarian nostalgia and the monumentalizing universalization that denies the individuality and particularity of the past, in *The Use and Abuse of History*, Nietzsche argued for a critical history, one that would "bring the past to the bar of judgment, interrogate it remorselessly" (1957, 20–1). He also made clear where he felt the only available standards of judgment were to come from: "*You can explain the past only by what is most powerful in the present*" (40). It is this kind of belief that Foucault brings to what he calls the New History (1972, 10–11). And his own version of this history is never a history of things, but of discourse, of the "terms, categories, and techniques through which certain things become at certain times the focus of a whole configuration of discussion and procedure" (Rajchman 1985, 51).

Clearly, then, there have been major attacks on historians' tendencies to fetishize facts and be hostile to theory. Hayden White has been the other major voice today working to lift the repression and to lay bare the "conceptual apparatus" which is the ordering and sense-giving principle of historiography (1976, 30). He has joined poststructuralist literary critics like Catherine Belsey (1980, 2–4) in arguing that there is no practice without theory, however much that theory be unformulated or seen as "natural" or even denied. For White, the question facing historians today is not "What are the facts?" but "How are the facts to be described in order to sanction one mode of explaining them rather than another?" (44). This is not unlike the kind of question that literary critics face in the new theoretically self-conscious climate of the 1980s. In both disciplines, it is getting increasingly difficult to separate history or criticism "proper" from philosophy of history or literary theory. Historical accounts and literary interpretations are equally determined by underlying theoretical assumptions. And in postmodern fiction too, theory interpenetrates with narrative and diachrony is reinserted into synchrony, though not in any simplistic way: the problematic concept of historical knowledge and the semiotic notion of language as a social contract are reinscribed in the metafictionally self-conscious and self-regulating signifying system of literature. This is the paradox of postmodernism, be it in theory, history, or artistic practice.

In these three areas, there have been direct cross-fertilizations as well as this kind of parallel or overlapping concern. Like Hayden White before him, Dominick LaCapra has recently been arguing for the commonality of interest in historiography and critical theory, and his intended aim is a "cognitively responsible historiography" (1985a, 11). This would involve a problematized rethinking of the nature of, for instance, historical documents. From this perspective, they would become "texts that supplement or rework 'reality' and not mere sources that divulge facts about 'reality'" (11). His account of the situation of crisis in contemporary historical studies will sound familiar to literary critics: the challenge to dominant humanist assumptions ("the postulates of unity, continuity, and mastery of a documentary repertoire" – 32), the contesting of the past as a transcendental signified, paradoxically considered objectively accessible to the historian (137), and the reconceptualization of historical processes to include the relations between texts and the contexts of reading and writing (106).

Historiography has had its impact on literary studies, not just in the New Historicism, but even in fields – such as semiotics – where history had once been formally banished. Just as history, to a semiotician, is not a phenomenal event, but "an entity producing meaning" (Haidu 1982, 188), so the semiotic production and reception of meaning have now been seen as only possible in a historical context (Finaly-Pelinski 1982). And historiographic metafiction like Eco's *The Name of the Rose* did as much to teach us this as any theoretical argument, though both theory and practice have worked to situate their own discourses economically, socially, culturally, politically, and historically. The general desire to get beneath or behind the "natural," the "given" (the assumptions which sustain historiography, theory, and art today) is shared by Barthesian de-mythologizing, Marxist and feminist contextualizing, and even, despite appearances at times, Derrida's deconstructing (cf. Lentricchia 1980, 177; 183; 185). Derrida defined deconstruction early on as a "question of . . . being alert to the implications, to the historical sedimentation of the language which we use" (in Macksey and Donato 1970, 1972, 271). Even Paul Ricoeur's argument, in the multiple volumes of *Temps et récit*, that time becomes human time by being narrated, turns out to belong to this general postmodern process of cross-fertilizing that leads to problematizing. Historiography and fiction are seen as sharing the same act of refiguration, of reshaping of our experience of time through plot configurations; they are complementary activities.

But nowhere is it clearer than in historiographic metafiction that there is also a contradiction at the heart of postmodernism: the formalist and the historical live side by side, but there is no dialectic. The unresolved tensions of postmodern aesthetic practice remain paradoxes, or perhaps more accurately, contradictions. Barthes's Utopian dream of a theory of the text that would be both formalist and historical (1981b, 45) is possible, but only if we are willing to accept problematic and doubled texts. Bakhtin (Medvedev) (1978) argued that form and history were interconnected and mutually determining, but in postmodernism this is true only if no attempt is made to unify or conflate the two. The Bakhtinian model of the dialogic is useful to keep in mind. The monologic discourses of power and authority are not the only responses possible to what has been called our age of recognition of the loss of certainties as the state of the human condition (Reiss 1983, 194). To operate paradoxically (to install and then subvert) may be less satisfying than to offer resolved dialectic, but it may be the only non-totalizing response possible.

Architectural theorist Manfredo Tafuri has argued that it is important today to engage in a "historical assessment of the present contradictions" but not necessarily a resolution of them (1980, 2). Postmodern architecture and visual arts, like literature must contend with modernism's attempts to be *outside* history – through pure form, abstractionism, or myth – or to *control* it through theoretical models of closure. In postmodern fiction, the literary and the historiographical are always being brought together – and usually with destabilizing, not to say unnerving, results. One final example of the disturbing consequences of postmodern problematizing of history: the hero of Angela Carter's *The Infernal Desire Machines of Doctor Hoffman* finds himself puzzled by a series of paintings in the diabolical doctor's home. He ponders:

> These pictures were heavily varnished oils executed in the size and style of the nineteenth-century academician and they all depicted faces and scenes I recognized from old photographs and from the sepia and olive reproductions of forgotten masterpieces. . . . When I read the titles engraved on metal plaques at the bottom of each frame, I saw they depicted such scenes as "Leon Trotsky Composing the Eroica Symphony"; the wire-rimmed spectacles, the Hebraic bush of hair, the burning eyes were all familiar. The light of inspiration was in his eyes and the crotchets and quavers rippled from his nib on to the sheets of manuscript paper which flew about the red plush cover of the mahogany table on which he worked as if blown by the fine frenzy of genius. Van Gogh was shown writing "Wuthering Heights" in the parlour of Haworth Parsonage, with bandaged ear, all complete. I was especially struck by a gigantic canvas of Milton blindly executing divine frescos upon the walls of the Sistine Chapel.
>
> (1972, 197–8)

Seeing his bewilderment, the doctor's daughter explains: "When my father rewrites the history books, these are some of the things that everyone will suddenly perceive to have always been true."

PART II

7

HISTORIOGRAPHIC METAFICTION: "THE PASTIME OF PAST TIME"

I

> We theoreticians have to know the laws of the peripheral in art.
> The peripheral is, in fact, the non-esthetic set.
> It is connected with art, but the connection is not causal.
> But to stay alive, art must have new raw materials. Infusions of the peripheral.
> *Viktor Shklovsky*

In the nineteenth century, at least before the rise of Ranke's "scientific history," literature and history were considered branches of the same tree of learning, a tree which sought to "interpret experience, for the purpose of guiding and elevating man" (Nye 1966, 123). Then came the separation that resulted in the distinct disciplines of literary and historical studies today, despite the fact that the realist novel and Rankean historicism shared many similar beliefs about the possibility of writing factually about observable reality (H. White 1976, 25). However, it is this very separation of the literary and the historical that is now being challenged in postmodern theory and art, and recent critical readings of both history and fiction have focused more on what the two modes of writing share than on how they differ. They have both been seen to derive their force more from verisimilitude than from any objective truth; they are both identified as linguistic constructs, highly conventionalized in their narrative forms, and not at all transparent either in terms of language or structure; and they appear to be equally intertextual, deploying the texts of the past within their own complex textuality. But these are also the implied teachings of historiographic metafiction. Like those recent theories of both history and fiction, this kind of novel asks us to recall that history and fiction are themselves historical terms and that their definitions and interrelations are historically determined and vary with time (see Seamon 1983, 212–16).

In the last century, as Barbara Foley has shown, historical writing and historical novel writing influenced each other mutually: Macauley's debt to

Scott was an overt one, as was Dickens's to Carlyle in *A Tale of Two Cities* (Foley 1986a, 170–1). Today, the new skepticism or suspicion about the writing of history found in the work of Hayden White and Dominick LaCapra is mirrored in the internalized challenges to historiography in novels like *Shame, The Public Burning,* or *A Maggot*: they share the same questioning stance towards their common use of conventions of narrative, of reference, of the inscribing of subjectivity, of their identity as textuality, and even of their implication in ideology. In both fiction and history writing today, our confidence in empiricist and positivist epistemologies has been shaken – shaken, but perhaps not yet destroyed. And this is what accounts for the skepticism rather than any real denunciation; it also accounts for the defining paradoxes of postmodern discourses. I have been arguing that postmodernism is a contradictory cultural enterprise, one that is heavily implicated in that which it seeks to contest. It uses and abuses the very structures and values it takes to task. Historiographic metafiction, for example, keeps distinct its formal auto-representation and its historical context, and in so doing problematizes the very possibility of historical knowledge, because there is no reconciliation, no dialectic here – just unresolved contradiction, as we have just seen in the last chapter.

The history of the discussion of the relation of art to historiography is therefore relevant to any poetics of postmodernism, for the separation is a traditional one. To Aristotle (1982, 1,451a–b), the historian could speak only of what has happened, of the particulars of the past; the poet, on the other hand, spoke of what could or might happen and so could deal more with universals. Freed of the linear succession of history writing, the poet's plot could have different unities. This was not to say that historical events and personages could not appear in tragedy: "nothing prevents some of the things that have actually happened from being of the sort that might probably or possibly happen" (1,451b). History-writing was seen to have no such conventional restraints of probability or possiblity. Nevertheless, many historians since have used the techniques of fictional representation to create imaginative versions of their historical, real worlds (see Holloway 1953; G. Levine 1968; Braudy 1970; Henderson 1974). The postmodern novel has done the same, and the reverse. It is part of the postmodernist stand to confront the paradoxes of fictive/historical representation, the particular/the general, and the present/the past. And this confrontation is itself contradictory, for it refuses to recuperate or dissolve either side of the dichotomy, yet it is more than willing to exploit both.

History and fiction have always been notoriously porous genres, of course. At various times both have included in their elastic boundaries such forms as the travel tale and various versions of what we now call sociology (Veyne 1971, 30). It is not surprising that there would be overlappings of concern and even mutual influences between the two genres. In the eighteenth century the focus of this commonality of concern tended to be the relation of ethics (not factuality) to truth in narrative. (Only with the passing of the Acts of Parliament that defined libel did the notion of historical "fact" enter this debate – L. J. Davis 1983.) It is not accidental that, "From the start the writers of novels seemed determined to pretend that their work is not *made*, but that it simply exists" (Josipovici 1971, 148); in fact, it was safer, in legal and ethical terms. Defoe's works made claims to veracity and actually convinced some readers that they were factual, but most readers today (and many then) had the pleasure of a double awareness of both fictiveness and a basis in the "real" – as do readers of contemporary historiographic metafiction.

In fact Michael Coetzee's novel, *Foe*, addresses precisely this question of the relation of "story"- and "history"-writing to "truth" and exclusion in the practice of Defoe. There is a direct link here to familiar assumptions of historiography: that

> every history is a history of some entity which existed for a reasonable period of time, that the historian wishes to state what is literally true of it in a sense which distinguishes the historian from a teller of fictitious or mendacious stories.
>
> (M. White 1963, 4)

Foe reveals that storytellers can certainly silence, exclude, and absent certain past events – and people – but it also suggests that historians have done the same: where are the women in the traditional histories of the eighteenth century? As we have seen, Coetzee offers the teasing fiction that Defoe did not write *Robinson Crusoe* from information from the male historical castaway, Alexander Selkirk, or from other travel accounts, but from information given him by a subsequently "silenced" woman, Susan Barton, who had also been a castaway on "Cruso"'s [sic] island. It was Cruso who suggested that she tell her story to a writer who would add "a dash of colour" to her tale. She at first resisted because she wanted the "truth" told, and Cruso admitted that a writer's "trade is in books, not in truth" (1986, 40). But Susan saw a problem: "If I cannot come foreward, as author, and swear to the truth of my tale, what will be the worth of it? I might as well have dreamed it in a snug bed in Chichester" (40).

Susan does tell Foe (he added the "De" only later, and so lost Coetzee's irony) her tale and his response is that of a novelist. Susan's reaction is irritation:

> You remarked it would have been better had Cruso rescued not only musket and powder and ball, but a carpenter's chest as well, and built himself a boat. I do not wish to be captious, but we lived on an island so buffeted by wind that there was not a tree did grow twisted and bent.
>
> (1986, 55)

In frustration, she begins her own tale: "The Female Castaway. Being a True Account of a Year Spent on a Desert Island. With Many Strange Circumstances Never Hitherto Related" (67), but discovers that the problems of writing history are not unlike those of writing fiction: "Are these enough strange circumstances to make a story of? How long before I am driven to invent new and stranger circumstances: the salvage of tools and muskets from Cruso's ship; the building of a boat . . . a landing by cannibals . . . ?" (67). Her final decision is, however, that "what we accept in life we cannot accept in history" (67) – that is, lies and fabrications.

The linking of "fictitious" to "mendacious" stories (and histories) is one with which other historiographic metafictions also seem to be obsessed: *Famous Last Words, Legs, Waterland, Shame.* In the latter, Rushdie's narrator addresses openly the possible objections to his position as insider/outsider writing about the events of Pakistan from England – and in English:

> *Outsider! Trespasser! You have no right to this subject!* . . . I know: nobody ever arrested me [as they did the friend of whom he has just written]. Nor are they ever likely to. *Poacher! Pirate! We reject your authority. We know you, with your foreign language wrapped around you like a flag: speaking about us in your forked tongue, what can you tell but lies?* I reply with more questions: is history to be considered the property of the participants solely? In what courts are such claims staked, what boundary commissions map out the territories?
>
> (1983, 28)

The eighteenth-century concern for lies and falsity becomes a postmodern concern for the multiplicity and dispersion of truth(s), truth(s) relative to the specificity of place and culture. Yet the paradox is still there: in *Shame* we learn that when Pakistan was formed, the *Indian* history had to be written out of the Pakistani past. But who did this work? History was rewritten by immigrants, in Urdu and English, the imported tongues. As the narrator puts it, he is forced – by history – to write in English "and so for ever alter what is written" (38).

There has also been another, long tradition, dating (as we have just seen) from Aristotle, that makes fiction not only separate from, but also superior to, history, which is a mode of writing limited to the representation of the contingent, and the particular. The romantic and modernist assertions of the autonomy and supremacy of art led, however, as Jane Tompkins (1980b) has shown, to a marginalization of literature, one that extremes of metafiction (like American surfiction or the French New New Novel) only exacerbate. Historiographic metafiction, in deliberate contrast to what I would call such late modernist radical metafiction, attempts to demarginalize the literary through confrontation with the historical, and it does so both thematically and formally.

For example, Christa Wolf's *No Place on Earth* is about the fictionalized meeting of two historical figures, dramatist Heinrich von Kleist and poet Karoline von Günderrode: "The claim that they met: a legend that suits us. The town of Winkel, on the Rhine, we saw it ourselves." The "we" of the narrating voice, in the present, underlines the metafictive historical recon- struction on the level of form. But on the thematic level too, life and art meet, for this is the theme of the novel, as Wolf's Kleist tries to break down the walls between "literary fantasies and the actualities of the world" (1982, 12), contesting his colleagues' separation of poets from praxis: "Of all the people here, perhaps there is none more intimately bound to the real world than I am" (82). It is he, after all, who is trying to write a romantic historical work about Robert Guiscard, Duke of Normandy. The metafictive and the historiographic also meet in the intertexts of the novel, for it is through them that Wolf fleshes out the cultural and historical context of this fictive meeting. The intertexts range from Günderrode's own letters to canonic romantic works like Hölderlin's *Hyperion*, Goethe's *Torquato Tasso*, and Brentano's *Gedichte* – but, in all, the theme is the conflict between art and life. This novel reminds us, as did Roland Barthes much earlier (1967) that the nineteenth century could be said to have given birth to both the realist novel and narrative history, two genres which share a desire to select, construct, and render self-sufficient and closed a narrative world that would be representational but still separate from changing experience and historical process. Today history and fiction share a need to contest these very assumptions.

II

> To the truth of art, external reality is irrelevant. Art creates its own reality, within which truth and the perfection of beauty is the infinite refinement of itself. History is very different. It is an empirical search for external truths, and for the best, most complete, and most profound external truths, in a maximal corresponding relationship with the absolute reality of the past events.   *David Hackett Fischer*

These words are not without their ironic tone, of course, as Fischer is describing what he sees as a standard historian's preconception about the relation of art to history. But it is not far from a description of the basic assumptions of many kinds of formalist literary criticism. For I. A. Richards, literature consisted of "pseudo-statements" (1924); for Northrop Frye (1957), art was hypothetical, not real – that is verbal formulations which imitate real propositions; not unlike Sir Philip Sydney, structuralists argued that

> literature is not a discourse that can or must be false . . . it is a discourse that, precisely, cannot be subjected to the test of truth; it is neither true nor false, to raise this question has no meaning: this is what defines its very status as "fiction".
>
> (Todorov 1981a, 18)

Historiographic metafiction suggests that truth and falsity may indeed not be the right terms in which to discuss fiction, but not for the reasons offered above. Postmodern novels like *Flaubert's Parrot*, *Famous Last Words*, and *A Maggot* openly assert that there are only *truths* in the plural, and never one Truth; and there is rarely falseness *per se*, just others' truths. Fiction and history are narratives distinguished by their frames (see B. H. Smith 1978), frames which historiographic metafiction first establishes and then crosses, positing both the generic contracts of fiction and of history. The postmodern paradoxes here are complex. The interaction of the historiographic and the metafictional foregrounds the rejection of the claims of both "authentic" representation and "inauthentic" copy alike, and the very meaning of artistic originality is as forcefully challenged as is the transparency of historical referentiality.

Postmodern fiction suggests that to re-write or to re-present the past in fiction and in history is, in both cases, to open it up to the present, to prevent it from being conclusive and teleological. Such is the teaching of novels like Susan Daitch's *L.C.*, with its double layer of historical reconstruction, both of which are presented with metafictional self-consciousness. Parts of the journal of the fictive protagonist, Lucienne Crozier, a woman implicated in yet marginalized as a witness of the historical 1848 revolution in Paris, are edited and translated twice: once by Willa Rehnfield and once by her younger assistant after her death. The recent interest in archival women's history is given an interesting new twist here, for the two translations of the end of Lucienne's diary are so vastly different that the entire activity of translation, as well as research, is called into question. In the more traditional Willa's version, Lucienne dies of consumption in Algiers, abandoned by her revolutionary lover. In the version of her more radical assistant (a veteran of Berkeley in 1968, being sought by the police for a terrorist bombing), Lucienne just stops writing, while awaiting arrest for revolutionary activities.

Other historiographic metafictions point to other implications of the rewriting of history. Ian Watson's *Chekhov's Journey* opens in the manner of a historical novel about Anton Chekhov's 1890 trip across Siberia to visit a convict colony. The next chapter, however, sets up a tension between this and a 1990 frame: at a Russian Artists' Retreat in the country, a film-maker, a scriptwriter, and a Chekhov look-alike actor meet to plan a film about that historical trip of 1890. The plan is to hypnotize the actor and tape his entry into Chekhov's personality and past. From these tapes, a script will emerge. However, they encounter a serious problem: the actor begins to *alter* the dates of verifiable historical events, moving the Tunguska explosion from 1888 to 1908. We are told that, from this point on, "the film project foundered further into a chaos of unhistory" (1983, 56). Suddenly a third narrative intervenes: a spaceship in the future is about to launch backwards into time past. (Meanwhile, at the Retreat, fog isolates the writing team in a timeless world; telephone circuits turn back on themselves; all links to the outside are cut.) The spaceship commander realizes that he is experiencing the rewriting of history: the 1908 explosion has regressed and become that of 1888, and both prefigure (repeat?) atomic blasts of an even later date. He is caught in a time loop which renders any firm sense of history or reality impossible. (At the Retreat, new books are found in the library, rewritten versions, not of history, but of literature: *Apple Orchard, Uncle Ivan, Three*

Cousins, Snow Goose. Not that history remains unscathed: Joan of Arc, Trotsky, and others get changed out of recognition, in an allegory of not only Russian revisionary history, but also all our rewritings of the past, deliberate and accidental.)

This world of provisionality and indeterminacy is made even more complex when a consultation with the *Soviet Encyclopedia* confirms the actor's altered version of the Tunguska expedition. The team decides that their film, to be entitled (like the novel) *Chekhov's Journey*, will not be the experimental one they had envisaged, but *cinéma vérité*, despite the reader's awareness that it was the hypnotic tampering with time that brought on the time warp that blasted the *Cherry Orchard* and mutated the *Sea Gull* into a *Snow Goose*. As one of the team says:

> Past events can be altered. History gets rewritten. Well, we've just found that this applies to the real world too. . . . Maybe the real history of the world is changing constantly? And why? Because history is a fiction. It's a dream in the mind of humanity, forever striving . . . towards what? Towards perfection.
>
> (1983, 174)

The text provides the ironic context in which to read this last statement: the next thing mentioned is Auschwitz, and the echo of Joyce in the passage reminds us that, for him, history was not a dream, but a nightmare from which we are trying to awaken.

The problematizing of the nature of historical knowledge, in novels like this, points both to the need to separate and to the danger of separating fiction and history as narrative genres. This problematizing has also been in the foreground of much contemporary literary theory and philosophy of history, from Hayden White to Paul Veyne. When the latter calls history "a true novel" (1971, 10), he is signalling the two genres' shared conventions: selection, organization, diegesis, anecdote, temporal pacing, and emplotment (14, 15, 22, 29, 46–8). But this is not to say that history and fiction are part of the "same order of discourse" (Lindenberger 1984, 18). They are different, though they share social, cultural, and ideological contexts, as well as formal techniques. Novels (with the exception of some extreme surfictions) incorporate social and political history to some extent, though that extent will vary (Hough 1966, 113); historiography, in turn, is as structured, coherent, and teleological as any narrative fiction. It is not only the novel but history too that is "palpably betwixt and between" (Kermode 1968a, 235). Both historians and novelists *constitute* their subjects as possible objects of narrative representation, as Hayden White (1978a, 56) has argued (for history alone, however). And they do so by the very structures and language they use to present those subjects. In Jacques Ehrmann's extreme formulation: "history and literature have no existence in and of themselves. It is we who constitute them as the object of our understanding" (1981, 253). This is the teaching of texts like Doctorow's *Welcome to Hard Times*, a novel about the attempt to write history that shows historiography to be a most problematic act: do we, in writing our past, even create our future? Is the return of the Bad Man from Bodie the past re-lived, or the past re-written?

Postmodernism deliberately confuses the notion that history's problem is verification, while fiction's is veracity (Berthoff 1970, 272). Both forms of narrative are signifying systems in our culture; both are what Doctorow once called modes of "mediating the world for the purpose of introducing meaning" (1983, 24). And it is the constructed, imposed nature of that meaning (and the seeming necessity for us to make meaning) that historiographic metafiction like Coover's *The Public Burning* reveals. This novel teaches that "history itself depends on conventions of narrative, language, and ideology in order to present an account of 'what really happened'" (Mazurek 1982, 29). Both history and fiction are cultural sign systems, ideological constructions whose ideology includes their appearance of being autonomous and self-contained. It is the metafictionality of these novels that underlines Doctorow's notion that

> history is kind of fiction in which we live and hope to survive, and fiction is a kind of speculative history . . . by which the available data for the composition is seen to be greater and more various in its sources than the historian supposes.
>
> (1983, 25)

Fredric Jameson has argued that historical representation is as surely in crisis as is the linear novel, and for much the same reasons:

> The most intelligent "solution" to such a crisis does not consist in abandoning historiography altogether, as an impossible aim and an ideological category all at once, but rather – as in the modernist aesthetic itself – in reorganizing its traditional procedures on a different level. Althusser's proposal seems the wisest in this situation: as old-fashioned narrative or "realistic" historiography becomes problematic, the historian should reformulate her vocation – not any longer to produce some vivid representation of history "as it really happened," but rather to produce the *concept* of history.
>
> (1984c, 180)

There is only one word I would change in this: the word "modernist" seems to me to be less apt than "postmodernist," though Jameson would never agree (see 1983; 1984a). Postmodern historiographic metafiction has done exactly what Jameson calls for here, though there is more a problematizing than just a production of a "*concept* of history" (and fiction). The two genres may be textual constructs, narratives which are both non-originary in their reliance on past intertexts and unavoidably ideologically laden, but they do not, in historiographic metafiction at least, "adopt equivalent representational procedures or constitute equivalent modes of cognition" (Foley 1986a, 35). However, there are (or have been) combinations of history and fiction which do attempt such equivalence.

III

> The binary opposition between fiction and fact is no longer relevant: in any differential system, it is the assertion of the space *between* the entities that matters.   *Paul de Man*

Perhaps. But historiographic metafiction suggests the continuing relevance of such an opposition, even if it be a problematic one. Such novels both install and then blur the line between fiction and history. This kind of generic blurring has been a feature of literature since the classical epic and the Bible (see Weinstein 1976, 263), but the simultaneous and overt assertion and crossing of boundaries is more postmodern. Umberto Eco has claimed that there are three ways to narrate the past: the romance, the swashbuckling tale, and the historical novel. He has added that it was the latter that he intended to write in *The Name of the Rose* (1983, 1984, 74–5). Historical novels, he feels, "not only identify in the past the causes of what came later, but also trace the process through which those causes began slowly to produce their effects" (76). This is why his medieval characters, like John Banville's characters in his *Doctor Copernicus*, are made to talk like Wittgenstein, for instance. I would add, however, that this device points to a fourth way of narrating the past: historiographic metafiction – and not historical fiction – with its intense self-consciousness about the way in which all this is done.

What is the difference between postmodern fiction and what we usually think of as nineteenth-century historical fiction (though its forms persist today – see Fleishman 1971)? It is difficult to generalize about this latter complex genre because, as theorists have pointed out, history plays a great number of distinctly different roles, at different levels of generality, in its various manifestations. There seems little agreement as to whether the historical past is always presented as individualized, particularized, and past (that is, different from the present) (see Shaw 1983, 26; 48; 148) or whether that past is offered as typical and therefore present, or at least as sharing values through time with the present (Lukács 1962). While acknowledging the difficulties of definition (see also Turner 1979; Shaw 1983) that the historical novel shares with most genres, I would define historical fiction as that which is modelled on historiography to the extent that it is motivated and made operative by a notion of history as a shaping force (in the narrative and in human destiny) (see Fleishman 1971). However, it is Georg Lukács' influential and more particular definition that critics most frequently have to confront in their defining, and I am no exception.

Lukács felt that the historical novel could enact historical process by presenting a microcosm which generalizes and concentrates (1962, 39). The protagonist, therefore, should be a type, a synthesis of the general and particular, of "all the humanly and socially essential determinants." From this definition, it is clear that the protagonists of historiographic metafiction are anything but proper types: they are the ex-centrics, the marginalized, the peripheral figures of fictional history – the Coalhouse Walkers (in *Ragtime*), the Saleem Sinais (in *Midnight's Children*), the Fevvers (in *Nights at the Circus*). Even the historical personages take on different, particularized, and ultimately ex-centric status: Doctor Copernicus (in the novel of that name), Houdini (in *Ragtime*), Richard Nixon (in *The Public Burning*). Historiographic metafiction espouses a postmodern ideology of plurality and recognition of difference; "type" has little function here, except as something to be ironically undercut. There is no sense of cultural universality. The protagonist of a postmodern novel like Doctorow's *Book of Daniel* is overtly specific, individual, culturally and familially conditioned in his response to history, both public and private. The narrative form enacts the fact that Daniel is not a type of anything, no matter how much he may try to see himself as representing the New Left or his parents' cause.

Related to this notion of type is Lukács's belief that the historical novel is defined by the relative unimportance of its use of detail, which he saw as "only a means of achieving historical faithfulness, for making concretely clear the historical necessity of a concrete situation" (1962, 59). Therefore, accuracy or even truth of detail is irrelevant. Many readers of historical fiction would disagree, I suspect, as have writers of it (such as John Williams – 1973, 8–11). Postmodern fiction contests this defining characteristic in two different ways. First, historiographic metafiction plays upon the truth and lies of the historical record. In novels like *Foe, Burning Water*, or *Famous Last Words*, certain known historical details are deliberately falsified in order to foreground the possible mnemonic failures of recorded history and the constant potential for both deliberate and inadvertent error. The second difference lies in the way in which postmodern fiction actually uses detail or historical data. Historical fiction (*pace* Lukács) usually incorporates and assimilates these data in order to lend a feeling of verifiability (or an air of dense specificity and particularity) to the fictional world. Historiographic metafiction incorporates, but rarely assimilates such data. More often, the process of *attempting* to assimilate is what is foregrounded: we watch the narrators of Ondaatje's *Running in the Family* or Findley's *The Wars* trying to make sense of the historical facts they have collected. As readers, we see both the collecting and the attempts to make narrative order. Historiographic metafiction acknowledges the paradox of the *reality* of the past but its *textualized accessibility* to us today.

Lukács's third major defining characteristic of the historical novel is its relegation of historical personages to secondary roles. Clearly in postmodern novels like *Doctor Copernicus, Kepler, Legs* (about Jack Diamond), and *Antichthon* (about Giordano Bruno), this is hardly the case. In many historical novels, the real figures of the past are deployed to validate or authenticate the fictional world by their presence, as if to hide the joins between fiction and history in a formal and ontological sleight of hand. The metafictional self-reflexivity of postmodern novels prevents any such subterfuge, and poses that ontological join as a problem: how do we know the past? What do (what can) we know of it now? For example Coover does considerable violence to the known history of the Rosenbergs in *The Public Burning*, but he does so to satiric ends, in the name of social critique. I do not think that he intends to construct a wilful betrayal of politically tragic events; perhaps, however, he does want to make a connection to the real world of political action through the reader – by making us aware of the need to question received versions of history. Historiographic metafiction's overt (and political) concern for its reception, for its reader, would challenge the following distinction:

> The discursive criterion that distinguishes narrative history from historical novel is that history evokes testing behavior in reception; historical discipline requires an author-reader contract that stipulates investigative equity. Historical novels are not histories, not because of a penchant for untruth, but because the author-reader contract denies the reader participation in the communal project.
>
> (Streuver 1985, 264)

In fact, as we have seen in Chapter 5, historiographic metafiction's emphasis on its enunciative situation – text, producer, receiver, historical, and social context – reinstalls a kind of (very problematic) communal project.

While the debates still rage about the definition of the historical novel, in the 1960s a new variant on the history/fiction confrontation came into being: the non-fictional novel. This differed from the treatment of recent factual events recounted as narrative history, as in William Manchester's *The Death of a President*. It was more a form of documentary narrative which deliberately used techniques of fiction in an overt manner and which usually made no pretence to objectivity of presentation. In the work of Hunter S. Thompson, Tom Wolfe, and Norman Mailer, the authorial structuring experience was often in the forefront as the new guarantee of "truth," as narrators individually attempted to perceive and impose pattern on what they saw about them. This metafictionality and provisionality obviously link the non-fictional novel to historiographic metafiction. But there are also significant differences.

It is probably not accidental that this form of the New Journalism, as it was called, was an American phenomenon. The Vietnam War created a real distrust of official "facts" as presented by the military and the media, and in addition, the ideology of the 1960s had licenced a revolt against homogenized forms of experience (Hellmann 1981, 8). The result was a kind of overtly personal and provisional journalism, autobiographical in impulse and performative in impact. The famous exception is Truman Capote's *In Cold Blood*, which is a modern rewriting of the realist novel – universalist in its assumptions and omniscient in its narrative technique. But in works like *The Electric Kool-Aid Acid Test, Fear and Loathing: On the Campaign Trail '72*, and *Of a Fire on the Moon*, there was a very "sixties" kind of direct confrontation with social reality in the present (Hollowell 1977, 10). The impact of the new mixing of fiction and fact is clear on popular, if not academic, history in the years following: in *John Brown's Journey,* Albert Fried broke the rules and showed the tentative groping movement of his becoming interested in his historical topic. The book is "marked by the feeling of an historian in the act of grappling with his subject" (Weber 1980, 144), as the subtitle underlines: *Notes and Reflections on His America and Mine.*

Perhaps, too, the non-fictional novel in its journalistic variety influenced writers like Thomas Keneally who write historical novels, often of the recent past. The self-consciousness of the author's note that prefaces *Schindler's Ark* makes clear the paradoxes of Keneally's practice:

> I have attempted to avoid all fiction, though, since fiction would debase the record, and to distinguish between reality and the myths which are likely to attach themselves to a man of Oskar's stature. Sometimes it has been necessary to attempt to reconstruct conversations of which Oskar and others have left only the briefest record.
>
> (1982, 9–10)

At the beginning of the novel, Keneally points to his reconstructions (which he refuses to see as fictionalizations) by self-reflexive references to the reader ("In observing this small winter scene, we are on safe ground." – 13) or by conditional verb forms. Nevertheless, there is a progression from initial statements of possibility and probability ("it is possible that . . ." and "[they] now probably paid attention") to a generalized use of the (historical) past tense and a single authoritative voice, as the story continues. This is not historiographic metafiction, however much it may seem so in its early pages. Nor is it quite (or not consistently) an example of the New Journalism, despite its commitment to the "authority of fact" (Weber 1980, 36).

The non-fictional novel of the 1960s and 1970s did not just record the contemporary hysteria of history, as Robert Scholes has claimed (1968, 37). It did not just try to embrace "the fictional element inevitable in any reporting" and then try to imagine its "way toward the truth" (37). What it did was seriously question who determined and created that truth, and it was this particular aspect of it that perhaps enabled historiographic metafiction's more paradoxical questioning. A number of critics have seen parallels between the two forms, but seem to disagree completely on the form that parallel might take. For one, both stress the overt, totalizing power of the imagination of the writers to create unities (Hellmann 1981, 16); yet, for another, both refuse to neutralize contingency by reducing it to unified meaning (Zavarzadeh 1976, 41). I would agree with the former as a designation of the non-fictional novel, though not of all metafiction; and the latter certainly defines a lot of contemporary self-reflexive writing more accurately than it does the New Journalism. Historiographic metafiction, of course, paradoxically fits both definitions: it installs totalizing order, only to contest it, by its radical provisionality, intertextuality, and, often, fragmentation.

In many ways, the non-fiction novel is another late modernist creation (see Smart 1985, 3), in the sense that both its self-consciousness about its writing process and its stress on subjectivity (or psychological realism) recall Woolf and Joyce's experiments with limited, depth vision in narrative, though in the New Journalism, it is specifically the author whose historical presence as participant authorizes subjective response. Postmodern novels like Rudy Wiebe's *The Scorched-Wood People* parody this stance, however: Pierre Falcon, the narrating participant in the historical action, was real, but is still fictionalized in the novel: he is made to tell the tale of the historical Louis Riel from a point of time after his own death, with all the insights of retrospection and access to information he could not possibly have had as participant.

There are non-fictional novels, however, which come very close to historiographic metafiction in their form and content. Norman Mailer's *The Armies of the Night* is subtitled *History as a Novel, the Novel as History*. In each of the two parts of the book there is a moment in which the narrator addresses the reader on the conventions and devices used by novelists (1968, 152) and historians (245). His final decision seems to be that historiography ultimately fails experience and "the instincts of the novelist" have to take over (284). This self-reflexivity does not weaken, but on the contrary, strengthens and points to the direct level of historical engagement and reference of the text (cf. Bradbury 1983, 159). Like many postmodern novels, this provisionality and uncertainty (and the wilful and overt constructing of meaning too) do not "cast doubt upon their seriousness" (Butler 1980, 131), but rather define the new postmodern seriousness that acknowledges the limits and powers of "reporting" or writing of the past, recent or remote.

IV

> History is three-dimensional. It partakes of the nature of science, art,
> and philosophy. *Louis Gottschalk*

Postmodern novels raise a number of specific issues regarding the interaction of historiography and fiction that deserve more detailed study: issues surrounding the nature of identity and subjectivity; the question of reference and representation; the intertextual nature of the past; and the ideological implications of writing about history. Although these will subsequently be treated in separate chapters, a brief overview at this point will show where these issues fit into the poetics of postmodernism.

First of all, historiographic metafictions appear to privilege two modes of narration, both of which problematize the entire notion of subjectivity: multiple points of view (as in Thomas's *The White Hotel*) or an overtly controlling narrator (as in Swift's *Waterland*). In neither, however, do we find a subject confident of his/her ability to know the past with any certainty. This is not a transcending of history, but a problematized inscribing of subjectivity into history. In a novel like *Midnight's Children*, nothing, not even the self's physical body, survives the instability caused by the rethinking of the past in non-developmental, non-continuous terms. To use the (appropriate) language of Michel Foucault, Saleem Sinai's body is exposed as "totally imprinted by history and the process of history's destruction of the body" (1977, 148). As we shall see in Chapter 10, postmodernism establishes, differentiates, and then disperses stable narrative voices (and bodies) that use memory to try to make sense of the past. It both installs and then subverts traditional concepts of subjectivity; it both asserts and is capable of shattering "the unity of man's being through which it was thought that he could extend his sovereignty to the events of the past" (Foucault 1977, 153). The protagonist's psychic disintegration in *Waterland* reflects such a shattering, but his strong narrative voice asserts that same selfhood, in a typically postmodern and paradoxical way. So too do the voices of those unreliable narrators of Burgess's *Earthly Powers* and Williams's *Star Turn*, the former "uncommitted to verifiable fact" (1980, 490) and the latter a self-confessed liar.

As we shall see in the next chapter, one of the postmodern ways of literally incorporating the textualized past into the text of the present is that of parody. In John Fowles's *A Maggot*, the parodic intertexts are both literary and historical. Interspersed throughout the book are pages from the 1736 *Gentleman's Magazine*, but there are many references to eighteenth-century drama as well, allusions that are formally motivated by the presence of actors in the plot. But it is to the fiction of the period that Fowles refers most often: its pornography, its prurient puritanism (as in Richardson's novels), but most of all, its mixing of fact and fiction, as in the writing of Defoe, whose "underlying approach and purpose" the narrator has consciously borrowed (1985, 449).

Postmodern intertextuality is a formal manifestation of both a desire to close the gap between past and present of the reader and a desire to rewrite the past in a new context. It is not a modernist desire to order the present through the past or to make the present look spare in contrast to the richness of the past (see Antin 1972, 106–14). It is not an attempt to void or avoid history. Instead it directly confronts the past of literature – and of historiography, for it too derives from other texts (documents). It uses and abuses those intertextual echoes, inscribing their powerful allusions and then subverting that power through irony. In all, there is little of the modernist sense of a unique, symbolic, visionary "work of art"; there are only texts, already written ones. Walter Hill's film *Crossroads* uses the biography and music of Robert Johnson to foreground the fictional Willie Brown and Lightening Boy, who pick up the Faustian challenge from the devil of his song, "Crossroads' Blues."

To what, though, does the very language of historiographic metafiction refer? To a world of history or one of fiction? It is commonly accepted that there is a radical disjunction between the basic assumptions underlying these two notions of reference. History's referents are presumed to be real; fiction's are not. But, as Chapter 9 will investigate more fully, what postmodern novels teach is that, in both cases, they actually refer at the first level to other texts: we know the past (which really did exist) only through its textualized remains. Historiographic metafiction problematizes the activity of reference by refusing either to bracket the referent (as surfiction might) or to revel in it (as non-fictional novels might). This is not an emptying of the meaning of language, as Gerald Graff seems to think (1973, 397). The text still communicates – in fact, it does so very didactically. There is not so much "a loss of belief in a significant external reality" (403) as there is a loss of faith in our ability to (unproblematically) *know* that reality, and therefore to be able to represent it in language. Fiction and historiography are not different in this regard.

Postmodern fiction also poses new questions about reference. The issue is no longer "to what empirically real object in the past does the language of history refer?"; it is more "to which discursive context could this language belong? To which prior textualizations must we refer?" This is true in the visual arts as well, where the issue of reference is perhaps clearer. Sherrie Levine has framed Andreas Feininger's photographs of real subjects and has called *her* work "Photographs by Andreas Feininger." In other words, she frames the existing discourse to create a double remove from the real. In dance, Merce Cunningham's influence has led to postmodern choreography that not only uses visual or musical discourses, but also looks to concepts that would make movement freer of direct reference, in either a sculptural or expressive sense (Kirby 1975, 3–4).

Postmodern art is more complex and more problematic than extreme late modernist auto-representation might suggest, with its view that there is no presence, no external truth which verifies or unifies, that there is only self-reference (B. H. Smith 1978, 8–9). Historiographic metafiction self-consciously suggests this, but then uses it to signal the discursive nature of all reference – both literary and historiographical. The referent is always already inscribed in the discourses of our culture. This is no cause for despair; it is the text's major link with the "world," one that acknowledges its identity as construct, rather than as simulacrum of some "real" outside. Once again, this does not deny that the past "real" existed; it only conditions our mode of knowledge of that past. We can know it only through its traces, its relics. The question of reference depends on what John Searle (1975, 330) calls a shared "pretense" and what Stanley Fish calls being party to a set of "discourse agreements which are in effect decisions as to what can be stipulated as a fact" (1980, 242). In other words, a "fact" is discourse-defined; an "event" is not.

Postmodern art is not so much ambiguous as it is doubled and contradictory. There is a rethinking of the modernist tendency to move away from representation (Harkness 1982, 9) by both installing it materially and subverting it. In the visual arts, as in literature, there has been a rethinking of the sign/referent relation in the face of the realization of the limits of self-reflexivity's separation from social practice (Menna 1984, 10). Historiographic metafiction shows fiction to be historically conditioned and history to be discursively structured, and in the process manages to broaden the debate about the ideological implications of the Foucaldian conjunction of power and knowledge – for readers and for history itself as a discipline. As the narrator of Rushdie's *Shame* puts it:

> History is natural selection. Mutant versions of the past struggle for dominance, new species of fact arise, and old, saurian truths go to the wall, blindfolded and smoking last cigarettes. Only the mutations of the strong survive. The weak, the anonymous, the defeated leave few marks. . . . History loves only those who dominate her: it is a relationship of mutual enslavement.
>
> (1983, 124)

The question of *whose* history survives is one that obsesses postmodern novels like Timothy Findley's *Famous Last Words*. In problematizing almost everything the historical novel once took for granted, historiographic metafiction destabilizes received notions of both history and fiction. To illustrate this change, let me take Barbara Foley's concise description of the paradigm of the nineteenth-century historical novel and insert in square brackets the postmodern changes:

> Characters [never] constitute a microcosmic portrayal of representative social types; they experience complications and conflicts that embody important tendencies [not] in historical development [whatever that might mean, but in narrative plotting, often traceable to other intertexts]; one or more world-historical figures enters the fictive world, lending an aura of extratextual validation to the text's generalizations and judgments [which are promptly undercut and questioned by the revealing of the true intertextual, rather than extratextual, identity of the sources of that validation]; the conclusion [never] reaffirms [but contests] the legitimacy of a norm that transforms social and political conflict into moral debate.
>
> (1986a, 160)

The premise of postmodern fiction is the same as that articulated by Hayden White regarding history: "every representation of the past has specifiable ideological implications" (1978b, 69). But the ideology of postmodernism is paradoxical, for it depends upon and draws its power from that which it contests. It is not truly radical; nor is it truly oppositional. But this does not mean it has no critical clout, as we shall see in Chapters 11 and 12. The Epiloguist of *A Maggot* may claim that what we have read is indeed "a maggot, not an attempt, either in fact or in language, to reproduce known history" (Fowles 1985, 449), but that does not stop him from extended ideological analyses of eighteenth-century social, sexual, and religious history. Thomas Pynchon's obsession with plots – narrative and conspiratorial – is an ideological one: his characters discover (or make) their own histories in an attempt to prevent themselves from being the passive victims of the commercial or political plots of others (Krafft 1984, 284). Similarly contemporary philosophers of history like Michel de Certeau have re-minded historiographers that no research of the past is free of socio-economic, political, and cultural conditions (1975, 65). Novels like *The Public Burning* or *Ragtime* do not trivialize the historical and the factual in their "game-playing" (Robertson 1984), but rather politicize them through their metafictional rethinking of the epistemological and ontological re-lations between history and fiction. Both are acknowledged as part of larger social and cultural discourses which various kinds of formalist literary criticism have relegated to the extrinsic and irrelevant. This said, it is also true that it is part of the postmodern ideology not to ignore cultural bias and interpretative conventions and to question authority – even its own.

All of these issues – subjectivity, intertextuality, reference, ideology – underlie the problematized relations between history and fiction in post-modernism. But many theorists today have pointed to narrative as the one concern that envelops all of these, for the process of narrativization has come to be seen as a central form of human comprehension, of imposition of meaning and formal coherence on the chaos of events (H. White 1981, 795; Jameson 1981a, 13; Mink 1978, 132). Narrative is what translates knowing into telling (H. White 1980, 5), and it is precisely this translation that obsesses postmodern fiction. The conventions of narrative in both historiography and novels, then, are not constraints, but enabling condi-tions of possibility of sense-making (W. Martin 1986). Their disruption or challenging is bound to upset such basic structuring notions as causality and logic – as happens with Oskar's drumming in *The Tin Drum*: narrative conventions are both installed and subverted. The refusal to integrate fragments (in novels like *The White Hotel*) is a refusal of the closure and telos which narrative usually demands (see Kermode 1966, 1967). In postmodern poetry too, as Marjorie Perloff has argued, narrative is used in works like Ashbery's "They Dream Only of America" or Dorn's *Slinger*, but used in order to question "the very nature of the *order* that a systematic plot structure implies" (1985, 158).

The issue of narrativity encompasses many others that point to the postmodern view that we can only know "reality" as it is produced and sustained by cultural representations of it (Owens 1982, 21). In historio-graphic metafictions, these are often not simple verbal representations, for *ekphrases* (or verbal representations of visual representations) often have central representational functions. For example in Carpentier's *Explosion in a Cathedral*, Goya's "Desastres de la guerra" series provides the works of visual art that actually are the sources of the novel's descriptions of revolutionary war. The seventh of that series, plus the "Dos de Mayo" and "Tres de Mayo," are particularly important, for their glorious associations are left aside by Carpentier, as an ironic signal of his own point of view. Of course, literary intertexts function in the narrative in a similar way. The details of Esteban and Sofía's house in Madrid come, in fact, from Torres

Villaroel's *Vida*, a book which Estaban had read earlier in the novel (see Saad 1983, 120–2; McCallum 1985).

Historiographic metafiction, like both historical fiction and narrative history, cannot avoid dealing with the problem of the status of their "facts" and of the nature of their evidence, their documents. And, obviously, the related issue is that of how those documentary sources are deployed: can they be objectively, neutrally related? Or does interpretation inevitably enter with narrativization? The epistemological question of how we know the past joins the ontological one of the status of the traces of that past. Needless to say, the postmodern raising of these questions offers few answers, but this provisionality does not result in some sort of historical relativism or presentism. It rejects projecting present beliefs and standards onto the past and asserts, in strong terms, the specificity and particularity of the individual past event. Nevertheless, it also realizes that we are epistemologically limited in our ability to know that past, since we are both spectators of and actors in the historical process. Historiographic metafiction suggests a distinction between "events" and "facts" that is one shared by many historians. Events, as I have been suggesting, are configured into facts by being related to "conceptual matrices within which they have to be imbedded if they are to count as facts" (Munz 1977, 15). Historiography and fiction, as we saw earlier, *constitute* their objects of attention; in other words, they decide which events will become facts. The postmodern problematization points to our unavoidable difficulties with the concreteness of events (in the archive, we can find only their textual traces to make into facts) and their accessibility. (Do we have a full trace or a partial one? What has been absented, discarded as non-fact material?) Dominick LaCapra has argued that all documents or artifacts used by historians are not neutral evidence for reconstructing phenomena which are assumed to have some independent existence outside them. All documents process information and the very way in which they do so is itself a historical fact that limits the documentary conception of historical knowledge (1985b, 45). This is the kind of insight that has led to a semiotics of history, for documents become signs of events which the historian transmutes into facts (B. Williams 1985, 40). They are also, of course, signs within already semiotically constructed contexts, themselves dependent upon institutions (if they are official records) or individuals (if they are eye-witness accounts). As in historiographic metafiction, the lesson here is that the past once existed, but that our historical knowledge of it is semiotically transmitted.

I do not mean to suggest that this is a radical, new insight. In 1910 Carl Becker wrote that "the facts of history do not exist for any historian until he creates them" (525), that representations of the past are selected to signify whatever the historian intends. It is this very difference between events (which have no meaning in themselves) and facts (which are given meaning) that postmodernism obsessively foregrounds. Even documents are selected as a function of a certain problem or point of view (Ricoeur 1984a, 108).

Historiographic metafiction often points to this fact by using the paratextual conventions of historiography (especially footnotes) to both inscribe and undermine the authority and objectivity of historical sources and explanations. Unlike the documentary novel as defined by Barbara Foley, what I have been calling postmodern fiction does not "aspire to tell the truth" (Foley 1986a, 26) as much as to question *whose* truth gets told. It does not so much associate "this truth with claims to empirical validation" as contest the ground of any claim to such validation. How can a historian (or a novelist) check any historical account against past empirical reality in order to test its validity? Facts are not given but are constructed by the kinds of questions we ask of events (H. White 1978b, 43). In the words of *Waterland*'s history teacher, the past is a "thing which cannot be eradicated, which accumulates and impinges" (Swift 1983, 109). What postmodern discourses – fictive and historiographic – ask is: how do we know and come to terms with such a complex "thing"?

8

INTERTEXTUALITY, PARODY, AND THE DISCOURSES OF HISTORY

Il y a plus affaire à interpréter les interprétations qu'à interpréter les choses, et plus de livres sur les livres que sur autre sujet: nous ne faisons que nous entregloser. *Montaigne*

In the wake of recent assaults by literary and philosophical theory on modernist formalist closure, postmodern fiction has certainly sought to open itself up to history, to what Edward Said (1983) calls the "world." But it seems to have found that it can no longer do so in any remotely innocent way, and so those un-innocent paradoxical historiographic metafictions situate themselves within historical discourse, while refusing to surrender their autonomy as fiction. And it is a kind of seriously ironic parody that often enables this contradictory doubleness: the intertexts of history and fiction take on parallel status in the parodic reworking of the textual past of both the "world" and literature. The textual incorporation of these intertextual pasts as a constitutive structural element of postmodernist fiction functions as a formal marking of historicity – both literary and "worldly." At first glance, it would appear that it is only its constant ironic signalling of difference at the very heart of similarity that distinguishes postmodern parody from medieval and renaissance imitation (see T. M. Greene 1982, 17). For Dante, as for Doctorow, the texts of literature and those of history are equally fair game. Nevertheless, a distinction should be made:

> Traditionally, stories were stolen, as Chaucer stole his; or they were felt to be the common property of a culture or community. . . . These notable happenings, imagined or real, lay outside language the way history itself is supposed to, in a condition of pure occurrence.

(Gass 1985, 147)

Today, there is a return to the idea of a common discursive "property" in the embedding of both literary and historical texts in fiction, but it is a return made problematic by overtly metafictional assertions of both history and literature as human constructs. The intertextual parody of historiographic metafiction enacts, in a way, the views of certain contemporary historiographers: it offers a sense of the presence of the past, but a past that can be known only from its texts, its traces – be they literary or historical.

Discussions on postmodernism these days do seem more prone than most to confusing self-contradictions, perhaps because of the paradoxical nature of the subject itself. Charles Newman, for instance, in his provocative book *The Post-Modern Aura* (1985), begins by defining postmodern art as a "commentary on the aesthetic history of whatever genre it adopts" (44). This, then, would be art which sees history only in aesthetic terms (57). However, when postulating an American version of postmodernism, he abandons this metafictional intertextual definition to call American litera-ture a "literature *without* primary influences," "a literature which lacks a known parenthood," suffering from the "anxiety of *non*-influence" (87). In this chapter I would like to focus my discussion primarily on American fiction in order to reply to Newman's claims by examining the novels of writers such as Toni Morrison, E. L. Doctorow, John Barth, Ishmael Reed, Thomas Pynchon, and others, all of which cast what I see as a reasonable doubt on any such pronouncements. On the one hand, Newman wants to argue that postmodernism at large is resolutely parodic; on the other, he asserts that the American postmodern deliberately puts "distance between itself and its literary antecedents, an obligatory if occasionally conscience-stricken break with the past" (172). Newman is not alone in his viewing of postmodern parody as a form of ironic rupture with the past (see Thiher 1984, 214), but, as in postmodernist architecture, there is always a paradox at the heart of that "post": irony does indeed mark the difference from the past, but the intertextual echoing simultaneously works to affirm – textually and hermeneutically – the connection with the past.

When that past is the literary period known as modernism, then, as we have seen in earlier chapters, what is both instated and then subverted is the notion of the work of art as a closed, self-sufficient, autonomous object deriving its unity from the formal interrelations of its parts. Postmodernism both asserts and then undercuts this view, in its characteristic attempt to retain aesthetic autonomy while still returning the text to the "world." But it is not a return to the world of "ordinary reality," as some have argued (Kern 1978, 216); the "world" in which these texts situate themselves is the "world" of discourse, the "world" of texts and intertexts. This "world" has direct links to the world of empirical reality, but it is not itself that empirical reality. It is a contemporary critical truism that realism is a set of conventions, that representation of the real is not the same as the real itself. What historiographic metafiction challenges is both any naive realist concept of representation but also any equally naive textualist or formalist assertions of the total separation of art from the world. The postmodern is self-consciously art "within the archive" (Foucault 1977, 92), and that archive is both historical and literary.

In the light of the work of writers like Fuentes, Rushdie, Thomas, Fowles, Eco, not to mention Coover, Doctorow, Barth, Heller, Reed, and other American novelists, it is hard to see why critics like Allen Thiher, for instance, "can think of no such intertextual foundations today" as those of Dante in Virgil (1984, 189). Are we really in the midst of a crisis of faith in the "possibility of historical culture" (189)? (Or rather, have we ever *not* been in such a crisis?) To parody is not to destroy the past; in fact to parody is both to enshrine the past and to question it. And this, once again, is the postmodern paradox.

The theoretical exploration of the "vast dialogue" (Calinescu 1980, 169) between and among literatures and histories that is postmodernism has, in part, been made possible by Julie Kristeva's (1969) reworking of the Bakhtinian notions of polyphony, dialogism, and heteroglossia – the multiple voicings of a text. Out of these ideas, she developed a more strictly formalist theory of the irreducible plurality of texts within and behind any given text, thereby deflecting the critical focus away from the notion of the subject (the author) to the idea of textual productivity. Kristeva and her colleagues at *Tel Quel* in the late 1960s and early 1970s mounted a collective attack on the "founding subject" (alias: the humanist notion of the author) as the original and originating source of fixed and fetishized meaning in the text. And, of course, this also put into question the entire notion of "text" as an autonomous entity, with immanent meaning.

In the United States a similar formalist impulse had provoked a similar attack much earlier in the form of Wimsatt and Beardsley's New Critical rejection of the "Intentional Fallacy" (Wimsatt 1954). Nevertheless, it would seem that, even though we may no longer be able to talk comfortably of authors (and sources and influences), we still need a critical language in which to discuss those ironic allusions, those re-contextualized quotations, those double-edged parodies both of genre and of specific works that proliferate in both modernist and postmodernist texts. This, of course, is where the concept of intertextuality has proved so useful. As later defined by Barthes (1977, 160) and Riffaterre (1984, 142–3), intertextuality replaces the challenged author–text relationship with one between reader and text, one that situates the locus of textual meaning within the history of discourse itself. A literary work can actually no longer be considered original; if it were, it could have no meaning for its reader. It is only as part of prior discourses that any text derives meaning and significance.

Not surprisingly, this theoretical redefining of aesthetic value has coincided with a change in the kind of art being produced. Postmodernly parodic composer George Rochberg, in the liner notes to the (Nonesuch) recording of his String Quartet Number Three articulates this change in these terms:

> I have had to abandon the notion of "originality," in which the personal style of the artist and his ego are the supreme values; the pursuit of the one-idea, uni-dimensional work and gesture which seems to have dominated the esthetics of art

in the 20th century; and the received idea that it is necessary to divorce oneself from the past.

In the visual arts too, the works of Arakawa, Rivers, Wesselman, and others have brought about, through parodic intertextuality (both aesthetic and historical), a real skewering of any humanist notions of subjectivity and creativity.

As in historiographic metafiction, these other art forms parodically cite the intertexts of both the "world" and art and, in so doing, contest the boundaries that many would unquestioningly use to separate the two. In its most extreme formulation the result of such contesting would be a "break with every given context, engendering an infinity of new contexts in a manner which is absolutely illimitable" (Derrida 1977, 185). While postmodernism, as I am defining it here, is perhaps somewhat less promiscuously extensive, the notion of parody as opening the text up, rather than closing it down, is an important one: among the many things that postmodern intertextuality challenges are both closure and single, centralized meaning. Its willed and wilful provisionality rests largely upon its acceptance of the inevitable textual infiltration of prior discursive practices. The typically contradictory intertextuality of postmodern art both provides and undermines context. In Vincent Leitch's terms:

> Intertextuality posits both an uncentered historical enclosure and an abysmal decentered foundation for language and textuality; in so doing, it exposes all contextualizations as limited and limiting, arbitrary and confining, self-serving and authoritarian, theological and political. However paradoxically formulated, intertextuality offers a liberating determinism.
>
> (1983, 162)

II

> The frontiers of a book are never clear-cut: beyond the title, the first lines, and the last full-stop, beyond its internal configuration and its autonomous form, it is caught up in a system of references to other books, other texts, other sentences: it is a node within a network. *Michel Foucault*

It has been claimed that to use the term intertextuality in criticism is not just to avail oneself of a useful conceptual tool: it also signals a "prise de position, un champ de référence" (Angenot 1983, 122). But its usefulness as a theoretical framework that is both hermeneutic and formalist is obvious when dealing with historiographic metafiction that demands of the reader not only the recognition of textualized traces of the literary and historical past but also the awareness of what has been done – through irony – to those traces. The reader is forced to acknowledge not only the inevitable textuality of our knowledge of the past, but also both the value and the limitation of the inescapably discursive form of that knowledge. Calvino's Marco Polo in

Invisible Cities (1978) both is and is not the historical Marco Polo. How can we, today, "know" the Italian explorer? We can only do so by way of texts – including his own (*Il Milione*), from which Calvino parodically takes his frame-tale, his travel plot, and his characterization (Musarra 1986, 141).

Roland Barthes once defined the intertext as "the impossibility of living outside the infinite text" (1975, 36), thereby making intertextuality the very condition of textuality. Umberto Eco, writing of his novel, *The Name of the Rose*, claims: "I discovered what writers have always known (and have told us again and again): books always speak of other books, and every story tells a story that has already been told" (1983, 1984, 20). The stories which *The Name of the Rose* retells are both those of literature (by Conan Doyle, Borges, Joyce, Mann, Eliot, and so on) and those of history (medieval chronicles, religious testimonies). This is the parodically doubled discourse of postmodernist intertextuality. However, this is not just a doubly introverted form of aestheticism: as we have seen, the theoretical implications of this kind of historiographic metafiction coincide with the recent historiographic theory about the nature of history writing as narrativization of the past and about the nature of the archive as the textualized remains of history (for a summary see H. White 1984).

In other words, yes, postmodern fiction manifests a certain introversion, a self-conscious turning toward the form of the act of writing itself; but, it is also much more than that. It does not go so far as to "establish an explicit relation with that real world beyond itself," as some have claimed (Kiremidjian 1969, 238). Its relationship to the "worldly" is still on the level of discourse, but to claim that is to claim quite a lot. After all, we can only "know" (as opposed to "experience") the world through our narratives (past and present) of it, or so postmodernism argues. The present, as well as the past, is always already irremediably textualized for us (Belsey 1980, 46), and the overt intertextuality of historiographic metafiction serves as one of the textual signals of this postmodern realization.

Patricia Waugh notes that metafiction like *Slaughterhouse-Five* or *The Public Burning* "suggests not only that writing history is a fictional act, ranging events conceptually through language to form a world-model, but that history itself is invested like fiction, with interrelating plots which appear to interact independently of human design" (1984, 48–9). Historiographic metafiction is particularly doubled, like this, in its inscribing of both historical and literary intertexts. Its specific and general recalls of the forms and contents of history-writing work to familiarize the unfamiliar through (very familiar) narrative structures (as Hayden White has argued – 1978a, 49–50), but its metafictional self-reflexivity works to render problematic any such familiarization. The ontological line between historical past and literature is not effaced (cf. Thiher 1984, 190), but rather is underlined. The past really did exist, but we can "know" that past today only through its texts, and therein lies its connection to the literary.

Historiographic metafiction, like postmodernist architecture and painting, is overtly and resolutely historical – though, admittedly, in an ironic and problematic way that acknowledges that history is not the transparent record of any sure "truth." Instead, such fiction corroborates the views of historians like Dominick LaCapra who argue that "the past arrives in the form of texts and textualized remainders – memories, reports, published writings, archives, monuments, and so forth" (1985a, 128) and that these texts interact with one another in complex ways. This does not in any way deny the value of history-writing; it merely redefines the conditions of value. Lately narrative history, with its concern "for the short time span, for the individual and the event" (Braudel 1980, 27), has been called into question by the work of, among others, the Annales school in France, as we have seen. But this particular model of narrative history was, of course, also that of the realist novel. Historiographic metafiction, therefore, represents a challenging of the (related) conventional forms of fiction and history writing through its acknowledgement of their inescapable textuality.

This formal linking throught the common denominators of intertextuality and narrativity is usually offered these days, not as a reduction or as a shrinking of the scope and value of fiction, but rather as an expansion. Or, if it is seen as a limitation – restricted to the always already narrated – this tends to be made into the primary value, as it is in Lyotard's "pagan vision" (1977, 78) wherein no one ever manages to be the first to narrate anything, to be the origin of even her/his own narrative. Lyotard deliberately sets up this "limitation" as the opposite of what he calls the capitalist position of the writer as original creator, proprietor and entrepreneur of her/his story. Much postmodern writing shares this implied ideological critique of the assumptions underlying nineteenth-century humanist concepts of author and text, and it is parodic intertextuality that is the major vehicle of that critique.

In Chapter 2, I argued that parody's contradictory ideological implications (as "authorized transgression," it can be seen as both conservative and revolutionary – Hutcheon 1985, 69–83) make it an apt mode of criticism for postmodernism, itself paradoxical in its conservative installing and then radical contesting of conventions. Historiographic metafictions, like García Márquez's *One Hundred Years of Solitude* or Grass's *The Tin Drum* or Rushdie's *Midnight's Children* (which has both of the former as intertexts), use parody not only to restore history and memory in the face of the distortions of the "history of forgetting" (Thiher 1984, 202), but also, at the same time, to put into question the authority of any act of writing by locating the discourses of both history and fiction within an ever-expanding intertextual network that mocks any notion of either single origin or simple causality.

When linked with satire, as in the work of Vonnegut, Wolf, or Coover, parody can certainly take on more precisely ideological dimensions. Here too, however, there is no direct intervention in the world: this is writing working through other writing, other textualizations of experience (Said 1975a, 237). (In many cases, intertextuality may well be too limited a term to describe this process; interdiscursivity would perhaps be a more accurate term for the collective modes of discourse from which the postmodern parodically draws: literature, the visual arts, history, biography, theory, philosophy, psychoanalysis, sociology, and the list could go on.) As we saw in Chapter 4, one of the effects of this discursive pluralizing is that the (perhaps illusory but once perceived as firm and single) center of both historical and fictive narrative is dispersed. Margins and edges gain new value. The "ex-centric" – as both off-center and de-centered – gets attention. That which is "different" is valorized in opposition both to élitist, alienated "otherness" and also to the uniformizing impulse of mass culture. And in American postmodernism, the different comes to be defined in particulariz-ing terms such as those of nationality, ethnicity, gender, race, and sexual orientation. Intertextual parody of canonical American and European classics is one mode of appropriating and reformulating – with significant change – the dominant white, male, middle-class, heterosexual, Euro-centric culture. It does not reject it, for it cannot. Postmodernism signals its dependence by its *use* of the canon, but reveals its rebellion through its ironic *abuse* of it. As Said (1986) has been arguing, there is a relation of mutual interdependence of the histories of the dominated and the dominators.

American fiction since the 1960s has been described by Malcolm Bradbury (1983, 186) as being particularly obsessed with its own past – literary, social, and historical. Perhaps this preoccupation is (or was) tied in part to a need to find a particularly American voice within a culturally dominant Euro-centric tradition (D'Haen 1986, 216). The United States (like the rest of North and South America) is a land of immigration. In E. L. Doctorow's words, "We derive enormously, of course, from Europe, and that's part of what *Ragtime* is about: the means by which we began literally, physically to lift European art and architecture and bring it over here" (in Trenner 1983, 58). This is also part of what American historiographic metafiction in general is "about." Critics have discussed at length the parodic intertexts of the work of Thomas Pynchon, including Conrad's *Heart of Darkness* (McHale 1979, 88) and Proust's first-person confessional form (Patteson 1974, 37–8) in *V*. In particular *The Crying of Lot 49* has been seen as directly linking the literary parody of Jacobean drama with the selectivity and subjectivity of what we deem historical "fact." Here the postmodern parody operates in much the same way as it did in the literature of the seventeenth century, and in both Pynchon's novel and the plays he parodies (Ford's *Tis Pity She's a Whore*, Webster's *The White Devil*, *The Duchess of Malfi*, and Tourneur's *The Revenger's Tragedy*, among others), the intertextual "received discourse" is firmly embedded in a social commentary about the loss of relevance of traditional values in contemporary life (S. Bennett 1985).

Just as powerful and even more outrageous, perhaps, is the parody of Dickens's *A Christmas Carol* in Ishmael Reed's *The Terrible Twos*, where political satire and parody meet to attack white Euro-centred ideologies of domination. Its structure of "A Past Christmas" and "A Future Christmas" prepares us for its initial Dickensian invocation – via metaphor, at first ("Money is as tight as Scrooge" – Reed 1982, 4), and then directly: "Ebenezer Scrooge towers above the Washington skyline, rubbing his hands and greedily peering over his spectacles" (4). He is less a character than the incarnation of 1980 Yuppie America. The novel proceeds to update Dickens's tale: the rich are cozy and comfortable ("Regardless of how high inflation remains, the wealthy will have any kind of Christmas they desire, a spokesman for Neiman-Marcus announces" – 5); the poor are not ("seven point eight million people will be unemployed" – 5). This is a 1980 replay of "Scrooge's winter," Americanized into a winter "as mean as a junkyard dog" (32).

The "Future Christmas" section takes place after monopoly capitalism has literally and officially captured Christmas, after a court case grants exclusive rights for Santa Claus to one entrepreneur. (Another court decision outlaws the naturalistic novel!) One strand of the complex plot continues the Dickensian intertext, but not without a detour through *The Divine Comedy*. The American President, a vacuous, alcoholic ex-model (male) is reformed by a visit from St Nicholas who takes him on a trip through hell, playing Virgil to his Dante and Marley to his Scrooge. There he meets past presidents and other politicians whose punishments, as in the *Inferno*, are always made to suit their crimes. A new man after this experience, the President spends Christmas day with the White House's (black) butler and his crippled grandson. Though unnamed, this Tiny Tim ironically out-sentimentalizes Dickens's: he has a leg amputated; he is black; and both parents have died in a car accident. In an attempt to save the nation from the ravages of capitalism, the President then goes on television to announce that "The problems of American society will not go away . . . by invoking Scroogelike attitudes against the poor or saying humbug to the old and to the underprivileged" (158). Nevertheless, the final echoes of the Dickens intertext are ultimately ironic: because of these mad ideas, the President is declared unfit to serve and is hospitalized by the business interests which really run the government. None of Dickens's optimism remains in this bleak satiric vision of the future.

It is significant that the intertexts of John Barth's *Letters* include not just the British eighteenth-century epistolary novel, *Don Quixote*, and other European works by Wells, Mann, and Joyce, but also texts by Thoreau, Hawthorne, Poe, Whitman, and Cooper. The specifically American past is as much a part of defining "difference" for contemporary American postmodernism as is the European past. The same parodic mix of authority and transgression, use and abuse, characterizes intra-American inter-textuality. For instance, Pynchon's *V.* and Morrison's *Song of Solomon*, in different ways, parody both the structures and theme of the recoverability of history in Faulkner's *Absalom! Absalom!*. Similarly Doctorow's *Lives of the Poets* both installs and subverts Roth's *My Life as a Man* and Bellow's *Herzog* (P. Levine 1985, 80).

The parodic references to the earlier, nineteenth-century or classic American literature are perhaps even more complex, however, since there is a long (and related) tradition of the interaction of fiction and history in, for example, Hawthorne's use of the conventions of romance to connect the historical past and the writing present. And indeed Hawthorne's fiction is a familiar postmodern intertext: *The Blithedale Romance* and Barth's *The Floating Opera* share the same moral preoccupation with the consequences of writers taking aesthetic distance from life, but it is the difference in their structural forms (Barth's novel is more self-consciously metafictional – Christensen 1981, 12) that points the reader to the real irony of the conjunction of the ethical issue.

Historiographic metafiction, like the non-fictional novel, also turns to the intertexts of history as well as literature. Barth's *The Sot-Weed Factor* manages both to debunk and to create the history of Maryland for its reader through not only the real Ebenezer Cooke's 1708 poem (of the same name as the novel) but also the raw historical record of the Archives of Maryland. From these intertexts, Barth rewrites history, taking considerable liberties: sometimes inventing characters and events, sometimes parodically inverting the tone and mode of the intertexts, sometimes offering connections where gaps occur in the historical record (see Holder 1968, 598–9). Berger's *Little Big Man* recounts all the major historical events on the American Plains at the end of the nineteenth century (from the killing of the buffalo and the building of the railway to Custer's Last Stand), but the recounting is done by a fictive, 111-year-old character who both inflates and deflates the historical heroes of the West and the literary clichés of the Western genre alike – since history and literature share a tendency to exaggerate in narrating the past. Berger makes no attempt to hide his intertexts, be they fictional or historical. Old Lodge Skins' mythic stature is meant to recall Natty Bumpo's and to parody it (Wylder 1969); the account of his death is taken almost word for word from John G. Neilhardt's report of Black Elk's demise, and Custer's final mad talk is lifted directly from his *My Life on the Plains* (Schulz 1973, 74–5). Even the fictional Jack Crabb is defined by his intertexts: the historical Jack Cleybourne and the fictive John Clayton from Will Henry's *No Survivors*, both of them temporally and geographically coextensive with Crabb.

III

It's simply that I have never shared the general admiration for his [Dvorak's] New World Symphony, which is, to be precise, a medley, as they say in popular music. . . . It will lead our composers astray. It won't be long before they're blowing the clarinet in Carnegie Hall like drunken Negroes in Chicago and calling it serious music.
Jim Huneker in Skvorecky's *Dvorak in Love*

Skvorecky is aware that Dvorak's work foreshadows the postmodern (including his own practice) both in its parodic intertextuality and in its mixing of popular and high art forms. In historiographic metafiction, it is not just (serious or popular) literature and history that form the discourses of postmodernism. Everything from comic books and fairy tales to almanacs and newspapers provide historiographic metafiction with culturally signifi-cant intertexts. In Coover's *The Public Burning*, the history of the Rosenbergs' execution is mediated by many different textualized forms. One major form is that of the various media, through which the concept of the disparity between "news" and "reality" or "truth" is foregrounded. *The New York Times* is shown to constitute the sacred texts of America, the texts that offer "orderly and reasonable" versions of experience, but whose apparent objectivity conceals a Hegelian "idealism which mistakes its own language for reality" (Mazurek 1982, 34). And one of the central intertexts for the portrayal of Richard Nixon in the novel is his famous televised "Checkers" speech, whose tone, metaphors and ideology provide Coover with the rhetoric and personality of his fictionalized Nixon.

Historiographic metafiction appears, then, willing to draw upon any signifying practices it can find operative in a society. It wants to challenge those discourses and yet to use them, even to milk them for all they are worth. In Pynchon's fiction, for instance, this kind of contradictory subversive inscribing is often carried to an extreme: "Documentation, obsessional systems, the languages of commerce, of the legal system, of popular culture, of advertising: hundreds of systems compete with each other, resisting assimilation to any one received paradigm" (Waugh 1984, 39). But Pynchon's intertextually overdetermined, discursively over-loaded fictions both parody and *enact* the totalizing tendency of all discourses to create systems and structures. The plots of such narratives become other kinds of plots, that is, conspiracies that invoke terror in those subject (as we all are) to the power of pattern. Many have commented upon this paranoia in the works of contemporary American writers, but few have noted the paradoxical nature of this particularly postmodern fear and loathing: the terror of totalizing plotting is inscribed within texts char-acterized by nothing if not by over-plotting and overdetermined intertextual self-reference. The text itself becomes the potentially closed, self-referring system.

Perhaps this contradictory attraction/repulsion to structure and pattern explains the predominance of the parodic use of certain familiar and overtly conventionally plotted forms in American fiction, for instance, that of the Western: *Little Big Man, Yellow Back Radio Broke-Down, The Sot-Weed Factor, Welcome to Hard Times, Even Cowgirls Get the Blues.* It has also been suggested that "the one thing the Western is always about is America rewriting and reinterpreting her own past" (French 1973, 24). But the ironic intertextual use of the Western is not, as some have claimed, a form of "Temporal Escape" (Steinberg 1976, 127), but rather a coming to terms with the existing traditions of earlier historical and literary articulations of American-ness. As such, obviously, parody can be used to satiric ends. Doctorow's *Welcome to Hard Times* recalls Stephen Crane's "Blue Hotel" in its underlining of the power of money, greed, and force on the frontier: through intertextuality, it is suggested that some noble myths have capitalistic exploitation at their core (Gross 1983, 133). In parodically inverting the conventions of the Western, Doctorow here presents a nature that is not a redemptive wilderness and pioneers who are less hardworking survivors than petty entrepreneurs. He forces us to rethink and perhaps reinterpret history, and he does so mainly through his narrator, Blue, who is caught in the dilemma of whether we make history or history makes us. To underline the intertextual intertwining of discourses, he writes his story in the ledger book where the town records are also kept (see P. Levine 1985, 27–30).

Ishmael Reed's consistently parodic fiction clearly asserts not just a critical and specifically American "difference" but also a racial one. And, on a formal level, his parodic mixing of levels and kinds of discourse challenges any notion of the different as either coherent and monolithic or original. It draws on both the black and white literary and historical narrative traditions, rewriting Hurston, Wright, and Ellison as easily as Plato or Eliot (see McConnell 1980, 145; Gates 1984c, 314), while also drawing on the multiple possibilities opened up by the folk tradition. Reed is always serious, beneath his funny parodic play. It is this basic seriousness that critics have frequently been blind to when they accuse postmodernism of being ironic – and therefore trivial. The assumption seems to be that authenticity of experience and expression are somehow incompatible with double-voicing and/or humor. This view seems to be shared, not only by Marxist critics (Jameson 1984a; Eagleton 1985), but also by some feminist critics. And yet it is feminist *writers*, along with blacks, who have used such ironic intertextuality to such powerful ends – both ideologically and aesthetically (if the two could, in fact, be so easily separated). Parody for these writers is more than just a key strategy through which "duplicity" is revealed (Gilbert and Gubar 1979a, 80); it is one of the major ways in which women and other ex-centrics both use and abuse, set up and then challenge male traditions in art. Alice Walker calls upon ironic versions of familiar fairy tales in *The Color Purple*: Snow White, the Ugly Duckling, Sleeping Beauty, and so on. But the significance of the parodies is not clear until the reader notices the gender and race reversal effected by her irony: the world in which she lives happily ever after is a female and black one (see Byerman 1985, 161).

The ex-centric in America is not just a matter of gender or race or nationality, but also one of class, for the fifty United States do not really constitute an economic and social monolith. Even within black or feminist novels, for instance, the issue of class enters. With intertextual echoes of Ike McCaslin in Faulkner's "The Bear," Milkman in *Song of Solomon* must be stripped of his physical symbols of the dominant white culture and submit to a trial by endurance in order to be accepted. The reason? The Blacks in Shalimar perceive the class issue beneath the racial one. They know that "he had the heart of the white men who came to pick them up in the trucks when they needed anonymous, faceless laborers" (1977, 269). And in the same novel, the petty bourgeois Ruth, the doctor's daughter, is shown to scorn her nouveau-riche husband. In Doctorow's *Ragtime*, the issues of ethnicity (Tateh) and race (Coalhouse) both merge with that of class. In *Loon Lake*, art itself is brought into the equation. Joe feels that it is his social background that prevents his full appreciation of Warren Penfield's poetry: "how could I have been listening with the attention such beautiful words demanded, people from my world didn't talk with such embellishment such scrollwork" (1979, 1980, 85). Readers may be tempted to equate grammar with class here until they notice that Penfield's poetry itself often lacks punctuation too.

Doctorow's fiction, like Reed's, reveals the kind of powerful impact, on both a formal and ideological level, that parodic intertextuality can have. Under enemy fire in 1918, *Loon Lake's* Warren Penfield, a signaler in the Signal Corps, sent – not the message desired by his commander – but the first few lines of Wordsworth's "Ode: Intimations of Immortality from Recollections of Early Childhood." The ironic appropriateness of the poem's themes of past glory and present reality makes Doctorow's point about war better than any didactic statement probably could have done. This novel presents us with all the kinds of intertextual parody that we have seen in American fiction in general: of genre, of the European tradition, of American canonical works (classic and modern), of the texts of popular culture and of history. On the level of genre, for instance, Joe is and is not the picaresque hero, both in his adventures on the road and in his narration of them: he usually narrates in the third person when recounting his past life, but often the first-person voice interferes.

Specifically British intertexts also abound in this novel, from the Wordsworthian signal message to D. H. Lawrence's *Sons and Lovers*: like Paul Morel, Warren Penfield grows up in a coal-mining community with a mother who feels he is special, "a rare soul, a finer being" (38). Doctorow demystifies and ironizes Lawrence's idealization by making his poet a clumsy, awkward man. And, like Morel, at the end of the novel it is not clear whether he is, in fact, a real artist or not. The opening of Joyce's *A Portrait of the Artist as Young Man* is recalled in *Loon Lake's* early passages about the infant's relations both to his body and language. But the parodic element enters with the differences: unlike Stephen Dedalus, this child recalls no names and is alone. He cannot place himself in his family, much less his universe. Yet both boys will end up poets. Or will they? No intertext used by Doctorow is without its cutting edge. His loon may indeed recall Keats's nightingale, but the cliché of "crazy as a loon" is never far away.

One of the protagonists, Joseph Korzeniowski, gives up his name to become the nominal son of F. W. Bennett. The use of Joseph Conrad's original name here is, of course, hardly accidental in a novel about identity and writing. But Joe hails from Paterson, NJ, a place which has other literary associations for Americans. Places, in fact, resound with intertextual echoes in *Loon Lake*. In American literature, lakes tend to be symbols of the purity of nature (Cooper's Lake Glimmerglass, Thoreau's Walden), but here they stand for corruption and, above all, economic commodity. Fittingly, this interpretation is prompted by another intertext: the Bennett estate unavoidably suggests Gatsby's, just as the young, indigent Joe with his dream of a woman follows the trail of that similar (yet different), self-made American literary hero.

But it is not just the literary canon that is drawn upon in this novel. In fact, the entire portrait of 1930s American is developed out of the popular culture of the period: Frank Capra comedies, gangster films, strike novels, Cain's melodramas (see Levine 1985, 67). The significance of this is both literary and historical: the novel actually enacts the realization that what we "know" of the past derives from the discourses of that past. This is not documentary realism: it is a novel about our cultural representations of the past, our discourse *about* the 1930s. I think this is what Doctorow meant by his inability to "accept the distinction between reality and books" (in Trenner 1983, 42). For him, there is no neat dividing line between the texts of history and literature, and so he feels free to draw on both. The question of originality obviously has a different meaning within this postmodern idea of writing.

The focus of *Ragtime* is America in 1902: Teddy Roosevelt's presidency, Winslow Homer's painting, Houdini's fame, J. P. Morgan's money, news of cubism in Paris. But the intertexts of history double up with those of literature, especially Heinrich von Kleist's "Michael Kohlhaas" and Dos Passos's *USA*. Doctorow himself has pointed critics to the Kleist text (in Trenner 1983, 39) and much work has been done already linking the two (P. Levine 1985, 56; Foley 1983, 166, 176–7n; Ditsky 1983). Doctorow's novel ironically transcodes the German feudal plot into American turn-of-century terms, complementing it with echoes of the climax of another intertext, George Milburn's *Catalogue*. In all these texts the focus is on people who cannot find justice in a society that pretends to be just. In both "Michael Kohlhaas" and *Ragtime*, historical characters mix with fictional: the hero meets Martin Luther in the one and Booker T. Washington in the other. But in neither, I would argue, does this imply any overvaluing of the fictional (cf. Foley 1983, 166). It is the narrativity and the textuality of our knowledge of the past that are being stressed; it is not a question of privileging the fictive or the historical, but of seeing what they share.

Again, many critics have teased out the connections between *Ragtime* and Dos Passos's *USA* (Foley 1983; Seelye 1976; Levine 1985). The echoes are thematic (the Laurence textile strike, San Diego free speech fight, portraits of events and personages like the Mexican Revolution and Red Emma), formal (fiction mixing with history; Boy/Camera Eye naively recording events), and ideological (a critique of American capitalism of the same period). But, the same critics have been careful to acknowledge serious differences, ones that, I would argue, the very intertextual echoes themselves force us to consider. Doctorow does not share his predecessor's trust in the objective presentation of history, and it is his ironic intermingling of the factual and the fictive and his deliberate anachronisms that underline this mistrust. As Barbara Foley notes, *USA* implies that historical reality is "knowable, coherent, significant, and inherently moving" (1983, 171). Doctorow, however, appears to feel, on the one hand, that fiction is as well, and on the other, that *both* need questioning in the light of these assumptions. Narrativized history, like fiction, reshapes any material (in this case, the past) in the light of present issues, and this interpretative process is precisely what historiographic metafiction calls to our attention:

> Walker's meeting with Booker T. Washington, for instance, echoes the contemporary debate between integrationists and black separatists. Similarly Henry Ford is described as the father of mass society and Evelyn Nesbit is depicted as the first goddess of mass culture.
>
> (Levine 1985, 55)

The ideological as well as epistemological implications of intertextuality are even clearer in Doctorow's earlier novel, *The Book of Daniel*. Here too we find the same range of kinds of parodic intertexts. The title cannot avoid pointing us to its biblical namesake: the alienation of modern Jews recapitulates their ancestors' fate (see Stark 1975). The first epigraph of the novel is from Daniel 3:4 about the King's call for all to worship the "golden image" or be cast into a "burning and fiery furnace." This sets the stage for the fate of those who challenge the new golden image of modern capitalism, since the Jews in this tale will ironically not survive in the Cold War climate of anti-semitic suspicion. The King who sentenced the biblical Daniel's brothers to the fiery furnace has become the more impersonal "state" which sentences the modern Daniel's parents to the electric chair. The Babylonian furnace image is picked up as well in the Isaacsons' apartment-building's furnace and its outcast black attendant. (The Nazi ovens – which do not have to be mentioned directly – are also clearly part of the historical intertext.)

The textual mentions of the biblical *Book of Daniel* are always ironic. Doctorow's Daniel calls his namesake "a Beacon of Faith in a Time of Persecution" (1971, 15). The irony here is two-fold: the present-day Daniel both persecutes his own wife and child, and seeks for faith – desperately; and the biblical Daniel was also marginalized, a "minor if not totally apocryphal figure" (21), a Jew in difficult times. He was not an actor in history, so much as an interpreter (with God's help) of the dreams of others, often remaining confused about his own. Such is the model of the writer for Doctorow's Daniel, who also tries to list "mysteries" and then examine them (26ff.) and who, as a survivor, is haunted by nightmares he cannot interpret. The result of their writing is also ironically similar. Daniel calls the biblical text one "full of enigmas," a mixture of familiar stories and "weird dreams and visions" (15), a disordered text with none of the closure of revelation or Truth. So too is Doctorow's *Book of Daniel*, in its generic mixture of journal form, history, thesis, and fiction. Both too are works *about* the act of interpreting – and then judging. The narrative voices in both move from impersonally omniscient third person to personally provisional first person, but the customary authority of the biblical omniscience is ironized into the modern Daniel's attempts at distance and self-mastery.

When their parents are first arrested, it is the black tender of the basement furnace who informs the Isaacson children. The text then immediately cites a Paul Robeson song, "Didn't my Lord deliver Daniel?" (143). But the rhetorical question is here rendered ironic by both its immediate context (the furnace attendant) and by our privileged knowledge of the fate of this Daniel's undelivered parents. The multiple, complex echoing points to the different possible functions of intertextuality in historiographic metafiction, for it can both thematically and formally reinforce the text's message *or* it can ironically undercut any pretensions to borrowed authority or legitimacy. "Daniel's Book" (318) actually ends as it began, self-conscious about being *"written in the book"* (319). Its final words of closure are of closure *sous rature*, so to speak, because they are not its own, but those of its biblical namesake: *"for the words are closed up and sealed till the time of the end"* (319). These two songs of lamentation and prophesy (Levine 1985, 49) come to the same end, as their words are opened up (not closed up) by our act of reading.

In a similar sense, the Isaacsons' fate opens up the Rosenbergs' case once again. The historical intertext for the reader here includes all the many books and articles written (before and after the novel) on that particular incident, including the book written by the Rosenberg children. Time has not resolved the doubts and questions that still surround this case. Analysts of all political persuasions line up to "prove" every possible perspective. These range from the view that the Rosenbergs were innocent victims of a specific (or general) anti-semitic (or even Jewish) plot to the view that Julius Rosenberg can be done proper justice by history only if we, in fact, accept his identity as a conscientious Soviet spy with his wife's devotion and support. What many seem to have come to see in the trial and its outcome is the social and ideological determination of so-called universal and objective justice. It is this that Doctorow enacts in his Daniel's tortured investigation of his "family truths." In Althusserian terms, both the Repressive and the Ideological State Apparatuses conspire to condemn the Isaacsons – and, by implication, perhaps, the Rosenbergs. The intertextual voices of official historical texts and Karl Marx's writings play off against each other with ironic and doubly undercutting force.

The importance of this historicizing parody is made clear – by contrast – in the novel's portrayal of Disneyland as the incarnation of a debased intertextuality, one that denies the historicity of the past. Disneyland is offered as a manipulative, consumerist transgression of the boundaries of art and life, of past and present. But, in itself, it is not a critical and parodic transgression that might provoke thought; it is intended for instant consumption as a spectacle voided of historical and aesthetic significance. It tames the past into the present. And it is the pasts of both literature and history that are being trivialized and recuperated:

> The life and life-style of slave-trading America on the Mississippi River in the 19th century is compressed into a technologically faithful steamboat ride of five or ten minutes. . . . The intermediary between us and this actual historical experience, the writer Mark Twain, is now no more than the name of the boat.
>
> (Doctorow 1971, 304)

Despite my focus in this chapter, I do not mean to suggest that this is true only for American fiction. Canadian writer Margaret Atwood's *The Handmaid's Tale* is as complex as any American text in her serious parodic echoing and inverting of the canonical *Scarlet Letter* (in setting, theme, and narrative frame) and of Zamyatin's *We*. And then there is Audrey Thomas's use and abuse of Virginia Woolf's *To the Lighthouse* and *The Waves* in *Intertidal Life* or Robert Kroetsch's ironic reworking of the conventions of the Western in *The Studhorse Man*. In contemporary British fiction, we need think only of the work of John Fowles, Anthony Burgess, Peter Ackroyd, Julian Barnes, or John Berger. In literature, intertextual parody crosses genre boundaries without reserve: Milan Kundera's play, *Jacques and his Master*, is subtitled *An Homage to Diderot in Three Acts* and represents what the author calls "an encounter of two writers but also of two centuries. And of the novel and the theater" (1985, 10). American writer Susan Daitch's novel *L.C.* offers an even more complex generic interaction that is directly tied to its dense intertextuality. As I mentioned in earlier discussions of this book, the core of the narrative is the journal of one Lucienne Crozier, (fictive) witness to the (real) 1848 Paris revolt. The first of two modern frames for this journal is that of Willa Rehnfield, its first translator. Her "Introduction" reminds us of the contradictions of 1848 in terms of two symbolic intertexts published that year: *Wuthering Heights* and the *Communist Manifesto*. And these are indeed the contradictions of the journal (at least as translated by Willa): Lucienne has strong socialist politics but is rendered ineffective by her marginalization (by the Left) and by her melodramatic fate, dying of tuberculosis and all but abandoned by her lover. Willa sees Lucienne as formed by "Marxism and fluff" (Daitch 1986, 2), that is by the *feuilletons*. But, in fact, the journal reveals Lucienne's critique of that popular literary form as being unfaithful to the social and economic realities of real life, despite their surface realism on the level of language (136–7).

Is this a radicalized Emma Bovary? The question is suggested by the text itself: "Madame Lucienne Crozier was doomed from the day she married" (207). So, of course, was Madame Bovary, as the novel's title constantly reminds us. But Lucienne is, if anything, a parodic inversion of Emma. Though they share a hatred of the provinces, it is their parallel extramarital affairs and their penchant for reading (though mutually motivated in both cases) that leads them in opposite directions: Emma into fantasy and a rejection of responsibility, and Lucienne into political action. This political connection is made clearer through the journal's second editor/translator who has taken the pseudonym of Jane Amme. The surname is obviously Emma backwards – but this is where the intertextual echoes proliferate: Emma Bovary is joined by Emma Goldman and *Jane* Austen's Emma. *Jane Eyre* is also not far in the background when a footnote refers us (with an anachronistic critical allusion) to "the mad woman in the attic, real or theoretical" (198n). This frame figure further defines herself as "the sort Jane Austen's characters would have called 'a most agreeable and obliging young lady'" (246), at least until her feminist radicalization at the hands of both the sexist male New Left at Berkeley in 1968 and the rapist who attacks and enrages her. Rejecting (as does Lucienne as well, at least in Amme's translation) the "mute role of an automatic participant" (246) that has traditionally been that of women, she bombs the home of the capitalist "global rapist" who is also her actual attacker. As well, she chooses to write her story, rejecting muteness both for herself and for the other women writers and characters whose intertexts are woven into the fabric of her text.

It is not just novels, though, which offer examples of postmodern intertextual echoing. Installations like Michelangelo Pistoletto's "Venus of Rags" and "Orchestra of Rags" suggest ironic postmodern critique. Pistoletto uses real rags (the end product of consumption): art represents the detritus of culture within the consumer ethic. His mica reproduction of the classical Venus may parodically represent the static, "universal" principle of aesthetic beauty, but here it faces – and is blocked by – a large pile of those rags. While many have argued that all paintings are intertextually connected to other paintings (e.g. Steiner 1985), postmodern ones by Mark Tansey or Sherrie Levine seem more tendentiously ironic in their interrelations. Even music, seen by most as the least representational of the arts, is being interpreted in terms of the intertextual linking of the past to the present as an analogue of the necessary linking of artistic form and human memory (Robert P. Morgan 1977, 51). Postmodernism clearly attempts to combat what has come to be seen as modernism's potential for hermetic, élitist isolationism that separated art from the world, literature from history. But it often does so by using the very techniques of modernist aestheticism against themselves. The autonomy of art is carefully maintained: metafictional self-reflexivity even underlines it. But through seemingly introverted intertextuality, another dimension is added by the use of the ironic inversions of parody: art's critical relation to the "world" of discourse – and through that to society and politics. History and literature both provide the intertexts in the novels examined here, but there is no question of a hierarchy, implied or otherwise. They are both part of the signifying systems of our culture, and therein lies their meaning and their value.

9

THE PROBLEM OF REFERENCE

I

In short, the net effect of thought about language, in the twentieth century, with its rejection of essence and such founding principles of history as causality and sufficient reason, has been to evacuate history from discourse. And with this evacuation the very idea of reference becomes problematic. *Allen Thiher*

In *Words in Reflection* (1984), his provocative study of the interacting parallels between modern language theories and contemporary fiction, Allen Thiher looks to Wittgenstein, Heidegger (and Derrida), and Saussure and their "critiques of the metaphysics of essence" for the reason for what he sees as the destruction of the intellectual foundations upon which traditional narrative history could be built (195). His analysis of these theorists is thorough and convincing, but what would happen if we began from the *texts* of postmodern art, instead of from the theory? And what if we looked at other theoretical discourses? Would we find a less negative view? I think that what we might find is less a destruction than a productive problematizing of the entire notion of the relation of language to reality – fictive or historical. Historiographic metafiction both underlines its existence as discourse and yet still posits a relation of reference (however problematic) to the historical world, both through its assertion of the social and institutional nature of all enunciative positions and through its grounding in the representational.

Modernist art – be it visual or verbal – tends to declare its status as art first, "autonomous from the language that lies buried in representational realism" (Harkness 1982, 9). The updated extreme of this view in literature can be seen in American surfiction, in the "textes" of *Tel Quel* in France, and in the works of the Gruppo 63 in Italy. These Italian writers share with postmodern artists a certain ideological impulse: the desire to challenge the

institutional structures of bourgeois society (usually seen as being reinforced by realism) by awakening readers to the political implications of
accepted literary practices. But the method they chose to bring this about is a
(late) modernist one which attempts to separate literary language from
reference. For Giorgio Manganelli and others, as Gregory Lucente has
argued,

> literature does not mean by any process of external reference. Literature's
> signifying elements, thus liberated from the illusion of their dependency on
> anything signified in the external universe of matter and sense, anything both
> worldly and prior, gain their importance and their particular value *because of* rather
> than *in spite of* their status as a lie, as an untruth that turns out to be both more
> engaging and more important than the supposed truth of the everyday world.
>
> (1986, 318)

This kind of separation is precisely what postmodernism, in turn, has
challenged by conflating this same kind of metafictive reflexivity with
documentary materials. Historiographic metafiction always asserts that its
world is both resolutely fictive and yet undeniably historical, and that what
both realms share is their constitution in and as discourse (Sparshott
1986, 154–5). Paradoxically this emphasis on what at first may appear to be a
kind of discursive narcissism is actually what connects the fictional to the
historical in a more material sense. Like Duchamp's ironic ready mades
which foreground the accepted, unexamined nature of the referential
function of sign systems, postmodern art forms work to "supplant the
legislative force of the referential context by the material assumption of a real
context, a reality which it had been the mission of representation to repress"
(Bois 1981, 31). Think of Jasper Johns's parodic flags and targets: do they
refer to real flags and targets or to the standard representations of them – or
both? When Magritte's painting of a pipe asserts "Ceci n'est pas une pipe," it
points toward what was to become a paradox of linguistic and visual
postmodern reference, with both its ontological and its epistemological
contradictions.

In historiographic metafictions like John Banville's *Doctor Copernicus* and
Kepler, the focus of the problem of reference is on the writing of history, for
in them history appears to have a double identity. On the one hand, its
discourse does seem to be ontologically separate from that of the self-
consciously fictional text (or intertexts) of fiction. This is an extension of the
common-sense distinction between two kinds of reference: what history
refers to is the actual, real world; what fiction refers to is a fictive universe.
This distinction can be found articulated in any introduction to fiction
written since at least the advent of New Criticism, if not before. On the other
hand, we have seen that there also exists quite another view of history in
postmodern art, but this time it is history as intertext. History becomes a
text, a discursive construct upon which fiction draws as easily as it does
upon other texts of literature. This view of history is the logical extension of

theories like those of Michael Riffaterre (e.g. 1984, 142) which argue that reference in literature is never anything but one of text to text and that, therefore, history as used in historiographic metafiction, for instance, could never refer to any actual empirical world, but merely to another text. At best, words refer, not to things, but to systems of signs that are "ready-made textual units" (159). And this is the way literature can challenge naive notions of representation. In postmodern fiction, these views of history – as intertextual and as extratextual – appear to co-exist and operate in tension.

The last few chapters have already examined how this issue of the textuality of the past has also become problematic in contemporary historiography and literary theory. Fredric Jameson articulates the very same ontological tension when he argues that history (that is, the past) is *not* a text – it is non-narrative, non-representational – but that history is "inaccessible to us except in textual form" (1981a, 82). Similarly Hayden White claims that any historical narrative "figures the body of events that serves as its primary referent and transforms these 'events' into intimations of patterns of meaning that any *literal* representation of them . . . could never produce" (1984, 22). History as narrative account, then, is unavoidably figurative, allegorical, fictive; it is always already textualized, always already interpreted. To see why these views should be so controversial, we need only remind ourselves once again of the strong materialist or realist view of history that has dominated the discipline in the last century. Here is Peter Gay:

> the objects of the historian's inquiry are precisely that, objects, out there in a real and single past. Historical controversy in no way compromises their ontological integrity. The tree in the woods of the past fell in only one way, no matter how fragmentary or contradictory the reports of its fall, no matter whether there are no historians, one historian, or several contentious historians in its future to record and debate it.
>
> (1974a, 210)

While both Jameson and White would agree that the past, obviously, did exist, they would contest our ability to *know* that past by any other means than textualized, interpreted "reports." White would go even further and argue that what we accept as "real" and "true" in historiography, as in fiction, is that which "wears the mask of meaning, the completeness and fullness of which we can only *imagine*, never experience" (1980, 24). In other words, only by narrativizing the past will we accept it as "true."

It is interesting that the work of Hayden White has arguably had more impact in literary than in historical circles. By opening history up to the rhetorical strategies of narrative, White has also raised questions that contemporary fiction has been asking. What constitutes the nature of reference in both history and fiction? (Is it the same? Totally different? Related?) How exactly does language hook onto reality? What our literary theory, our literature, and our philosophy of history are doing these days is becoming part of an already existing and now general problematizing of the entire idea of reference. They join semiotics and analytic philosophy in *their* recent intense interest in reference. That aesthetic practice and theoretical discourse in general should focus on the same issues is not at all surprising, as I have tried to argue throughout this study, if we posit that there can exist a poetics of postmodernism that would contain and constitute the common denominators among our various ways of writing and thinking about our writing. Historiographic metafiction explicitly and even didactically asks the same central questions about the nature of reference that are being asked in many other fields today. Does the linguistic sign refer to an actual object – in literature, history, ordinary language? If it does, what sort of access does this allow us to that actuality? *Reference* is not *correspondence*, after all (see Eco 1979, 61). Can any linguistic reference be unmediated and direct?

What a novel like Rudy Wiebe's *The Temptations of Big Bear* suggests, by its very form as well as its content, is that what language refers to – any language – is a textualized and contextualized referent: the Big Bear we come to know is not really the Big Bear of actuality (for how can we know that today?) but the Big Bear of history texts, newspaper accounts, letters, official and unofficial reports, but also of imagination and legend. The very fabric of the novel refuses any naive separation of fictional reference from that of so-called "scientific" descriptions of the past that many critics still want to make (e.g. Harshaw 1984). But it also refuses, just as firmly, any formalist or deconstructive attempt to make language into the play of signifiers discontinuous with representation and with the external world (e.g. Caramello 1983, 10). There *was* a Big Bear, a famous Cree Indian orator and leader – though we can know him today only from texts. The novel is both a referential inscription and an imaginative invention of a world.

That frequent and common denial of representation, however, merits more consideration here because this is what is usually associated (I think wrongly) with the concept of postmodernism. It seems to be the case that this entire question of reference has recently been re-opened in the wake of various kinds of formalism which bracketed it, even to the point of declaring interest in it illegitimate. Roland Barthes's famous gallic overstatement is typical of this repression of reference: "'What takes place' in a narrative is from the referential (reality) point of view literally *nothing*; 'what happens' is language alone, the adventure of language, the unceasing celebration of its coming" (1977, 124). It is out of this view of language that most theories of postmodernism seem to have been derived. But I have argued that this formalism is the defining expression of *modernism*, not postmodernism. In both art and theoretical discourse today there is what Peter Brooks has called "a certain yearning for the return of the referent" (1983, 73), but it can never be a naive and unproblematic return: "there has been an end to innocence concerning the status of and access to the referent in discourses of all types" (74).

Historiographic metafiction, in fact, works to short-circuit what critics like to call the "referential fallacy" (Eco 1976, 58). The metafictional impulse of novels like *Famous Last Words* – initially signalled by having a protagonist called Hugh Selwyn Mauberley – suggests that, yes, it is a fallacy, that the referents of the novel's language are clearly fictive and intertextual. But the co-presence of the Duke and Duchess of Windsor and Ezra Pound in the same novel complicates considerably the metafictional fallaciousness of reference. This kind of use and abuse of our notions of reference is not unlike the Derridean strategy of writing *sous rature* (Derrida 1976): it makes you want to have your historical referent and erase it too. This is not really a devaluing of the referential dimension of language at all, as many theorists of postmodernism assert (e.g. Russell 1980a, 183). Nor is it an unproblematic revelling in factual immediacy, as in so-called fact or information fiction (the novelization of sociology, psychiatry, economics, or anthropology). Historiographic metafiction renders problematic both the denial and the assertion of reference. It blurs the distinction which Richard Rorty (1985) makes between "texts" and "lumps" – things made and things found, the domains of interpretation and epistemology. It suggests that there *were* lumps – historical personages and events – but that we know them only as texts today.

As Nelson Goodman (1978, 2–3) asserts, then, frames of reference appear to be a matter of systems of description rather than of things described. This does not deny that lumps exist (or existed), but it does suggest that our understanding of those lumps is predicated on our available ways of describing. The very term, referent, of course, implies that the "reality" to which we refer is not a given, a lump, but rather "that of which we speak." In other words, perhaps by definition, the referent is a discursive entity. In Lyotard's terms, the object of history is the referent of the proper name (Ezra Pound) and this is not the same thing as the object of perception (the empirical, once alive, Ezra Pound) (Lyotard 1984c, 12). It is this distinction that historiographic metafiction foregrounds in its paradoxical use and abuse of the conventions of novelistic and historiographic reference.

Of course, this debate about reference is not a particularly new one, though its intensity has increased considerably lately. Think of Henry James attacking Trollope for his metafictional breaking of the referential illusion. The novelist, according to James, had to "relate events that are assumed to be real" (1948, 59). The historical novel has always carried this even one step further. Mary McCarthy argued that referential accuracy of historical detail was crucial to the novel genre: "if Tolstoy was all wrong about the Battle of Borodino or the character of Napoleon, *War and Peace* would suffer" (1961, 263). But does *Famous Last Words* "suffer" because Findley was "wrong about" (or fictionalized about) the Duke and Duchess of Windsor? E. L. Doctorow replied for all historiographic metafictionists, perhaps, when he responded to attacks on his fictionalizations of Freud, Morgan, and Ford, among others, in *Ragtime*: "I'm satisfied that everything I made up about Morgan and Ford is true, whether it happened or not. Perhaps truer because it didn't happen" (in Trenner 1983, 69). The writer is "independent witness" – as are all, even eye-witnesses. This is what the philosophy of history has recently been asserting about historiography as well: the act of telling about the past, of writing history, makes the "given" into the "constructed" (de Certeau 1975, 13). That border between past event and present praxis is where historiographic metafiction self-consciously locates itself. As we have seen at length, that past *was* real, but it *is* lost or at least displaced, only to be reinstated as the referent of language, the relic or trace of the real.

Postmodernist reference, then, differs from modernist reference in its overt acknowledgement of the *existence*, if relative inaccessibility, of the past real (except through discourse). It differs from realist reference in its – again – overt assertion of that relative *inaccessibility* of any reality that might exist objectively and prior to our knowledge of it. In this it approaches a long philosophical tradition which argues that, while reality may exist 'out there,' it is unavoidably ordered by the concepts and categories of our human understanding (Norris 1985, 54). Historiographic metafiction, while teasing us with the existence of the past as real, also suggests that there is no direct access to that real which would be unmediated by the structures of our various discourses about it. Semioticians have recently questioned whether even the most direct of facts used by historians can be assumed to refer directly and unproblematically to a real past world. The counter-assertion is that even these direct reports are conventional and stylized, culturally mediated by prefabricated discursive models (Even-Zohar 1980, 66). In its most straightforward articulation, this view takes the form that "What literary or non-literary fiction or reality *is* depends on conventionalized criteria within systems of social action, and *not* on reality as such or art as such" (Schmidt 1984, 273). Historiographic metafiction does not deny that reality *is* (or *was*), as does this kind of radical constructivism (according to which reality is only a construct); it just questions how we *know* that and how it is (or was). In doing so, it simultaneously opposes and joins forces with Marxists (T. E. Lewis 1979) and common-sense advocates who resist the splitting off of language from reality. This is the paradox of its very nature as historiographic metafiction.

II

In the historical narrative the systems of meaning-production peculiar to a culture or society are tested against the capacity of any set of "real" events to yield to such systems. If these systems have their purest, most fully developed, and formally most coherent representations in the "literary" or "poetic" endowment of modern, secularized cultures, this is no reason to rule them out as *merely* imaginary constructions. To do so would entail the denial that literature and poetry have anything valid to teach us about "reality". *Hayden White*

Two major intellectual forces have operated in our century to combat any very simple referential notion of a "natural" and one-to-one relationship of words to things: analytic philosophy and Saussurian structuralism. Although hermeneutics has addressed the issue in works like Ricoeur's *Interpretation Theory: Discourse and the Surplus of Meaning* (1976) (see also Ricoeur 1984a, 77–82), it has been analytic philosophy that has been the site of the most vigorous debates, for reference is central to the philosophical debate between "realism" and "nominalism" in both fictive and ordinary language discourses (see Davidson 1980 and McGinn 1980): one thinks of the work of Russell, Searle, Donnellan, Parsons, Strawson, Kripke, and so many others (see Rorty 1982 for a complete discussion of this issue regarding fictional language). It is inevitably the theories of Frege that come to the fore here, for they offer a way of going beyond the impasse of Russell's denial of fictional reference (as "empty" terms). Frege (1952) distinguished between the "sense" and the "reference" of a sign. Sense precedes reference in that it constitutes the semantic criteria which we need to identify the object referred to by the reference. His famous example is that of the Morning Star and the Evening Star: they have the same reference, but different senses. What defines reference is not empirical existence (abstract numbers have reference), but a set of internally consistent criteria which constitute the truth-conditions of a discourse. But, for Frege, imaginary or fictive terms could have no reference – only sense – because they do not pose questions about truth or falsehood.

Yet *Famous Last Words* or *Ragtime*, as historiographic metafictions, implicitly do pose exactly that kind of question in their tensions between what is known about history and what is narrated in the text. For Frege, literature lacked truth value and, therefore, could aim only at aesthetic delight, not knowledge. What seriously didactic postmodern literature like Williams's *Star Turn* and Wiebe's *The Scorched-Wood People* does, however, is to prevent any such easy separation of the cognitive from the poetic. Truth-value is both implied and blocked. Wiebe's Batoche both is and is not the actual historical Batoche. Historiographic metafiction demands what "possible world" semantics calls "cross-world identifications" (Doležel 1986) and the semiotic mediation is effected through the recognition that our knowledge of that past, real Batoche comes to us today only from other texts, other discourses.

The debate over the existence and nature of reference in fiction has taken a number of forms, ranging from denial of truth-value to the granting of special status to the fictive (see Rorty 1982). The "denial of truth-value" point of view argues that the language of fiction is syntactically and semantically indistinguishable from that of ordinary language, and that therefore we must turn to intentionality (Lange 1969; Harshaw 1984, 237) to assert difference, thereby concluding that, thanks to different "intentional acts," the historian and the novelist aim at different referents: "the fictional narrative statement is immune to judgments of truth or falsity; in fiction, they are suspended" (Banfield 1982, 258). Historiographic metafiction, in which the producer's position is one of both novel writer and narrative historian, certainly complicates such a neat distinction. And the familiar view – that if a historian were to go into the mind of a historical personage or use any other clearly narrative technique in writing, then "we would find ourselves in a novel" (Hamburger 1973, 82–3) – is hardly a view that can satisfy the reader of historiographic metafiction, or for that matter, of history. As Francis Sparshott (1967, 3) pointed out in his attack on Joseph Margolis's (1965, 155) contention that fiction cannot embody truth-claims, what exactly do we do – even in realist fiction – with statements about the actual world that appear in fiction (Paris is the capital of France; the Second World War began in 1939, and so on)? Are these no longer truth-claims? Or are these not to be considered part of the story?

The other approach is not to deny reference to fiction, but to grant the fictive a separate referential status. There are many versions of this stand: Ohmann's (1971) theory that literature "purportedly" imitates speech acts which have no other existence; Searle's (1975) designation of literature as "as if" assertions; Frye's (1957) idea of the literary as the hypothetical; Richards's (1924) "pseudo-statements," and so on. From this perspective, as Rorty explains: "If we agree that [Sherlock] Holmes is a fictional character, we shall settle debates about his habits by turning to Conan Doyle, we shall not inquire whether he and Gladstone ever met" (1982, 118). But *Famous Last Words* asks us to consider precisely what happens when Ezra Pound meets (and interacts with) Hugh Selwyn Mauberley (his own real – that is fictional – creation). It both demands and challenges our ability as readers to imagine any statement about either as prefaced by an intensional operator ("In such-and-such a fiction . . . " – D. Lewis 1978, 37) and then to proceed to operate as if both were equally factual (in that context). But I would argue that they do *not* have the same referential weight: Pound and Mauberley have different representational resonances, for their initial contexts (historical and literary) differ. So, while analytic philosophy has raised the same questions as postmodernist fiction regarding reference, from the point of view of historiographic metafiction it too seems to offer no definitive answers – just more problematizing questions.

Like much contemporary philosophy, Saussurian structuralism accepts that language is a structure of signifying relations between words and concepts, rather than between words and things (see Norris 1985 on the similiarities between Frege and Saussure). However, while analytic philosophy still seems nevertheless to want an account of representation and reference (Rorty 1982, 128), structuralism does not; indeed, it is content to bracket these concerns. In a Saussurian context, language is a system of signs, of signifiers and signifieds. The referent is not part of this system. This does not, however, deny the *existence* of a referent of language: it is presumed to exist, but is not necessarily immediately accessible through knowledge.

Saussure's systematic, synchronic linguistics took as a new investigative strategy the bracketing of the referent. As Christopher Norris has argued, so has post-structuralism, but what was a methodological convenience for linguistics has become a "high point of philosophical principle" for literary theory and philosophy (1985, 62). He is clearly thinking of Derrida's famous contention that there is nothing preceding, nothing outside the text and of Foucault's general unwillingness to accept language as referring (as reduced to referring) to any first-order reference, anything, that is that would ground it in any foundational "truth." But we must be careful to note that neither statement is a denial of the real world, past or present. They both merely question its accessibility to us in terms of signification. Derrida's denial of the transcendental signified is not a denial of reference or a denial of any access to extra-textual reality. However, it is meant to suggest that *meaning* can be derived only from within texts through deferral, through *différance*. This kind of post-structuralist thinking has obvious implications for historiography and historiographic metafiction. It radically questions the nature of the archive, the document, evidence. It separates the (meaning-granted) facts of history-writing from the brute events of the past.

Facts in historiography are discursive, already interpreted (granted meaning). In linguistic terms, the refusal to accept this separation of fact from event involves what Barthes (1982b, 20) called a conflation of the signified and the referent which elides the former in order to provide the illusion that the signifier of history writing is in a direct relation with the referent. For Barthes, the same illusionary elision is also present in realist fiction. What historiographic metafiction does is reinstate the signified through its metafictional self-reflexivity about the function and process of meaning-generation while at the same time not letting the referent disappear. Such postmodernist fiction, however, also refuses to allow the referent to take on any original, founding, controlling function: Ezra Pound is made to meet Hugh Selwyn Mauberley. The facts of history, as portrayed in historiographic metafiction, are overtly discursive. Often this is formally and thematically worked out within the narrative itself: think of the different and contradictory "factual" (in this sense of the word) accounts of the same events in *The Temptations of Big Bear* or *Antichthon*. It is one of the lessons of postmodernism that, while all knowledge of the past may be provisional, historicized, and discursive, this does not mean we do not make meaning of that past.

III

Language is . . . more powerful as an experience of things than the experience of things. Signs are more potent experiences than anything else, so when one is dealing with the things that really count, then you deal with words. They have a reality far exceeding the things they name. *William Gass*

Facts versus events: how language hooks onto reality. The questions raised by historiographic metafiction regarding reference in language (fictive or ordinary) are similar to those raised by these theoretical discourses today. John Banville's *Doctor Copernicus* focuses directly on the relations between facts and events or, more specifically, between names and things, scientific theories and the universe. And the intertextual allusions to Wittgenstein in the novel point to the broad implications of this theme. In Coetzee's *Foe*, it is Robinson Cruso's [sic] tongueless Friday who is the focus of the question of the relation of language to reality. Foe suggests a utilitarian approach to the issue of how much language Friday needs to know in order to survive. "Because we cannot say in words what an apple is, it is not forbidden to eat the apple. It is enough that we know the names of our needs and are able to use these names to satisfy them" (1986, 149). However, in contrast, Friday's protectress wants to help him express "the urgings of [his] heart" (149). The final scene of the novel returns to this debate about the nature and function of linguistic expression and reference and manages to problematize even further the entire novel's relation to fictive and intertextual, as well as political reality. The book, like the imagined underwater world being "described" (that is, created), becomes a paradoxical world of silent meaning: "But this is not a place of words. . . . This is a place where bodies are their own signs. It is the home of Friday" (157). That the silenced Friday is black and Coetzee South African is part of the literary and material/political context of the novel.

A similarly complex view of the world/word relationship can be seen in the work of Jean-François Lyotard, the one analyst of postmodernity who has consistently addressed the question of reference. In his early, phenomenologically inspired work, he – like metafictionists from John Barth to Paolo Volponi – investigated what he felt to be the impossibility of language ever being able to grasp the non-linguistic. Instead of going in the direction of Derrida and suggesting that our interest should therefore be in language itself or textuality, Lyotard saw in this impossibility the fundamental limitations of language. In *Discours, figure* (1971), he contested several prevailing theories of reference: Merleau-Ponty's implication of an elective affinity between language and the world; Derrida's relegating of the referential to secondary and derivative status (traces); and the Saussurian bracketing of the referent (for a critical discussion of this, see Dews 1984, 42–4). For Lyotard, language does not articulate the meaning of the world; it constantly excludes what it tries to grasp (1971, 125). This self-contradicting situation is reminiscent of the general postmodernist paradox of a discourse which uses and ironically abuses, asserts and denies the conventions within which it operates.

In his more recent work, Lyotard's interest in reference takes place within the context of a pragmatics of narrative that includes the producer of the narrative, its receiver, the narrative itself, and all the complex interactions of these components. In this enunciative context, the referents of narrative are presented as referring inevitably to other narratives (or discourses), and not to any brute reality: they are narrative facts not events. Just as the term "I" always refers to the speaker of the particular enunciation or discursive act (Benveniste 1971, 226), so the "reality" to which the language of historiographic metafiction refers is always primarily the reality of the discursive act itself (hence its designation as metafiction) but also the reality of other past discursive acts (historiography).

Both in this kind of fiction and in current philosophical inquiry, the question of reference often includes the issue of naming (Davidson 1980, 134). Maxine Hong Kingston's *China Men* foregrounds the relation of the name to the bearer of the name through its recounting of the experience of the narrator's father. When he sat the Imperial Examination in China, he replaced his family name with an invented one:

> His new name brought him enough luck, and so he kept it; the name he has now is that name: Think Virtue, my father's name. I hesitate to tell it; I don't want him traced and deported. Even MaMa rarely calls him by name and not this one but other vocatives, like So-and-so's Father. Friends call him Uncle or Brother or Teacher. Anyway, a translation, Think Virtue, is nothing like this name; the English words are like fiction, that is, their sounds are dissimilar from the Chinese sounds. Nobody would call anyone else by a translation, Think Virtue. . . . He is still disguised.
>
> (1980, 24)

When he arrived in the United States, her father again named himself, this time, as Ed (after Thomas Edison), a name which his Chinese wife translates into "Eh-Da-Son. Son as in *sage* or *immortal* or *saint*" (69). When the police raid the gambling house which he operates in Stockton, California, her father just invents new names each time he is run in, because to the whites, all Chinese – and their names – look alike. His young daughter, however, attributes more power than cynicism to his act: "He had the power of naming" (241). So too does she, as writer.

Perhaps women have been more aware of naming in relation to reference because they have traditionally been designated by paternal and spousal surnames. In certain cultures, such as some African ones, the name is seen as the expression of the soul (Byerman 1985, 201). Both of these contexts are directly relevant to Toni Morrison's problematizing of the name/person relationship in *Song of Solomon*. The protagonist's life-denying family's appropriate surname is "Dead"; it was given this by a drunken soldier during the Civil War. As one character puts it, "white folk name Negroes like race horses" (1977, 245). The women of the family get their first names from a process of random selection of a word in the Bible, and the results are, to say the least, unorthodox: First Corinthians, Pilate. Milkman gets his name from his mother's refusal to wean him – at least until she is shamed into it. But it is Milkman's trip to Shalimar that is the focus of the naming-theme of the novel. In deciphering a children's song, he learns the history of his family and his people, embedded and distorted in the folktale of Solomon, the flying African slave. The novel's epigraph is "The fathers may soar/And the children may know their names." In Shalimar, Milkman learns his and his race's history through their names: "Names they got from yearnings, gestures, flaws, events, mistakes, weaknesses. Names that bore witness" (335).

In addition to this general problematizing of the issue of naming, some postmodern fiction asks more precisely: what is the relation between names in novels and people in history – the Duke and Duchess of Windsor, Copernicus, Giordano Bruno? The most common theory one finds (Lyotard 1984c, 10; Kripke 1980) is that proper names are "rigid designators" of reality. In historiography, this would be the assumption behind the use of names like Freud or the Duchess of Windsor, the former Wallis Simpson: the referent is a constant, despite different connotations for different readers. But what we do with these two statements: "Wallis Simpson married Edward" and "Wallis Simpson was a friend of Hugh Selwyn Mauberley"? Can "Wallis Simpson" effect a "trans-world identification," as the terminology of possible-world semantics would have it? Are the referents of the name in history and fiction exactly the same? Lyotard (1984c, 11) makes a distinction between names whose referents are real (Duchess of Windsor) and names whose referents are not (Mauberley). But will this neat separation work in historiographic metafiction? Lyotard does not consider the question, but his separation clearly presents problems. He argues that

> Every time a phrase (of a historian, of a philosopher, of a philologist) occurs in which *Aristotle* [or the Duchess of Windsor] or one of his admitted equivalents [Plato's disciple – or, the former Wallis Simpson] is signified, a new expression turns out to be by that very fact substitutable for *Aristotle* or his equivalents under the same logical conditions.
>
> (1984c, 12)

But what if the phrase is that, not of a historian, but of a historiographic metafictionist? Does "friend of Mauberley" become substitutable for "the Duchess of Windsor"? The "logical conditions" have indeed changed, yet the existence of "friend of Mauberley" as an equivalent of Wallis Simpson in *Famous Last Words* relies on our understanding of all the other equivalents of that name. My point is that historiographic metafiction's complex referential situation does not seem to be fully covered by any of the theories of reference offered in today's theoretical discourse. Postmodernist fiction neither brackets nor denies the referent (however defined); it works to problematize the entire activity of reference.

IV

> The real, the real. If only I had you once more, I would not be writing this. Instead, I would be rejoicing at you. The lovely image of the real. The real itself, mirror-source of the image. The true real, a real devoid

of world, empty in the fullness of itself. That real for which we
laboriously compensate, piling on. The nature of the real. A real thing
burning in unreality.   *Marvin Cohen*

This passage comes from an intensely metafictional piece entitled "What Is
the Real, Really? What Does It Mean? Or Do We Only Think It? Is There a
Real? But What Is 'Is'? And What Does It Mean?". Generally speaking, all
metafictional self-reflexivity and auto-representation act to question the
very existence as well as the nature of extratextual reference. But *historiographic* metafiction complicates this questioning. History offers facts –
interpreted, signifying, discursive, textualized – made from brute events. Is
the referent of historiography, then, the fact or the event, the textualized
trace or the experience itself? Postmodernist fiction plays on this question,
without ever fully resolving it. It complicates the issue of reference in two
ways, then: in this ontological confusion (text or experience) and in its
overdetermination of the entire notion of reference (we find autoreferen-
tiality, intertextuality, historiographic reference, and so on). There is a
tension, then, not only between the real and the textualized, but also among
a number of kinds of reference.

Georges Lavis (1971) has argued the distinction between real and fictive
referents (on the level of *parole*). Referents can be fictive either because they
are imaginary or because they are falsehoods. It is not accidental that one of
the constant themes of historiographic metafiction is that of lying: will
Mauberley tell the "truth" in his writing on the wall (as Quinn believes) or
will he lie (as Freyburg believes)? On the level of narration, falsehood is also
an issue for the reader: did George Vancouver really die before returning to
England? (No, despite *Burning Water*.) Were the Duke and Duchess of
Windsor involved in a plot called Penelope? (No, despite the "evidence"
offered in *Famous Last Words*.) Here it is the historiographical event that
complicates the reference question. Metafiction teaches its reader to see all
referents as fictive, as imagined. The equivalent formalist critical perspective
argues, as does Genette (1980, 227–30), that in all fiction historical characters
can coexist with fictional ones within the context of the novel because *there*
they are subject only to the rules of fiction. But I would still maintain that
there is a significant difference in allusive resonance between the "Duke of
Windsor" and "Mauberley." What they have in common is that their
allusions are to intertexts: historical, on the one hand, and literary, on the
other. They both, in other words, refer (now) to textualized entities.

In novels like *Ragtime*, there is no realist pretense that the referent could be
brute experience, although there is no denial that J. P. Morgan or Henry
Ford did exist. There is, instead, an acknowledgement that we know
Morgan or Ford only from their textualized traces in history. The metafictional elements undermine any *"effet de réel"* (Barthes 1968a): the *"avoir-été-là
des choses"* is no longer *"un principe suffisant de la parole."* Now it is the
"avoir-été-écrit" that founds novelistic and – by implication – historiographic
reference. As Paul Veyne (1971, 309) has argued, even the event closest to us

personally can be known to us afterwards only by its remains: memory can create only texts. There is no such thing as the *reproduction* of events by memory: "As a symbolic structure, the historical narrative does not reproduce the event is describes; it tells us in what direction to think about the events" (H. White 1978a, 52). Historiographic metafiction does not pretend to reproduce events, but to direct us, instead, to facts, or to new directions in which to think about events.

The study of such a mixture of (themselves already referentially complicated) entities – the historiographic and the metafictional – requires some theoretical model like Nelson Goodman's (1981) "routes of reference." However, various referential models already exist to deal with fiction and non-fiction, and all tend to be binary. Mas'ud Zavarzadeh (1976) regards the non-fictional novel, for example, as "bi-referential" in that it refers to itself and to reality, thereby suggesting the fact/fiction polarity is ontologically questionable. At first glance, historiographic metafiction is but a more self-conscious version of such doubleness. However, it would challenge any attempt to argue, as does Zavarzadeh, that such bi-referential narratives "form open dynamic systems in active tension with the experiential world outside the book" (58). Postmodernist fiction, while not denying the existence of that experiential world, contests its availability to us: how do we know that world? We know it only through its texts.

Nevertheless, this binary model is a popular one, appearing in various guises in current theory. Malmgren's (1985) terminology is "out-referential" and "in-referential": referents which are verifiably extra-textually existent and those which are non-existent, counterfactual, and thus fictionally justified, rather than factually true. Again historiographic metafiction radically problematizes that seemingly simple concept: "*verifiably* extra-textual." Malmgren sees that a narrative could exist which was referential in both ways, but such a fiction would be "anomalous and cause no end of problems for the narrative typologist" (28). Such are the limits of narrative typologies, perhaps. Other binary models have been offered which are considerably more formalistic. Instead of confronting the fictive with the non-fictive, Inge Crosman (1981) argues that the two referential networks which operate and indeed intersect to form the text's reference are "intertextual" and "intra or autotextual." While this is a valuable addition to the more realist version of the binary model, it too does not deal with the complexity of postmodernist historical reference. Perhaps we have to move to a multi-term model, since the reference of historiographic metafiction appears to be multiple and over-determined. If we do, at least five directions of reference would seem to have to be taken into account: intra-textual reference, self-reference, inter-textual reference, textualized extra-textual reference, and what we might call "hermeneutic" reference.

There are many theories that argue the intra-textual reference of fiction: that is that fictional language refers first and foremost to the universe of reality of fiction, independent of how closely or distantly it be modeled on the empirical world of experience (Rabinowitz 1981, 409). This is the argument that rests on a view of intentionality similar to that of Searle or Ohmann: the intended framework of fiction is fiction. It is also an argument that validates fiction through its autonomous, internally consistent, formal unity. Murray Krieger claims: "we must feel that Tolstoy's Kutuzov – or, for that matter, Shakespeare's Henry V – has a different 'material' status from that of history's Kutuzov (or Henry)" (1974, 344). History's Kutuzov derives his status, by this argument, from "evidence" outside even the system of historical discourse; Tolstoy's Kutuzov has only a "feigned" materiality, an imaginative identity controlled by the "form-giving power" of the author's imagination. Krieger, like many others, uses this autonomous-world basis of intratextual reference in order to transcend history: "man's [sic] capacity to create forms and to impose them on matter in a way that brings it to organic life can free him from history by allowing him to reshape it as he will" (347). The implication is that "history's Kutuzov" is not reshaped in any way, that historical discourse has direct access to the real and does not deviate from or transform brute reality, as does fiction (355). Historiographic metafiction questions both these assumptions. The Ambrose Bierce of Fuentes's *The Old Gringo* both is and is not the Bierce of history – in its many textualized forms or its "historiettes," to use Lyotard's term. It is this paradoxical identity that makes it postmodern, and that makes this referential model here have to be expanded.

A second kind of reference operative in historiographic metafiction is clearly not only to the coherent fictional universe but also to the fiction as fiction. This auto-representation or self-reference suggests that language cannot hook directly onto reality, but is primarily hooked onto itself. In postmodernist fiction, it is the kind of reference that makes the very name of the protagonist of *Famous Last Words*, Hugh Selwyn Mauberley, into a marker of metafictionality.

Related to this kind of reference is a third kind, the intertextual. Mauberley's name does not just signify metafiction; it points to a specific intertext, Pound's poem. But that novel abounds in other layers of intertextual reference: among the texts to which this postmodern fiction refers us are the biblical Book of Daniel and the work of Alexandre Dumas, Ernest Hemingway, Joseph Conrad, and many others. The reference can be on the level of word (*mene, mene, tekel upharsim*) or of structure (Conrad's Lord Jim jumps, and Marlow's ambivalence in recounting its consequences are intertextually linked to the moral leap of Mauberley [and his father] and Quinn's problematic ambivalence as our reading surrogate in the novel). Among these intertexts, however, are those of historiography: those "texts" – both specific and general – by which we know that the German concentration camps existed, that Edward abdicated the British throne for Wallis Simpson, and so on.

This intertextuality is, in fact, close to the fourth, the textualized extratextual kind of reference. The difference is one of emphasis. The first is history as intertext; the second is historiography as presentation of fact, as the textualized tracing of event. Here history allows some – mediated – access to what semioticians call "External Fields of Reference" (Harshaw 1984, 243–4), all the while acknowledging that historiography itself is a form of reshuffling, reforming, in short, mediating the past. This is not the kind of reference that attempts to derive authority from documentary data; instead it offers extratextual documents as traces of the past.

Just as each of these four kinds of reference borders on or overlaps with others in these historiographic metafictional "routes of reference," so this textualized extratextual reference suggests a fifth part of the network, one which I have called hermeneutic. In Peter Ackroyd's postmodernist detective novel, *Hawksmoor*, the reader gradually catches on that the recurring sign "M SE M" (which marks the sight of some of the novel's action) omits the U – the "you" – need to make sense of the plot. This points overtly to why a static model of reference must be avoided, for we cannot ignore the role of the hermeneutic process of reading: historiographic metafiction does not just refer in textual (that is, product) ways (intra-, inter-, auto-, extra-). The postmodernist's text's self-conscious return to performative process and to the entirety of the enunciative act demands that the reader, the *you*, not be left out, even in dealing with the question of reference.

There is a kind of reference, then, to the discursive situation of the reader that moves the study of the referent away from the level of individual words and names to that of discourse. Inge Crosman defines the referent of fiction as "a floating, conceptual construct that gradually emerges during the reading process" (1983, 96). This is not quite what I mean by hermeneutic reference, though the two concepts are related. What I mean is something closer to Kendall Walton's (1978) discussion of the interaction of the fictive world with the real world of the reader. Words hook onto the world, at one level, at least, through the reader, and this would be as true of historiography as of fiction. It is at this level that the ideological critique, the demystifying of the "natural" and the "given" can operate. In this way historiographic metafiction avoids the "cul-de-sac of self-reference" (Sukenick 1985, 77), the danger of becoming a "self-voiding narrative" (Doležel 1986). Any ideologically radical possibility for change – in a Brechtian sense – would be tied up directly with this kind of hermeneutic reference.

These five kinds of referentiality all demand to be considered by historiographic metafiction's complexity of representation. The cross-processing within this kind of model involves overlap and overdetermination, a "route" more than a static model of reference. What we witness is a self-conscious problematization of what has always been a truism of the novel as a genre: it has always "exemplified an uneasy cohabitation between the empirical and the fictional impulses" (Newman 1985, 138). The self-conscious problematizing of the question of reference in philosophy, linguistics, semiotics, historiography, literary theory, and fiction is part of a contemporaneous realization that many things we once took for granted as "natural" and common-sensical (like the word/world relationship) must be scrutinized very carefully. Recently the serious questioning of epistemology – by writers like Hindess (1977) and Hindess and Hirst (1977) – has meant that "no special class of statements about how language and reality are linked is itself privileged, immune from revision, hence suitable to serve as the sort of guaranteeing metalanguage epistemology classically has sought" (J. O. Thompson 1981, 92). Postmodern discourses both install and then contest our traditional guarantees of knowledge, by revealing their gaps or circularities. They suggest no privileged access to reality. The real exists (and existed), but our understanding of it is always conditioned by discourses, by our different ways of talking about it.

We are emerging from a resolutely formalist age – which some call modernism. Its questioning of and simultaneous yearning for some order which would have a privileged explanatory power is exactly what has forced *post*modernism to try to move beyond this "referential agnosticism" (Norris 1985, 69). Its attempts to do so are always self-reflexive; they may be mutually contradictory at times; they may raise more questions than they answer. But that is the only way they can approach what Thomas Pynchon once called "pulsing Stelliferous Meaning."

10

SUBJECT IN/OF/TO HISTORY
AND HIS STORY

Continuous history is the indispensable correlative of the founding
function of the subject: the guarantee that everything that has eluded
him may be restored to him; the certainty that time will disperse
nothing without restoring it in a reconstituted unity; the promise that
one day the subject – in the form of historical consciousness – will once
again be able to appropriate, to bring back under his sway, all those
things that are kept at a distance by difference, and find in them what
might be called his abode. Making historical analysis the discourse of
the continuous and making human consciousness the original subject
of all historical development and all action are two sides of the same
system of thought. *Michel Foucault*

For the last twenty years, perhaps since the advent of structuralism's
rejection of the "pretensions of the Cartesian . . . *cogito*" (Jameson
1972, 135), the topic of "man as the concrete universal," to use Said's term
(1975a, 287), has hovered over our various intellectual enterprises, descend-
ing now and again to become the basis of some attack or other on the
humanist tradition. Theorists of all political propensities have recently
pointed out the trendiness of the subject of the "subject" in both criticism
and literature. Jameson calls the fragmentation and death of the subject a
"fashionable theme" of contemporary theory, marking the "end of the
autonomous bourgeois monad or ego or individual" (1984a, 63). Gerald
Graff had earlier defined the essence of the avant-garde aesthetic in terms of
"a refusal of the entire bourgeois view of reality, epitomized by the
subject-object paradigm of rationalist epistemology" (1975, 321). The coincidence of the concerns of criticism and art – their shared focus on the
ideological and epistemological nature of the human subject – marks
another of those points of intersection that might define a postmodernist
poetics. More specifically, this is a point of challenge to any aesthetic theory

or practice that either assumes a secure, confident knowledge of the subject or elides the subject completely. And both theory and art effect this challenge through their awareness of the need to situate or contextualize the discussion of subjectivity carried on by any discursive activity (including their own) within the framework of both history and ideology.

The philosophical, "archaeological," and psychoanalytic de-centering of the concept of the subject has been led by Derrida, Foucault, Lacan, among others. To decenter is not to deny, however. Postmodernism does not, as Terry Eagleton asserts, mistake "the disintegration of certain traditional ideologies of the subject for the subject's final disappearance" (1985, 70). Its historicizing of the subject and of its customary (centering) anchors radically problematizes the entire notion of subjectivity, pointing directly to its dramatized contradictions. Cindy Sherman's photographs of herself expose the fiction of selfhood underlying both photography's representation of reality and its status as art. The humanist notion of the unitary and autonomous subject is both installed (in each individual photo) and then subverted (by its context within an entire discontinuous series) (see Crimp 1980, 99). As Derrida insists: "The subject is absolutely indispensable. I don't destroy the subject; I situate it" (in Macksey and Donato 1970, 1972, 271). And to situate it, as postmodernism teaches, is to recognize differences – of race, gender, class, sexual orientation, and so on. To situate is also both to acknowledge the ideology of the subject and to suggest alternative notions of subjectivity (Huyssen 1986, 213).

Luce Irigaray has pointed out that theories of the subject always seem to turn out to be theories of the masculine (1974, 165). But they also tend to be theories of bourgeois, white, individual, western "Man" too. This is what really defines the so-called universal and timeless humanist subject. In this context, neither man nor woman is an autonomous, coherent free agent; neither can be separated from cultural systems or what Kaja Silverman calls "historically circumscribed signifying operations" (1983, 129) which prove to have priority over the subject. Human reality, for both sexes, is a construct. Obviously such a view is bound to pose problems for traditional humanist notions of the stability of the self and of the equation of the self with consciousness. To reinsert the subject into the framework of its *parole* and its signifying activities (both conscious and unconscious) within an historical and social context is to begin a force a redefinition not only of the subject but of history as well.

When Michel Foucault and others introduced a kind of historical analysis based on categories of discontinuity and difference, the cry went up that this was a murdering of history, but, as Foucault saw it later:

> one must not be deceived: what is being bewailed with such vehemence is not the disappearance of history, but the eclipse of that form of history that was secretly, but entirely related to the synthetic activity of the subject; what is being bewailed is the "development" (*devenir*) that was to provide the sovereignty of the consciousness

with a safer, less exposed shelter than myths, kinship systems, languages, sexuality, or desire.

(1972, 14)

What contemporary self-reflexive, discontinuous, and often difficult historiographic metafiction does is work to subvert this very view of history that much poststructualist thought is also contesting. And, not surprisingly, it has been received with much the same vehement response from those for whom the novel too – like history – represents and presents a coherent and motivated inscription of a unifed subjectivity.

However, many of these postmodern novels (*The White Hotel*, *The French Lieutenant's Woman*, *Blackout*, among others) are contestatory on yet another level: they overtly pose questions about subjectivity that involve the issues of sexuality and sexual identity and of the representation of women. And they do so in political terms. The kind of poststructuralist feminist analysis that Teresa de Lauretis (1984) and Kaja Silverman (1983) bring to film is exactly what is needed to study this kind of fiction. Like modern films, these novels have reformulated the questions of the enunciation (or the contextualized production and reception of texts); therefore, they should help us to re-examine notions of address and of "subject processes" (de Lauretis 1984, 28) in the same way that film has provoked its theorists. Surely *The White Hotel* is as much about the impossibility of a "fixed subject-vision" and the "uncertainty of vision" as is Oshima's *In the Realm of the Senses*. How we read is not unrelated to how we see – at least from the point of view of subjectivity.

II

> The erratic and devious presence of the unconscious, without which the position of the subject cannot be understood, insists on heterogeneity and contradictions within the subject itself. Therefore it provides the most rigorous criticism of the presupposition of a consistent, fully finished subject, and of the social sciences that base themselves on such a presupposition.   *Rosalind Coward and John Ellis*

Perhaps the most obvious point at which to begin to study that overlap of viewing and reading is with the analogy between the "look" or eye of the camera and point of view in the novel, since the latter has traditionally been the guarantee of subjectivity in narrative (D.Carroll 1982). In historiographic metafiction, as with metafiction in general, such is not the case. Its subversion of the stability of point of view, the inheritance of modernist experiments (Faulkner, Woolf, Joyce), takes two major forms. On the one hand, we find overt, deliberately manipulative narrators; on the other, no one single perspective but myriad voices, often not completely localizable in the textual universe. In both cases, the inscription of subjectivity is problematized, though in very different ways. Both are movements away from the French New Novel's "'splendid anonymity' . . . within a lottery of constantly shifting pronouns" (Jardine 1982, 57), although they are equally effective ways of contesting the traditional realist novel's inscription of the subject. In place of anonymity, we find over-assertive and problematizing subjectivity, on the one hand, and, on the other, a pluralizing multivalency of points of view. As we shall see shortly, in *The White Hotel*, the female protagonist is not fully or consistently a traditional Jamesian centre of consciousness with whom the reader can identify as subject. Nor does she seem to be the reflection of any authorial subjectivity upon which she might be based. Instead she is presented as the "read" subject of her own and of others' interpretations and inscriptions of her. She is literally the female product of readings.

It is this female subject who is addressed as both product and viewer, as spectacle and spectator, in de Lauretis's analysis of film as well. Although left implicit, feminist reading (it is suggested) as well as feminist viewing, can be turned into performance rather than representation (1984, 36); both activities can be the site of productive relations, of the engagement of subjectivity in meaning and values (51). In both, the problems of identification, of the relation of subjectivity to the representation of sexual difference, and of the positions available to women form part of the conditions of meaning-production (75). In both reading and viewing, we are already socially constituted as women and men (121), not just in the sense of being simply female or male, but in the sense of being each armed with a semiotic history (personal and social), a series of previous identifications by which we have been en-gendered (145). Heath's theory of the "gaze" of the camera's eye (137–9) has its analogy in the novelistic texts, as de Lauretis's work on narrativity could be seen to imply. She suggests that the female (reader) spectator identifies with both the subject and the object of the "gaze" at the same time. Her own conclusion suggests the broader implications of her theory:

> This, I think, is in fact the operation by which narrative and cinema solicit the spectators' consent and seduce women into femininity: by a double identification, a surplus of pleasure produced by the spectators themselves for cinema and for society's profit.
>
> (1984, 143)

Is this how *The White Hotel* "hails" (in an Althusserian sense) its female reader? This is a concern to which I shall return shortly, for it is directly involved in the putting into question of both history and subjectivity by historiographic metafiction.

Often those two types of metafictional narration – the resolutely singular and disconcertingly plural – come together, as in Salman Rushdie's *Midnight's Children* and, as a result, both the male subject and history are simultaneously decentered, along with the narrative itself. Despite the presence of a single, insistent, controlling narrator – a writer who knows he both reports and creates public and private history – the (male) center of this novel is constantly displaced and dispersed. The search for unity (narrative, historical, subjective) is constantly frustrated. Saleem Sinai would like to reduce history to autobiography, to reduce India to his own consciousness, but the fact that he never can or will is underlined by the constant presence of *Tristram Shandy* as a parodic intertext: contingency shall rule. The autobiographical memoir has a long history in fiction as a form of asserting the primacy of individual experience (Watt 1957), but this novel, by trying to make that individual experience the source of public history as well, subverts both this traditional inscription of male subjectivity and, at the same time, the traditional notion of history as non-contradictory continuity.

In fact, the implications of *Midnight's Children*'s presentation of history and history writing can best be glossed by Foucault's description of Nietzsche's "effective" history. Saleem learns that the

> forces operating in history are not contolled by destiny or regulative mechanisms, but respond to haphazard conflicts. They do not manifest the successive forms of a primordial intention and their attraction is not that of a conclusion, for they always appear through the singular randomness of events.
>
> (Foucault 1977, 154–5)

The incredible plethora of detail, both fictive and historical, in Saleem's account of the man and nation both born at midnight on August 15, 1947 offers a new view of the notions of historical events and their ordering:

> The world we know is not this ultimately simple configuration where events are reduced to accentuate their essential traits, their final meaning, or their initial and final value. On the contrary, it is a profusion of entangled events. If it appears as a "marvelous motley, profound and totally meaningful," this is because it began and continues its secret existence through a "host of errors and phantasms."
>
> (1977, 155)

Faced with the hermeneutic problem of dealing with Saleem's fragments of memories (just as he must deal with the many voices of the Midnight's Children's Conference, the "essence of multiplicity"), readers of either sex might well feel driven to acknowledge that perhaps we *do* want narrators, like historians, "to confirm our belief that the present rests upon profound intentions and immutable necessities" (155). What Saleem's account offers instead, however, is what Foucault calls the "true historical sense," the one that "confirms our existence among countless lost events, without a landmark or a point of reference" (155). Despite his insistent, male narrative voice, Saleem offers no final point of reference; all he affirms is personal and historical "knowledge as perspective" (156), in Foucault's terms. And he does so to the insistent, controlling female narratee, Padma, whose desire he cannot satisfy.

Instead of satisfaction, he offers her sublimation; instead of History, he offers Padma his histories. By overtly "producing" these histories for her, Saleem subverts both the causality and continuity of what is traditionally conceived of as patriarchal History. Similarly he is forced to challenge the limitations of the linearity and continuity of his own tale by trying to satisfy at least Padma's narrative demands. He is reduced to using multiple plots, sometimes carried on in alternate paragraphs, sometimes within interrupting parentheses. Finally he is driven to exclaim: "Interruptions, nothing but interruptions! The different parts of my somewhat complicated life refuse, with a wholly unreasonable obstinacy, to stay neatly in their separate compartments" (1981, 187). And part of the responsibility for these textual ruptures lies with his female listener. Saleem begins writing with the assumption that autobiography, like fiction, allows for a "natural unfolding" of a tale. For Padma and for the reader, however, his attempts to suggest multiplicity and simultaneity through syntax ("While" this was happening, so was . . .), combined with the numerous intertextual echoes provoked by each page of the narration, allow no coherence; no unity is permitted her or us.

But it is not just history and narrative that are denied their traditional humanist structures and functions: the unified male writing subject is not only decentered and radically split, but is actually splitting. Like Foucaldian archaeology which "shortens its vision to those things nearest to it – the body, the nervous system, nutrition, digestion, and energies" (Foucault 1977, 155), the "chutnification of history" in *Midnight's Children* turns on the actual body of the male subject, a body that, like his feminized country (his "subcontinental twin sister" – 1981, 385), cannot remain whole and is constantly splitting. Saleem loses part of a finger and a piece of his scalp and hair; his skin begins to crack, like the land of India during periods of drought. But the real analogy is to India as a nation founded in 1947 and subsequently split. The ideal may well be wholeness, as Saleem argues, wholeness on every level – political, historical, physical, narrative:

> And now I, Saleem Sinai, intend briefly to endow myself-then with the benefits of hindsight; destroying the unities and conventions of fine writing, I make him cognizant of what was to come, purely so that he can be permitted to think the following thoughts: "O eternal opposition of inside and outside! Because a human being, inside himself, is anything but a whole, anything but homogeneous; all kinds of everywhichthing are jumbled up inside him, and he is one person one minute and another the next. The body, on the other hand, is homogeneous as anything. . . . It is important to preserve this wholeness."
>
> (1981, 236–7)

But that wholeness cannot be attained, much less preserved. Saleem's subjectivity can only be multiple, and even that is tied to the multiplicity of India, the nation born with him and subsequently split to create Pakistan:

> in a country where the truth is what it is instructed to be, reality quite literally ceases to exist, so that everything becomes possible except what we are told is the case; and maybe this was the difference between my Indian childhood and Pakistani adolescence – that in the first I was beset by an infinity of alternative realities, while

in the second I was adrift, disoriented, amid an equally infinite number of falsenesses, unrealities and lies.

(1981, 326)

A head injury empties Saleem, however, of memory and therefore of this multiple subjectivity. With this erasure of multiplicity comes, paradoxically, a doubling of narration, for Saleem the narrator (to whom memory has been restored) can only refer to this unified, whole, single (but memoryless) subject as "I, he" in a manner reminiscent of Benveniste's (1971) insights into the linguistic foundations of subjectivity. It is in this particular state, split off from memory and history, that Saleem becomes a citizen of Pakistan, the country that itself was physically split at that historical moment:

In those days, the country's East and West Wings were separated by the unbridgeable land-mass of India; but past and present, too, are divided by an unbridgeable gulf. Religion was the glue of Pakistan, holding the halves together; *just as consciousness, the awareness of oneself as a homogeneous entity in time, a blend of past and present, is the glue of personality, holding together our then and our now.*

(1981, 351, italics mine)

Losing this historical and personal consciousness, Saleem can be referred to only as "I, he" – at least until a snake bite jolts him into a different "unity" (364) that is paradoxically a multiplicity. At this point he is "rejoined to the past" by the act of narrating the tales of his life, the tales we too have been reading, the ones he calls "the pouring-out of what-was-inside-me" (383).

In the end, despite all his efforts to make his story into history, to make the multiple single, he is forced to acknowledge that the inverse has come to pass:

I am the sum total of everything that went before me, of all I have been seen done, of everything done-to-me. I am everyone everything whose being-in-the-world affected was affected by mine. I am anything that happens after I've gone which would not have happened if I had not come. Nor am I particularly exceptional in this matter; each "I," every one of the now-six-hundred-million-plus of us, contains a similar multitude.

(1981, 383)

This does not deny subjectivity; but it does challenge the traditional notion of its unity and its function. The totalizing power of narrative, of history, and of our notions of the subject is subverted by the end of this novel, told by "a broken creature spilling pieces of itself into the street, because I have been so-many too-many persons, life unlike syntax allows one more than three" (463).

As the "I" of the narrative act, Saleem invokes the masculine Cartesian subject, attempting to postulate himself as the origin of meaning – both public and private. But he speaks in a discursive context, and he knows it, or at least comes to know it in the course of the telling and writing of his autobio-graphical/fictional/historical narrative. This kind of historiographic metafic-tion contests the *cogito* in ways that recall the strategies of a Lacan or a

Foucault. Just as the French language allowed the New New Novel to make the leap from "je" to "jeux," so the English language enables the transition from "I" to "eye" in a way that critics of the cinema like de Lauretis, Silverman, and other writers for journals like *Screen* can exploit to great advantage in their analyses of cinematic modes of subjectivity. What feminist film theory offers in addition, however, is a concept of the enunciative apparati of visual representation that helps us approach an understanding of *gendered* subjectivity. Citing Freud's masculine privileging of the visual, Jane Gallop has asserted: *"Sexual difference takes its decisive significance from a sighting"* (1982, 27). The inscription of female subjectivity by what is argued to be the masculine gaze of the camera could well be compared to the inscription of that same femininity in historiographic metafictions about women that are written by men. The feminist critique of patrimony and the postmodernist critique of representation (in all art forms) can be seen to intersect at the point of the issue of gender and sexual difference (Owens 1983, 59; 61–2). Both feminist poststructuralist theory and postmodernist fiction address and radically problematize the same issues. For example both novels like *The White Hotel* and theoretical studies like those of de Lauretis, Silverman, or Catherine Belsey treat women as particularly contradictory subjects. In the theory's terms, women "participate both in the liberal humanist discourse of freedom, self-determination and rationality and at the same time in the specifically feminine discourse offered by society of submission, relative inadequacy and irrational intuition" (Belsey 1980, 65). Both theory and fiction here imply the positing of what Alice Jardine calls *"gynesis"*: "the putting into discourse of 'woman' as that process beyond the Cartesian Subject, the Dialectics of Representation, or Man's Truth" (58).

In the practice and theory of the visual arts too today, the postmodern is defined as that art which works to "undermine the notions of the self-sufficient art object and the concommitant transcendental artistic subject that is outside of any social, political or sexual history" (M. Lewis 1984, 66). As in literary theory and fiction, here too there is "a sense of informed and avowed radical critique of both 'mastery' and 'universal truths'" (67) through the study of sexual difference, through the demonstration within art itself of how meaning and sexual identity are fixed through and by representation, and are therefore inherently unstable. There are many who feel that all of our cultural forms today contribute to what film theorists see as the contesting of the voyeuristic masculine gaze of patriarchal society that idealizes and fetishizes woman. Certainly fiction does. In order to investigate this ideological construction of subjectivity, I choose a postmodern novel whose controversial reception has perhaps signalled its problematic nature: D. M. Thomas's *The White Hotel*. I select this, not as a good or bad novel, but as one which many, if not most, readers have found upsetting. The reasons given are numerous: its sado-masochistic sexuality, its tampering with history, its plagiarism of the documents of history (see Letters to the Editor, *The Times Literary Supplement*, from March 26, 1982, to April 30, 1982). I suspect, however, that all these responses are, to some extent, displacements, for this is in some ways a profoundly anti-humanistic novel that problematizes the same issues as poststructuralist theory, and, not surprisingly, it has been received with the same defensive reactions. Its metafictional aspects make evident the illusory nature of any narrative that pretends to transparency, to concealing the "apparatuses of enunciation" (Silverman 1983, 215). It profoundly disturbs and disperses the notion of the individual, coherent subject and its relation to history, to social formation, and even to its own unconscious. It is the presence of "Freud" as a character in the novel that underlines the specifically male inscription of subjectivity by psychoanalysis. But this text never resolves any of the issues it raises: it offers no totalizing solution because it both cannot and will not. All it can do is contextualize and confront the contradictions of history, both public and private.

Both *The White Hotel* and much feminist theory today confront the relation of non-coincidence between the discursive construct of "woman" and the historical subjects called "women" (de Lauretis 1984, 5). Both expose this as a culturally determined relationship, intimately related to cultural notions of femininity. And both suggest that the representation of woman must now be destabilized and altered. Where a critic like de Lauretis studies how narrative works to engender the subject in the movement of its discourse, how it defines positions of meaning, identification, and desire (10), the novel *enacts* that engendering, even unto the horrible death of its protagonist. Just as it was a woman – albeit a victim – who lived to be the sole surviving witness to the massacre of Babi Yar and whose voice is "borrowed" by the narrator of the novel, so women are no longer to be "absented" from history and cultural process, as de Lauretis laments that they have been (13).

The White Hotel is a novel which both enacts and thematizes one of the issues that most concerns de Lauretis: that of the woman as spectacle, of woman as the result of the inscriptions of her subjectivity by herself and by others. This is a novel about how we produce meaning in fiction and in history. Its multiple and often contradictory forms and points of view (first-person poem, third-person expansion of it in prose, "Freudian" case history, third-person limited narration, first-person epistolary form used by many characters) call attention to the impossibility of totalizing narrative structures in a more overt way than did the resolutely insistent, but inadequately ordering, male voice of Saleem Sinai, but the challenge to the illusion of unity on all levels remains just as potent: the narrative's dispersion becomes the objective correlative of the decentering of the female (as well as male) subject and of history. The metafictional stress on writing, reading, and interpreting emphasizes the fact that the gendered subject is where meanings are formed, even though meanings are what constitute the subject. How we produce (socially established) meanings in history is here an important issue. Like poststructuralist feminist theory, this novel addresses the need to understand sociality and subjectivity as implicated in the production and reproduction of meaning, value and ideology. It is signifying processes that create "subject positions": the subject is "continually engaged, represented, and inscribed in ideology" (de Lauretis 1984, 37) – be it a male or female subject.

In short, *The White Hotel* is, like much current theory, a contestation of many of the bases of humanistic discourse. Here Man is literally not the individual source of meaning or action: *woman* is, on one level, and *collective history* is, on another. And the various narrative inscriptions of woman as subject are anything but unified and coherent. Human experience is no longer the guarantee of meaning, especially if it is taken outside of the context of the history of women. The empirical basis of the humanist and positivist concepts of knowledge – trust in observation and experiment – is called into question through the novel's challenge to "Freud"'s psycho-analytic reading of the protagonist's ailments: the cause of her pain is not to be found in her individual (but universalizable) psychic past as a human, but rather in her collective (though individually suffered) future as a Jew at a certain moment in history.

The White Hotel creates a curious doubling effect as narrative: it manages to offer both a vivid and concrete rendering of the world of a Jamesian center of consciousness (witness the power of the Babi Yar scene) and a subversion of it through its multiple points of view. The reader is both offered and refused a comfortable position "from which the text is most 'obviously' intelligible, the position of a transcendent subject addressed by an autonomous and authoritative author" (Belsey 1980, 55). The overt use of multiple intertexts – Freud's case histories, *Beyond the Pleasure Principle* (1920), Anatoli Kuz-netsov's *Babi Yar* (1966, 1967), the operas *Don Giovanni* and *Eugene Onegin* – suggests a textualized refusal to "express" either singular subjectivity or single meaning. As Said has claimed, the image of writing has changed from one of unique inscribing to one of parallel script (1983, 139). What much recent theory has argued, this novel (as typical of much historiographic metafiction) has put into action: through its intertextuality, it suggests that knowledge is discursively produced.

Even the eye-witness account of Babi Yar by Dina Pronicheva is offered in a slightly altered version, re-fictionalized once again as the protagonist's experience: *re*-fictionalized, because Kuznetsov's narrative account of it is already twice removed from any historical reality. It is his version of her later narrativization of her experience. In neither case, however, is there any guarantee outside of discourse – or, at least, not any more. The narrative unity within each section of the novel is disrupted by the start of another section with a different point of view. At any given moment, the text seems hypothetical, ready to accept the impossibility of its own coherence and completion; the protagonist's identity, likewise. Althusser has argued that bourgeois ideology stresses the fixed identity of the individual subject, and here Freudian determinism seems to be meant to stand for that bourgeois – and male – ideology. Its final subverting moves *The White Hotel* into a distinctly poststructualist frame of reference where the subject is viewed as a process and as the site of contradictions.

III

> Language is . . . the possibility of subjectivity because it always
> contains the linguistic forms appropriate to the expression of
> subjectivity, and discourse provokes the emergence of subjectivity
> because it consists of discrete instances.   *Emile Benveniste*

What contemporary theory and fiction have both undergone (or instigated) is what I earlier called the revenge of *parole*: speech-act theory, pragmatics, discourse analysis, and other formalizations on the level of theory are matched by historiographic metafiction's stress on the enunciation, on the subject's use of language and the multiple contexts in which that use situates itself. Basing her theory on that of Benveniste, Kaja Silverman claims that we cannot isolate language from discourse or discourse from subjectivity. In his much-quoted paper on "Subjectivity in Language," Benveniste (1971) argued the necessity of taking into account *parole*, concrete discursive situations, in determining what personal pronouns like "I" and "you" mean. Postmodern novels like Puig's *Kiss of the Spider Woman* point to the problematic nature of these designations of speaker and listener (I/you) as revealed through the dialogue format in which one of the male characters refers to himself in the third person and as female. Molina claims: "I can't talk about myself like a man because I don't feel like one" (Puig 1978, 1979, 60). Benveniste articulated the consequence of this enunciative act of self-identification through language in terms of a definition of subjectivity as the "capacity of the speaker to posit himself as 'subject'" (1971, 224). In other words, subjectivity is a fundamental property of language: "It is in and through language that man constitutes himself as a *subject*, because language alone establishes the concept of 'ego' in reality, in *its* reality" (224). This view of subjectivity has immense consequences not only for any general theory of the subject but also for any attempts to inscribe or interpret that subject in literature or criticism: "there is no other objective testimony to the identity of the subject except that which he himself thus gives about himself" (226). While the Benvenistian insight that the subject is constituted in language could obviously lead to an aestheticist privileging of language *per se*, in postmodern theory and practice it is language as *discourse* that is foregrounded, as we shall see in more detail in the next chapter.

This theory is the basis of Kaja Silverman's expansion of Benveniste's concepts of the speaking subject and of the subject of speech. To these she adds a third element – the spoken subject. First of all, the speaking subject is itself not as unproblematic an entity as it may appear (as is evident in *Midnight's Children*). If the speaking subject is constituted in and by language, s/he cannot be totally autonomous and in control of her or his own subjectivity, for discourse is constrained by the rules of the language and open to multiple connotations of anonymous cultural codes (Silverman 1983, 50). *The White Hotel*'s inscriptions of its female protagonist make this abundantly clear. What the novel also underlines is the role of the unconscious for each speaking subject, a role which splits the subject in a radical way. In "Language and Freudian Theory," Benveniste argued that the Freudian model of the divided subject (conscious/unconscious) and its discourse (manifest/latent) means that each split part must take its meaning from the whole of the signifying system (1971, 67–8). Silverman merges these insights with those of the Lacanian model to argue the relational nature of subjectivity – both male and female – as induced by discourse (1983, 52).

This speaking subject as the agency of discourse is distinguished from the subject of speech, the "I" of the discourse itself which acts as the anchor for the subjectivity of that speaking subject. To these two Benvenistian entities, Silverman adds that of the spoken subject: "the subject who is constituted through identification with the subject of the speech, novel, or film" (47). This is the subject produced *through* discourse. At various points in *The White Hotel*, this is Lisa, the protagonist, literally produced through her own and others' discourses; it is also the reader. But, like the viewer of film in Silverman's theory, this reader too has no stable continuous subjectivity (or even gender), but rather one that is "activated intermittently, within discourse" (48). The entire enunciative situation is self-consciously brought to our attention and the awareness of the discursive exchange in action is what engages the reader and speaks her/him as subject (48), though not a subject in the usual stable and continuous humanist sense of the term. Because of the confusion of diverse "hailings," the only subject that the reader can recognize is a problematized and doubly gendered one, for Lisa is inscribed both by herself and by "Freud."

As in film, it is more than the producer and the text that are implicated in signifying practices: the reader, like the spectator, can have no other identity than as subject of those discursive practices (de Lauretis 1984, 79), than as "the *subject in (and of) ideology*" (Belsey 1980, 57). *The White Hotel* can be seen as a novel that overtly challenges both the realist novel's representation of the world of consistent subjects who offer an origin of meaning and action and also its presentation of a reader position from which the text is easily understandable (since the reader too is thus reinforced as a coherent source of shared meaning). There is no closed, coherent, non-contradictory world or subjectivity either inside or outside the novel. The multiple points of view prevent any totalizing concept of the protagonist's subjectivity, and simultaneously prevent the reader from finding or taking any one subject position from which to make the novel coherent. Asked to confront and not evade contradictions, the reader cannot but feel ill at ease and disturbed. As spoken subject s/he finds no anchor in discourse for her/his own (gendered) subjectivity through identification.

Benveniste's insights into the discontinuous nature of the linguistic subject have many similarities with the Lacanian notion of the object as a function within a symbolic order, as structured by language as difference, instead of as a unified autonomous consciousness. Lacan's merging of Freudian and structuralist models leads to a focus that is important for postmodernism, a focus on the subject *in process* and on its relation to ideological formations (see Coward and Ellis 1977, 93–100). But, since Benveniste's model of the subject (which has no existence outside the discursive moments in which it emerges) avoids any transcendent positioning of the unconscious and any valorizing of the (despite protestations to the contrary) unavoidably male Lacanian phallus, it may be, in a sense, more flexible and less potentially totalized a view of subjectivity than Lacan's for the purposes of analysis of the gendered subject in literature, as in film. My main reason, though, for not using a Lacanian model here is that so much fine feminist analysis already exists that does so and does so at much greater length than I can here (see Mulvey 1975; Gallop 1982; J. Mitchell 1974; J. Mitchell and Rose 1982; Kuhn 1982).

I would, therefore, agree with Silverman that Benveniste's

> discontinuous subject may depend for its emergence upon already defined discursive positions, but it has the capacity to occupy multiple and even contradictory sites. This descriptive model thus enables us to understand the subject in more culturally and historically specific ways than that provided by Lacan – i.e. in terms of a range of discursive positions available at a given time, which reflect all sorts of economic, political, sexual, artistic, and other determinants, instead of in terms of a monolithic symbolic order.
>
> (1983, 199)

It is these areas of political, artistic, and especially sexual determination that both poststructuralist feminist theory and postmodernist metafiction address, and both have worked to relocate the problematic of the subject within language, within discourse. The fiction enacts what the theory calls for. In David Carroll's terms,

> A truly radical questioning of the subject, and the resulting emergence of processes, areas of theory and practice, and strategies not totally dependent on the subject can only be realized by a repeated *working through* and undermining of the premises on which the subject depends and which depend on it.
>
> (1982, 26)

Historiographic metafiction, like *The White Hotel*, is just such a "working through" of these premises. It recognizes that even its own self-reflexivity does not eliminate the problems of subjectivity; indeed, if anything, it foregrounds them.

IV

> it is the subject itself, as an individual or collectivity (type) that depends on teleological views of history for its support. The derivation of the individual subject itself . . . is problematical when history is not accepted in its "domesticated," rational, metaphysical form as the optimistic resolution of contradictions: as either History or Rhetoric.
> *David Carroll*

The White Hotel presents the process of the constitution of its protagonist, Lisa, as a *gendered* subject, subject to history. What "engenders" Lisa is a series of discourses. Some of these deliberately inscribe her as a unified, coherent subject: "Freud"'s overtly male naming and creation of Frau Anna G., in his case history, as the female neurotic whose symptoms are rooted in her individual but universalizable past, and the third-person narrator's account that primarily uses Lisa as a center of consciousness in the last half of the novel. But along with (and often within) these totalizing discourses appear two others which suggest more contradictory and multiple ways to confer subjectivity. The first is her own series of self-inscriptions: the first-person poetic "Don Giovanni" section; the third-person expansion, "The Gastein Journal" (requested by "Freud"), in which she changes from the subject to the object of her own inscription; and her autobiographical letter to "Freud" which contradicts both his case history and information she herself had earlier offered as "facts" to enable his interpretations.

The second disrupting set of discourses is constituted by the many intertextual contexts overtly addressed by the text, all of which contribute on the surface to the thematic overdetermination of the structuring matrix of both the Freudian Eros/Thanatos opposition and the concept of repetition compulsion discussed within the novel itself. *Don Giovanni*, the opera score between whose staves Lisa copies her "obscene" poem for "Freud," is an opera about passion and death, also involving a Donna (Frau) Anna; it too has a literally hellish end, followed by a moralizing finale after the death of the protagonist. The opera that Lisa sings, *Eugene Onegin*, is equally about passion and death, and also about the *writing* of that passion and its consequences. Aside from these intertexts from art, however, there are others whose discursive nature is not as straightforward. The acknowledgment on the copyright page of Thomas's debt to Anatoli Kuznetsov's *Babi Yar* (1966, 1967) signals more than a borrowing of historical information. Kuznetsov's "documentary novel," with its stress on "authenticated facts and documents . . . not the slightest literary invention" (xv), insists constantly on the truth of its eye-witness reports: "none of this is fiction" (213). As we have seen, Thomas draws from Kuznetsov's retelling of Dina Pronicheva's account of her survival of Babi Yar. Although Kuznetsov insists that her story is "exactly as she told it, without adding anything" (63), he does not take into account the discursive context of her account (the 1946 Ukraine war crimes trial) or the fact that he (a male) has re-inscribed her (female) experience or that her narrativization (from memory) is already a distancing from anything resembling her real past experience. Certain scenes in section V of the novel are directly from *Babi Yar* but are never taken quite verbatim: the effect is that of reading a second translation of the same source. Compare Kuznetsov's "Suddenly an open car drove up carrying a tall, well-knit, elegant officer carrying a riding crop. At his side was an interpreter" (74) to Thomas's "Suddenly an open car drew up and in it was a tall, well-built, smartly turned-out officer with a riding crop in his hand. At his side was a Russian prisoner" (1981, 216).

What all of these intertexts do is contest any claim to the humanist notions of singularity and originality which the reader might want to ascribe to the novel. The Freudian intertexts (the case histories and *Beyond the Pleasure Principle*) function in much the same way. Lisa's multiple self-inscriptions and the extensive intertextual layerings all work to combat any fixed identity for either protagonist or text, and thus any fixed identification for the reader. Lisa creates herself as a gendered subject in the first two sections of the novel: her fantasies are female – as will be her mode of death (a scene *not* taken from Pronicheva's account of Babi Yar). Her sexual fantasies appear on the surface much more amenable to a (female) Kleinian analysis in terms of the mother and the breast than to a (male) Freudian one in terms of the phallus or the lack thereof. Indeed it is "Freud"'s inscription of her that provokes the autobiographical impulse in Lisa: she writes to "Freud" not only to clarify points he (unavoidably?) misinterprets, but also to leave the trace of her own inscription of her own subjectivity.

In combining these multiple and contradictory intertextual and (female) autobiographical discourses with those of third-person representations of coherent, unified subjectivity (one of which, "Freud"'s, is overtly male), the text problematizes the notions of both the subject of speech and the spoken subject – for both novel character and reader. In another (Barthesian) set of terms, *The White Hotel* turns out to be both readerly and writerly. The recourse to historical personages (Freud, Sachs, Ferenczi) and events (Babi Yar) and to the traditional, realist fiction staples of biographical and epistolary form is a comforting, readerly lure that is made into a writerly trap by the sheer multiplicity of points of view and interpretations offered of the validity and indeed of the reality of that comfortable familiarity. The metafictional self-consciousness about the hermeneutic power actually to constitute subjectivity finally points to the foregrounding of the text's "cultural inscription" (Silverman 1983, 246), to its awareness that its discursive situation cannot ignore, by definition, the cultural and historical nature of its own utterance. And such an awareness cannot but involve, therefore, the issue of the gender of the subject constituted.

Teresa de Lauretis argues that feminist theory and film should both work to "articulate the relations of the female subject to representation, meaning, and vision" (1984, 68). Historiographic metafiction also contexts the notion of a transcendental male subject as a unique and autonomous source of meaning. In *The White Hotel*, Lisa is both the subject of and subject to "Freud"'s male inscription of her as woman and as neurotic. Similarly she is the subject of and subject to history: the victim, the perverted, parodic object of desire in her death. But she does manage to constitute her own subjectivity too, through her own discourses. That these are contradictory and multiple may be a symptom of what de Lauretis calls "the 'impossible' place of female desire" (1984, 69). *The White Hotel*, in fact, enacts what de Lauretis argues to be true of all narrative and its relation to the subject: "subjectivity is engaged in the cogs of narrative and indeed constituted in the relation of narrative, meaning, and desire . . . the very work of narrativity is the engagement of the subject in certain positionalities of meaning and desire" (106). Both the subject of speech and the spoken subject in that novel actualize those very positionalities. We could even say that this puts into action within the fiction what de Lauretis calls for in narrative theory: the need "to envisage a materially, historically, and experientially constituted subject, a subject engendered, we might say, precisely by the process of its engagement in the narrative genres" (106). "Freud" and Lisa herself read and interpret differently, not just because one is the analyst and one, the analysand; they interpret differently because they are also already socially constituted as male and female – as are we as readers of *The White Hotel*. As de Lauretis argues regarding film, it is this engendering that determines what forms of identification are even possible for us, and the text's own contradictory inscriptions of subjectivity further complicate the issue.

Nevertheless, there is one moment in the novel where Lisa does seem to perceive her own identity as subject as whole and coherent. That this occurs in the third-person narrative may suggest that the unity is, at least in part, not of Lisa's making. But, in a very Proustian moment, just before the beginning of the Babi Yar section in which she will die, Lisa smells pine trees and her past floods back to her:

> For as she looked back through the clear space to her childhood, there was no blank wall, only an endless extent, like an avenue, in which she was still herself, Lisa. She was still there, even at the beginning of all things. And when she looked in the opposite direction, towards the unknown future, death, the endless extent beyond death, she was there still.
>
> (1981, 190)

The final words of the novel, at the end of the "endless extent beyond death," are: "She smelt the scent of a pine tree. She couldn't place it. . . . It troubled her in some mysterious way, yet also made her happy" (240). Perhaps the suggestion is that only in that "endless extent" is such a sense of subjectivity possible: in the time of the novel, something is about to intervene that will radically challenge Lisa's sense of her self, and that something is history.

In Braudel's words, history "makes men and fashions their destiny – anonymous history" (1980, 10). History makes women too in this same way. In both cases the individual subject is transcended. In *The White Hotel*, the realist novel's concept of the subject, both in history and in fiction, is openly contested. This is most evident if we compare the experience of the inscription of subjectivity and its relation to history in this novel to David Carroll's description of the previous century's novelistic practice:

> The individual or collective subject is clearly indicated as the vital force of history and the novel in this period, as the origin of its own life and actions, a unity (small and large) whose "life" is the matter of history and the novel. The "life" of this subject is

assumed to be a continuous, temporal process with a definite beginning and end, and the *récit* which narrates this "life" is necessarily one which attempts to be as continuous and uninterrupted as history or "life" itself is assumed to be.

(1982, 19–20)

Just as nineteenth-century assumptions about narrative *history* writing have been challenged, so novels themselves are now questioning the assumptions of the past about *novel* writing. Neither act of inscribing is seen as neutral, and both put the priority of the subject into question.

One way to look at the writing of history, they both suggest, is in terms of how memory defines and gives meaning to the subject. *The White Hotel* further complicates this relation of the subject to history through memory by inverting the function of the act of remembering: here it is clairvoyant foresight that is needed and that supplants memory as the power that explains. The irony of this inversion is emphasized by the central role of "Freud" in the novel, for, of course, memory plays a crucial part in the hermeneutics of psychoanalysis. The patient's memories form the basis upon which psychoanalytic practice constructs and reconstructs his (or, more commonly, her) personal history (Schafer 1980, 29–30), and the case history is the form of that reconstruction. What *The White Hotel* makes clear is what de Lauretis elaborates as the metahistorical nature of the case history: as a form of biography, it is a metadiscursive operation in which the analysand participates (de Lauretis 1984, 130), but whose structures are controlled by narrative itself, not by the analyst or the analysand (Schafer 1980, 53). Like Freud's Dora, "Freud"'s Lisa questions the account of the analyst, thereby denying narrative closure to the case history. The context of the novel as a whole (the sections both preceding and following "Freud"'s case history) also works to subvert any hermeneutic closure. What we learn as readers when we struggle with the contradictions of Lisa's inscribed subjectivity is that in interpreting the novel we too are engaged in a historically and socially constituted, gendered subjectivity, just as "Freud" (and indeed Freud) was.

The entire notion of a "case history" involves further complications. Its basic nature is private (one patient's case); but its import is intended to be universal or public (hence its publication as a "scientific" document). *The White Hotel* is both private and public in much the same way. Lisa's private, unique, but female fantasies are made to partake of those of the human unconscious (in Kleinian more than Freudian terms); her individual fate partakes of that of her race: "A quarter of a million white hotels in Babi Yar" (1981, 221). Given the limits of his knowledge, "Freud" did not and could not comprehend this public and historical dimension of Lisa's life. Like the historical Freud, the novel's "Freud" is working on *Beyond the Pleasure Principle* (1920) at the same time that he is treating Lisa. The mention of Lisa's feeling of being beset by a "'demon' of repetition" (1981, 117) is one of many intertextual echoes back to that work which help to explain both "Freud"'s and Freud's limits. Freud claims that neurotics give the impression of "being pursued by a malignant fate or possessed by some 'daemonic' power; but psychoanalysis has always taken the view that their fate is for the most part arranged by themselves and determined by early infantile influences" (1920, 21). Such a totalized and totalizing view of subjectivity leaves no room for Lisa's subjection to history. Caught in the confines of analytico-referential discourse (Reiss 1982), the male Freud can believe only that a "great deal of what might be described as the compulsion of destiny seems intelligible on a rational basis" (1920, 23).

A second reading of the novel, aided by hindsight that corresponds in part to Lisa's foresight, subverts any such faith in patriarchal rationality and in memory of the past as the key to understanding: it is knowledge of the future that is needed. "Freud"'s authority as interpreter is undermined in this novel; so, by implication, is Freud's. Or is it? On another level of the text, certain of Freud's concepts are actually enacted in fictional structures. Recurring images and situations suggest his concept of repetition compulsion, a concept which helped Freud form the theory that "the aim of all life is death" (1920, 38). If the normal drive of life is toward inertia, we are forced to re-assess, according to Freud (and the novel), the instincts of self-preservation, self-assertion, and mastery (39). The overdetermination of the textual matrices both of violent death and of sexual passion in *The White Hotel* recalls Freud's description of two kinds of instincts: "those which seek to lead what is living to death, and others, the sexual instincts, which are perpetually attempting and achieving a renewal of life" (46). He goes on to link the "Eros of poets," however, to sadistic tendencies through their common relation to the death instinct (54) in a way that perhaps casts some light on the final grotesque death of Lisa, her parodic and violent rape which at last explains all her earlier physical pains which "Freud" had sought to interpret through the reconstruction of a private past history. It is as much the historical limitations of the closure of the male Freud's system as the lack of correct information from the analysand that prevent "Freud" from correctly interpreting Lisa's story.

So "Freud" and Freud are both undermined and installed as figures of authority in the novel, just as the narration is both writerly and readerly. The subject is both a coherent, unified whole and a contradictory, dispersed multiplicity. *The White Hotel*'s concerns would seem to coincide with the researches of psychoanalysis, linguistics, and ethnology, according to Michel Foucault, in the decentering of the subject "in relation to the laws of his [and her] desire, the forms of his [and her] language, the rules of his [and her] action, or the games of his [and her] mythical or fabulous discourse" (1972, 13). I have deliberately and awkwardly added what the novel forces us to add: the *female* subject. Freud may have radically shifted consciousness from the center of humanist endeavor, but in practice, Freudian theories have been used to recuperate that subjectivity into a way of sustaining the social order, integrating the once "sick" patient (usually female) back into bourgeois society. *The White Hotel* enacts both the radical decentering and the recuperation: we come to see both the new role posited for the unconscious in the split subject and "Freud"'s and Freud's determinism, sexism, and bourgeois social values. This ambivalence recalls the terms of Teresa de Lauretis's evaluation of the contribution of Freud. She writes of his "valiant effort" (1984, 125) to tell "*her* story" and also of his limits, bound as he was within the plot structures of a patriarchal culture that always wants to make her story into his story (while eliding her from history).

Both *The White Hotel* and poststructuralist feminist theory work to continue that attempt to tell the story of female subjectivity, to confront both the Freudian challenge and recuperation. And both insist that this be done within the framework of a theory of the gendered subject. It has been argued that "because the analyst 'normalizes,' introducing the patient into an acceptable cultural position, he is within this framework necessarily 'male' – i.e. aligned with the father, the law, discursive power" (Silverman 1983, 132). In *The White Hotel* the presence of "Freud" as the embodiment of this male power structure does not, perhaps, in the end, represent the most disturbing infringement on female subjectivity. In Babi Yar, Lisa's experience merges with that of the sole survivor of the massacre (also a woman); she becomes an object, yet therein subject to historical forces beyond her control. The voyeuristic male soldiers reassert their patriarchal power over woman as object in perhaps a more immediately effective way than "Freud"'s equally patriarchal inscription of her as subject. But the two are not unrelated. As Silverman explains, the female subject in Freud's work is "'ideally' passive, masochistic and exhibitionistic to fit male aggression, sadism and voyeurism" (1983, 143–4). The power of history (as we have constituted it) may be anonymous, but it may not be as gender-innocent as it is traditionally conceived. It appears here to victimize women more than men: Lisa and "Freud"'s sisters die in the Holocaust, but Freud and "Freud" survive.

The White Hotel's curious double resonance (writerly/readerly; installing and subverting of both the subject and of authority) acts as a problematizing mechanism that continues right through to the last pages of the novel. The final section, "The Camp," appears to be set in that timeless realm that Freud ascribed to the unconscious mental processes (1920, 28) and its logic certainly seems to be that of dreams, ordered by condensation, displacement, and symbolization. This section is the perfect anti-closure closure. All the narrative ends are tied up: characters meet and sort out their difficulties (even the abandoned cat reappears). Yet it is fundamentally inexplicable by normal narrative logic, and its time (after Lisa's death?) and place (Israel?) cannot be fixed with any certainty. What this ending does is foreground the arbitrariness of traditional novelistic closure, while nevertheless allowing, even demanding, it.

It continues the ambivalence of doubling that prevents us from confirming our own subjectivity as coherent, non-contradictory spoken subjects. And this, perhaps, is the real reason why *The White Hotel* is such a disturbing novel. It is indeed sadistic and plagiaristic (or parodic); but it is also militantly anti-humanistic in its installation but simultaneous subversion of the female subject. Lisa's self-inscriptions and her final fate teach that woman – like man – is not an autonomous, coherent subject outside the dictates of society and history, just as the novel, as a whole, further contests the closure inherent in our humanist narratives – both fictional and historical. The corollary of historiographic metafiction's challenge to the realist assumption of the transitivity of language and of narrative as an unmediated way to represent history (or some reality that exists outside discourse) is its challenge to the traditional transparency of the first-person pronoun as a reflection of subjectivity and of the third-person pronoun as the guarantee of objectivity.

In *La Révolution du langage poétique* (1974), Julia Kristeva argued that the avant-garde texts of Lautréamont and Mallarmé revealed the subject in crisis. Postmodern fiction is the heir to that crisis, though its use of narrative does inevitably condition its potential radicality: the multiple and heterogeneous come directly up against the totalizing order of narrative, and so complicate and compromise the text in a way that the genre of poetry could almost avoid. Almost. Just as the art of Robert Rauschenberg and Jasper Johns challenges the traditional lyricism of abstract expressionism, so poetry like that of John Ashbery breaks down the conventional oppositions, such as the one between the lyrical and the ironic, in the articulation of subjectivity in literary language (Altieri 1986). Duane Michals's various photographic narrative image series both assert subjectivity (his own handwriting supplies a text which surrounds and comments upon each photo) and implicitly undercut it (by the use of the technology of the distancing and objectifying camera). These too are the paradoxes of postmodernism. But what novels like *The White Hotel* or *Midnight's Children* explicitly do is to undermine the ideological assumptions behind what has been accepted as universal and trans-historical in our culture: the humanist notion of Man as a coherent and continuous subject. Like poststructuralist feminist theory and recent historiography, this fiction investigates how, in all these discourses, the subject of history is the subject in history, subject to history and to his story.

11

DISCOURSE, POWER,
IDEOLOGY: HUMANISM AND
POSTMODERNISM

I

Figurations, usually of an ideological origin whether acknowledged or
not, will be found in history as well as in the history-like.
Frank Kermode

In the postmodern "history-like," the ideological and the aesthetic have
turned out to be inseparable. The self-implicating paradoxes of historiographic metafiction, for instance, prevent any temptation to see ideology as
that which only others fall prey to. What postmodern theory and practice
has taught is less that "truth" is illusory than that it is institutional, for we
always act and use language in the context of politico-discursive conditions
(Eagleton 1986, 168). Ideology both constructs and is constructed by the way
in which we live our role in the social totality (Coward and Ellis 1977, 67) and
by the way we represent that process in art. Its fate, however, is to appear as
natural, ordinary, common sense. Our consciousness of ourselves is
usually, therefore, uncriticized because it is familiar, obvious, transparent
(Althusser 1969, 144).

When these practical norms move from asserting how things are to
claiming how they ought to be, we can begin to see the connections between
ideology and existing relations of power. From the earlier Marxist notion of
ideology as false consciousness or as an illusory belief system, current
critical discourse has moved to a different notion of ideology as a general
process of production of meaning (R. Williams 1977, 55). In other words, all
social practice (including art) exists by and in ideology and, as such,
ideology comes to mean "the ways in which what we say and believe
connects with the power-structure and power-relations of the society we
live in" (Eagleton 1983, 14). Much of the impetus to this redefining of
ideology and to its newly important position in recent discussions of art has
come from a reaction against the liberal humanist suppression of the
historical, political, material, and social in the definition of art as eternal and

universal. Postmodern theory and practice have worked to contest this suppression, but in such a way that their implication in the underlying humanism value system cannot be ignored.

Historiographic metafiction foregrounds the problematic and complex relationship that has always existed between the formal concept of the text and the socio-political one of ideology (see Hamon 1982). It also demands a concept of ideology that is concerned equally with dominant and with oppositional strategies (Kress 1985, 29), for it incarnates the contradictions of their interaction. The romantic and modernist heritage of non-engagement insists that art is art and that ideological discourse has no place in the literary (see Graff 1983). Added to this historical separation is a suspicion of the artistic, general in much of the Anglo-American world, a view that sees art as trivial, insignificant, imaginative and therefore cut off from the social and historical realities of real life. This is a view implicitly shared by many commentators from both ends of the political spectrum, from neoconservative to Marxist.

Nevertheless, postmodernist art and theory have self-consciously acknowledged their ideological positioning in the world and they have been incited to do so, not only in reaction to that provocative accusation of triviality, but also by those previously silenced ex-centrics, both outside (post-colonial) and within (women, gays) our supposedly monolithic western culture. These are ex-centrics whose marginalization has taught them that artists indeed have inherent political status: think of that scene in Salman Rushdie's *Shame* in which the narrator attends a production of Georg Büchner's play, *Danton's Death*, in a largely empty theater: "Politics empties theatres in Old London town" (1983, 240). However, his three guests, visitors from Pakistan, love just being in a country where such plays could even be performed. They tell the story of the military censors at home preventing a production of *Julius Caesar* because it depicted the assassination of a Head of State – until a British diplomat was persuaded to play Caesar and Shakespeare's play could become a patriotic call for the overthrowing of imperialism.

It is the novel genre in particular that has become the battleground for much of this asserting – and contesting – of liberal humanist beliefs about the status and identity of art. Ian Watt's (already ideological) analysis of the rise of the English novel, for instance, has been further politicized lately by those readings of the genre in the light of class and, of course, gender. Lennard Davis has shown that the prevailing *theory* of the novel at its beginnings (as moral, conservative) must be contrasted with the reality of the *form* itself (as morally ambiguous and ambivalently both radical and conservative) (1980, 113). This would suggest that those postmodern paradoxes of historio-graphic metafiction are perhaps inherent in the novel as a genre – as defined by Davis as a doubled discourse which ambiguously embodies opposing political and moral functions. That is to say, the novel is potentially dangerous not just because it is a reaction against social repression, but because it also works to authorize that very power of repression at the same time (117). What postmodern fiction does, however, is to reverse that doubled process: it installs the power, but then contests it. Nevertheless, the contradictory doubleness remains.

The literary history of the novel has been inseparable from that of realism. Today, many want to claim that realism has failed as a method of novelistic representation because life today is just too horrific or too absurd. But surely Dickens saw nineteenth-century London as both horrific and absurd, but he used realism as his mode of ordering and understanding what he saw and thus of creating what we read. It is perhaps this function of realism that we have come to question today, in our self-consciousness about (and awareness of the limits of) our structuring impulses and their relation to the social order. Gerald Graff once tied the declaration of the obsolescence of fictional realism by Eliot (in his review of Joyce's *Ulysses*) to the end of the "world-view of liberal bourgeois individualism, with its optimistic belief in progress and the rational intelligibility of experience" (1975, 306). Postmodernism suggests that the language in which realism – or any other mode of representation – operates cannot escape such ideological "contamination." However, it also reminds us, by its very paradoxes, that awareness of ideology is as much an ideological stand as common-sense lack of awareness of it (cf. Waugh 1984, 11). The link between realism and the ideology of liberal humanism is a historically validatable one (see Belsey 1980; Waugh 1984), but the postmodern contesting of both is just as ideologically inspired, and considerably more ambivalent. The postmodern novel, in other words, does not (as Bakhtin claimed of the genre a whole) begin "by presuming a verbal and semantic decentering of the ideological world" (1981, 367). It begins by creating and centering a world – Saleem Sinai's India (*Midnight's Children*) or Tom Crick's fen country (*Waterland*) – and then contesting it. Historiographic metafictions are not "ideological novels" in Susan Suleiman's sense of the word: they do not "seek, through the vehicle of fiction, to persuade their readers of the 'correctness' of a particular way of interpreting the world" (1983, 1). Instead they make their readers *question* their own (and by implication others') interpretations. They are more "romans à hypothèse" than "romans à thèse."

Art and ideology have a long history of mutual interaction – and recuperation – that undercuts the humanist and the more recent formalist separation of the two. Verdi's Israelite chorus, singing of its desire for a homeland (in *Nabucco*), was greeted by its first northern Italian audiences as singing *their* song, in an allegory of their desire to free themselves from Austro-Hungarian rule; it remains the unofficial national anthem of Italy today. In John Berger's postmodern novel, *G.*, the revolutionary crowds gather in northern Italian cities around statues of Verdi, whose very name has come to stand for freedom (but only for some – it means oppression for others): V(ictor) E(mmanuele) R(e) D' I(talia). Berger's text's own overtly ideological focus calls our attention to this (changing but real) history of art's implication in the political.

In this novel there is also a Livornese statue which plays an important allegorical role in the conjoining of the political and the aesthetic. It is a seventeenth-century representation of Ferdinand I, complete with naked and chained slaves adorning each of the four corners. These slaves, we are told, were modelled after local prisoners. This statue comes to be connected to the Risorgimento and then to the revolt of the new slaves – the workers – who have cast off their chains and come to life, in an ironic echoing (ironic because of the class inversion) of the Commendatore's statue in Mozart's *Don Giovanni*. But there are several levels of irony here. First of all, the "slaves" who come to life are not just workers. Berger makes the connection between the ethnically oppressed of northern Italy – the slavs or *sc'iavi* – and these slaves (or *schiavi*). The hero (known only by the initial G.), though he may die for his political activities, is no resurrected Garibaldi, despite his nickname and his partly Italian blood. He is, if anything, a Don Giovanni, so his death makes intertextual, if ironic, sense. Yet the historical Garibaldi's absent presence haunts the novel from its early claim that its "principal protagonist was conceived four years after Garibaldi's death" (1972, 20). This statement is followed by a long section on the importance of Garibaldi's particular blend of innocence and patriotism to Italian identity and politics. The novel's G. is neither innocent nor patriotic, however, so the link is again a deliberately ironic one.

Postmodern fiction – like Brecht's drama – often tends to use its political commitment in conjunction with both distancing irony like this and technical innovation, in order both to illustrate and to incarnate its teachings. Cortázar's *A Manual for Manuel* becomes a didactic collage of a manual for both the revolutionaries' son, Manuel, and the reader, both of whom "come of age" in the reading of this text. The "aura" of the original, genuine, single work of genius is replaced, as Benjamin foresaw, by the mechanical reproduction of fragments of history – here, of newspaper clippings. But what is gained is an ideological awareness both of the political, social, and linguistic repression in Latin America and also of the modes of possible resistance (see D'Haen 1983, 70–1). The social and historical contexts are made part of the physical text we read, thereby shifting "the previous social context of rebellion to the social text of ideology" (Russell 1985, 253).

II

Criticism and interpretation, the arts of explanation and understanding, have a deep and complex relation with politics, the structures of power and social value that organize human life.   W. J. T. *Mitchell*

Just as metafictional self-consciousness is nothing new (think of *Tristram Shandy*, not to mention *Don Quixote*), so this merging of the ideological and the self-reflexively literary in terms of the "presence of the past" is not radically innovative in itself: witness Shakespeare's history plays' self-consciously critical involvement of their audience in the questioning of social action and authority, past and present (Belsey 1980, 95–102). But the particular concentration of these concerns in the theory and practice of today suggests that here there may be something else that is part of a poetics of postmodernism. Other genres and art forms would support such a view. Postmodern poetry, for example, has been called "irrevocably worldly and social" (Mazzaro 1980, viii). In the visual arts, the much-heralded "return of content" has included a return to the political and the social. Artists and critics have worked in both visual and literary domains to challenge the canon, to expose the system of power which (though unacknowledged) authorizes *some* representations while blocking others (M. Lewis 1984; Owens 1983). Works like Hans Haacke's "Taking Stock" use formal parody to satirize Thatcherite values in such a way as to foreground, in a very postmodern way, the political and economic determinants involved in how we value art, but also its own inevitable implication in those very values. Postmodernism raises the uncomfortable (and usually ignored) question of the ideological power behind basic aesthetic issues such as that of representation: *whose* reality is being represented (Nochlin 1983)?

Even music, usually considered the least representational of art forms, has not escaped this kind of questioning. Composers like Frederic Rzewski and Christian Wolff have made the performance situation into "a kind of laboratory for the cultivation of political awareness" (Robert P. Morgan 1977, 51). Rzewski's "The People United Will Never Be Defeated" overtly works variations on a Bolivian revolutionary song; Wolff's "Accompaniments" features a Maoist text about a peasant woman. Others (like del Tredici and Kenze) work even more clearly within the conventions of traditional high art or bourgeois music in order to express and contest its assumptions (Falck 1987), usually in the context of an Adornian sociology of music which underlines, rather than denies, the relation of the musical to the social, and of the present to the past. Although the term postmodernism is not usually used by musicologists and composers (for reasons, see Rochberg 1984, 330–2; J. D. Kramer 1984, 347), such music fits the description offered here of postmodern art. So too does dance choreography like Harry Streep's "Number Two" where three men, with faces painted black, yellow and white, dance ceremonial movements and manage (symbolically and literally) to smudge their individual colors onto the skins of the others.

If I keep coming back to the literary and the fictional, however, it is not only because of my particular competences and interests. The self-consciously linguistic, narrative and historical nature of postmodern fiction raises, for me, more issues than any one of these other art forms does individually. Berger's play on *schiavi/sc'iavi* and its interlocking with the Livornese/Mozartian statue within a self-consciously provisional narrative about politics (class, sexual, national, ethnic) is an example of the complexity entailed by historiographic metafiction. This is why I have used it most in the second part of this study. Its mixing of the self-reflexive and the ideological allows (forces?) a merging of what are usually kept separate in humanist thought. As Bakhtin once put it: "the study of verbal art can and must overcome the divorce between an abstract 'formal' approach and an equally abstract 'ideological' approach" (1981, 259). Postmodern fiction is the form that, for me, best illustrates the value of such an attempt. Its self-consciousness about its form prevents any suppression of the literary and linguistic, but its problematizing of historical knowledge and ideology work to foreground the implication of the narrative and the representational in our strategies of making meaning in our culture.

One caution is in order, however. I am not saying that self-consciousness is, by definition, revolutionary or even progressive. Metafiction does not inevitably lead to cultural relevance (cf. Waugh 1984, 18) any more than self-demystifying theory is inherently radical. It is perhaps liberal to believe that any subversion or undermining of a system of thought is healthy and good, but it would also be naive to ignore that art can just as easily confirm as trouble received codes, no matter how radical its surface transgressions. Texts could conceivably work to dismantle meaning and the unified humanist subject in the name of right-wing irrationalism as easily as left-wing defamiliarizing critique: think of the works of Céline, Pound, and others (whose politics tend to get ignored by the French theorists who prize their radical form).

Nevertheless, it has become almost a truism of postmodern *criticism* today that the deconstruction effected by metafictional self-consciousness is indeed revolutionary "in the deepest sense" (Scholes 1980, 212). But the *art* of postmodernism itself suggests a somewhat less sure sense of the inherently revolutionary value of self-reflexivity. The interpretation given to its modes of distancing and critique just might depend on *what* is being deconstructed and analyzed. The humanist faith in the power of language can be turned in on itself, for historiographic metafiction often teaches that language can have many uses – and abuses. It can also, however, be presented as limited in its powers of representation and expression. The self-conscious narrator of Berger's *G.* offers a verbal description of an event and then tells us:

> The description so far as it goes is accurate. But my power to select (both the facts and the words describing them) impregnates the text with a notion of choice which encourages the reader to infer a false range and type of choice. . . . Descriptions distort.
>
> (1972, 80)

The important things, we learn, are beyond words, but are still intensely real, indeed, more real because they are not articulated or named (159). Yet paradoxically, the narrating writer has only language to work with and knows he is unavoidably "a prisoner of the nominal, believing that things are what I name them" (137). Other historiographic metafictions – by writers as diverse as John Banville and Graham Swift – also frequently foreground the practical and theoretical consequences of that humanist faith in language through their thematization and formal working-out of the ideological issues implicit in the novel genre's representational and narrative identity.

One of the most extreme examples of metafictional self-theorizing about this and other humanist certainties is to be found in Ian Watson's novel, *The Embedding*, where the linguistic theories of Chomsky, the anthropological structuralism of Lévi-Strauss, and the political perspective of Marx meet to explicate and theorize the narrative's enactment of their implications regarding human mental processes, cultural action, and social organization. All of these theories are shown to be human constructs which can be made to operate in the interests of political power as well as "disinterested" knowledge: they are all – potentially – discourses of manipulation. The constant intertextual presence of the intensely self-reflexive work of Raymond Roussel suggests the further contamination of both ideology with art and art with scientific knowledge, past and future. The real power of both self-referring language and knowledge turns out to be their shared ability to distance us from that brute reality with which no one in the novel seems able to cope. Fiction like this can be read from the perspective of a poetics of postmodernism within which language is inextricably bound to the social and ideological (Kress and Hodge 1979, 15). Like much contemporary theory, it argues that we need to examine critically the social and ideological implications operative in the institutions of our disciplines – historical, literary, philosophical, linguistic, and so on. In Terry Eagleton's terms:

> Discourses, sign-systems and signifying practices of all kinds, from film and television to fiction and the languages of natural science, produce effects, shape forms of consciousness and unconsciousness, which are closely related to the maintenance or transformation of our existing systems of power.
>
> (1983, 210)

What postmodernism's focus on its own context of enunciation has done is to foreground the way we talk and write within certain social, historical, and institutional (and thus political and economic) frameworks. In other words, it has made us aware of "discourse." As Colin MacCabe has pointed out, the use of this word has become a kind of ideological flag in film (and other) criticism, signifying that the critic does not accept to analyze the formal articulation of a genre independently of its political and ideological address (1978–9, 41). As such, then, "discourse" becomes an important and unavoidable term in discussions of postmodernism, of the art and theory that also will not let us ignore social practices, the historical conditions of meaning, and the positions from which texts are both produced and received (see Macdonell 1986, 12). The diverse theoretical perspectives usually grouped together under the label of "discourse analysis" share a mode of study which looks at authority and knowledge in their relation to power and also at the consequences of the moment in history when "truth moved over from the ritualized act . . . of enunciation to settle on what was enunciated itself: its meaning, its form, its object and its relation to what it referred to" (Foucault 1972, 218).

In Chapter 5 I suggested that the suppression of the enunciative act (and its responsibility) has led to the separation of discourse from the exercize of power. Both postmodern art and theory work, instead, to reveal the complicity of discourse and power by re-emphasizing the enunciation: the *act* of saying is an inherently political act, at least when it is not seen as only a formal entity (or in terms of *what* was said). In Foucault's words, this is a move to "restore to discourse its character as an event" (1972, 229) and thus to enable analysis of the controls and procedures by which discourse operates (216), both interpersonally and institutionally (Fowler 1981, 7). Art, theory, criticism are not really separable from the institutions (publishing houses, galleries, libraries, universities, and so on) which disseminate them and which make possible the very existence of a field of discourse and its specific discursive formations (the system of norms or rules that govern a certain way of thinking and writing at a certain time and place). So, when we speak of discourse, there is also a concrete material context implied.

Discourse, then, is both an instrument and an effect of power. This paradox is why it is so important to postmodernism. What Doctorow's Daniel learns by writing *The Book of Daniel* is that discourse is, in Foucault's terms, "a hindrance, a stumbling-block, a point of resistance and a starting point for an opposing strategy" (1980, 101). Discourse is not a stable, continuous entity that can be discussed like a fixed formal text; because it is the site of conjunction of power and knowledge, it will alter its form and significance depending on who is speaking, her/his position of power, and the institutional context in which the speaker happens to be situated (Foucault 1980, 100). Historiographic metafiction is always careful to "situate" itself in its discursive context and then uses that situating to problematize the very notion of knowledge – historical, social, ideological. Its use of history is not a modernist look to the "authorizing past" (Conroy 1985) for legitimation. It is a questioning of any such authority as the basis of knowledge – and power.

Given this contextualized concern for power and its relation to knowledge, it is not surprising that postmodernism has entered the classroom, usually through the issue of literary theory. In the classroom, authority (that of the teacher and of the canon) has been challenged by changes in the assumptions and practices of literary pedagogy, which can now be seen as operating in terms of discursive practices, rather than teachable methodologies (Nelson 1986b, xiii). This too is part of the postmodern problematizing of our relation to "facts" or to knowledge and its "natural" hierarchies. With this has come the suggestion that nothing is "natural" or normal in our curricula. Everything is "concocted and thus alterable" (Leitch 1986, 53). That things are not eternal and universal, that they can be changed – this is the radical potential, if not reality, of the postmodern discursive impact on education in an age of increasing self-consciousness: "We not only need to know things, we also need to know that we know them and how we know them, questions of authority that contemporary fiction takes into account as do philosophy, science, linguistics, sociology, and other disciplines" (Sukenick 1985, 79). This is the message of the many discourses that would constitute the basis of a poetics of postmodernism.

It was, of course, Michel Foucault who was most responsible for problematizing the relation of discourse to power. Power, he argued, is omnipresent, not because it embraces all human action, but because it is constantly *being produced*: "it is the moving substrate of force relations which, by virtue of their inequality, constantly engender states of power" (1980, 93). Power is not a structure or an institution. It is a process, not a product. But postmodern thought inverts the power arrangements described by Foucault. He claims there is a doubled discourse: a disavowal and then reinscription of control or power. In postmodern art, there is, instead, a simultaneous avowal or inscription, plus a challenge to that. It too is doubled discourse but the terms differ, perhaps because it never sees itself as outside power relations – the necessary position from which to be able to disavow.

Power is also, of course, a dominant theme in historiographic metafiction's investigations of the relation of art to ideology. In William Kennedy's *Legs*, Jack Diamond's desire for power over people (and money) is matched by Kiki's sexual power and is shared by those in his employ: "Wasn't it funny how fast Fogarty [Jack's man] could turn somebody's head around? Power in the word. In any word from Fogarty" (1975, 224). The power in the word (or the law) will not save Diamond, however, from the power of politics. But power is not just a general novelistic theme in this kind of postmodern fiction. It also takes on potent critical force in the incorporated and overt discourse of protest, especially that of class, gender and racial protest. Toni Morrison's *Tar Baby*, in fact, studies all three – class, racial, sexual power – in their wide range of manifestations and consequences, both present and historical. Language is once again shown to be a social practice, an instrument as much for manipulation and control as for humanist self-expression (see Fowler 1985, 61). There is no way that power here can be abstracted from material circumstances (cf. Kroker and Cook 1986, 73–113), for it is incarnate in the very bodies of the protagonists.

The postmodern interrogates and demystifies those totalizing systems that unify with an aim to power. Historiographic metafictions like Banville's *Doctor Copernicus* or *Kepler* challenge science in particular as a dominant totalizing system, as the positivist adjunct to humanism, and they do so through an investigation of the role language plays in both knowledge and power. Of course, theory – from Vattimo's "pensiero debole" to the neo-Nietzscheans' apocalyptic lamentations – has been doing the same thing. While the visual arts, music, dance and architecture contest received ideological notions as well, metafiction and what we might call "meta-theory" do it specifically in terms of language, and in such a way, as we have seen, as to link language to politics in a manner which humanistic and positivistic thought have both resisted. In Salman Rushdie's *Shame*, that link is established in these terms:

> Islam might well have proved an effective unifying force in post-Bangladesh Pakistan, if people hadn't tried to make it into such an almighty big deal. . . . Few mythologies survive close examination, however. . . . So-called Islamic "funda-mentalism" does not spring, in Pakistan, from the people. It is imposed on them from above. Autocratic regimes find it useful to espouse the rhetoric of faith, because people respect that language, are reluctant to oppose it. This is how religions shore up dictators; by encircling them with words of power, words which the people are reluctant to see discredited, disenfranchised, mocked.
>
> (1983, 251)

The linguistic and the political, the rhetorical and the repressive – these are the connections postmodernism places in confrontation with that humanist faith in language and its ability to represent the subject or "truth," past or present, historical or fictional. For instance in Coover's *The Public Burning*, the novel's "Richard Nixon" is neither excused nor derided. Instead the novel focuses on the ideology that formed "Nixon" (and Nixon) and does so "in a context which foregrounds the problematic (and rhetorical) nature of historical interpretation" (Mazurek 1982, 33). The relations between language and fiction, language and history, language and criticism were once accepted as relatively unproblematic ones. Postmodernism attempts to change that.

III

> Each class which puts itself in the place of the one ruling before it, is compelled, merely in order to carry through its aim, to represent its interests as the common interests of all members of society, that is, expressed in an ideal form: it has to give its ideas the form of unversality and represent them as the only rational, universally valid ones. *Marx and Engels*

For many today today, it is the "rationally, universally valid" ideas of our liberal humanist tradition that are being called into question. And post-modern art and theory are both playing a role in that questioning, while still acknowledging that they are inevitably, if unwillingly, part of that tradition. In other words, they have not yet seen themselves as being in the "position of the one ruling before" them, and so have not needed to "idealize" their position, but rather have contented themselves with a challenge from within, though from the margins. And they have contested these humanist values in full knowledge that these same values have also been under attack from many other directions. As postmodern novels like *Star Turn* and *Gravity's Rainbow* show, there is considerable anti-humanism to be found in mechanized, technocratic bureaucracies and in most regimes of power, be they capitalist, totalitarian, or socialist.

In a much-quoted essay called "Marxism and Humanism," Althusser outlines how Marx, in 1845, broke with his earlier theories that based history and politics on an essence of "Man" in order to argue that this bourgeois humanism – the view that each individual carries the whole of a timeless human essence within her/himself – was an ideology, that what had seemed transparent and unquestionable was neither. But what is of particular interest, from a postmodern perspective, is that, while Marx rejected the humanist pretensions to both (individual) empirical subjectivity and (universal) idealist essence, he also understood the practical function of both as ideology (Althusser 1969, 229). What historiographic metafiction also often does is to show how these humanist notions are unavoidably connected as well to direct political and aesthetic issues.

The narrator of *Shame* considers trying the liberal humanist line that art is universal and timeless in his defense of the book he could have written, one that would have included more "real-life material" (1983, 69). However, he realizes the secret incompatibility of humanism and realism at a political level: "By now, if I had been writing a book of this nature, it would have done me no good to protest that I was writing universally, not only about Pakistan. The book would have been banned" (70). He ironically tells the reading authorities (including us) that what he has written is only fiction, "a sort of modern fairy-tale" and so "No drastic action need be taken" (70). At the end, he returns to this ironic and protective frame and makes clear the political grounds upon which humanist assumptions are being contested:

> Well, well, I mustn't forget I'm only telling a fairy-story. My dictator will be toppled by goblinish, faery means. "Makes it pretty easy for you," is the obvious criticism; and I agree, I agree. But add, even if it does sound a little peevish: "*You* try and get rid of a dictator some time".
>
> (1983, 257)

On one level, this is clearly not what Mas'ud Zavarzadeh calls a "liberal-humanist novel" that claims to totalize, to offer an integrated view of existing realities (1976, 4)., Yet, on another level, it is. It does offer *a* view of existing realities, though it is one revealed to be deliberately contingent. It does order the chaos of experience, though it then challenges that shaping process and the product of it, in very self-conscious ways.

Postmodern theory today has also challenged humanism's assumptions, and by "postmodern theory" here I do not mean just the obvious: deconstruction, feminism, Marxism, and poststructuralism. The meta-theoretical contesting of the assumption of timeless universality behind both art and much writing about art has also become frequent in semiotics, in art history, in psychoanalytic, sociological, and other fields, often organized around the concept of representation (see, for example, Doležel 1986 and Owens 1982) and its relation to subjectivity. How does culture represent the subject? How does it form part of the social processes of "differentiation, exclusion, incorporation and rule" (Owens 1982, 10) that make representation the "founding act" of culture?

Theory like this, along with novels like *The White Hotel* or *The French Lieutenant's Woman*, works to define the subject in terms that are rather different, in the end, from those of liberal humanist individualism and human essence. There is no transcending of the particularities of the historical and social system. The subject, in a novel like *Midnight's Children*, is constituted in a way that postmodern theory would define as "the individual in sociality as a language-using, social and historical entity" (Coward and Ellis 1977, 1). Such a definition almost must, if not preclude, then at least challenge, the humanist faith in the individual as free, unified, coherent, and consistent. As we saw in the last chapter, the work of Benveniste, Lacan, and Kristeva has been important in changing how we can think about the subject. And such a change affects how we consider both literature and history, as the representations and recordings of subjectivity in language. Both become unstable processes in meaning-making, no longer final products of past and fixed meaning. In historiographic metafictions, all the various critically sanctioned modes of talking about subjectivity (character, narrator, writer, textual voice) fail to offer any stable anchor. They are used, inscribed, entrenched, yes, but they are also abused, subverted, undermined. These novels are perhaps upsetting to many readers for exactly this reason.

Much contemporary theory is also upsetting, and maybe for a related reason. Edward Said suggests as much when he writes of Foucault's disturbing effect on current theory:

> If we are inclined to think of man as an entity resisting the flux of experience, then because of Foucault and what he says of linguistics, ethnology, and psychoanalysis, man is dissolved in the overarching waves, in the quanta, the striations of language itself, turning finally into little more than a constituted subject, a speaking pronoun, fixed indecisively in the eternal, ongoing rush of discourse.
>
> (1975a, 287)

In the light of Foucault's later work, though, a caveat must be added. Like postmodern fiction, postmodern theory is perhaps unavoidably contradictory: Foucault's anti-totalizing and anti-essentializing impulses appear to lead to the paradox of the transhistorical essentializing of the non-essentializable: power. (Some would say that "ideology" has the same function in the work of Althusser, as does "simulacrum" in that of Baudrillard and "écriture" in that of Derrida.) None of these contradictions, however, invalidates the actual critique of liberal humanism. They do condition the degree of radicality of those contestations, perhaps, as does the fact that such critique can, in fact, be recuperated in the name of a liberal humanist openness to all that is human.

As Rosalind Krauss has noted, in art, values such as complexity, universality, authenticity, and originality have served much wider ideological interests and are thus fueled by more diverse institutions than just the restricted circles of "professional art-making" (1985, 162). The museum, the historian, and, I would add, the publisher, the library, the university – all have shared in this humanist "discourse of authenticity" that has certified the original and repressed the notion of repetition and copy (that gives any idea of originality its force). Postmodern art has challenged this repression in its parodic intertextuality, and nowhere more overtly than in the photographic pirating of Sherrie Levine and Richard Prince. That they deliberately violate copyright points to the fact that there are ideological and economic underpinnings to the idea of originality, and that these lie in the concept of ownership. The photos they rephotograph are themselves frequently pictures of other works of art, and so the historical context of that critique is underlined as well (Crimp 1980, 98–9). In literary terms, the much-celebrated and lamented death of the author has not meant an end to novelists, as we all know. It has meant a questioning of authority or, in William Gass's amusing terms, a decline in "theological power, as if Zeus were stripped of his thunderbolts and swans, perhaps residing on Olympus still, but now living in a camper and cooking with propane. He *is*, but he is no longer a god" (1985, 265).

To stress the unavoidably textual and intertextual nature of both literature and history is not to obliterate the producer; it does change her/his status and role. In historiographic metafiction, the novelist and the historian are shown to write in tandem with others – and with each other. In *G.* the narrator overlaps his own narration with the words of Collingwood: "the condition of [events] being historically known is that they should vibrate in the historian's mind" (J. Berger 1972, 55). The novel is not just plagiarizing Collingwood's text (in fact some of the sources or intertexts, including this one, are provided in an introductory acknowledgement, as is the case in Banville's *Doctor Copernicus* as well). The novel shares the historian's view of historiography as both a contemporary event and related to self-knowledge. Just as the novel mixes historical and fictive events and personages, so its textual fabric mixes the historiographic and the novelistic.

Sometimes, however, postmodern fiction even more obviously uses the specific values of humanism in order to let them subvert themselves: the stubborn assertion and equally insistent undermining of both individuality and universality in Saleem Sinai's narrative in *Midnight's Children* is perhaps the most blatant example. I am not at all sure that the result of this process is the "revitalizing" of these particular parts of the humanist tradition because they "deserve" to last (A. Wilde 1985, 347); I think the end result of the demystifying paradoxes is to ask us to question, but not to resolve. Like all parody, such subversion also inscribes what it undercuts, however, and so it may ironically work toward the enshrining of those values it exists to contest. But just as the postmodern is not automatically radical, despite its often leftist rhetoric of oppositionality (Foley 1986b), it does not automatically revitalize the tradition. It sits on the fence; it literally becomes a point of interrogation. Its ironies implicate and yet critique. It falls into (or chooses) neither compromise nor dialectic. As I see it, postmodernism remains questioning, and, for many, is unsatisfactory for that reason. This judgment is itself, perhaps, a comment on the strength of our liberal humanist heritage.

Artist and theorist Victor Burgin has recently articulated the paradox of the postmodern in these terms:

> The "post-modernist" subject must live with the fact that not only are its languages "arbitrary" but it is *itself* an "effect of language", a precipitate of the very symbolic order of which the humanist subject supposed itself to be the master. "Must live with", *but nevertheless* may live "as if" its condition were other than it is; may live "as if" the grand narratives of humanist history . . . were not yet, long ago, over.
>
> (1986, 49)

I think I would add only that this postmodernist subject lives as well in full knowledge both of the power of and desire for those humanist master narratives and also of their impossibility, except as they are acknowledged to be necessary (if illusory) consolations.

When postmodern artists and theorists argue for a return to the collective and historical and to the past conventions of art (e.g. Portoghesi 1983), this is not a nostalgic return to humanist universal history; it cannot be, because, for the postmodernist, art is considered not as the product of original genius or even of individual artisanal activity, but as a "set of operations performed in a *field* of signifying practices" (Burgin 1986, 39) which have a past as well as a present, a public as well as a personal dimension. In terms of theory, the closest both to postmodern paradoxes and to this awareness of the historico-cultural conditioning of thought is likely to be found in the work of Gianni Vattimo and the Italian philosophers of *pensiero debole* or "weak thought," who attempt to work with, rather than be paralyzed by, the loss of stability and unicity of the Cartesian order (Vattimo and Rovatti 1983, 10). Fundamentally contradictory and provisional, this is philosophy which knows it cannot dismiss "reason-domination" because it is implicated in it, but neither does it seek to avoid the challenges to the Enlightenment project, as some have accused Habermas of doing.

IV

> Postmodernism is about art's dispersal, its plurality, by which I certainly do not mean pluralism. Pluralism is, as we know, that fantasy that art is free, free of other discourses, institutions, free, above all, of history. And this fantasy of freedom can be maintained because every

work of art is held to be absolutely unique and original. Against this
pluralism of originals, I want to speak of the plurality of copies.
Douglas Crimp

Copies, intertexts, parodies – these are among the concepts which have challenged humanist notions of originality and universality. Together with positivistic science, humanism has also tended to mask what current theory wants to unmask: the idea that language has the power to constitute (and not only to describe) that which it represents. According to this perspective, there can be no value-neutral discourses – not even science or history, and certainly not literary criticism and theory. These are the kind of issues that postmodern theory and practice bring to our attention. The art's interrogation of the values underlying our cultural practices, however, is always overt, always on the surface, not hidden in the depths to be unearthed by the discerning (deconstructing) critic. Indeed the art sometimes even acts as a contesting of the criticism or theory. The disciplines of history and literary studies are being challenged by historiographic metafiction's problematizing of both historical knowledge and literary representation, by its foregrounding of the process of the production of facts out of events through definite ideological and literary practices (see Adler 1980, 250).

Both novels like Hubert Aquin's *The Antiphonary* and historiography like Natalie Zemon Davis's *The Return of Martin Guerre* complicate any naive view of how we understand both the past and the present. Yet, oversimplifications persist:

> In contrast to the scattered and baffling contradictory reality of present-day America, the preceding eras of human history – notwithstanding disruptions, valuational crises, and upheavals occasioned by natural and social disasters – enjoyed a cohering system of belief rooted in their integrative conceptual frame of reference and vision of reality.
>
> (Zavarzadeh 1976, 9)

Perhaps. But the past too probably felt confused, at least as it was being lived. As it was written about later, of course, the totalizing power of history writing managed to construct order; this too will likely be the fate of our present, confused and contradictory though it may feel as we live it. The related and common invocation of the notion of entropy in the criticism of postmodernism might best be regarded in itself as, in fact, a totalizing metaphor, as controlling as that of system or order. This, of course, is one of the postmodern teachings of the work by Thomas Pynchon.

But, if postmodernism no longer privileges continuities and values humanist essences, this does not mean that it is not more than willing to exploit the power of both. It is part of the paradox of both the fiction and the theory I have been calling postmodern that it is willing to acknowledge, even as it contests, the relation of its writing to legitimacy and authority. For Hayden White, even to narrativize the events of the past is already to moralize and to impose closure on a story which did not end and whose constructed end suggests that there is a moral meaning inherent in those events (rather than in the narrative structuring of the historian) (1980, 18; 24; 27). Though challenged by Louis Mink (1981, 778) on the grounds that every story permits, but does not demand, a moral interpretation, White's point holds for the ideological, if not the specifically moral, as he himself argued earlier: "there is no value-neutral mode of emplotment, explanation, or even description in any field of events, whether imaginary or real" (1976, 34). The shift from the humanist concern for the moral to a postmodern concern for the ideological is visible in White's work – as it is in much recent theory in other fields as well. Even the use of language itself is seen by White to entail less a moral than a particular political positioning of the user in relation to the world: "all language is politically contaminated" (35). What Catherine Belsey challenges in the humanist reading of literature could apply to the reading of history:

> What we do when we read, however "natural" it seems, presupposes a whole theoretical discourse, even if unspoken, about language and about meaning, about the relationships between meaning and the world, meaning and people, and finally about people themselves and their place in the world.
>
> (1980, 4)

But the perspective here is ideological, rather than moral. Despite obvious similarities, the contexts differ considerably.

The inheritance of liberal humanism's conjunction with positivistic science in the last century was the notion of the possibility of literary criticism and history being objective, apolitical disciplines. The negative response in both fields to the mixing of the historical and the literary in historiographic metafiction, on the one hand, and to attempts to theorize the disciplines, on the other, marks the parallel site of the postmodern challenges. What Hayden White says of historians of historical thought holds for many literary critics: "[they] often lament the intrusion of . . . manifestly ideological elements into earlier historians' efforts to portray the past 'objectively'. But more often they reserve such lamentation for the assessment of the work of historians representing ideological positions different from their own" (1978b, 69).

In a provocative article on Robert Coover's *The Public Burning*, Raymond Mazurek offers an alternative to this view of the ideological, one aware of the debates raging in both historiography and literary studies today. *The Public Burning*, he argues,

> while presenting history as discursive . . . also presents a model of the history within which Nixon and the Rosenbergs act and are trapped. The bridge between the metafictional techniques and the historical content of Coover's novel is provided by its criticism of American ideology: by emphasizing the limits of historical discourse in the America of the 1950's [sic], it points to the limits of American ideology and the use of language as power.
>
> (1982, 30)

The novel overtly presents the protean Uncle Sam as the paradoxically one-dimensional incarnation of American ideology and the Rosenbergs as the victims of that single vision.

But, from a humanist perspective, the strong ideological impact of that novel's problematizing of notions of historical truth, political power, and the individual's role in society has been ignored: instead it is described as a novel which is said to "disclaim external evidence, eschew the reciprocal, the reportorial, the historical, and at times even the felt" (Newman 1985, 90–1). But, I would argue that this rejection is based on the fact that what *The Public Burning* does is, respectively, to problematize the entire notion of external evidence, to question the objectivity of the reportorial, and to complicate the fragile and often unexamined concepts of the historical and the "felt" within the humanist discourses of both history and literature. This novel may indeed be fascinated by "the power of history to subjugate events to pattern – to create connections, causal relationships, and stories when most observers can find no meaning at all" (McCaffery 1982, 87), but the fascination coexists with a serious critique of the literally lethal results of such totalizing. Here history enters the text as ideology. "Richard Nixon" is, ironically, the one to see that the prosecutor at the "Rosenbergs'" trial has tried to "make what might later seem like nothing more than a series of overlapping fictions cohere into a convincing semblance of historical continuity and logical truth" (Coover 1977, 122), but this message is a very postmodern one of the ideological consequences of totalization, one shared by many contemporary theorists of both history and literature, as well as by other historiographic metafictionists.

Postmodern novels like this question the possibility, as well as the desirability, of the humanist separation of history and art from ideology. So too have the works of Kurt Vonnegut, from *Mother Night* to *Cat's Cradle* to *Slaughterhouse-Five*, all of which, though in different ways, investigate the unavoidable ideological consequences of fictions and their making. They also suggest both the dangers and the comforting temptation of evasion, of seeing fiction as a withdrawal from history. We have seen that, in architecture, modernism began with just such a withdrawal, a rejection of the historical city, and that postmodernism marks the awareness of the ideological consequences of that rejection of the history of society's relation to space. Transcoded into literary terms, this insight becomes that of Cassandra in Christa Wolf's novel of the same name. Cassandra fears that she will "disappear without a trace" (1984, 78) and so tells her tale in order to fill in the historical record of Troy (which we read as literature today). The story of women – of the concerns of human relations rather than war – is what she fears will never be told: "The scribes' tablets, baked in the flames of Troy, transmit the palace accounts, the records of grain, urns, weapons, prisoners. There are no signs for pain, happiness, love. That seems to me an extreme misfortune" (78). She begs Clytemnestra to let her tell this story to a "young slave woman" (81), an ex-centric outsider like herself, who will both understand and pass on the story to her own daughter. This is the history of women: oral, provisional, and personal.

On another level, the Homeric accounts, of course, are Greek; the Trojan experience is a silenced one and, Wolf suggests, a misinterpreted one. For example the Greeks had no idea of what Cassandra's prophesies could mean and the reason here is linguistic: "We have no name for what spoke out of me," says the Trojan Cassandra (106). But the Greeks feel the need to name it and, since they (like us) have only a binary system for dealing with such utterances (truth and lies), they claim she spoke truth, but truth that the Trojans took for lies. This is only one of the reasons why she fears that "Their singers will pass on none of all this" (197). And, of course, Homer did not. Only the war, the experience of patriarchy, got narrated there, whereas here there is an entire parallel world of women living in caves outside Troy and it is Cassandra – the ex-centric woman artist figure – who tells its history. The Logos had been the domain of the male until this strange, inside-outsider appeared to give voice to the (patriarchally incomprehensible) matriarchy. In her essay, "Conditions of a Narrative," which accompanies the translation of this novel, Wolf links both men's writing about women (Aeschylus' about Cassandra) and their silencing of the world of women (Homer's) to the patriarchal structures of both thought and government that have created both the oppression of an entire gender and the potential destruction of humanity (the arms race) – then and now. Troy becomes a metaphor of contemporary society. Postmodern historical awareness is this "presence of the past," as the architects claimed. The past can no more be denied than unproblematically returned to. This is not nostalgia; it is a critical revisiting. We see it not only in historiographic metafiction and architecture, but in the New Art History and the New Historicism as well. The labels themselves incarnate the paradox of being implicated in yet contesting of what went before. And the assertion of the "New" is articulated in the postmodern move from the concern with the moral to the ideological.

V

> It is comparatively recently that the perception and definition of the field of the "political" has undergone a radical expansion beyond the traditional ghetto of party politics and considerations of "class struggle" to now include, amongst other things, considerations of sexuality. *Victor Burgin*

As Wolf's *Cassandra* shows, the ex-centric or the different has been one of the postmodern forces that has worked to reconnect the ideological with the aesthetic. Race, gender, ethnicity, sexual preference – all become part of the domain of the political, as various manifestations of centralizing and centralized authority are challenged. While some French poststructuralist theory has argued that the margin is the ultimate place of subversion and transgression (e.g. Kristeva 1980b, 92), another branch has shown how the margin is both created by and part of the center (Foucault 1973, 10), that the "different" can be made into the "other." As we have been seeing, postmodernism tends to combat this by asserting the plurality of the "different" and rejecting the binary opposition of the "other." Though *Cassandra*'s paradigm is clearly male/female and thus unavoidably binary, its model is an expanded one (like Engels's, in which the marital relationship and its inherent inequality is the model for class conflict). For Wolf, the gender opposition is the model for national (Greek/Trojan or east/west today) and class power relations (230). Her Cassandra makes contact with all the socially and ethnically heterogeneous minority groups around the Trojan palace, and in so doing, loses any privileges of centrality her birth grants her. This is the destiny of the ex-centric.

Postmodern metafictions have looked to both the historiographic and fictional accounts of the past in order to study the ideological inscriptions of difference as social inequality. In *A Maggot* the twentieth-century narrator fills in the background of the eighteenth century's sexism and classism as it is needed in order to explain his characters' actions – such as the "crudely chauvinistic contempt" (Fowles 1985, 227) of the middle-class English lawyer, Ayscough, for his poor Welsh witness, Jones. We are told that the roots of such contempt lie in the real religion of the century, the "worship, if not idolatry" of property (227): "this united all society but the lowest, and dictated much of its behaviour, its opinions, its thinking" (228), including its notion of justice. Like many other postmodern fictions, this one is not content to say something about the past and stop at that. Like *Cassandra*, this novel forges a link with the present:

> Jones is a liar, a man who lives from hand to mouth . . . [yet] he is the future and Ayscough the past; and both are like most of us, still today, equal victims in the debtors' prison of History, and equally unable to leave it.
>
> (1985, 231)

The overt didacticism of Fowles's novel(s) is, in the work of others, replaced by a more indirect satiric mode, but the ideological implications of the representations of the marginal and the different are just as clear. Ishmael Reed's *Mumbo Jumbo* is as much an attack on the present as on the Harding years, for the simple reason that there has been little but stasis in terms of the white American establishment view of black consciousness as subversive and alien (R. Martin 1980, 20–1). In *The Terrible Twos*, the satiric attack on the economic and political situation of 1980s America is vehicled by what is called, in the text itself, "the right metaphor" (Reed 1982, 106): white America is like a 2-year-old child. It is demanding and harbors "cravings that have to be immediately quenched" (24). The list of its qualities builds up as the novel progresses: 2-year-olds "have very bad taste" (25) and "Life to them is a plaything anyway" (82). "Two-year-olds are what the id would look like if the id could ride a tricycle" (28), we learn. The reader is "hailed" (in Althusser's sense) into the text as "you" in order for her/him to recognize

America in this guise: "You know how two-year-olds are. Their plates will be full but they'll have their eyes on everybody else's plates" (115). The narrative fleshes out the image of a greedy, egocentered, demanding, and dangerous society.

Reed uses the metaphor both to illustrate and to undercut the power of the center. "Machotots" are what he calls the "Competitors for the Great Teat whose conversations revolve around themselves. Bully the blacks, bully the women" (108). But the second-person address by the black narrator and that "hailing" of the reader implicates us, even if it becomes clear that the "you" being addressed is a male, white lawyer, married and with a 2-year-old child, a former 1960s radical who does not find black people "interesting" any more. We may not fit the description, but we cannot fail to get the point of our implication in the satiric attack on the 1980s as "grand times for white men" (146). The narrative's ideological inscription of both difference and inequality covers both past and present and includes race (native and black), gender, and class.

Reed uses his metaphor of the "terrible twos" in much the same way as Grass had used little Oskar's refusing to grow beyond the size of a 3-year-old. While the allegorical nature of both the image and the wildly imaginative satiric plot is clear in Reed's novel, it is somewhat more problematic in Grass's. As Patricia Waugh has asked: "Is Oskar . . . a 'real' midget . . . or is he an allegorical reflection, in an otherwise realistic fiction, of the anarchic, destructive, libidinous infantilism of Danzig society as it partakes in the rise of Nazism?" (1984, 141). I would question if it really is "an otherwise realistic fiction," given the intensely metafictive nature of the text: we are always aware of Oskar's (later) writing – and fictionalizing – of his past. Nevertheless, the general point stands. How are we to interpret Oskar? Probably in the same way as we interpret the insomnia plague in *One Hundred Years of Solitude*. In other words, clearly fictional creations they may be, but this does not mean that they do not have ideological implications for the "real," as Waugh's second interpretation, in fact, suggests. The insomnia plague is a lesson in the dangers of forgetting the personal and public past, as is the more obvious revisionary history that wipes out Macondo's experience of economic exploitation ending in massacre.

Those in power control history. The marginal and ex-centric, however, can contest that power, even as they remain within its purvey. Ishmael Reed's "Neo-HooDoo Manifesto" exposes these power relations in both history and language. But in several ways, he reveals the inside-ness of his inside-outsider marginalized position. On the one hand, he offers another totalizing system to counter that of white western culture: that of voodoo. And, on the other hand, he appears to believe strongly in certain humanist concepts, such as the ultimately free individual artist in opposition to the political forces of oppression. This is the kind of self-implicated yet challenging critique of humanism, however, that is typical of postmodernism. The position of black Americans has worked to make them especially aware of those political and social consequences of art, but they are still part of American society.

Maxine Hong Kingston's articulation of this same paradoxical positioning is in terms of Chinese Americans. When these ex-centrics visit China, she claims, "their whole lives suddenly made sense. . . . They realize their Americanness, they say, and 'You find out what a China Man you are'" (1980, 295). This is the contradictory position too of Wiebe's Métis, Rushdie's Indian, Kogawa's Japanese-Canadian, and of the many women, gays, hispanics, native peoples, and members of the working class, whose inscription into history since the 1960s has forced a recognition of the untenable nature of any humanist concepts of "human essence" or of universal values that are not culturally and historically dependent. The postmodern attempts to negotiate the space between centers and margins in ways that acknowledge difference and its challenge to any supposedly monolithic culture (as implied by liberal humanism).

Feminist theories have clearly been among the most potent decentering forces in contemporary thought, and their rhetoric has been largely oppositional (gender's binary oppositions are perhaps not that easily surmounted). Witness the opening of Judith Fetterley's *The Resisting Reader*: "Literature is political. It is painful to have to insist on this fact, but the necessity of such insistence indicates the dimensions of the problem" (1978, xi). Feminisms have, in fact, almost replaced the more traditionally political concerns (such as nationalism) in places like Quebec, where women artists and theorists are rearticulating power relations in terms of gender and language. Historiographic metafiction has participated in this politicizing process in typically postmodern ways, insisting on both the history of the ideological issues and their continuing relation to art and society. The heroine of Susan Daitch's *L.C.* receives her political education through the aesthetic and the personal. The novel is set in Paris in 1848, so the public dimension is overt. But it is the personal relations which the fictive Lucienne Crozier has with various artists, including the historical Delacroix, that teach her both about the role of art in politics and about the marginalized role of women in both domains: they are muses, models, observers, diversions. The novel's complex framing relates Berkeley 1968 to Paris 1848 (equally marked as revolutionary contexts). But the conclusions of both story and frame – outside of those marked contexts – question the patriarchal values underlying (male) revolutions, but offer no positive substitute. Just as Cassandra must beg to have her story told, so Lucienne's journal manuscript is used and abused by those whose political and economic interests it can serve.

In historiographic metafiction, this kind of exposition is often directly connected to that of other similarly unequal oppositions, such as race and class. In Michael Coetzee's *Foe*, as we have seen in other chapters, the enabling conceit of the text is that Defoe's *Robinson Crusoe* was indeed a real tale told to its author, but the teller was a woman, Susan Barton, and the tale somewhat different from the one we have come to know. In this novel, however, her awareness of the inequalities of gender do not save Susan from other ideological blind spots: she berates Cruso [sic] for not teaching Friday how to speak: "you might have brought home to him some of the blessings of civilization and made him a better man" (Coetzee 1986, 22). The narrative's exploration of these "blessings" and of Friday's status in their regard makes it another of the challenges to the liberal humanist – and imperialist – heritage that lives on in Coetzee's South Africa, as elsewhere. Like Susan, Friday cannot tell his own story, but it is not because he has been silenced by a controlling male writer: here it is the white slave traders who literally and symbolically have removed his tongue. Susan shares the assumptions of her age, but her gender helps her see a little, at least, of her own ideological motivations:

> I tell myself I talk to Friday to educate him out of darkness and silence. But is that the truth? There are times when benevolence deserts me and I use words only as the shortest way to subject him to my will.
>
> (1986, 60)

Language paradoxically both expresses and oppresses, educates and manipulates. Though the writer, Foe, denies her charge, she asserts that his ignoring of her "true" castaway story of Cruso is comparable to the slavers' robbing Friday of his tongue (150). What she learns is to question the humanist assumptions underlying her own ironic claim that she is "a free woman who asserts her freedom by telling her story according to her own desire" (131): her sex, like Friday's race and Foe's class, conditions her freedom.

In Puig's *Kiss of the Spider Woman*, the protagonists' freedom (or rather their lack thereof) is literally determined by their sexual and political roles in Argentinian society. But the revolutionary politics of Valentin and the sexual politics of Molina are as closely connected as are the fates of the two very different men who share a prison cell. There is, in this novel, a set of paratextual footnotes to psychoanalytic theories of domination operative in patriarchal society that makes us aware of the double political repression the narrative works to combat: that of gay sexuality and that of women. Molina sees the female as the opposite of all that is evil and unjust in society and persists in referring to himself with feminine pronouns. He teaches Valentin the parallel between the struggle for class liberation and the struggle for sexual liberation, and he does so as much by his narration of illustrative movie plots as by his acts of kindness and didactic lessons.

In terms of theory, the work of feminists, Marxists, and black critics, among others, have argued this kind of interaction of the discourses of the marginalized. They have done so in such a powerful way that many feel today that they have created a new cultural hegemony, in the Gramscian sense of a new set of values and attitudes which validates what is now a dominant class in its power. But within each group there is little sense of unity or power: some claim that feminism is the discourse of the white, middle-class woman. Alice Walker calls her fiction "womanist" to set it apart from this discourse (see Bradley 1984, 35). But there is a black feminist discourse, a Marxist feminist discourse, and, of course, a humanist feminist discourse. From a metatheoretical point of view, it is this plurality of feminisms that makes the postmodern valuing of difference possible. Though no acceptable non-totalizing alternatives may be available, the questioning of the existing order should not cease for that reason. The interrogations of the ex-centric form their own discourses, ones that attempt to avoid the unconscious traps of humanist thought, while still working within its power-field, as Teresa de Lauretis has recently been arguing (1987). Like feminists, post-colonial theorists and artists now have their own discourse, with its own set of questions and strategies (see Bhabha 1983, 198). Black and gay critics now possess quite a long discursive history. And all of these marginalized ex-centrics have contributed to definition of the postmodern heterogeneous different and to its inherently ideological nature. The new ideology of postmodernism may be that everything is ideological. But this does not lead to any intellectual or practical impasse. What it does is underline the need for self-awareness, on the one hand, and on the other, for an acknowledgement of that relationship – suppressed by humanism – of the aesthetic and the political. In E. L. Doctorow's words: "a book can affect consciousness – affect the way people think and therefore the way they act. Books create constituencies that have their own effect on history" (in Trenner 1983, 43).

12

POLITICAL DOUBLE-TALK

I

I've never been able to endure anything but contradiction.
Bertolt Brecht

Given my general modelling of the postmodern on its architecture, the basic defining feature of postmodernism in this study has been its paradoxical, not to say, contradictory nature. In both formal and ideological terms, as we have seen, this results in a curious mixture of the complicitous and the critical. I think it is this 'inside-outsider' position that sets the postmodern up for the contradictory responses it has evoked from a vast range of political perspectives. What frequently seems to happen is that one half of the paradox gets conveniently ignored: postmodernism becomes either totally complicitous or totally critical, either seriously compromised or polemically oppositional. This is why it has been accused of everything from reactionary nostalgia to radical revolution. But when its doubleness is taken into account, neither extreme of interpretation will hold. In order to understand the political ambivalence of postmodernism, it might be wise to look once again at the 1960s, the years of formation of most of the postmodern thinkers and artists, because these years are also contradictorily interpreted, or perhaps it would be more accurate to say, contradictorily encoded: self-indulgent versus engaged; bourgeois solipsism versus sit-ins, teach-ins, May 1968, flower power. For some critics today, the 1960s were both uncritical and unhistorical (Huyssen 1981, 29–30). In other words, to be political does not insure ideological awareness or a sense of history. In fact, for many of us who lived through those years, it was the age of now, of the present. What postmodernism has added, however, is precisely a historical consciousness mixed with an ironic sense of critical distance.

Postmodern fiction like Doctorow's *Book of Daniel* explores these differences between postmodernism and its 1960s roots. That novel is able to

contextualize for us the limits of the American New Left, whose middle-
class student membership determined its limitations in political terms,
making it quite a different grouping from that of the Old Left. It shared some
of its forerunner's romantic defiance and nihilistic desperation, but tended
to define political, public issues in personal terms (Lasch 1969). Postmodernism too renegotiates the borders between the public and the personal, but
aims to replace individualistic idealism with institutional analysis. What
Daniel comes to see about America (through his analysis of Disneyland) at
the end of the novel is a far cry from his sadistic solipsism in the opening
pages. He comes to see that "cultural politics" cannot be separated from
"real" politics or practical life. They share the same semiotic domain of signs,
images and meanings (see Batsleer *et al.* 1985, 9). This is where the political
and the personal meet, as they had in the women's and civil rights
movements. What Daniel also learns is that he cannot isolate himself – as
writer – from the practical world of everyday life or from political life. He
must leave the stacks of Columbia University library at the end of the novel.
Doctorow's text is postmodern, but its roots lie both in the 1960s and in a
critique of those years.

The basic postmodernist stance – of a questioning of authority – obviously
is a result of the ethos of the 1960s. Out of the demands for engagement and
relevance in these years, came the American non-fictional novel which
"took on" everything from the New York élite playing with poverty
programs (in Tom Wolfe's *Radical Chic and Mau-Mauing the Flak Catchers*) to
the Pentagon and the Vietnam War (Norman Mailer's *The Armies of the Night*,
a significant intertext for Doctorow's novel). These were also the years of the
black protest literature and the beginnings of feminist writings. Paradoxically the 1960s also marked the international recognition of the challenge of
the French New Novel, a different mode of writing entirely, but one which,
at least indirectly, shared certain political concerns with other fiction of the
time. Raymond Federman (1981c) has argued that the New Novel's roots are
in Sartrean existentialist engagement: the novelist participates in the
shaping of history; literature is a *prise de position* because writing is a form of
liberation (294). What postmodernism has done with each of these beliefs is
question their idealism, while still aiming – more modestly, perhaps – at
changing consciousness through art. In some ways, as I have already
argued, the New Novel is therefore much more radical in form than any
postmodern fiction. It assumes that its readers know the conventions of the
realist novel, and so goes about subverting them – without the postmodern
inscribing of them. Both aim to show the conventional nature of our usual
ways of constructing novelistic worlds, but historiographic metafiction both
asserts and then undermines those worlds and their constructing. This may
explain why postmodern novels have frequently been best-sellers. Their
complicity guarantees accessibility. I do not mean this as a cynical remark.
Perhaps the most potent mode of subversion is that which can speak directly
to a "conventional" reader, only then to chip away at any confidence in the

transparency of those conventions. The ultra-formalism of the texts of *Tel Quel*, the Gruppo 63, and American surfictionists, for instance, may be ineffective because their "purity" of material and social critique are ultimately self-marginalizing because hermetic.

Postmodern thinkers and artists today grew up (after the experience of the 1960s) increasingly suspicious of "heroes, crusades, and easy idealism" (Buford 1983, 5). They learned something, in other words, from those years. As Doctorow's *Book of Daniel* once again shows, one of the things that the postmodern has learned is irony: it has learned to be critical, even of itself. In that novel, the ironically named revolutionary, Sternlicht, represents the 1960s' rejection of history, its repudiation of the past (even the radical Left past). What discredits him in the novel is equally his self-indulgent romanticism and his ineffectual politics. Daniel and Susan, as the children of the Isaacsons (read: Rosenbergs), cannot reject their personal past, which is also intimately connected to their country's political past. This novel has been accurately called "a meditation on American politics in the form of a novel, an imaginative revisioning of the radical movement which attempts to bridge the generation gap and reconnect the new radicalism to its history" (P. Levine 1985, 38).

Other of Doctorow's novels are also either overtly or covertly dealing with 1960s' issues from a postmodern point of view. In *Ragtime*, as Barbara Foley (1983, 168) has noted, the terrorist bombings of the Coalhouse gang, its self-designation as the Provisional American Government, and its occupation of the Morgan mansion as a symbolic political gesture are strategies of the 1960s, not of the ragtime era: Coalhouse Walker is made into a proto-Black Panther. Doctorow's deliberate anachronisms are ways of "commenting upon the age of Wilson by importing a dramatic example from the age of Nixon, and his point is, quite clearly, that the forms of present-day racism have their roots in the past" (167). It is this "haunting continuity of the past in the present" (168) that is the basis of the postmodern rewriting of the ahistorical, but politically engaged, 1960s. Postmodernism was made possible by these years, as much as by modernism. But many of the concepts of those years have needed serious analysis and criticism: everything from its ahistorical presentism to its idealist or essentialist belief in the value of the "natural" and "authentic." With the help of Roland Barthes, Michel Foucault, and others, the postmodern argues that what we so valued is a construct, not a given, and, in addition, a construct that occupies a relation of power in our culture. The postmodern is ironic, distanced; it is not nostalgic – even of the 1960s.

II

There can't be any doubt about it any longer: the struggle against ideology has become a new ideology. *Bertolt Brecht*

Like the 1960s, postmodernism has been interpreted in opposite, mutually contradictory ways. There is little doubt that any politics – Right or Left – has the power to appropriate: Abstract Expressionism's liberational radical form can be read as the *"aesthetic paradigm* of social freedom – democracy" (Barber 1983–4, 35), since it was aggressively marketed as such by the American government, the Museum of Modern Art, and the CIA in Europe, through the early mass touring exhibits which aimed to sustain the image of American cultural power and freedom under capitalism. Another more obvious and, in some ways (since the death of Warhol) more controversial example of the contradictory possible ways of interpreting art can be seen in the conflicting views of Pop Art. Is it totally and cynically commodified in its use of the techniques of advertising and comics? Or does the work of Warhol and Lichtenstein ironically appropriate that commodified American life in order to effect a critical reappraisal of mass culture and to comment upon the commodification of daily life under capitalism?

The art of postmodernism is perhaps even more problematic than this because its radically paradoxical nature self-consciously leaves itself open to both kinds of readings. For example Graves's Humana Building in Louisville has been praised for retaining the vernacular of Main Street and thus enabling the visual reinstatment of the values of community and continuity. It has also been attacked for using this inscription of classic American values cynically – to mask the capitalist version of health care that is carried out in the building. Both are right and both are wrong, I would argue. Both interpretations are certainly possible and defensible, but neither takes into account both the inscription and ironic challenging of various values that are equally produced by the use of the local idiom, in conjunction with the formal language of modernism. Like all parody, this postmodern architecture can be read as conservative and nostalgic (and indeed has, by many), but it has also been seen as revitalizing and revolutionary in its ironies and implied criticism of its culture. What I would argue is that we cannot write off these conflicting ways of evaluating and understanding postmodern art by putting them down to different critical or even political perspectives: the art and thought itself is doubly encoded and allows for such seemingly mutually contradictory interpretations.

There is yet another complication to be dealt with, however. Even within the same general political perspective – say, the Left – there can be mutually contradictory ways of viewing the relation of art to culture: as direct expression of it (e.g. Lukács) or as potentially or inherently oppositional and critical (e.g. the Frankfurt School). The Left is no more a monolith than the Right. In other words, it is difficult to talk about Right or Left readings of postmodernism, given the range of possible positions within each political perspective. To this must be added the problem created by the terminological confusions within the debates about the postmodern. "Neoconservative" is what Habermas labels French poststructuralists like Derrida and Foucault on the grounds that

> They claim as their own the revelations of a decentered subjectivity, emancipated from the imperatives of work and usefulness, and with this experience they step outside the modern world. On the basis of modernistic attitudes they justify an irreconcilable antimodernism. They remove into the sphere of the far-away and the archaic the spontaneous powers of imagination, self-experience and emotion.
> (Habermas 1983, 14)

Many have questioned this equation of the neoconservative and the postmodern, especially in the light of Habermas's own almost unqualified endorsement of a definition of the modernist project as reaffirming the values of the Enlightenment (Giddens 1981, 17; Calinescu 1986, 246). His own language suggests at least a romantic ("spontaneous powers of imagination, self-experience and emotion"), if not more conventionally considered humanist conservatism underlying his own writing. As Andreas Huyssen has remarked, Habermas ignores the fact that the very idea of modernity that he espouses, with its implied totalizing view of history, "has become anathema in the 1970s, and precisely not on the conservative right" (1981, 38). It could also be argued that it might be either conservative or radical to claim that everything is culturally bound or that there are social and ideological determinations of all thought and knowledge (see Norris 1985, 23–5, on Lyotard, Rorty, Gadamer). Postmodernism, of course, argues precisely this stand, and its paradoxes of form (historical and yet self-reflexive) are thus mirrored by equally strong paradoxes of politics. Given this, it may not, in fact, be very fruitful to discuss these contradictions in terms which they both encompass and *surpass*.

Because they are always paradoxically both inside and outside, compromised and critical, postmodern challenges have proved – as most do – to be what Gerald Graff (1983, 603) once called politically "ambidextrous," open to appropriation from the Right, Left, or Center. (An additional problem is that, in the current intellectual climate, the definitions of those political positions are fluid ones: in the face of feminist and poststructuralist theory, those who have always seen themselves as the "left liberals" of liberal humanism start to look like beleagured traditionalists, not to say right-wing conservatives.) Most of the issues raised by postmodernism are actually doubly encoded. Most are by definition ambivalent, though it is also true that there are few notions which cannot be formulated in opposing political terms. The devaluing of the individual in the name of the "collective," for instance, can be a socialist ideal or a bureaucratic (even fascist) nightmare. A number of the fundamental concerns of postmodernism are particularly vulnerable to this kind of hermeneutic doubling: I am thinking, in particular, of innovation, self-consciousness, and power. Perhaps a better way in which to discuss these terms might be to call them politically "unmarked," rather than ambivalent. That is to say, they can be "marked" (in the linguistic sense of the term) in a number of political ways. Experimentation or innovation in form, for instance, can be used either commercially (advertising thrives on novelty) or oppositionally (as in the work of Brecht, and Piscator and Meyerhold before him). Postmodern art plays on this "unmarked" quality in order to create ambivalences or paradoxes which ask us to question our automatic responses to the new, to query if any theory which displaces another dominant one must necessarily be progressive.

Similarly, as we saw in the last chapter, we are asked to decide if self-reflexiveness is really inherently activist and revolutionary, whether it necessarily sets itself up in opposition to "the sense of oppression by the endless systems and structures of present-day society – with its technologies, bureaucracies, ideologies, institutions and traditions" (Waugh 1984, 38). It may be "explicitly engagé" (Fogel 1984, 15), but is the political direction of its engagement necessarily to the Left, as is often implied? Textual self-consciousness certainly can be (and has been) used as a deliberate strategy to "provoke readers to critically examine all cultural codes and established patterns of thought" (McCaffery 1982, 14), but must it necessarily do so? Could it not, instead (as too many others have argued to list), be a form of solipsistic navel-gazing and empty ludic game-playing? Certainly Marxist critics have tended to read metafiction in terms of an aestheticist separation from the historical and political (Jameson 1984a, Eagleton 1985). But there have been others, also on the Left, who have seen in metafictional self-reflexivity an anti-repressive liberation of the reader from conventions which were representations of dominant social and political institutions. The underlying belief here is clearly that self-awareness combats self-delusion (Marcuse 1978, 13), and that (even in textualized form) it can be a form of resistance to the power of homogenizing mass culture and of traditional strategies of representation. But, as the Brechtian epigraph to this section suggests, this resistance to the dominant culture and its ideology is itself an ideology.

This is the lesson of postmodern fiction's inscribing of the political doubleness of demystification through its self-conscious but also overtly manipulative narrators and narratives. It suggests that we ask what the difference (if any) might be between the fashionable view of the reader's freedom to "actively politicize the text" (T. Bennett 1979, 168) in choosing an interpretation and the somewhat less fashionable notion of propaganda (the author's freedom actively to politicize the text). Novels like *Shame* and *The Tin Drum* actively play upon this double-directed freedom, with its resultant establishment of the paradox of the social and ideological determinism of all art and the individual reader's freedom. Postmodern fiction has often explored, on a thematic level, the issues of freedom and responsibility (in novels as diverse as Fowles's *The French Lieutenant's Woman* and Clarence Major's *Reflex and Bone Structure*). It has problematized these issues by showing how narratorial (and authorial) freedom is, in terms of characters (and readers), really another name for power. And power is another of these doubled or "unmarked" terms of discourse. As Doctorow (1983) once explained, there are two different kinds of power: the power of the régime and the power of freedom. His novels, like those of other historiographic metafictionists, work to investigate the overlappings of, as well as the distinctions between, these kinds of power.

Despite the political ambidexterity of most concepts underpinning the postmodern, the entire debate on postmodernism has taken place in terms of political positions, primarily Left and neo-conservative. The fact that the two extremes seem to be describing different phenomena when they write is perhaps directly attributable to the paradoxes or the politically "unmarked" (or doubly encoded) nature of postmodern discourse. I would argue that each sees only half of the contradiction: its complicity with the dominant or its challenge to it. The Left position will be treated in more detail in the next section, but it should be mentioned, by way of introduction, that it is postmodernism's complicity with capitalist consumer culture that is the focus of attacks. Yet I would argue that, although postmodern art does indeed acknowledge the commodification of art in capitalist culture, it does so in order to enable a critique of it through its very exploitation of its power. Martha Rosler's *The Bowery in Two Inadequate Descriptive Systems* (in Rosler 1981) is a series of photographs of Bowery doorways and storefronts which have been voided of the drunks and derelicts usually associated in our minds with that part of New York. What we look at in these pictures becomes clear through their juxtaposition with the "lexicon of drunkenness" (Solomon-Godeau 1984, 85), that is with texts on drunkenness in the language of the working class or the poor: what we see in both "descriptive systems" is the Bowery as "socially mediated ideological construction" (Sekula 1978, 867). The title of Rosler's work points to her critical parody of the genre of the social documentary with its humanist, liberal "concerned" tone mixed with formalist premises (Walker Evans's shanties as form). Here the social victims of the Bowery are strong but absent presences, as if Rosler were agreeing with Foucault that one can never speak for others. To represent, postmodernism argues, is to image others as spectacle – be they drunks, blacks, the poor, or women.

Clearly this is political art. It is, I would argue, more interesting and more ideologically contestatory as a stand than Eagleton's (1985) implied Adornian retreat into modernist high art and its élitist, hermetic escape from economic use. Is withdrawal the only possible challenge? Postmodern art suggests not. Rosler's photography, like historiographic metafiction, harkens back to the documentary and the historical as aesthetic techniques, challenging the boundaries set up between art and these other modes of discourse by the humanist privileging (and self-marginalizing) of the imagination and the aesthetic. This postmodernist practice is also, however, a challenging *and* an exploiting of the commodification of art by our consumer culture. Fredric Jameson's immensely influential readings of the postmodern (1981b, 1982, 1983, 1984a, 1984b) see only the second half of that paradox, however. And there is another problem: from what position can one attack this implication of the postmodern in consumer culture? Is there a position outside it from which Jameson can speak? Certainly traditionally conservative cultural critics, contemplating the canon from their ivory towers, have made a position for themselves from which, for example, to condemn all non-high art as non-art, as the product of commercial culture. If we transcode "commercial" into "commodified capitalist culture," would we have the equivalent Marxist perspective and would it ensure one such a privileged externality, without the dangers of the ivory tower? If one shares the Adornian view of the total and utter domination and manipulation of the culture industry over everything, how can even a Marxist perspective really escape contamination? Postmodernism's paradoxes challenge both this almost paranoid view of the power of the totalized concept of the culture industry and any attempt to set oneself up in a position outside it. In other words, if the commodification processes were as dominant as is argued, the entire controversy regarding the definition and value of the postmodern could not even take place.

These are only some of the complications built into the debate on postmodernism and politics. Lyotard sees the reaction against the post-modern as a conservative call to unity, order, identity, security, consensus (1986, 17). And, we have seen that historiographic metafiction and other forms of postmodern art certainly do challenge each of these re-called values, even if they also assert them. That act of asserting is, of course, the basis of the view that it is not the *reaction against* postmodernism, but *postmodernism itself* that is neoconservative, particularly in its return to history. But what this view misses is the critical, rather than affirmative, stance of the postmodernist problematizing (as opposed to humanist valorizing) of the notions of history and tradition. It makes the assumption that any recall of the past today must be a sign of nostalgia or antiquarianism or "a pastiche of historical consciousness, an exercise in bad faith" (Lawson 1984, 157). But should we therefore also accuse anyone from Picasso and Joyce, back through Shakespeare and Dante of the same sins? There seems no reason not to, by this argument. And also, from a historical perspective, the so-called re-discovery of history is not at all (despite claims to the contrary) particularly typical of times of economic recession and political conservatism (cf. Buchloh 1984, 108). The combining of the new and the old is not an innovation, nor is it necessarily subversive – or affirmative. It can be either; it is not, *by definition*, negative, however.

Habermas is the name most often associated with the interpretation of the postmodern as neoconservative, but what he is calling postmodern is a largely West German phenomenon. He focuses on the prefix "post" because, according to him, in West Germany "posthistory" is what the neoconservatives call culturally explosive modernity in order to deactivate it – and dismiss it, by declaring it passé (post) (1985a, 87; 90). While this may be true in West Germany, it is not at all true of the rest of Europe and North America. But what, then, are we to make of the Habermasian generalizations about the *entirety* of postmodernism based on one *particular and local* experience of it? I would argue that it is, in fact, the postmodern demand for contextualization of discourse that would contest or at least condition any Habermasian claim to generality. For instance is the postmodern really a reaction against the loss of authority of central social institutions (Habermas 1985a, 81), or is it part of the challenge to the authority of all those too powerful and arbitrary institutions? Must tradition's legacy be kept (87) or is that particular formulation of the issue of history going to lead to an immobilizing nostalgia rather than a critical reformulating and revisiting of tradition? Must we seek social cohesion (92) when that is, in fact, what has been masking social difference in the name of a dominant power group? Postmodernism, I would argue, challenges everything Habermas wants to use as a compensation for the moral crisis he perceives as the state of the world: "a straightforward common sense, historical consciousness, and religion" (88). "Common sense," be it Leavisite or Habermasian, has been revealed as anything but "common" and shared: it is the ideology of a dominant group. "Historical consciousness" cannot be an unproblematic issue after historiographic metafiction's questionings. "Religion" and other systems of belief have been called into question as essentializing totalizations which create power relations.

Postmodernism marks a challenge to received ideas, but it also acknowledges the power of those ideas and is willing to exploit that power in order to effect its own critique. Rather than seeing this complicity as recuperation, we might see it as the site of internalized challenge. The postmodern problematizing of the issue of historical knowledge is, I think, a reaction against the neoconservative appropriation of history to its own ends (a nostalgic traditionalism and need for authority). To question how we can even *know* the past is to undermine an unexamined faith in (or desire for) continuity and certainty. But postmodern art and theory also realize their implication in the economic and political realities of the communications industry (cf. Newman 1985, 168; Rawson 1986, 723); they know that their interrogations of culture themselves form an ideology. They are, in fact, suspicious of theories and practices which claim to transcend the culture from which they spring. It is this that makes them less radical than many would like. There is contradiction, but no dialectic in postmodernism. And it is essential that the doubleness be maintained, not resolved (cf. Ryan 1982 vs Leitch 1986, 54). It is the doubleness that renders unlikely the possible extremes of both political quietism and radical revolution.

Gerald Graff has accused the postmodern imagination of indulging "in the trivializing freedom of infinite fabulation, trivializing in that the writer is not taken seriously enough to be held to verifiable standards of truth" (1975, 307). But, postmodernism challenges precisely this idea of "verifiable standards of truth," by asking such questions as: verifiable by whom? By whose standards? What is meant by "truth"? Why do we want standards? To what ends are they to be put? In a later work, Graff (1979) argues that the relativizing of belief is not a liberating strategy but one which dissolves all authority, including those which resist dogmatic systems of thought. In other words, postmodernist questioning of authority will pave the way for the mass manipulation of society. Novelist and critic Ronald Sukenick has answered this objection:

> But very much of what Graff says is reversible. Is it a critical relativism that smooths the path to totalitarianism, or is it, in our society, acceptance of political dogma and consumerist cliché? Is it radical esthetics that encourages a mindless consumer society, or is it that conventional mimetic realism which provides the basis for all those blockbusters in the box office and on the best seller list? . . . Is it not all the more urgent, given the pressures of that [consumerist] manipulation, to present the reader with a literature that gives him models for a creative truth of "construction" rather than a passive truth of "correspondence," for confrontation and recreation rather than reconciliation and adjustment through the identification and catharsis inherent in mimetic theory – a Brechtian model rather than an Aristotelian one?
>
> (1985, 236)

Sukenick is right in pointing here to Brecht, for postmodernism has indeed used a version of the Brechtian model, as we shall soon see. First, however, what should be addressed is the apparent contradiction of a cultural phenomenon that could be structured on Brechtian principles but still condemned by many Marxist critics.

III

> It is not too much to say that bad conscience about revolution is the
> specific malady of art today.   *Harold Rosenberg*

The Left's response to the postmodern has, in fact, run the gamut from approval of its radical potential to total condemnation of its complicity in capitalist culture. In the debate about postmodernism, as soon as a critic (of any political persuasion) invokes either mass consumer culture or late capitalism, the second step seems always to be to condemn the postmodern as their expression (rather than contestation). And the next step is almost always to lament the "unserious" nature of ironic, parodic postmodernism, conveniently ignoring the history of art that teaches that irony and parody have always been used as potent political (and very serious) weapons by satirists. The current distrust of the radical potential of irony (and humor) is reminiscent of Jorge da Borgos in Eco's *The Name of the Rose* who fears the disruptive irreverence of laughter enough to resort to murder. Bakhtin (1968) theorized at length the carnivalesque power of what is certainly not a trivial or trivializing force, as Jorge knew. But it is also not possible to entomb forces we do not like by rejecting them. Both irony and parody are double-voicings, for they play one meaning off against another. To call such complexity "unserious" may well mask a desire to void that doubleness in the name of the monolithic – of any political persuasion.

But it is Marxist attacks from this position that have had the most impact on the debate here. Their roots are in Adorno's tireless stressing of the powers of recuperation of the fetishistic "culture industry" (a theory which presumably is offered from a position outside it). Yet, as many (and not only postmodernists) have reminded us, the very academics and scholars who take this position are themselves part of the "teaching industry" or the Ideological State Apparatus of education, and *that* cannot be separated from the culture industry (Rosenberg 1973, x). I do not say this necessarily in agreement with the Adornian view here, however. I would rather say, with Ronald Sukenick, that our implication is inevitable, but not necessarily a negative: "Literary values serve the interests of classes, groups, professions, institutions, industries, and this is neither bad nor avoidable" (1985, 49).

For example a look at the underlying assumptions of Fredric Jameson's critique of postmodernism reveals its own complicity with the (unavoidable) dominant academic context of humanism. He links the "pathology" of self-referential art with the jeopardizing of the "position of the artist" (1981b, 103) and what he means by that position seems to be a very humanist or even romantic notion, in the end. He does not see that the postmodern translation of precisely such an individual artistic "aura" into a process of production should be of interest to him, were he not caught in a humanist notion of aesthetic authenticity and its related notion of authorial authority. He could understand only as pastiche (that threatens such authority) a work like Hans Haacke's "Seurat's 'Les Poseuses.'" This is a photograph of Seurat's study of several nudes within a suite of panels tracing the history of the *original* (authentic) picture's ownership (see P. Smith 1985, 195). In other words, here postmodern parody becomes a means to question the economic underpinnings of those same humanist notions of originality and authenticity that are suggested by Jameson's view of the "position of the artist."

Despite the loud and vigorous general denunciation of postmodernism by some Marxists, there has been very little actual analysis of specific postmodern art works by them. I think the reason is not just sly evasion. Postmodern texts make overt what certain kinds of Marxist criticism (and deconstruction too) claim is hidden and only revealed by their particular kinds of analysis. In historiographic metafiction, though, for example, the ideological is *not* the silent "non-said," in Macherey's terms. The model is more a Brechtian one and the ideological challenges are as open (and foregrounded) as are the textual aporias. Postmodern texts contest the view that the role of criticism is to enunciate the latent or hidden, be it ideological or rhetorical. They decode themselves by foregrounding their own contra-dictions.

Yet, clearly, a Marxist understanding of how ideological systems contain within themselves the seeds of their own contradiction and destruction (the Frankfurt School's "negative dialectics") is of significant value in considering postmodern paradoxes (see Buck-Morss 1977). The Althusserian Marxist view of literature as having the ability both to reveal and to disrupt *from within* the dominant ideology is (potentially) equally important to an analysis of postmodernism. But postmodern art cannot be fully explained either by the view that art is totally complicitous with the prevailing mass culture (Jameson 1984a) or by the view that "real art" posits a distance from ideology in order to allow us to perceive it critically (Althusser 1971, 219). It does both, usually addressing the issues directly, either thematically or in terms of its form.

The main issue on which Marxists have taken postmodernism to task is that of history. While arguing that the formal experience of art must be regrounded in the social and the historical, this particular attack has ignored the fact that what I am calling postmodernism does precisely that. But the history to which the postmodern returns – in historiographic metafiction like *Star Turn* or *Hawksmoor* or *Terra Nostra* – is a very problematic and problematized one. Perhaps it is *this*, in fact, that is being reacted against, though (on the surface at least) it is more the actual return to the past itself that seems to be under seige. This particular assault might revealingly be placed within the context of the long tradition from Hegel and Marx through Lukács to Eagleton that tends to see only the past as the site of positive values (though what the past is changes – from the classic novel to modernism), always in direct contrast to the capitalist present (and that too changes) which, by definition, must be incapable of great art. This line of descent values only the past and rejects the art of the present as being totally complicitous with capitalism, while (implicitly) positioning *itself* safely outside it. *This* is the kind of recalling of the past that I would call nostalgic, and it is very different from the postmodern historically problematic engagement with the past in terms of how we can come to know it today. To Jameson's lament that the historical novel can no longer "set out to represent the historical past" (1984a, 71), novels like *The Public Burning* and *Ragtime* reply that it never could – except by means of seemingly transparent conventions. To his lament that all fiction today can do is "'represent' our ideas and stereotypes about that past" (71), these novels reply that this is all they ever have been able to do, and that this is the lesson of the entire crisis in contemporary historiography. The postmodern problematizing of historical knowledge prevents statements such as: "The past, simpler than the present, offers a kind of model from which we can begin to learn the realities of history itself" (Jameson 1973, xiv). This, if anything, is nostalgia. The past was never "simpler"; it has only been simplified.

It is also the case, however, as Jonathan Arac remarked in his introduction to the *Boundary 2* symposium on "Engagements: Postmodernism, Marxism, Politics," that post-1960s Marxism and postmodernism "share the conviction that literature and theory and criticism are not only contemplative, not mere superstructures, but active; they share commitments to human life in history. In short, they share the world" (1982–3, 2). Postmodern art and Marxist theory also share more specific concerns that point to an overlap of the kind which I have argued might constitute the basis for defining a poetics of the postmodern. First of all, both are engaged in contextualized, institutional critique. But postmodern art also sees *itself* as institutionalized and thus deeply implicated in the logic of bourgeois society (Bürger 1984; Kroker and Cook 1986), in the "agencies of production, transmission, and administration of knowledge as dominant cultural institutions" (Newman 1985, 185). The second point of overlap involves history: when Jameson asserts that "there is nothing that is not social and historical . . . [and] 'in the last analysis' political" (1981a, 20), he is in a sense echoing what a historiographic metafiction like Berger's *G.* both thematizes and theorizes about – historical and social context. This can be seen, for example, in a didactic statement from the novel such as: "Sexual passion may have varied little throughout recorded history. But the account one renders to oneself about being in love is always informed and modified by the specific culture and social relations of the time" (1972, 151). This kind of fiction does not so much invent "imaginary or formal 'solutions' to unresolvable social contradictions" (Jameson 1981a, 79) as foreground those very contradictions – in both social and formal terms. History and ideology are equally inescapable in postmodernism.

The third area of overlapping concern is what we might generally call "materialist" in focus. Postmodernism is actually materialist in a sense that Marxism sometimes is not: it implies an anti-idealist distinction between the real past and the past as object of knowledge (Macdonell 1986, 79). It is also materialist, though, in a more Marxist sense in that it presents literature, for instance, as the result of particular discursive practices operative in a culture, practices which define what "literature" is and which make literature into something valued. It also emphasizes the particularities of enunciation, its textual (but still material) communicative existence. Its institutional critique involves a challenging of those institutionalized discourse boundaries (history, literature, theory, philosophy, sociology) whose academic entrenchment has meant the privileging or trivializing of certain discursive practices. The fourth concern shared by both postmodern art and Marxism is for the importance of contradictions. Postmodern art uses its contradictions, on the one hand, to ensure both accessibility and access to the prevailing ideology and, on the other, to enable a critique of that ideology. Marxism offers a model that stresses contradiction and process, and this is what is of value for postmodernism. However, there is no such thing as a postmodern dialectic in the sense of a "continual unification of opposites, in the complex relation of parts to a whole" (R. Williams 1983, 103), though there is indeed a sense of a doubled and active struggle of contraries (Coward and Ellis 1977, 88). In addition, the postmodern is not transformative in aspiration or totally oppositional in strategy. It remains content to critique through ironic contextualization and through demystification of its own (and others') signifying practices.

There are even more acute differences than these between the post-modern and Marxist positions, however. Postmodernism takes an inter-rogative stand against totalizing systems and, while it has been argued by some that dialectical materialism is actually unable to be totalizing (or continuous or centered) knowledge because it places the class struggle in the foreground (Macdonell 1986, 88), precisely the act of placing *one* struggle – that of class – in a foregrounded position is to totalize, at least in the sense of excluding other struggles which many see as equally basic (those of gender, sexual preference, and race, for instance). One could argue that class is to Marxism what gender is to feminism, power to Foucault, writing to Derrida, the Name of the Father to Lacan: that is, despite the anti-totalizing aim of all of these decentered (postmodern) theories, there is still an essentializing center around which totalities can be constructed. Witness Jameson's (1981a) capitalized History as the great collective human story and Wil-liams's definition of dialectical materialism as the "progressive unification through the contradiction of opposites" (1983, 107). Jameson, Eagleton, and even Habermas share a universalizing gesture toward a totalizing notion of modernity to which they oppose the postmodern (Huyssen 1986, 175). In addition, Cornel West (1982–3, 178) has pointed to Jameson's "nearly dogmatic" belief in commodification and reification – his Lukácian roots. He also argues that Jameson is painfully (and postmodernly, I would say) aware of the idealism inherent in the Marxist search for totalized order (181), but certainly in *The Political Unconscious*, his view that Marxism subsumes all other systems and becomes the "absolute horizon of all reading and all interpretation" (1981a, 17) is totalizing and centered. West sees that Jameson wants to preserve that which postmodernism questions: the Christian and Marxist notion of History as meaningful. But postmodern fictions like *Star Turn* or *Waterland* historicize such a desire, placing it into a Utopian and essentialist context, showing how little in the past actually supports such a desire and hope. It substitutes for History the value of histories, revealing how it is we who give meaning to the past, how it is we who make histories into History.

When Jameson calls for a new realism to "resist the power of reification in consumer society and to reinvent that category of totality which, systemati-cally undermined by existential fragmentation on all levels of life and social organization today, can alone project structural relations between classes" (1977, 212), he is calling for the opposite of the postmodern as I have defined it. He does not want the contradictions and paradoxes; he does not want questioning. Instead he wants answers, totalizing replies – which post-modernism cannot and will not offer. In fact it challenges and radically problematizes that which Jameson sees as satisfying about the Marxist vision of history: "that for it the events of man's reign on earth can tell a single story and share a common theme, encourage us in a solidarity with the works and deeds of vanished or alien cultures and generations" (1973, xiv). While the postmodern and the Marxist do share a recognition of the contradictions in social and aesthetic practice, postmodernism has no dialectic, no tool with which to effect a return to any ideal totality. In fact, it refuses such a tool as it refuses any (Marxist or other) claim "to be an all-embracing view of human reality whose multiple aspects can be understood only if they are consistently dealt with from the point of view of the whole" (Arvon 1973, 24). Any single dominant discourse is hard to defend in a postmodern context which privileges difference and interrogation (Bové 1982–3, 160).

I have been writing as if "Marxism" were a monolith, instead of a label we give for convenience to a wide range of Marx-inspired theories and practices. Doctorow's *The Book of Daniel*, for instance, problematizes the entire notion of the Left as a political stand. In its presentation of the relations between the American Old Left and the New Left, neither wins the confrontation of generations; both are submitted to a serious critique that, in turn, paradoxically gives them status and value. The bourgeois middle-class students of the New Left have the leisure to march for their beliefs; their parents (in a specific and general sense) had to live their beliefs in the working class, for, as immigrants, they were part of it. Their commitment, though, was intellectual as well as emotional. Their austere and fervent belief is contrasted with the drugs, decadence and solipsism of the newer generation. If this were where the novel stopped its analysis, it would be banal enough. But it does not: it, in fact, then inverts the judgment to which it seemed to be building up. The New Left is seen as at least wanting to try to change the system, as wanting to use action, not words. The Old Left is presented as ultimately self-defeating, paranoid, overly intellectual. However, it is they who are killed by the threatened State; the New Left (Susan) seems content to kill itself. In this, the novel can also be seen as putting into question the Marxist orientation toward the future. There is little of the Utopian in the postmodern, given the lessons of the past. This is what many find depressing about postmodernism, and perhaps rightly so.

Both ends of the political spectrum have accused postmodernism of being peripheral, in the sense that it is said to fail to address major social and economic issues. I never know what actual texts are being referred to in this kind of generalized condemnation. What the novels I have been discussing here do is reveal very overtly that they are indeed "closely related to" postindustrial consumer society with its social fragmentation and obliteration of historical memory (Jameson 1983), but only in the sense that they work to *counteract and question* precisely that unavoidable relation. In other words, "related to" can mean many things, and not all of them are affirmational. It is just too facile to connect (and then condemn), through the verbal link, the *post*modern and the *post*industrial, as Susan Suleiman (1986) accuses Jameson of doing. In contrast, we need only look at a trenchantly ironic passage like the following one from Doctorow's *Loon Lake*. It follows one of the novel's computer data-poems, one about capitalism in which its

positive powers are enumerated. The passage's cumulative effect is intensified by its disruptive lack of punctuation:

> The periods of economic stability also ensure a greater degree of popular political
> freedom and among the industrial Western democracies today despite the
> occasional suppressions of free speech quashing of dissent corruption of public
> officials and despite the tendency of legislation to serve the interests of the ruling
> business oligarchy the poisoning of the air water the chemical adulteration of food
> the obscene development of hideous weaponry the increased costs of simple
> survival the waste of human resources the ruin of cities the servitude of backward
> foreign populations the standards of life under capitalism by any criterion are far
> greater than under state socialism in whatever forms it is found British Swedish
> Cuban Soviet or Chinese. Thus the good that fierce advocacy of personal wealth
> accomplishes in the historical run of things outweighs the bad.
>
> (1979, 1980, 160)

Ironic works like this defy the postmodern-bashers' attempts to relegate
them to the dust-heap of self-disenfranchized, apolitical, solipsistic nostalgia. They prevent any ignoring of class or general economic issues. Susan
Daitch's *L.C.* foregrounds both of these, right from its initial introduction
where the frame translator of Lucienne Crozier's journal tells us of the class
background to the 1848 revolution in Paris: "Workers don't own the means
of production. . . . The stories which illuminated the lives of Paris's
working class had, when it came to happy endings, little basis in truth"
(1986, 2). In this novel, women (especially) are treated as economic victims.
Lucienne writes: "You grow up, the family needs money, they send you to
Paris to marry into a rich family" (13). Dutifully, she does so: "I try to think of
my marital enterprise as a job, the repetitive fabrication of images for a
salary" (28).

But it not just marriage that is coded in economic terms in this novel.
Through her love affair with Delacroix she learns of art's implication in the
economic and political worlds. Though the artist denies art's complicity in
the commodification of culture (65), his own evasions are themselves
complicitous: "Suffocating miners, permanently bent weavers, children
worked to death, hoards of destitute unemployed, oppression by the
dominant class, the owners of the means of production. . . . He is so aloof
with his Moroccan buccaneers, medieval knights, Faust, Orlando Furioso"
(66). Art and history can be an escape too – but a politically indefensible one,
according to Lucienne. Her relationship with the revolutionary Jean de la
Tour and her involvement, through him, with the *14 Juillet* group are what
make her see that the Left too, whatever its discourse of economic equality,
wilfully ignores the social and therefore economic inequalities lived by
women. Gender and class cannot be viewed separately. Caught in male
power patterns, Lucienne feels she cannot deal with the class issue until the
more basic injustices of the gender one are addressed (106).

In a novel like Carpentier's *Explosion in a Cathedral*, the issue of race, of
slavery's relation to class revolution, is added. These are all examples of the

kind of challenges to the Marxist totalizing of class (over gender, race, and so on) that postmodern fiction offers. In this it joins other theoretical arguments – black, ethnic, gay, feminist – which argue against a sole privileging of class, suggesting that there are social and aesthetic contradictions which cannot be entirely explained in terms of the material exploitation of the working class under capitalism. This does not mean that the Marxist analysis is invalid; it just challenges its claim to total and totalizing explanatory power. This brings me back to an earlier point: if Adorno's "culture industry" or Enzensberger's "consciousness industry" (1974) is indeed inescapable, then from what position can one claim to have any total explanation, unless one is somehow outside it ? I keep returning to this question of the position, the "outside" from which much Marxist theorizing seems to come, because postmodern contextualizing contests its very possibility. In doing so, of course, it does circumscribe its own radicality. It admits that it does not itself work outside the institutions which it nevertheless seeks to interrogate. It suggests that there is no "outside" to be found.

Marxism, these historiographic metafictions suggest, does not guarantee its adherents a place outside history. Nor does it have a monopoly on political action. In volume III of Peter Weiss's *Die Ásthetik des Widerstands*, this long novel's historical reconstruction of the collective history of the working-class movement after the First World War is turned over to the voice of women, for communism and capitalism share one thing – the structures of patriarchy (see Huyssen 1986, 121). Postmodernism suggests that to discuss only class is to ignore other, perhaps even more basic differences: those of gender and race, in particular. This is one of the most important lessons of the postmodern re-evaluation of the ex-centric and the different.

IV

Only conservatives believe that subversion is still being carried out in the arts and that society is being shaken by it. *Harold Rosenberg*

Toril Moi's recent attack on Julia Kristeva's "grossly exaggerated confidence in the political importance" (1985a, 172) of avant-garde movements might act as a warning to any attempt to romanticize the postmodern (however ex-centric) into the necessarily oppositional. The paradoxes of postmodernism's ideological positioning and its subsequent openness to opposing political appropriations complicate and condition the potentially radical nature of its contestations. Both criticism (e.g. Booth 1982, 49) and art itself (e.g. Findley's *Famous Last Words*) have recently called into question the moral and political implications of an equally (if differently) double-talking modernism: both its anti-ethical, apolitical aestheticism and its overtly conservative, even fascist engagement. In a postmodern perspective, both are ideological stands. In other words, modernism too was often overtly political (we need only recall the names of Pound, Céline, Eliot, Yeats), despite Terry Eagleton's (1985) claim that a concern for politics was not characteristic of the movement as a whole. It was, even if its politics were not always Eagleton's (see Lucas 1986, 731).

But the same period also spawned Brecht and the historical avant-garde. It provided challenges to the institutions and conventions of both art and history: Duchamp's ready mades, Mallarmé's *Un Coup de dés*, Joyce's *Ulysses* (Barber 1983–4, 33). And these are what provide the link with the postmodern today. While the so-called high modernists, like Eliot and Ortega y Gasset, worked to "salvage the purity of high art from the encroachments of urbanization, massification, technological modernization, in short, of modern mass culture" (Huyssen 1981, 27), it was the historical avant-garde who offered to the postmodern an example of the possible subversion and democratization of high art, of aestheticist hermeticism, and of nostalgia politics. I do not mean to suggest that postmodernism is merely a revival or a neo-avant-garde. There is none of the overt and defining oppositionality of the avant-garde in the postmodern. There is no desire to break with the past, no desire to "destroy not only history, but even itself as an historical object" (Tafuri 1980, 7), but rather an attempt to inscribe a new historicity and a new problematizing of the notion of historical knowledge. The postmodern also shares none of the avant-garde's Utopian orientation toward the future, despite its propensity for revolutionary rhetoric, at times. It has little faith in art's ability to change society *directly*, though it does believe that questioning and problematizing may set up the conditions for possible change.

This said, it is also true that the historical avant-garde offers to the postmodern a model for contesting the fixity of the borders between art and life, a model that openly acknowledges its own inevitable institutionalization as art, however. Like the postmodern, the avant-garde was both oppositional and affirmative of certain modernist tenets (Buchloh 1986, 45), but among their common challenges is the one to modernism's "strategy of exclusion" or "anxiety of contamination" (Huyssen 1986, vii) that resulted in the separation of high art from mass culture, a separation still supported by both neoconservative and Leftist critics. The avant-garde shared with modernism, however, a general focus on the individual subject, personal speech, and the specific text, for which postmodernism would substitute an interest in culture, in collective discourse, and in semiotic codes or aesthetic conventions (Russell 1985, 246). Of course, there was a contemporary of both the high modernists and the avant-garde who was also interested in precisely these things: Bertolt Brecht. Nevertheless, this is a name that rarely appears in the postmodern debate, not even in Marxist arguments. Perhaps Brecht's celebrated opposition to Lukács (1977) is what conditions the manifest antipathy to him in the work of someone like Jameson (1977, 199–200), for instance. Brecht had also presented problems for Adorno earlier, partly because he tried to go beyond the power of negative dialectics by self-reflexively acknowledging his own implication in, as well as reaction against, the dominant values of bourgeois capitalism. Brecht's work accepts, and indeed thrives, on these contradictions: Puntilla or Grusha want to change, but give in to prevailing social conditions. While the contradictions are very postmodern ones, Brecht's work united the epistemological self-consciousness of modernism with a revolutionary political praxis (Foley 1986a, 203) in a much more radical way than postmodernism ever could.

I do not mean to suggest that Brecht's work is Utopian. As Charles Russell has argued, Brecht

> explicitly located himself, his work, and his audience in the midst of a terribly complex, and not necessarily successful struggle with the prevailing ideological and political conditions of his society, conditions which could not easily be transcended by an avant-garde appeal to a utopian future.
>
> (1985, 207)

This is similar to the position of the postmodern, always aware of the contradictions of its inside-outsider role. And there are postmodernist parallels both to the self-conscious didacticism of the *Lehrstücke* and to epic theater's *Verfremdungseffekt*, with its attack on the seemingly transparent and seamless unity of the work of art and the world of the audience. A good example of the connection in form would be, once again, Cortázar's *A Manual for Manuel*. Throughout the novel, real newspapers clippings are paratextually inserted in the text we read. All of these function to alienate the reader from the realist illusion of a coherent and closed fictive world, and all point to the larger world of South American politics. The conclusion of one of these, one reporting and documenting political torture in Brazil, is repeated in the privileged position of the end of the chapter and in capital letters: "THE PUBLIC OPINION OF CIVILIZED COUNTRIES HAS A REAL POSSIBILITY TODAY OF FORCING AN END, BY MEANS OF REPEATED AND PRECISE DENUNCIATIONS, TO THE INHUMAN PRACTICES OF WHICH SO MANY MEN AND WOMEN IN BRAZIL ARE THE OBJECT" (1978, 248). This functions, as do the posters, captions, and songs in Brecht's plays, to engage the reader in that "public opinion" and in the acknowledging of the responsibility of art to speak out politically.

Brecht made it possible for self-reflexivity (or the baring of convention) to be considered as potentially politically progressive, rather than as just having a formal (or formally evolutionary) function, as the Russian Formalists had suggested. Historiographic metafiction, in particular, offers many parallels with epic theatre. Both, for instance, place the receiver in a paradoxical position, both inside and outside, participatory and critical: we are to be thoughtful and analytic, rather than either passive or unthinkingly empathetic. Both are equally accessible and entertaining, and equally didactic. For Brecht, the entire act of enunciation was important: the text's reception and production as well as the social and cultural relations in which they operate, and in Chapter 5, we saw that the same is the case with postmodernism. The "particular historical field of human relations" (Brecht 1964, 190) in which art is written, received and in which its action takes place is central to both, though in Brecht's work there is more of a sense that these relations are open to change *by art itself*.

Epic theater and postmodernist art also share challenges to the concepts of linearity, development, and causality which, Brecht argued, all work to reinforce the dominant ideology in power (1964, 37). Contradiction, "zigzag" form, and "the instability of every circumstance" (277) were some of the techniques Brecht used to wake up the audience to the possibilities of change. When the contradictions are to be found in character portrayal, we get a further contesting of the notion of the coherent unified bourgeois subject – one that is consonant with that of postmodernism: "The continuity of the ego is a myth" (15). There is no masking of ideology, no smoothing out of contradiction, either in character or plot. The subject is an object of inquiry – and problematization. It is not taken for granted; it is not unchanging or unchangeable. Brecht's theater and postmodernist art further contest that entire set of assumptions we have seen to derive from the humanist concept of subjectivity: originality, uniqueness, authority, universality. Both parodically rewrite the historical events and works of art of the past, thereby questioning the stability of the meaning of both. By incorporating known historical events and personages within their texts, both manage to problematize historical knowledge and to break any illusionist frame.

Because the work of Brecht, like that of postmodernism, values process ("the course") over product ("the finish") (37), the text *qua* formal text has no fixed and final value in and for itself. It is not a closed and fetishized object, but an open process with an enunciative situation that changes with each receiver, whose ideological positioning as consumer (by both realist theater and fiction) is what epic theater and postmodernism attempt to subvert. Perhaps the postmodern tends to exploit as well as subvert more than Brecht would ever have allowed, though: it usually installs the consumer subject-position and then undermines it by making the receiver aware of the modes of representation operative in the text. Its self-reflexivity still points, however, to the fact that art does not innocently reflect or convey reality; rather, it creates or signifies it, in the sense that it makes it meaningful. This is how the "combative" (277) *Verfremdungseffekt* was intended to function, moving the receiver from "general passive acceptance to a corresponding state of suspicious inquiry" (192).

Postmodern art functions in a similar way. Catherine Belsey has suggestively given the label of "interrogative text" to such Brechtian works:

> The interrogative text . . . disrupts the unity of the reader by discouraging identification with a unified subject of the enunciation. The position of the "author" inscribed in the text, if it can be located at all, is seen as questioning or as literally contradictory. Thus, even if the interrogative text does not precisely . . .

seek "to obtain information" [as the adjective would suggest] from the reader, it does literally invite the reader to produce answers to the questions it implicitly or explicitly raises.

(1980, 91)

Though I think the final remark about an invitation to produce answers more a wishful projection than a reality, postmodern art certainly asks those questions, and it does so by revealing the contradictions within (and collusions with) the prevailing ideology.

The combination of intense self-reflexivity and political commitment that characterized Brecht's plays is what David Caute (1972) has argued as a model for fiction. He has called this "dialectical literature." This is not quite what I have been calling historiographic metafiction, for it would apply to all metafiction, according to his formulation. It is the act of textual self-questioning and self-exposing that is seen as inherently radical: "the real potentialities and limitations of literature as an expression of socio-political commitment can be achieved only if the writer and reader alike understand *what writing is*" (145). Historiographic metafiction both questions this certainty and takes the concept itself one step further: a work like Elsa Morante's *History* directly addresses political issues through its interrogations of the writing of both literature and history, and thus places the burden of responsibility for understanding on the reader (Lucente 1986, 264). For Caute, a "dialectical" novel, as its label suggests, would bring together, in a higher synthesis, literature and life (251). Postmodern fiction, however, suggests no such dialectic: the borders between art and reality are indeed challenged, but only because the borders are still there – or so we think. Instead of synthesis, we find problematization. It may not be much, but, once again, it may be all we have.

13

CONCLUSION: A POETICS OR A PROBLEMATICS?

Theory is never more than an extension of practice. *Charles Bernstein*

The art and theory that I have been labelling as postmodernist are not, perhaps, as revolutionary as either their own rhetoric or their supporters' suggest. Nor, however, are they as nostalgically neoconservative as their detractors would have it. Whether we use a model of double encoding or one of ideological "unmarking," the point is that postmodernism has been both acclaimed and attacked by both ends of the political spectrum because its inherently paradoxical structure permits contradictory interpretations: these forms of aesthetic practice and theory both install and subvert prevailing norms – artistic and ideological. They are both critical and complicitous, outside and inside the dominant discourses of society. This kind of contradiction is what seems to me to be what shows up at those points of intersection of art and theory today, and it is these that I have been using here to suggest the basis for a poetics of postmodernism, an open and flexible descriptive structure by which to order our current cultural knowledge. Theorized from these points of intersection, a postmodern poetics would account for the theory and art that recognize their implication in that which they contest: the ideological as well as aesthetic underpinnings of the cultural dominants of today – both liberal humanism and capitalist mass culture. Despite all the apocalyptic rhetoric of a Charles Newman, a Jean Baudrillard, or an Arthur Kroker, I see little in the postmodern, as I have defined it, to warrant such statements as:

Ours is a *fin-de-millenium* consciousness which, existing at the end of history in the twilight time of ultramodernism (of technology) and hyperprimitivism (of public moods), uncovers a great arc of disintegration and decay against the background radiation of parody, kitsch, and burnout.

(Kroker and Cook 1986, 8)

This neo-Nietzschean celebratory lament grants to the present a status that almost any past age could also have argued for itself, if it tried. While a delight to read, such rhetorical flourishes may presume too much.

But this "dark side of postmodernity" (Kroker and Cook 1986, 171) has now become the fashionable view, particularly among more sociologically oriented critics. Deriving at once their tone and their theories from the patron saints of apocalyptic thought, from the nihilistic theorists of excess and decay (Nietzsche, Bataille, Baudrillard), they often do not take into account the position from which they themselves lament, or the complexities of the cultural phenomena they claim to be describing. One of the lessons of the doubleness of postmodernism is that you cannot step outside that which you contest, that you are always implicated in the value, you *choose* to challenge. And, while the bold assertion that the postmodern is "dehistoricized" has made for great headlines for both these critics and Marxist ones, it is a claim that has little relation to the actual works of postmodern art, especially to what I have been calling historiographic metafiction, for these are novels whose self-reflexivity works in conjunction with their seeming opposite (historical reference) in order to reveal both the limits and powers of historical knowledge. To challenge history or its writing is not to deny either.

Baudrillard's immensely influential article, "The Precession of Simulacra" (1984), also substitutes for analysis of actual postmodern practice a generalized apocalyptic vision which collapses differences and rejects the possible creative and contestatory impulses within the postmodern. He has argued that mass media has neutralized reality for us and it has done so in stages: first reflecting, then masking reality, and then masking the absence of reality, and finally, bearing no relation to reality at all. This is the simulacrum, the final destruction of meaning. What I would want to argue is that postmodern art works to contest the "simulacrization" process of mass culture – not by denying it or lamenting it – but by problematizing the entire notion of the representation of reality, and by therein suggesting the potentially reductive quality of the view upon which Baudrillard's laments are based. It is not that truth and reference have ceased to exist, as Baudrillard claims; it is that they have ceased to be unproblematic issues. We are not witnessing a degeneration into the hyperreal without origin or reality, but a questioning of what "real" can mean and how we can *know* it. The function of the conjunction of the historiographic and the metafictive in much contemporary fiction, from that of Fowles and Doctorow to that of Eco and García Márquez, is to make the reader aware of the distinction between the *events* of the past real and the *facts* by which we give meaning to that past, by which we assume to know it. Baudrillard's simulacrum theory is too neat; it resolves tensions which I see as ongoing and unresolvable and which perhaps should form the basis of any definition of postmodernism that pretends to be faithful to actual cultural practice.

Baudrillard himself is aware of some contradictions that cannot be resolved, however. He accepts that all culture, whatever its overt claims to the contrary, acts in accord with the political logic of the capitalist system. But postmodernism, I think, inverts the terms of that paradox. It does not pretend to operate outside that system, for it knows it cannot; it therefore overtly acknowledges its complicity, only to work covertly to subvert the system's values from within. It is what Michael Ryan (1982, 218) has called an "enclave" or a pocket within the dominant that can contest it through a strategy of pluralized and diversified struggles. It is not apolitical, then, any more than it is ahistorical. It partakes of what Edward Said (1983, 241–2) labels "critical consciousness," for it is always aware of differences, resistances, reactions. The postmodern does not deny that all discourses (including this one – and also Baudrillard's) work to legitimize power; instead, it questions how and why, and does so by self-consciously, even didactically, investigating the politics of the production and reception of art. To challenge a dominant ideology, it recognizes, is itself another ideology. To claim that questioning is a value in itself is ideological: it is done in the name of its own power investment in institutional and intellectual exchanges within academic and critical discourse. And, of course, the very act of questioning is one of inscribing (and then contesting) that which is being queried. In other words, the very form of interrogation enacts the postmodern paradox of being both complicitous with and critical of the prevailing norms – which it has inscribed. This is the ideology from which this study of the postmodern has been written, unavoidably implicated as it too is in that which it investigates.

The paradoxes of postmodernism work to instruct us in the inadequacies of totalizing systems and of fixed institutionalized boundaries (epistemological and ontological). Historiographic metafiction's parody and self-reflexivity function both as markers of the literary and as challenges to its limitations. Its contradictory "contamination" of the self-consciously literary with the verifiably historical and referential challenges the borders we accept as existing between literature and the extra-literary narrative discourses which surround it: history, biography, autobiography. This challenge to the limitations of the humanist privileging (and simultaneous marginalizing) of the literary has had repercussions that have intersected with feminist and other "minoritarian" contestings of the canon as a stable, fixed body of eternally and universally accepted "great" works. The point of intersection here is in the realization shared by both theory and practice that "literariness depends crucially not on the formal properties of a text in themselves but on the position which those properties establish for the text within the matrices of the prevailing ideological field" (T. Bennett 1979, 59).

Instead of a "poetics," then, perhaps what we have here is a "problematics": a set of problems and basic issues that have been created by the various discourses of postmodernism, issues that were not particularly problematic before but certainly are now. For example we now query those boundaries between the literary and the traditionally extra-literary, between fiction and non-fiction, and ultimately, between art and life. We can interrogate these borders, though, only because we still posit them. We think we know the difference. The paradoxes of postmodernism serve to call to our attention both our continuing postulation of that difference and also a newer epistemological doubt. (*Do* we know the difference? *Can* we?) The focus of this doubt in postmodern art and theory is often on the historical, as we have seen. How can we know the past today? The question of historical knowledge is obviously not a new one, but the powerful and unignorable conjunction of multiple challenges to any unproblematic concept of it in art and in theory today is one of those intersections that, I think, define the postmodern. This is not a throwback to the romantic period when, as Linda Orr has argued, history was the common denominator of concern among "epic, utopia, political economy, political philosophy, religion, fiction, and lyricism" (1986, 3). The intervening years have witnessed the separation of these various discourses into individual institutionalized disciplines. Today, postmodernism represents the attempt to re-historicize – not de-historicize – art and theory. But it both uses and abuses the modes of historiography we had come to consider "natural": continuous narrative, inevitable development, universal (in other words, recognizable) patterns of action. We find today an investigation of specific conditions of specific change, a contextualized interrogation of ideological assumptions.

Considerations of this postmodern poetics or problematics would also include the many issues which result from these challenges to the knowing and writing of history, issues such as the textuality of the archive and the inevitable intertextuality of all writing. And it is not only literature that is involved in this contesting. What Renato Barilli (1986) has dubbed the art of the "Nuovi Nuovi" (New New) in Italian painting is reappraising the past of both local and international art and its relation to global informational mass culture. Similarly postmodern architecture's parodic return to the history of architectural form is an ironic (not nostalgic) reworking of both the structural and ideological inheritance that was deliberately wiped out of architectural memory by high modernism. Parody is the ironic mode of intertextuality that enables such revisitations of the past. Such self-reflexive, parodic interrogating of history has also brought about a questioning of the assumptions beneath both modernist aesthetic autonomy and unproblematic realist reference. The entire notion of reference in art has been problematized by the postmodern mingling of the historical and the self-reflexive. This is most obvious, perhaps, in historiographic metafictions like *Ragtime*, where Sigmund Freud and Karl Jung can ride through the Coney Island Tunnel of Love together in a way they historically did not, but symbolically perhaps always had. What is the referent of the language of this fiction – or of any fiction, or, for that matter, of historiography? How can we come to know the past real? Postmodernism does not deny that it existed; it merely questions how we can know real past events today, except through their traces, their texts, the facts we construct and to which we grant meaning.

I have also argued that postmodernism's questioning of humanist notions of history also involves challenges to its implied notion of subjectivity. In Victor Burgin's terms: "The 'individual' presupposed in humanism is an autonomous being, possessed of self-knowledge and an irreducible core of 'humanity', a 'human essence' in which we all partake, an essence which strives over history progressively to perfect and realize itself" (1986, 32). Any contestation of this basic belief – from Freud's to the postmodernists' – has been attacked as "the enemy of civilised aspirations." But feminist and black theory and practice, to name only the most evident, have qualified the (male, white, Euro-centered) poststructuralist rejection of the *cogito* and bourgeois subjectivity: they cannot reject that which they do not have, that to which they have not been allowed access. Feminist theory and art, for instance, know they must first inscribe female subjectivity before they can contest it. And this is how this and other ex-centric discourses have such an important impact on the postmodern – through their inevitable and productive contradictions. In other words, in dealing with the overlappings of theory and practice we need to go beyond the now obligatory association of the postmodern with the poststructuralist. Admittedly Habermas (1983) is largely responsible for promoting the association and the two terms did enter North American theoretical debates at about the same time. They were also greeted with the same hostility by Marxists, traditionalists, and neoconservatives alike. But, while there are significant overlappings of concern between these two most polemical "posts" today, to equate them would be to ignore the very strong connections between postmodernism and other modes of contemporary theory: discourse analysis; feminist, black, ethnic, gay, post-colonial, and other ex-centric theories; psychoanalysis; historiographic theory; and even analytic philosophy.

Whether this study has outlined a poetics or a problematics, it has based its analysis on both theory and art, working on the assumption that theory and criticism should take into account "the structure of critical propositions in their relations to the artifacts they describe" (Thurley 1983, 1). Theory and practice are too often separated – in the classroom and in the research we do – and one of the lessons of postmodernism is that we should question any such institutionalized separations, and that we should learn to theorize from the site of practice. Novels like John Berger's *G.* overtly theorize (as they narrativize) all the notions to be found in the theories of Jameson or Lyotard, but today many are almost more likely to read (and legitimate) the theory than the fiction. As Manfredo Tafuri has written, "there exists an intimate complicity between criticism and activity" (1980, 1), between theory and practice, and it is therefore not surprising that many of the most illuminating studies of the postmodern have come from artist-theorists: Paolo Portoghesi, Charles Jencks, Victor Burgin, Rosalind Krauss, David Antin.

John Fekete has recently called for an "anti-foundational interpretive project" which would be "pluralist, rational, pragmatic" (1984b, 245), but I think this already exists in the conjunction of theory and art that is postmodernism. In both discourses there is clearly an "ideological commitment to the 'worldliness' of art and criticism" (Bové 1982–3, 156–7) that cannot be separated from their conjunction and their shared self-consciousness of their own positions in cultural practice. That these positions are ex-centric, paradoxically both inside and outside the dominant they contest, is no cause for despair or apocalyptic wailing. The postmodern view is that contradictions are inevitable and, indeed, the condition of social as well as cultural experience. To smooth them over would be bad faith, even if it would also be our normal reaction within a humanist context. The narrator of Salman Rushdie's novel, *Shame*, puts it this way: "I myself manage to hold large numbers of wholly irreconcilable views simultaneously, without the least difficulty. I do not think others are less versatile" (1983, 242). Postmodernism refuses to eliminate (and indeed foregrounds) "the productive tension between the political and the aesthetic, between history and the text" (Huyssen, 1986, 221), and it does so by historicizing and contextualizing the separation between those discourses, which for humanism, have been seen as almost mutually incompatible.

I have concentrated on fiction, particularly in the second part of this study, partly because many others writing on postmodernism have also done so, and partly because it overtly (because verbally) articulates and problematizes the assumptions of our dominant culture. The self-reflexivity of historiographic metafiction may have its roots in the modernist assertion of the autonomy of art and its separation from the contamination of life and history, but, as the Russian Formalists saw, it also has the effect of demystifying artistic illusion, of decreasing the distance between art and life. It challenges what Benjamin (1968) saw as "auratic" art, which isolated and fetishized the aesthetic. When conjoined with historical references to actual events and personages, this demystifying auto-representation engages a problematizing of historical knowledge and of the borders between fact and fiction, conducted within the powers and limits of narrativization.

While privileging historiographic metafiction in this study, then, I have tried to discuss the parallel manifestations of postmodern paradoxes in the other arts. A painting like Mark Tansey's "Achilles and the Tortoise" is as much a postmodernist allegory of the historical race between culture and nature, between scientific theory and the universe, as is Banville's *Doctor Copernicus* or *Kepler*. A rocket soars in the background, but a foregrounded pine tree exceeds its height. An intertextual homage to Zeno of Elia's paradox (the basis of the allegory), this painting also portrays the actual scientists Mitchell Feigenbaum, Benoit Mandelbrot, and Albert Einstein. Their represented presence is important to the ideological message of the work: for instance Feigenbaum's paradoxical-sounding theories of the dimensions of irregularities in geometry and physics prove the "fallibility of reality models in the face of the inevitability of turbulence" (McCormick 1987, 95). Any challenge to given "reality models" is of relevance to a painting which forces a number of their mimetic equivalences into ironic confrontation with each other: photographic realism, pictorial and painterly conventions, illustrational techniques. In other words, Tansey's painting both inscribes the authority of realistic representation and ironically contradicts it.

But painting is not the only medium used to postmodernly paradoxical ends. Perhaps the most inherently contradictory of all art forms, one which has therefore come into its own in postmodernism, is that of photography (see Rosler 1984, 328). Like historiographic metafiction, it is now self-consciously as well as inherently referential. It has an irreducible documentary status. But today, in the work of Martha Rosler, Barbara Kruger, Heribert Berkert, Victor Burgin, Sherrie Levine, and others, it is also self-consciously and inherently framed or self-referential. It is constructed space. An additional postmodern paradox (within that of the rise of photography as a high art form today) is that this is taking place at a time when the photograph is the most common of all cultural artifacts. We are surrounded by them; we constantly produce and consume photographic images.

To admit this is not the same as claiming that these simulacra, in Baudrillard's terms, are all we have. Postmodern photography foregrounds its inevitable identity as simulacrum in a special way, overtly offering both its obvious intertextuality and its undeniable nature as multiply reproducible mass media as challenges to "auratic" art and to the related humanist assumptions of subjectivity, authorship, singularity, originality, uniqueness, and autonomy. Of course, it was preceded and enabled in this by the work of Duchamp and Pop artists, by both the ready made and the "already made" (Solomon-Godeau 1984, 76). It is interesting that it has frequently been women photographers who have been the most obviously radical in their contesting of the institutional and ideological framework of high art by mixing it with mass media images – from advertisements, fashion magazines, and film. This is another of the points of intersection of theory and practice, for the work of Silvia Kolbowski, Cindy Sherman, and others have specifically addressed in their art the same issues as some feminist theory: the commodification and fetishization of images of women, in both high and mass culture.

The same ideological effects of boundary-testing can be felt in postmodern dance as well: Karole Armitage conflates classical ballet and modern dance into something that questions the autonomous and quasi-sacred designation of only certain kinds of dance as high art and she does so in the context, not only of contemporary music and painting, but also of fashion and other forms of mass culture. In addition, throughout this study, I have tried to bring in examples of postmodern architecture, music, and film, where relevant, to illustrate the defining contradictions which I feel characterize the discourses of the postmodern. But in all, the major locus of the study of these paradoxes here has been in the points of intersection of theory and practice. In the light of postmodern art, I have argued that what we might label postmodern theory would be inherently self-contradictory: what I earlier called those Foucaldian totalizing negations of totalization and essentializations of the inessentializable (power) or those Lyotardian master narratives about our loss of faith in master narratives. The debate around the definition and value of the postmodern has involved many of these theories. In the early terms of the debate – as articulated by Lyotard (1984a) and Habermas (1983) – what I would call postmodernism sits on the fence, both asserting a metanarrative with precise values and premises (à la Habermas) and then problematizing both the process and product of such a procedure (à la Lyotard).

Postmodernism offers what Habermas seeks: that is "a *changed constellation* of art and the life-world" (1985b, 202), but it does so in a problematic and provisional, not certain or definite way. But Habermas's interest in the dialogic nature of communicative acts is in tune with the postmodern reinstating of the complexity of enunciation, and there are surely other aspects of his work that are also potentially postmodernist: his own critical practice of challenging the philosophical tradition and his emphasis on the need to differentiate distinctions and differences, rather than blur them in the name of unities. Nevertheless, as is also the case with Marxism, there is a universalizing impulse in Habermas's thought that is tied to his being a dialectical thinker. And it is this that Lyotard has responded to and which postmodernism contests. But it is too simplistic to reduce Habermas to an example of the "traumatized German mind," unable to bear the historical conjunction of reason and irrationalism, taking shelter in the "rationalist citadel" of "rationalized ethics" (Kroker and Cook 1986, 255). The contradictions of his thought are symptomatic of much of the writing on and around postmodernism, contradictions it shares with the object of its study.

It is for this reason that the latest doxa – the simulacrum theory – rings false to me. It is too absolute, too dogmatic for the provisional and decentered phenomena it pretends to describe. The impact of Baudrillard's view, however, has been immense. For some, the simulacrum has rendered "questions about 'the real thing' at once obsessive and irrelevant" (Orvell 1980, 64). Postmodern questions about "the real thing" are indeed obsessive because they are now problematic; but they are by no means irrelevant. The act of problematizing is, in a way, an act of restoring relevance to something ignored or taken for granted. The "real thing" has, however, had a problematic relation to art ever since Plato. What postmodernism does is not only to remind us of this, but also to investigate our amnesia.

What postmodernism questions, then, is not just liberal humanism's assertion of the real but the apocalyptic murder of the real. Merely to dismiss reality, as does Baudrillard (1984, 253), is not the same as proving that it has degenerated into hyperreality. The postmodern discourses I have been studying here do not "liquidate referentials" so much as force a rethinking of the entire notion of reference that makes problematic both the traditional realist transparency and this newer reduction of reference to simulacrum. It suggests that all we have ever had to work with is a system of signs, and that to call attention to this is not to deny the real, but to remember that we only *give meaning to* the real within those signifying systems. This is no radical new substitution of signs for the real, as Baudrillard argues. Postmodern art merely foregrounds the fact that we can know the real, especially the past real, only through signs, and that is not the same as wholesale substitution.

The postmodern still operates, in other words, in the realm of representation, not of simulation, even if it constantly questions the rules of that realm. In writing of the avant-garde, Lyotard has used the image of psychoanalysis: the attempt to understand the present by examining the past (1986, 125). The same image is suggestive for postmodernism's orientation toward the "presence of the past" and its deliberate rejection of either a positive Utopian (Marxist) or negative apocalyptic (neo-Nietzschean) orientation toward the future. Its aims are more limited: to make us look to the past from the acknowledged distance of the present, a distance which inevitably conditions our ability to know that past. The ironies produced by that distancing are what prevent the postmodern from being nostalgic: there is no desire to return to the past as a time of simpler or more worthy values. These ironies also prevent antiquarianism: there is no value to the past in and of itself. It is the conjunction of the present and the past that is intended to make us question – analyze, try to understand – both how we make and make sense of our culture. Postmodernism may well be, as so many want to claim, the expression of a culture in crisis, but it is not in itself any revolutionary breakthrough. It is too contradictory, too wilfully compromised by that which it challenges.

Postmodern theory, criticism, and art today are all engaged in contesting the modernist (humanist) premises of art's apolitical autonomy and of theory and criticism as value-free activities. The postmodern paradoxes both reveal and question prevailing norms, and they can do so because they incarnate both processes. They teach that, for example, representation cannot be avoided, but it can be studied to show how it legitimates certain kinds of knowledge and, therefore, certain kinds of power. Postmodern art self-consciously acknowledges that, like mass culture, it is ideologically loaded because of its representational (and often narrative) nature. In other words, "it is not that representations possess an inherently ideological content but that they carry out an ideological function in determining the production of meaning" (Wallis 1984b, xv). This is the lesson of the ex-centrics (of women, ethics, gays, blacks, postcolonials) and it comes from the margins of (but within) the dominant culture.

This does not mean that the postmodern cannot be or has not been appropriated and recuperated by either (or both) of the extremes of that dominant: capitalist mass culture or humanist high art. As I have argued, I think its double encoding as both contestatory but also complicitous is what enables such co-option. There can be little doubt that the postmodern has been commercialized, that the aesthetic has been turned into the fashionable. It might be wise, however, to make some distinction between art and what the art-promotional system does to it. From the fate of even hermetic modernism, it seems clear that any aesthetic practice can be assimilated and neutralized by both the high art market and mass media culture. My question would be, why is this separation that is usually made in discussions of modernism (between the art itself and its commodification) not made as well in considerations of the postmodern? I think that, in all fairness, a separation must be made between Charles Moore's Piazza d'Italia and all those trendy classical arches pasted on the front of modernist buildings.

Instead of looking to totalize, this study has tried to interrogate the limits and powers of postmodernist discourse, by investigating the overlappings within a plurality of manifestations in both art and theory, overlappings that point to the consistently problematized issues that I think define this poetics (or problematics) of postmodernism: historical knowledge, subjectivity, narrativity, reference, textuality, discursive context. I would agree with Habermas that this art does not "emit any clear signals" (1985a, 90), but, then again, it does not try to. It tries to problematize and, thereby, to make us question. But it does not offer answers. It cannot, without betraying its anti-totalizing ideology. Yet both the detractors and promoters of post-modernism have found answers, because the paradoxes of postmodern do allow for answers – though only if you ignore the other half of the paradox. To Habermas's question: "But where are the works which might fill the negative slogan of 'postmodernism' with a positive content?" (90), I would reply: everywhere – in today's fiction, painting, film, photography, dance, architecture, poetry, drama, and video. In their contradictions we may find no answers, but the questions that will make any answering process even possible are at least starting to be asked.

BIBLIOGRAPHY

Ackroyd, Peter (1985) *Hawksmoor*, London: Hamish Hamilton.

Adler, Louise (1980 "Historiography in Britain: 'une histoire en construction,'" *Yale French Studies* 59: 243–53.

Alloula, Malek (1986) *The Colonial Harem*, Minneapolis: University of Minnesota Press.

Alter, Robert (1975) *Partial Magic: The Novel as a Self-Conscious Genre*, Berkeley: University of California Press.

Althusser, Louis (1969) *For Marx*, trans. Ben Brewster, New York: Pantheon.

—— (1971) *Lenin and Philosophy and Other Essays*, trans. Ben Brewster, London: New Left Books.

Altieri, Charles (1973) "From Symbolist Thought to Immanence: The Ground of Postmodern American Poetics," *Boundary 2* 1, 3: 605–41.

—— (1984) *Self and Sensibility in Contemporary American Poetry*, Cambridge: Cambridge University Press.

—— (1986) "What Ashbery Makes of the Challenges of Post-Modern Visual Arts," paper to Modern Language Association of America meeting, New York, December.

Angenot, Marc (1983) "L'intertextualité': enquête sur l'émergence et la diffusion d'un champ notionnel," *Revue des sciences humaines* 189, 1: 121–35.

Antin, David (1972) "Modernism and Postmodernism: Approaching the Present in American Poetry," *Boundary 2* 1, 1: 98–133.

—— (1980) "Is There a Postmodernism?" in Garvin (1980): 127–35.

Aquin, Hubert (1974) *Blackout*, trans. Alan Brown, Toronto: Anansi.

—— (1983) *The Antiphonary*, trans. Alan Brown, Toronto: Anansi.

Arac, Jonathan (1982–3) "Introduction" to *Engagements: Postmodernism, Marxism, Politics* issue of *Boundary 2* 11, 1–2: 1–4.

Aristotle (1982) *Poetics*, trans. James Hutton, London and New York: Norton.

Aronowitz, Stanley (1984) "When the New Left Was New" in Sayres *et al.* (1984): 11–43.

Arvon, Henri (1973) *Marxist Esthetics*, trans. Helen R. Lane, Ithaca, NY and London: Cornell University Press.

Atwood, Margaret (1985) *The Handmaid's Tale*, Toronto: McClelland & Stewart.

Baird, George (1969) "'La Dimension Amoureuse' in Architecture" in Jencks and Baird (1969): 78–99.

Bakhtin, Mikhail (1968) *Rabelais and His World*, trans. Hélène Iswolsky, Cambridge, Mass: MIT Press.

—— (V. N. Voloshinov) (1973) *Marxism and the Philosophy of Language*, trans. Ladislaw Matejka and I. R. Titunik, New York and London: Seminar Press.

—— (P. N. Medvedev) (1978) *The Formal Method in Literary Scholarship: A Critical Introduction to Sociological Poetics*, trans. Albert J. Wehrle, Baltimore, Md and London: Johns Hopkins University Press.

—— (1981) *The Dialogic Imagination: Four Essays by M. M. Bakhtin*, ed. Michael Holquist, trans. Caryl Emerson and Michael Holquist, Austin, Tex. and London: University of Texas Press.

Banfield, Ann (1982) *Unspeakable Sentences: Narration and Representation in the Language of Fiction*, Boston, Mass. and London: Routledge & Kegan Paul.

Banville, John (1976) *Doctor Copernicus*, New York: Norton.

—— (1981) *Kepler*, London: Secker & Warburg.

Barber, Bruce Alistair (1983–4) "Appropriation/Expropriation: Convention or Intervention?" *Parachute* 33: 29–39.

Barilli, Renato (1984) "Una generazione postmoderna," *Il Verri* 1–2, 7th series: 15–55.

—— (1986) *Icons of Postmodernism: The Nuovi-Nuovi Artists*, Torino: Allemandi.

Barker, Francis, *et al*. (eds) (1983) *The Politics of Theory*, Colchester: University of Essex.

Barnes, Julian (1984) *Flaubert's Parrot*, London: Jonathan Cape.

Barth, John (1956) *The Floating Opera*, New York: Avon.

—— (1960) *The Sot-Weed Factor*, New York: Doubleday.

—— (1967) "The Literature of Exhaustion," *The Atlantic* 220, 2: 29–34.

—— (1979) *Letters* New York: Putnam's Sons.

—— (1980) "The Literature of Replenishment: Postmodernist Fiction," *The Atlantic* 245, 1: 65–71.

Barthes, Roland (1967) *Writing Degree Zero*, trans. Annette Lavers and Colin Smith, London: Jonathan Cape.

—— (1968a) "L'Effet de réel," *Communications* 11: 84–9.

—— (1968b) "Drame, poème, roman" in *Tel Quel: Théorie d'ensemble*, Paris: Seuil: 25–40.

—— (1972) *Critical Essays*, trans. Richard Howard, Evanston, Ill: Northwestern University Press.

—— (1973) *Mythologies*, trans. Annette Lavers, London: Granada.

—— (1974) *S/Z*, trans. Richard Miller, New York: Hill & Wang.

—— (1975) *The Pleasure of the Text*, trans. Richard Miller, New York: Hill & Wang.

—— (1977) *Image Music Text*, trans. Stephen Heath, New York: Hill & Wang.

—— (1981a) *Camera Lucida: Reflections on Photography*, trans. Richard Howard, New York: Hill & Wang.

—— (1981b) "Theory of the Text" in Young (1981a): 31–47.

—— (1982a) *A Barthes Reader*, ed. Susan Sontag, New York: Hill & Wang.

—— (1982b) "Le Discours de l'histoire," *Poétique* 49: 13–21.

Batsleer, Janet, Davies, Tony, O'Rourke, Rebecca, and Weedon, Chris (1985) *Rewriting English: Cultural Politics of Gender and Class*, London and New York: Methuen.

Baudrillard, Jean (1980) "Forgetting Foucault," trans. Nicole Dufresne, *Humanities in Society* 3, 1: 87–111.

—— (1984) "The Precession of Simulacra" in Wallis (1984a): 253–81.

Becker, Carl (1910) "Detachment and the Writing of History," *Atlantic Monthly* 106: 524–36.

Beebe, Maurice (1972) "*Ulysses* and the Age of Modernism," *James Joyce Quarterly* 10 (Fall): 172–88.

—— (1974) "What Modernism Was," *Journal of Modern Literature* 3, 5: 1,065–84.

Begnal, Michael H. (1973) "James Joyce and the Mythologizing of History" in Weintraub and Young (1973): 211–19.

Belsey, Catherine (1980) *Critical Practice*, London: Methuen.

Benjamin, Walter (1968) "The Work of Art in the Age of Mechanical Reproduction" in his *Illuminations*, ed. Hannah Arendt, trans. Harry Zohn, New York: Schocken: 217–51.

—— (1973) *Understanding Brecht*, trans. Anna Bostock, London: New Left Books.

—— (1978) *Reflections*, New York: Harcourt Brace Jovanovich.

Bennett, Susan (1985) "Horrid Laughter," paper to Canadian Comparative Literature Association, Montreal.

Bennett, Tony (1979) *Formalism and Marxism*, London and New York: Methuen.

—— (1984) "Texts in History: The Determinations of Reading and their Texts," *Australian Journal of Communication* 5–6: 3–12.

Benveniste, Emile (1971) *Problems in General Linguistics*, trans. Mary Elizabeth Meek, Coral Gables, Fla: University of Miami Press.

Berger, John (1972) *G.*, New York: Pantheon.

Berger, Thomas (1964) *Little Big Man*, New York: Dial Press.

Bergonzi, Bernard (ed.) (1968) *Innovations: Essays on Art and Ideas*, London: Macmillan.

Bernstein, Richard J. (ed.) (1985) *Habermas and Modernity*, Cambridge, Mass: MIT Press.

Bertens, Hans (1986) "The Postmodern *Weltanschauung* and its Relation with Modernism: An Introductory Survey" in Fokkema and Bertens (1986): 9–51.

Berthoff, Warner (1970) "Fiction, History, Myth: Notes toward the Discrimination of Narrative Forms" in Bloomfield (1970): 263–87.

Bhabha, Homi K. (1983) "Difference, Discrimination and the Discourse of Colonialism" in Barker *et al.* (1983): 194–211.

Bird, Jon (1986) "On Newness, Art and History: Reviewing *Block* 1979–85" in Rees and Borzello (1986): 32–40.

Black, Max and Geach, P. T. (eds) (1952) *Translations from the Philosophical Writings of Gottlob Frege*, Oxford: Blackwell.

Blake, Peter (1977) *Form Follows Fiasco*, Boston, Mass. and Toronto: Little, Brown.

Bloom, Harold (1973) *The Anxiety of Influence*, New York: Oxford University Press.

Bloomfield, M. W. (ed.) (1970) *The Interpretation of Narrative: Theory and Practice*, Cambridge, Mass: Harvard University Press.

Boelhower, William (1984) *Through a Glass Darkly: Ethnic Semiosis in American Literature*, Venezia: Helvetia.

Bois, Yve-Alain (1981) "The Sculptural Opaque," *Sub-Stance* 31: 23–48.

Bolton, Richard (1986) "The Modern Spectator and the Postmodern Participant," *Photocommuniqué* 8, 2: 34–45.

Booth, Wayne C. (1982) "Freedom of Interpretation: Bakhtin and the Challenge of Feminist Criticism," *Critical Inquiry* 9, 1: 45–76.

Bové, Paul A. (1982–3) "The Ineluctability of Difference: Scientific Pluralism and the Critical Intelligence," *Boundary 2* 11, 1–2: 155–76.

Bowering, George (1980) *Burning Water*, Don Mills, Ontario: General Publishing.

Bowles, Gloria and Duelli Klein, Renate (eds) (1983) *Theories of Women's Studies*, London and Boston, Mass: Routledge & Kegan Paul.

Bradbury, Malcolm (1973) *Possibilities: Essays on the State of the Novel*, London, Oxford, and New York: Oxford University Press.

—— (1983) *The Modern American Novel*, Oxford and New York: Oxford University Press.

Bradley, David (1984) "Novelist Alice Walker: Telling the Black Woman's Story," *New York Times Magazine* 8 January: 25–37.

Braudel, Fernand (1980) *On History*, trans. Sarah Matthews, Chicago, Ill: University of Chicago Press.

Braudy, Leo (1970) *Narrative Form in History and Fiction: Hume, Fielding and Gibbon*, Princeton, NJ: Princeton University Press.

Brecht, Bertolt (1964) *Brecht on Theatre: The Development of an Aesthetic*, ed. and trans. John Willett, New York: Hill & Wang; London: Methuen.

—— (1977) "Against Georg Lukács" in Taylor (1977): 68–85.

Bremner, Robert H. (ed.) (1966) *Essays on History and Literature*, np: Ohio State University Press.

Broadbent, Geoffrey (1969) "Meaning into Architecture" in Jencks and Baird (1969): 51–75.

Brooke-Rose, Christine (1981) *A Rhetoric of the Unreal: Studies in Narrative and Structure, Especially of the Fantastic*, Cambridge and New York: Cambridge University Press.

Brooks, Peter (1983) "Fiction and its Referents: A Reappraisal," *Poetics Today* 4, 1: 73–5.

Buchloh, Benjamin H. D. (1984) "Figures of Authority, Ciphers of Regression: Notes on the Return of Representation in European Painting" in Wallis (1984a): 106–35.

—— (1986) "The Primary Colors for the Second Time: A Paradigm Repetition of the Neo-Avant-Garde," *October* 37: 41–52.

Buck-Morss, Susan (1977) *The Origin of Negative Dialectics*, New York: Free Press.

Buford, Bill (1983) "Editorial," *Dirty Realism: New Writing from America, Granta* 8: 4–5.

Bürger, Peter (1984) *Theory of the Avant-Garde*, trans. Michael Shaw, Minneapolis: University of Minnesota Press.

Burgess, Anthony (1980) *Earthly Powers*, New York: Avon.

Burgin, Victor (1986) *The End of Art Theory: Criticism and Postmodernity*, Atlantic Highlands, NJ: Humanities Press International.

Butler, Christopher (1980) *After the Wake: An Essay on the Contemporary Avant-Garde*, Oxford: Oxford University Press.

Byerman, Keith E. (1985) *Fingering the Jagged Grain: Tradition and Form in Recent Black Fiction* Athens Ga and London: University of Georgia Press.

Calinescu, Matei (1977) *Faces of Modernity*, Bloomington: Indiana University Press.

—— (1980) "Ways of Looking at Fiction" in Garvin (1980): 155–70.

—— (1983) "From the One to the Many: Pluralism in Today's Thought" in Hassan and Hassan (1983): 263–88.

—— (1986) "Postmodernism and Some Paradoxes of Periodization" in Fokkema and Bertens (1986): 239–54.

Calvino, Italo (1978) *Invisible Cities*, trans. William Weaver, New York and London:

Harcourt Brace Jovanovich.

Canary, Robert H. and Kozicki, Henry (eds) (1978) *The Writing of History: Literary Form and Historical Understanding*, Madison: University of Wisconsin Press.

Capote, Truman (1965) *In Cold Blood*, New York: Random House.

Caramello, Charles (1983) *Silverless Mirrors: Book, Self and Postmodern American Fiction*, Tallahassee: University Presses of Florida.

Carpentier, Alejo (1963) *Explosion in a Cathedral*, trans. John Sturrock, London: Gollancz.

Carrard, Philippe (1985) "Writing the Past: Le Roy Ladurie and the Voice of the New History," *Studies in 20th Century Literature* 10, 1: 9–30.

Carroll, Berenice A. (ed.) (1976) *Liberating Women's History: Theoretical and Critical Essays*, Urbana: University of Illinois Press.

Carroll, David (1978a) "The Subject of Archaeology or the Sovereignty of the Epistémè," *Modern Language Notes* 93, 4: 695–722.

—— (1978b) "History as Writing," *Clio* 7, 3: 443–61.

—— (1982) *The Subject in Question: The Languages of Theory and the Strategies of Fiction*, Chicago, Ill: University of Chicago Press.

—— (1983) "The Alterity of Discourse: Form, History, and the Question of the Political in M. M. Bakhtin," *Diacritics* 13, 2: 65–83.

Carter, Angela (1972) *The Infernal Desire Machines of Doctor Hoffman*, Harmondsworth: Penguin.

—— (1984) *Nights at the Circus*, London: Picador.

Caton, Charles E. (ed.) (1963) *Philosophy and Ordinary Language*, Urbana: University of Illinois Press.

Caute, David (1972) *The Illusion*, New York: Harper & Row.

Chénetier, Marc (1985) "Charting Contemporary American Fiction: A View from Abroad," *New Literary History* 16, 3: 653–69.

Christensen, Inger (1981) *The Meaning of Metafiction: A Critical Study of Selected Novels by Sterne, Nabokov, Barth and Beckett*, Bergen, Oslo: Universitetsforlaget.

Christian Barbara (1980) *Black Women Novelists: The Development of a Tradition, 1892–1976*, Westport, Conn. and London: Greenwood.

—— (1985) *Black Feminist Criticism: Perspectives on Black Women Writers*, New York: Pergamon.

Clarke, Graham (1980) "Beyond Realism: Recent Black Fiction and the Language of 'The Real Thing'" in Lee (1980): 204–21.

Coetzee, J. M. (1986) *Foe*, Toronto: Stoddart.

Cohen, Sande (1978) "Structuralism and the Writing of Intellectual History," *History and Theory* 17, 2: 175–206.

Collingwood, R. G. (1946) *The Idea of History*, Oxford: Clarendon.

Conroy, Mark (1985) *Modernism and Authority: Strategies of Legitimation in Flaubert and Conrad*, Baltimore, Md: Johns Hopkins University Press.

Coover, Robert (1977) *The Public Burning*, New York: Viking.

Cornillon, Susan Koppelman (ed.) (1972) *Images of Women in Fiction: Feminist Perspectives*, Bowling Green, Ohio: Bowling Green University Popular Press.

Cortázar, Julio (1978) *A Manual for Manuel*, trans. Gregory Rabassa, New York: Pantheon.

Coward, Rosalind and Ellis, John (1977) *Language and Materialism: Developments in Semiology and the Theory of the Subject*, Boston, Mass., London, and Henley: Routledge & Kegan Paul.

Cox, Christoph (1985) "Barthes, Borges, Foucault, Utopia," *Subjects/Objects* 3: 55–69,

Crimp, Douglas (1979) "Pictures," *October* 8: 75–88.

—— (1980) "The Photographic Activity of Postmodernism," *October* 15: 91–101.

—— (1983) "On the Museum's Ruins" in Foster (1983): 43–56.

Crosman, Inge (1981) "Poétique de la lecture romanesque," *L'Espirit Créateur* 21, 2: 70–80.

—— (1983) "Reference and the Reader," *Poetics Today* 4, 1: 89–97.

Culler, Jonathan (1982a) "Structuralism and Grammatology" in Spanos, Bové, and O'Hara (1982): 75–86.

—— (1982b) *On Deconstruction: Theory and Criticism after Structuralism*, Ithaca, NY: Cornell University Press.

—— (1983, 1984) "At the Boundaries: Barthes and Derrida" in Sussman (1983, 1984): 23–41.

Cunliffe, Marcus (ed.) (1975) *American Literature Since 1900*, London: Sphere.

Daiches, David (1971) "Politics and the Literary Imagination" in Hassan (1971a): 100–16.

Daitch, Susan (1986) *L.C.*, London: Virago.

Danto, Arthur C. (1968) *Analytical Philosophy of History*, New York: Columbia University Press.

Davidson, Donald (1980) "Reality without Reference" in Platts (1980): 131–40.

Davis, Douglas (1977) *Artculture: Essays on the Post-Modern*, New York: Harper & Row.

Davis, Lennard J. (1980) "Wicked Actions and Feigned Words: Criminals, Criminality, and the Early English Novel," *Yale French Studies* 59: 106–18.

—— (1983) *Factual Fictions: The Origins of the English Novel*, New York: Columbia University Press.

Davis, Natalie Zemon (1980) "Gender and Genre: Women as Historical Writers, 1400–1820" in Labalme (1980): 153–82.

—— (1983) *The Return of Martin Guerre*, Cambridge, Mass: Harvard University Press.

de Certeau, Michel (1975) *L'Ecriture de l'histoire*, Paris: Gallimard.

de Lauretis, Teresa (1984) *Alice Doesn't: Feminism, Semiotics, Cinema*, Bloomington: Indiana University Press.

—— (1985) "Gaudy Rose: Eco and Narcissism," *SubStance* 47: 13–29.

—— (1987) "The Technologies of Gender", course, International Summer Institute of Structuralism and Semiotics, Toronto.

de Lauretis, Teresa, Huyssen, Andreas, and Woodward, Kathleen (eds) (1980) *The Technological Imagination: Theories and Fictions*, Madison, Wis: Coda Press.

Deleuze, Gilles and Guattari, Félix (1980) *Mille Plateaux*, Paris: Minuit.

Derrida, Jacques (1970, 1972) "Structure, Sign, and Play in the Discourse of the Human Sciences" in Macksey and Donato (1970, 1972): 247–65.

—— (1974) *Glas*, Paris: Galilée.

—— (1976) *Of Grammatology*, trans. Gayatri Spivak, Baltimore, Md: Johns Hopkins University Press.

—— (1977) "Signature Event Context," *Glyph* 1: 172–97.

—— (1978) *Writing and Difference*, trans. Alan Bass, Chicago, Ill: University of Chicago Press.

—— (1980) "La Loi du genre/The Law of Genre," *Glyph* 7: 202–29.

—— (1981a) *Positions*, trans. Alan Bass, Chicago, Ill: University of Chicago Press.

— (1981b) *Dissemination*, trans. Barbara Johnson, Chicago, Ill: University of Chicago Press.

—— (1984) "Voice ii" (letter to verena andermatt conley), *Boundary 2* 12, 2: 76–93.

Dews, Peter (1984) "The Letter and the Line: Discourse and its Other in Lyotard," *Diacritics* 14, 3: 40–9.

D'Haen, Theo (1983) *Text to Reader: A Communicative Approach to Fowles, Barth, Cortázar and Boon*, Amsterdam: John Benjamins.

—— (1986) "Postmodernism in American Fiction and Art" in Fokkema and Bertens (1986): 211–31.

Ditsky, John (1983) "The German Source of *Ragtime*: A Note" in Trenner (1983): 179–81.

Doctorow, E. L. (1960) *Welcome to Hard Times*, New York: Simon & Schuster.

—— (1971) *The Book of Daniel*, New York: Bantam.

—— (1975) *Ragtime*, New York: Random House.

—— (1979, 1980) *Loon Lake*, New York: Random House.

—— (1983) "False Documents" in Trenner (1983): 16–27.

—— (1984) *Lives of the Poets*, New York: Random House.

Doležel, Lubomir (1986) "Possible Worlds and Literary Fictions," address to Nobel Symposium, Stockholm.

Donovan, Josephine (1984) "Toward a Women's Poetics," *Tulsa Studies in Women's Literature* 3, 1–2: 99–110.

Doyle, Nannie (1985) "Desiring Dispersal: Politics and the Postmodern," *Subjects/Objects* 3: 166–79.

DuBois, Barbara (1983) "Passionate Scholarship: Notes on Values, Knowing and Method in Feminist Social Science" in Bowles and Duelli Klein (1983): 105–16.

DuBois, W. E. B. (1973) *The Souls of Black Folk: Essays and Sketches*, repr. Millwood, NY: Kraus-Thomson.

Dundes, Alan (ed.) (1973) *Mother Wit from the Laughing Barrel: Readings in the Interpretation of Afro-American Folklore*, Englewood Cliffs, NJ: Prentice-Hall.

Eagleton, Terry (1976a) *Criticism and Ideology: A Study in Marxist Literary Theory*, London: New Left Books, Verso.

—— (1976b) *Marxism and Literary Criticism*, Berkeley: University of California Press.

—— (1983) *Literary Theory: An Introduction*, Oxford: Blackwell.

—— (1985) "Capitalism, Modernism and Postmodernism," *New Left Review* 152: 60–73.

—— (1986) *Against the Grain: Essays 1975–1985*, London: New Left Books, Verso.

Eco, Umberto (1976) *A Theory of Semiotics*, Bloomington: Indiana University Press.

—— (1979) *The Role of the Reader: Explorations in the Semiotics of Texts*, Bloomington: Indiana University Press.

—— (1983) *The Name of the Rose*, trans. William Weaver, New York: Harcourt Brace Jovanovich.

—— (1983, 1984) *Postscript to The Name of the Rose*, trans. William Weaver, San Diego, Calif., New York, and London: Harcourt Brace Jovanovich.

Egbert, Donald, D. (1970) *Social Radicalism and the Arts*, New York: Knopf.

Ehrmann, Jacques (1981) "The Death of Literature," trans. A. James Arnold, in Federman (1981a): 229–53.

Eisenstein, Hester (1983) *Contemporary Feminist Thought*, Boston, Mass: G. K. Hall.

Ellmann, Mary (1968) *Thinking About Women*, New York: Harcourt Brace Jovanovich.

Enzensberger, Hans Magnus (1974) *The Consciousness Industry: On Literature, Politics and the Media*, selected by Michael Roloff, New York: Seabury.

Even-Zohar, Itamar (1980) "Constraints of Realeme Insertability in Narrative," *Poetics Today* 1, 3: 65–74.

Falck, Robert (1987) "The Second Aging of the New Music: Postscript to Adorno," paper to University College Symposium on "Our Postmodern Heritage," Toronto.

Federman, Raymond (ed.) (1981a) *Surfiction: Fiction Now . . . and Tomorrow*, 2nd edn, Chicago, Ill: Swallow.

—— (1981b) "Surfiction: Four Propositions in Form of an Introduction" in Federman (1981a): 5–15.

—— (1981c) "Fiction Today or the Pursuit of Non-Knowledge" in Federman (1981a): 291–311.

Fekete, John (ed.) (1984a) *The Structural Allegory: Reconstructive Encounters with the New French Thought*, Minneapolis: University of Minnesota Press.

—— (1984b) "Modernity in the Literary Institution: Strategic Anti-Foundational Moves" in Fekete (1984a): 228–47.

Fetterley, Judith (1978) *The Resisting Reader: A Feminist Approach to American Fiction*, Bloomington and London: Indiana University Press.

Fiedler, Leslie (1975) "Cross the Border – Close that Gap: Post-modernism" in Cuncliffe (1975): 344–66.

Findley, Timothy (1977) *The Wars*, Toronto: Clarke, Irwin.

—— (1981) *Famous Last Words*, Toronto and Vancouver: Clarke, Irwin.

Finlay-Pelinski, Marike (1982) "Semiotics or History: From Content Analysis to Contextualized Discursive Practice," *Semiotica* 40, 3–4: 229–66.

Fischer, David Hackett (1970) *Historians' Fallacies: Toward a Logic of Historical Thought*, New York: Harper & Row.

Fish, Stanley (1972) *Self-Consuming Artifacts: The Experience of Seventeenth-Century Literature*, Berkeley: University of California Press.

—— (1980) *Is There a Text in This Class? The Authority of Interpretive Communities*, Cambridge, Mass. and London: Harvard University Press.

—— (1986) "Critical Self-Consciousness or Can We Know What We Are Doing?" lecture, McMaster University, Ontario.

Fisher, Dexter (ed.) (1977) *Minority Language and Literature: Retrospective and Perspective*, New York: Modern Languages Association.

Fisher, Dexter and Stepto, Robert B. (eds) (1979) *Afro-American Literature: The Deconstruction of Instruction*, New York: Modern Languages Association.

Fitzsimmons, Matthew A., Pundt, Alfred G., and Nowell, Charles E. (eds) (1954) *The Development of Historiography*, Harrisburg, Pa: Stackpole.

Fleishman, Avrom (1971) *The English Historical Novel: Walter Scott to Virginia Woolf*, Baltimore, Md: Johns Hopkins University Press.

Fletcher, Angus (ed.) (1976) *The Literature of Fact*, New York: Columbia University Press.

Flynn, Elizabeth A. and Schweickart, Patrocinio P. (eds) (1986) *Gender and Reading: Essays on Readers, Texts and Contexts*, Baltimore, Md and London: Johns Hopkins University Press.

Fogel, Stanley (1984) *A Tale of Two Countries: Contemporary Fiction in English Canada and the United States*, Toronto: ECW Press.

Fokkema, Douwe (1984) *Literary History, Modernism, and Postmodernism*, Amsterdam and Philadelphia, Pa: John Benjamins.

—— (1986a) "Preliminary Remarks" in Fokkema and Bertens (1986): 1–8.

—— (1986b) "The Semantic and Syntactic Organization of Postmodernist Texts" in Fokkema and Bertens (1986): 81–98.

Fokkema, Douwe and Bertens, Hans (eds) (1986) *Approaching Postmodernism*, Amsterdam and Philadelphia, Pa: John Benjamins.

Foley, Barbara (1982) "Fact, Fiction, Facism: Testimony and Mimesis in Holocaust Narratives," *Comparative Literature* 34, 4: 330–60.

—— (1983) "From *U.S.A.* to *Ragtime*: Notes on the Forms of Historical Consciousness in Modern Fiction" in Trenner (1983): 158–78.

—— (1986a) *Telling the Truth: The Theory and Practice of Documentary Fiction*, Ithaca, NY and London: Cornell University Press.

—— (1986b) "Textual 'Subversion' and Political Oppositionality," paper to Modern Languages Association meetings, New York.

Foster, Hal (ed.) (1983) *The Anti-Aesthetic: Essays on Postmodern Culture*, Port Townsend, Wash: Bay Press.

—— (1985) *Recodings: Art, Spectacle, Cultural Politics*, Port Townsend, Wash: Bay Press.

Foucault, Michel (1970) *The Order of Things: An Archaeology of the Human Sciences*, New York: Pantheon.

—— (1972) *The Archaeology of Knowledge and the Discourse on Language*, trans. A. M. Sheridan Smith, New York: Pantheon.

—— (1973) *Madness and Civilization: A History of Insanity in the Age of Reason*, trans. Richard Howard, New York: Random House.

—— (1977) *Language, Counter-Memory, Practice: Selected Essays and Interviews*, trans. Donald F. Bouchard and Sherry Simon, Ithaca, NY: Cornell University Press.

—— (1980) *The History of Sexuality: Volume I: An Introduction*, trans. Robert Hurley, New York: Vintage.

—— (1982) *This Is Not a Pipe*, trans. and ed. James Harkness, Berkeley, Los Angeles, and London: University of California Press.

—— (1985) *The Use of Pleasure*, vol. 2 of *The History of Sexuality*, trans. Robert Hurley, New York: Pantheon.

Fowler, Roger (1981) *Literature as Social Discourse*, London: Batsford.

—— (1985) "Power" in van Dijk (1985a): 61–82.

Fowles, John (1969) *The French Lieutenant's Woman*, Boston, Mass. and Toronto: Little, Brown.

—— (1974) *The Ebony Tower*, Boston, Mass. and Toronto: Little, Brown.

—— (1985) *A Maggot*, Toronto: Collins.

Frampton, Kenneth (1983) "Towards a Critical Regionalism: Six Points for an Architecture of Resistance" in Foster (1983): 16–30.

Frege, Gottlob (1952) "On Sense and Reference" in Black and Geach (1952): 56–78.

French, Philip (1973) *Westerns*, London: Secker & Warburg.

Freud, Sigmund (1920) *Beyond the Pleasure Principle*, in *The Standard Edition of the Complete Psychological Works of Sigmund Freud*, vol. 18, ed. James Strachey, London: Hogarth Press and Institute of Psycho-Analysis, 1955, 1–64.

Fried, Michael (1969) "Manet's Sources: Aspects of his Art, 1859–1865," *Artforum* 7, 7: 28–82.

Frye, Northrop (1957) *Anatomy of Criticism*, Princeton, NJ: Princeton University Press.

Fuentes, Carlos (1964) *The Death of Artemio Cruz*, trans. Sam Hileman, New York: Farrar, Straus, & Giroux.

—— (1985) *The Old Gringo*, trans. Margaret Sayers Peden and the author, New York: Farrar, Straus, & Giroux.

Gaillard, Françoise (1980) "An Unspeakable (Hi)story," trans. Timothy Reiss, *Yale French Studies* 59: 137–54.

Gallop, Jane (1982) *The Daughter's Seduction: Feminism and Psychoanalysis*, Ithaca, NY: Cornell University Press.

García Márquez, Gabriel (1970) *One Hundred Years of Solitude*, trans. Gregory Rabassa, New York: Avon.

—— (1982) *Chronicle of a Death Foretold*, trans. Gregory Rabassa, New York: Ballantine.

Garvin, Harry R. (ed.) (1980) *Romanticism, Modernism, Postmodernism*, Lewisburg, Pa: Bucknell University Press; London: Associated University Press.

Gass, William H. (1985) *Habitations of the Word: Essays*, New York: Simon & Schuster.

Gates, Henry Louis, Jr (ed.) (1984a) *Black Literature and Literary Theory*, London and New York: Methuen.

—— (1984b) "Criticism in the Jungle" in Gates (1984a): 1–24.

—— (1984c) "The Blackness of Blackness: A Critique of the Sign and the Signifying Monkey" in Gates (1984a): 285–321.

—— (1985) "Editor's Introduction: Writing 'Race' and the Difference It Makes," *Critical Inquiry* 12, 1: 1–20.

Gay, Peter (1974a) *Style in History*, New York: Basic.

—— (1974b) "History and the Facts," *Columbia Forum* ns, 3, 2: 7–14.

Genette, Gérard (1980) *Narrative Discourse: An Essay on Method*, trans. Jane E. Lewin, Ithaca, NY: Cornell University Press.

Ghose, Zulfikar (1983) *The Fiction of Reality*, London: Macmillan.

Giddens, Anthony (1981) "Modernism and Post-Modernism," *New German Critique* 22: 15–18.

Gilbert, Sandra and Gubar, Susan (1979a) *The Madwoman in the Attic: The Woman Writer and the Nineteenth-Century Literary Imagination*, New Haven, Conn: Yale University Press.

—— (eds) (1979b) *Shakespeare's Sisters*, Bloomington: Indiana University Press.

Gilligan, Carol (1982) *In a Different Voice: Psychological Theory and Women's Development*, Cambridge, Mass.: Harvard University Press.

Goodman, Nelson (1978) *Ways of Worldmaking*, Indianapolis, Ind.: Hackett.

—— (1981) "Routes of Reference," *Critical Inquiry* 8, 1: 121–32.

Gossman, Lionel (1978) "History and Literature: Reproduction or Signification," in Canary and Kozicki (1978): 3–39.

Gottschalk, Louis (1969) *Understanding History: A Primer of Historical Method*, 2nd edn, New York: Knopf.

Graff, Gerald (1973) "The Myth of the Postmodernist Breakthrough," *TriQuarterly* 26: 383–417.

—— (1975) "Babbitt at the Abyss: The Social Context of Postmodern American Fiction," *TriQuarterly* 33: 305–37.

—— (1979) *Literature Against Itself*, Chicago, Ill.: University of Chicago Press.

—— (1983) "The Pseudo-Politics of Interpretation," *Critical Inquiry* 9, 3: 597–610.

Graham, Joseph F. (1982) "Critical Persuasion: In Response to Stanley Fish" in Spanos, Bové and O'Hara (1982): 147–58.

Grass, Günter (1962) *The Tin Drum*, trans. Ralph Manheim, New York: Pantheon.

Gray, Alasdair (1969, 1981) *Lanark: A Life in Four Books*, New York: Harper & Row.

Green, Martin (1975–6) "Nostalgia Politics," *American Scholar* 45: 841–5.

Greene, Gayle and Kahn, Coppélia (eds) (1985) *Making a Difference: Feminist Literary Criticism*, London and New York: Methuen.

Greene, Thomas M. (1982) *The Light in Troy: Imitation and Discovery in Renaissance Poetry*, New Haven, Conn.: Yale University Press.

Greer, Colin (1984) "The Ethnic Question" in Sayres *et al.* (1984): 119–36.

Griffin, Susan (1980) *Woman and Nature: The Roaring Inside Her*, New York: Harper & Row.

—— (1981, 1982) "The Way of All Ideology" in Keohane, Rosaldo, and Gelpi (1981, 1982): 273–92.

Gross, David S. (1983) "Tales of Obscene Power: Money and Culture, Modernism and History in the Fiction of E. L. Doctorow" in Trenner (1983): 120–50.

Gutman, Herbert G. (1981) "Whatever Happened to History?" *The Nation* 21 November: 521, 553–4.

Habermas, Jürgen (1983) "Modernity – An Incomplete Project" in Foster (1983): 3–15.

—— (1985a) "Neoconservative Culture Criticism in the United States and West Germany: An Intellectual Movement in Two Political Cultures" in Bernstein (1985): 78–94.

—— (1985b) "Questions and Counterquestions" in Bernstein (1985): 192–216.

Haidu, Peter (1982) "Semiotics and History," *Semiotica* 40, 3–4: 187–228.

Hamburger, Käte (1973) *The Logic of Literature*, trans. M. Rose, Bloomington and London: Indiana University Press.

Hamon, Philippe (1982) "Texte et idéologie: pour une poétique de la norme," *Poétique* 49: 105–25.

Harkness, James (1982) "Translator's Introduction" in Foucault (1982): 1–12.

Harrison, Bernard (1985) "Deconstructing Derrida," *Comparative Criticism* 7: 3–24.

Harrison, John (1967) *The Reactionaries: A Study of the Anti-Democratic Intelligentsia*, New York: Schocken.

Harshaw (Hrushovski), Benjamin (1984) "Fictionality and Fields of Reference: Remarks on a Theoretical Framework," *Poetics Today* 5, 2: 227–51.

Hassan, Ihab (ed.) (1971a) *Liberations: New Essays on the Humanities in Revolution*, Middletown, Conn.: Wesleyan University Press.

—— (1971b) "POSTmodernISM," *New Literary History* 3, 1: 5–30.

—— (1975) *Paracriticisms: Seven Speculations of the Times*, Urbana: University of Illinois Press.

—— (1980a) *The Right Promethean Fire: Imagination, Science, and Cultural Change*, Urbana: University of Illinois Press.

—— (1980b) "The Question of Postmodernism" in Garvin (1980): 117–26.

—— (1982) *The Dismemberment of Orpheus: Toward a Postmodern Literature*, 2nd edn, Madison: University of Wisconsin Press.

—— (1983) "Postmodernism: A Vanishing Horizon," paper to Modern Language Association of America, New York.

—— (1986) "Pluralism in Postmodern Perspective," *Critical Inquiry* 12, 3: 503–20.

Hassan, Ihab and Hassan, Sally (eds) (1983) *Innovation/Renovation: New Perspectives on the Humanities*, Madison: University of Wisconsin Press.

Hayman, David (1978) "Double Distancing: An Attribute of the 'Post-Modern' Avant-Garde," *Novel* 12, 1: 33–47.

Heath, Stephen (1974) "Lessons from Brecht," *Screen* 15, 2: 103–28.

—— (1978) "Difference," *Screen* 19, 3: 51–112.

Hellmann, John (1981) *Fables of Fact: The New Journalism as New Fiction*, Urbana: University of Illinois Press.

Henderson, Harry B. (1974) *Versions of the Past: The Historical Imagination in American Fiction*, New York: Oxford University Press.

Hindess, Barry (1977) *Philosophy and Methodology in the Social Sciences*, Hassocks: Harvester.

Hindess, Barry and Hirst, Paul (1977) *Mode of Production and Social Formation*, London: Macmillan.

Hoffmann, Gerhard (1986) "The Absurd and its Forms of Reduction in Postmodern American Fiction" in Fokkema and Bertens (1986): 185–210.

Hoffmann, Gerhard, Hornung, Alfred, and Kunow, Rüdiger (1977) "'Modern,' 'Postmodern,' and 'Contemporary' as Criteria for the Analysis of Twentieth-Century Literature," *Amerikastudien* 22: 19–46.

Hohendahl, Peter Uwe (1982) *The Institution of Criticism*, Ithaca, NY: Cornell University Press.

Holder, Alan (1968) "'What Marvelous Plot .. . . Was Afoot?' History in Barth's *The Sot-Weed Factor*," *American Quarterly* 20, 3: 596–604.

Holloway, John (1953) *The Victorian Sage*, New York: Norton.

Hollowell, John (1977) *Fact and Fiction: The New Journalism and the Nonfiction Novel*, Chapel Hill: University of North Carolina Press.

Hook, Sidney (ed.) (1963) *Philosophy and History: A Symposium*, New York: New York University Press.

Hough, Graham (1966) *An Essay on Criticism*, New York: Norton.

Hubbard, William (1980) *Complicity and Conviction: Steps Toward an Architecture of Convention*, Cambridge, Mass. and London: MIT Press.

Hutcheon, Linda (1980) *Narcissistic Narrative: The Metafictional Paradox*, Waterloo, Ontario: Wilfrid Laurier University Press.

—— (1985) *A Theory of Parody: The Teachings of Twentieth-Century Art Forms*, London and New York: Methuen.

Huyssen, Andreas (1981) "The Search for Tradition: Avant-Garde and Postmodernism in the 1970s," *New German Critique* 22: 23–40.

—— (1986) *After the Great Divide: Modernism, Mass Culture, Postmodernism*, Bloomington: Indiana University Press.

Irigaray, Luce (1974) *Speculum de l'autre femme*, Paris: Minuit.

Jacobs, Jane (1961) *Death and Life of Great American Cities*, New York: Vintage.

Jacobus, Mary (ed.) (1979a) *Women Writing and Writing About Women*, London: Croom Helm.

—— (1979b) "The Difference of View" in Jacobus (1979a): 10–21.

Jakobson, Roman (1960) "Closing Statement: Linguistics and Poetics" in Sebeok (1960): 350–77.

James, Henry (1948) *The Art of Fiction and Other Essays*, New York: Oxford University Press.

Jameson, Fredric (1971) *Marxism and Form: Twentieth-Century Dialectical Theories of Literature*, Princeton, NJ: Princeton University Press.

—— (1972) *The Prison-House of Language: A Critical Account of Structuralism and Russian*

Formalism, Princeton, NJ: Princeton University Press.
—— (1973) "Introduction" in Arvon (1973): vii–xxiv.
—— (1977) "Reflections in Conclusion" in Taylor (1977): 196–213.
—— (1979) "Marxism and Historicism," *New Literary History* 11, 1: 41–73.
—— (1981a) *The Political Unconscious: Narrative as a Socially Symbolic Act*, Ithaca, NY: Cornell University Press.
—— (1981b) "'In the Destructive Element Immerse': Hans-Jürgen Syberberg and Cultural Revolution," *October* 17: 99–118.
—— (1982) "Progress Versus Utopia; or, Can We Imagine the Future?" *Science-Fiction Studies* 9, 2: 147–58.
—— (1983) "Postmodernism and Consumer Society" in Foster (1983): 111–25.
—— (1984a) "Postmodernism, Or The Cultural Logic of Late Capitalism," *New Left Review* 146: 53–92.
—— (1984b) "Foreword" in Lyotard (1984a): vii–xxi.
—— (1984c) "Periodizing the 60s" in Sayres *et al.* (1984): 178–209.
Jardine, Alice (1982) "Gynesis," *Diacritics* 12, 2: 54–65.
Jauss, Hans Robert (1969) "Paradigmawechsel in der Literaturwissenschaft," *Linguistische Berichte* 3: 44–56.
Jencks, Charles (1973) *Le Corbusier and the Tragic View of Architecture*, London: Allen Lane.
—— (1977) *The Language of Post-Modern Architecture*, London: Academy.
—— (1980a) *Post-Modern Classicism: The New Synthesis*, London: Academy.
—— (1980b) *Late-Modern Architecture and Other Essays*, London: Academy.
—— (1982) *Architecture Today*, New York: Abrams.
Jencks, Charles and Baird, George (1969) *Meaning in Architecture*, New York: Braziller.
Johnson, Barbara (1985) "Thresholds of Difference: Structures of Address in Zora Neale Hurston," *Critical Inquiry* 12, 1: 278–89.
Jones, Ann Rosalind (1985) "Inscribing Femininity: French Theories of the Feminine" in G. Greene and Kahn (1985): 80–112.
Jones, Gayl (1976) *Corregidora*, New York: Random House.
Josipovici, Gabriel (1971) *The World and the Book: A Study of Modern Fiction*, London: Macmillan.
—— (1977) *The Lessons of Modernism and Other Essays*, London: Macmillan.
—— (1982) *Writing and the Body*, Princeton, NJ: Princeton University Press.
Kahler, Erich (1968) *The Disintegration of Form in the Arts*, New York: Braziller.
Kamuf, Penny (1982) "Replacing Feminist Criticism," *Diacritics* 12, 2: 42–7.
Kaplan, Cora (1985) "Pandora's Box: Subjectivity, Class and Sexuality in Socialist Feminist Criticism" in G. Greene and Kahn (1985): 146–76.
Kawin, Bruce F. (1982) *The Mind of the Novel: Reflexive Fiction and the Ineffable*, Princeton, NJ: Princeton University Press.
Kellman, Steven G. (1980) *The Self-Begetting Novel*, London: Macmillan.
Keneally, Thomas (1982) *Schindler's Ark*, London: Hodder & Stoughton.
Kennard, Jean E. (1986) "Ourself behind Ourself: A Theory for Lesbian Readers" in Flynn and Schweickart (1986): 63–80.
Kennedy, William (1975) *Legs*, Harmondsworth: Penguin.
Keohane, Nannerl O., Rosaldo, Michelle Z., and Gelpi, Barbara C. (eds) (1981, 1982) *Feminist Theory: A Critique of Ideology*, Chicago, Ill.: University of Chicago Press.

Kermode, Frank (1966, 1967) *The Sense of an Ending*, London and New York: Oxford University Press.

—— (1968a) "Novel, History and Type," *Novel* 1, 3: 231–8.

—— (1968b) "Modernisms" in Bergonzi (1968): 66–92.

—— (1971) "Revolution: The Role of the Elders" in Hassan (1971a): 87–99.

—— (1979) *The Genesis of Secrecy: On the Interpretation of Narrative*, Cambridge, Mass. and London: Harvard University Press.

Kern, Robert (1978) "Composition as Recognition: Robert Creeley and Postmodern Poetics," *Boundary 2* 6, 3 and 7, 1: 211–30.

Kibbins, Gary (1983) "The Enduring of the Artsystem," *Open Letter* 5th series, 5–6: 126–39.

Kingston, Maxine Hong (1976) *The Woman Warrior: Memories of a Girlhood Among Ghosts*, New York: Knopf.

—— (1980) *China Men*, New York: Ballantine.

Kirby, Michael (1975) "Post-Modern Dance Issue: An Introduction," *Drama Review* 19, 1: 3–4.

Kiremidjian, G. D. (1969) "The Aesthetics of Parody," *Journal of Aesthetics and Art Criticism* 28, 2: 231–42.

Klinkowitz, Jerome (1980) *Literary Disruptions: The Making of a Post-Contemporary American Fiction*, 2nd edn, Urbana: University of Illinois Press.

—— (1984) *The Self-Apparent Word: Fiction as Language/Language as Fiction*, Carbondale: Southern Illinois University Press.

—— (1985) *Literary Subversions: New American Fiction and the Practice of Criticism*, Carbondale and Edwardsville: Southern Illinois University Press.

Kogawa, Joy (1981) *Obasan*, Toronto: Lester & Orpen Dennys.

Köhler, Michael (1977) "'Postmodernismus': Ein begriffsgeschichtlicher Überblick," *Amerikastudien* 22, 1: 8–18.

Kosinski, Jerzy (1977) *Blind Date*, Boston, Mass.: Houghton Mifflin.

—— (1986) "Death in Cannes," *Esquire* March: 81–9.

Krafft, John (1984) "Thomas Pynchon" in Sayres *et al.* (1984): 283–5.

Kramer, Hilton (1982) "Postmodern: Art and Culture in the 1980s," *The New Criterion* 1, 1: 36–42.

Kramer, Jonathan D. (1984) "Can Modernism Survive George Rochberg?" *Critical Inquiry* 11, 2: 341–54.

Krauss, Rosalind (1980) "Poststructuralism and the 'Paraliterary,'" *October* 13: 36–40.

—— (1985) *The Originality of the Avant-Garde and Other Modernist Myths*, Cambridge, Mass. and London: MIT Press.

Kress, Gunther (1985) " Ideological Structures in Discourse" in van Dijk (1985a): 27–42.

Kress, Gunther and Hodge, Robert (1979) *Language as Ideology*, London and Boston, Mass.: Routledge & Kegan Paul.

Krieger, Murray (1974) "Fiction, History, and Empirical Reality," *Critical Inquiry* 1, 2: 335–60.

—— (1976) *Theory of Criticism: A Tradition and its System*, Baltimore, Md: Johns Hopkins University Press.

—— (1982) "Poetic Presence and Illusion II: Formalist Theory and the Duplicity of Metaphor" in Spanos, Bové and O'Hara (1982): 95–122.

Kripke, Saul (1980) *Naming and Necessity*, Cambridge, Mass.: Harvard University Press.

Kristeva, Julia (1969) *Sēmēiotikē: Recherches pour une sémanalyse*, Paris: Seuil.
—— (1974) *La Révolution du langage poétique*, Paris: Seuil.
—— (1980a) "Postmodernism?" in Garvin (1980): 136–41.
—— (1980b) *Desire in Language*, trans. Thomas Gora, Alice Jardine, and Leon S. Roudiez, Oxford: Blackwell; New York: Columbia University Press.
Kroetsch, Robert (1969) *The Studhorse Man*, Toronto: Macmillan.
Kroker, Arthur and Cook, David (1986) *The Postmodern Scene: Excremental Culture and Hyper-Aesthetics*, Montreal: New World Perspectives.
Krysinski, Wladimir (1981) *Carrefour de signes: Essais sur le roman moderne*, The Hague: Mouton.
Kuhn, Annette (1982) *Women's Pictures*, London and Boston, Mass.: Routledge & Kegan Paul.
Kundera, Milan (1985) *Jacques and his Master: An Homage to Diderot in Three Acts*, trans. Michael Henry Heim, New York: Harper & Row.
Kuwabara, Bruce (1987) "A Problem for Post-Modern Architecture: Which Heritage to Preserve?"; panel at University College Symposium on "Our Postmodern Heritage," Toronto.
Kuznetsov, Anatoli (1966, 1967) *Babi Yar*, trans. Jacob Guralsky, New York: Dial Press.
Labalme, Patricia H. (ed.) (1980) *Beyond their Sex: Learned Women of the European Past*, New York and London: New York University Press.
LaCapra, Dominick (1985a) *History and Criticism*, Ithaca, NY: Cornell University Press.
—— (1985b) "On Grubbing in My Personal Archives: An Historiographical Exposé of Sorts (Or How I Learned to Stop Worrying and Love Transference)," *Boundary 2* 13, 2–3: 43–67.
Lacoue-Labarthe, Philippe (1984) "Talks," trans. Christopher Fynsk, *Diacritics* 14, 3: 24–37.
Lange, Victor (1969) "Fact in Fiction," *Comparative Literature Studies* 6, 3: 253–61.
Lasch, Christopher (1969) *The Agony of the American Left*, New York: Knopf.
Lavis, Georges (1971) "Le Texte littéraire, le référent, le réel, le vrai," *Cahiers d'analyse textuelle* 13: 7–22.
Lawson, Thomas (1984) "Last Exit: Painting" in Wallis (1984a): 152–65.
Lee, A. Robert (ed.) (1980) *Black Fiction: New Studies in the Afro-American Novel Since 1945*, London: Vision Press.
Lefebvre, Henri (1968) *La Vie quotidienne dans le monde moderne*, Paris: Gallimard.
Le Goff, Jacques and Nora, Pierre (eds) (1974) *Faire de l'histoire*, 3 vols, Paris: Gallimard.
Leitch, Vincent B. (1983) *Deconstructive Criticism: An Advanced Introduction*, New York: Columbia University Press.
—— (1986) "Deconstruction and Pedagogy" in Nelson (1986a): 45–56.
Lemaire, Gérard-Georges (1981) "Le Spectre du post-modernisme," *Le Monde Dimanche* 18 octobre: xiv.
Lentricchia, Frank (1980) *After the New Criticism*, Chicago, Ill.: University of Chicago Press.
Lerner, Gerda (1979) *The Majority Finds its Past: Placing Women in History*, London: Oxford University Press.
Le Roy Ladurie, Emmanuel (1979) *Carnival in Romans*, trans. Mary Feeney, New York: Braziller.

Lethen, Helmut (1986) "Modernism Cut in Half: The Exclusion of the Avant-garde and the Debate on Postmodernism" in Fokkema and Bertens (1986): 233–8.

Levine, George (1968) *The Boundaries of Fiction: Carlyle, Macaulay, Newman*, Princeton, NJ: Princeton University Press.

Levine, Paul (1966) "Reality and Fiction," *Hudson Review* 19, 1: 135–8.

—— (1985) *E. L. Doctorow*, London and New York: Methuen.

Lewis, David (1978) "Truth in Fiction," *American Philosophical Quarterly* 15, 1: 37–46.

Lewis, Mark (1984) "Covering Up Some Old Wounds," *Parachute* 36: 66–9.

Lewis, Philip (1982) "The Post-Structuralist Condition," *Diacritics* 12, 1: 2–24.

Lewis, Thomas E. (1979) "Notes Toward a Theory of the Referent," *PMLA* 94, 3: 459–75.

Lindenberger, Herbert (1984) "Toward a New History in Literary Study," *Profession 84*: 16–23.

Lippard, Lucy R. (1984) "Trojan Horses: Activist Art and Power" in Wallis (1984a): 340–58.

Lodge, David (1977) *The Modes of Modern Writing: Metaphor, Metonymy, and the Typology of Modern Literature*, London: Edward Arnold.

Logan, Marie-Rose (1980) "Rethinking History . . .," *Yale French Studies* 59: 3–6.

Longenbach, James (1987) *Modernist Poetics of History: Pound, Eliot, and the Sense of the Past*, Princeton, NJ: Princeton University Press.

Lucas, John (1986) "Irony of Ironies," *Times Literary Supplement* (London), 4 July: 731.

Lucente, Gregory L. (1986) *Beautiful Fables: Self-consciousness in Italian Narrative from Manzoni to Calvino*, Baltimore, Md and London: Johns Hopkins University Press.

Lukács, Georg (1962) *The Historical Novel*, trans. Hannah and Stanley Mitchell, London: Merlin.

Lyotard, Jean-François (1971) *Discours, figure*, Paris: Klincksieck.

—— (1977) *Instructions païennes*, Paris: Galilée.

—— (1978) "One of the Things at Stake in Women's Struggles," trans. D. J. Clarke, W. Woodhull and J. Mowitt, *Sub-Stance* 20: 9–16.

—— (1979) *Le Mur du Pacifique*, Paris: Galilée.

—— (1983) *Le Différend*, Paris: Minuit.

—— (1984a) *The Postmodern Condition: A Report on Knowledge*, trans. Geoff Bennington and Brian Massumi, Minneapolis: University of Minnesota Press.

—— (1984b) "Answering the Question: What is Postmodernism?" trans. Régis Durand, in Lyotard (1984a): 71–82.

—— (1984c) "The *Différend*, the Referent, and the Proper Name," trans. Georges Van Den Abbeele, *Diacritics* 14, 3: 4–14.

—— (1984d) "Interview," with (and trans.) Georges Van Den Abbeele, *Diacritics* 14, 3: 16–21.

—— (1986) *Le Postmoderne expliqué aux enfants: Correspondance 1982–1985*, Paris: Galilée.

Lyotard, Jean-François and Francken, Ruth (1983) *L'Histoire de Ruth*, Paris: Le Castor Astral.

Lyotard, Jean-François and Adami (1983) *Peintures récentes; On dirait qu'une ligne. . . . Repères, cahiers d'art contemporain* 6, Paris: Galerie Maeght.

Lyotard, Jean-François and Arakawa (1984) *Padiglione d'arte contemporanea; Longitude 180' W or E*, trans. Maurizio Ferraris and Mary Ann Caws, Milan: Edizioni Nava Milano.

MacCabe, Colin (1974) "Realism and the Cinema: Notes on Some Brechtian Theses," *Screen* 15, 2: 7–27.

—— (1978–9) "The Discursive and the Ideological in Film: Notes on the Conditions of Political Intervention," *Screen* 19, 4: 29–43.

McCaffery, Larry (1982) *The Metafictional Muse*, Pittsburgh, Pa: University of Pittsburgh Press.

McCallum, Pamela (1985) "Benjamin on Allegory: Carpentier's *Explosion in a Cathedral*," lecture at McMaster University, Ontario.

MacCannell, Dean and MacCannell, Juliet Flower (1982) *The Time of the Sign: A Semiotic Interpretation of Modern Culture*, Bloomington: Indiana University Press.

McCarthy, Mary (1961) *On the Contrary*, New York: Farrar, Straus, & Cudahy.

McConnell, Frank (1980) "Ishmael Reed's Fiction: Da Hoodoo Is Put on America" in Lee (1980): 136–48.

McCormick, Carlo (1987) "Fracts of Life," *Artforum* 25, 5: 91–5.

Macdonell, Diane (1986) *Theories of Discourse: An Introduction*, Oxford: Blackwell.

McGinn, Colin (1980) "Truth and Use" in Platts (1980): 19–40.

McHale, Brian (1979) "Modernist Reading, Post-Modern Text: The Case of *Gravity's Rainbow*," *Poetics Today* 1, 1–2: 85–110.

—— (1982) "Writing about Postmodern Writing," *Poetics Today* 3, 3: 211–27.

—— (1986) "Change of Dominant from Modernist to Postmodernist Writing" in Fokkema and Bertens (1986): 53–79.

—— (1987) *Postmodernist Fiction*, London and New York: Methuen.

Macherey, Pierre (1978) *A Theory of Literary Production*, trans. Geoffrey Wall, London: Routledge & Kegan Paul.

MacKinnon, Catherine A. (1981, 1982) "Feminism, Marxism, Method, and the State: An Agenda for Theory" in Keohane, Rosaldo, and Gelpi (1981, 1982): 1–30.

Macksey, Richard and Donato, Eugenio (eds) (1970, 1972) *The Structuralist Controversy: The Languages of Criticism and the Sciences of Man*, Baltimore, Md: Johns Hopkins University Press.

Mailer, Norman (1968) *The Armies of the Night: History as a Novel, the Novel as History*, New York: New American Library.

—— (1970) *Of a Fire on the Moon*, Boston, Mass.: Little, Brown.

Major, Clarence (1975) *Reflex and Bone Structure*, New York: Fiction Collective.

Malmgren, Carl Darryl (1985) *Fictional Space in the Modernist and Postmodernist American Novel*, Lewisburg, Pa: Bucknell University Press.

Manganelli, Giorgio (1981) *Amore*, Milano: Rizzoli.

Marcuse, Herbert (1978) *The Aesthetic Dimension*, Boston, Mass.: Beacon Press.

Margolis, Joseph (1965) *The Language of Art and Art Criticism*, Detroit, Mich.: Wayne State University Press.

Marks, Elaine and de Courtivron, Isabelle (eds) (1980) *New French Feminisms*, Amherst: University of Massachusetts Press.

Marrou, Henri I. (1966) *The Meaning of History*, trans. Robert J. Olsen, Baltimore, Md: Helicon.

Martin, Richard (1980) "Clio Bemused: The Uses of History in Contemporary American Fiction," *SubStance* 27: 13–24.

Martin, Wallace (1980) "Postmodernism: Ultima Thule or Seim Anew" in Garvin (1980): 142–54.

—— (1986) *Recent Theories of Narrative*, Ithaca, NY: Cornell University Press.

Marxist-Feminist Literature Collective (1978) "Women's Writing: *Jane Eyre, Shirley,*

Villette, Aurora Leigh," *Ideology and Consciousness* 1, 3: 27–48.

Massumi, Brian (1985) "The Power of the Particular," *Subject/Objects* 3: 6–23.

Mazurek, Raymond A. (1982) "Metafiction, the Historical Novel, and Coover's *The Public Burning*," *Critique* 23, 3: 29–42.

Mazzaro, Jerome (1980) *Postmodern American Poetry*, Urbana: University of Illinois Press.

Mellard, James M. (1980) *The Exploded Form: The Modernist Novel in America*, Urbana: University of Illinois Press.

Menna, Filiberto (1984) "Gli anni Settanta," *Il Verri* n. 1–2, 7th series: 9–14.

Metscher, Thomas (1972) "Ästhetik als Abbildtheorie. Erkenntnistheoretische Grundlagen materialistischer Kunsttheorie und das Realismusproblem in den Literaturwissenschaften," *Das Argument* 77: 919–76.

—— (1975) "Ästhetische Erkenntnis und realistische Kunst," *Das Argument* 90: 229–58.

Miller, J. Hillis (1974) "Narrative and History," *ELH* 41: 455–73.

Miller, Nancy K. (1982) "The Text's Heroine: A Feminist Critic and her Fictions," *Diacritics* 12, 2: 48–53.

Miller, R. Baxter (ed.) (1981) *Black American Literature and Humanism*, Lexington: University Press of Kentucky.

Mink, Louis O. (1978) "Narrative Form as a Cognitive Instrument" in Canary and Kozicki (1978): 129–49.

—— (1981) "Everyman His or Her Own Annalist," *Critical Inquiry* 7, 4: 777–83.

Mitchell, Juliet (1974) *Psychoanalysis and Feminism*, Harmondsworth: Penguin.

Mitchell, Juliet and Rose, Jacqueline (eds) (1982) *Feminine Sexuality: Jacques Lacan and the Ecole Freudienne*, trans. Juliet Mitchell and Jacqueline Rose, London and New York: R. W. Norton.

Mitchell-Kernan, Claudia (1973) "Signifying" in Dundes (1973): 310–28.

Moi, Toril (1985a) *Sexual/Textual Politics: Feminist Literary Theory*, London and New York: Methuen.

—— (1985b) "Power, Sex and Subjectivity: Feminist Reflections on Foucault," *Paragraph* 5: 95–102.

Morante, Elsa (1977) *History: A Novel*, trans. William Weaver, New York: Vintage.

Moreno, César Fernández (ed.) (1974) *América Latina en su Literatura*, 2nd edn, Buenos Aires: Siglo XXI.

Morgan, Robert P. (1977) "On the Analysis of Recent Music," *Critical Inquiry* 4, 1: 33–53.

Morgan, Robin (ed.) (1970) *Sisterhood is Powerful: An Anthology of Writings from the Women's Liberation Movement*, New York: Vintage.

Morrison, Toni (1974) *Sula*, New York: Knopf.

—— (1977) *Song of Solomon*, New York: Signet.

—— (1981) *Tar Baby*, New York: Signet.

Moser, Walter (1984) "Mode-Moderne-Postmoderne," *Études Françaises* 20, 2: 29–48.

—— (forthcoming) "Gianni Vattimo's 'Pensiero Debole' Or: Avoiding the Traps of Modernity?" *Occasional Papers of Center for Humanistic Studies, University of Minnesota*.

Mulvey, Laura (1975) "Visual Pleasure and Narrative Cinema," *Screen* 16, 3: 6–18.

—— (1979) "Feminism, Film and the *Avant-Garde*" in Jacobus (1979a): 177–95.

Munich, Adrienne (1985) "Notorious Signs, Feminist Criticism and Literary Tradition" in G. Green and Kahn (1985): 238–59.

Munro, Alice (1972) *Lives of Girls and Women*, New York: McGraw Hill.

Munz, Peter (1977) *The Shapes of Time*, Middletown, Conn.: Wesleyan University Press.

Musarra, Ulla (1986) "Duplication and Multiplication: Postmodernist Devices in the Novels of Italo Calvino" in Fokkema and Bertens (1986): 135–55.

Nabokov, Vladimir (1962) *Pale Fire*, New York: Putnam's Sons.

Nead, Lynda (1986) "Feminism, Art History and Cultural Politics" in Rees and Borzello (1986): 120–4.

Nelson, Cary (ed.) (1986a) *Theory in the Classroom*, Urbana and Chicago: University of Illinois Press.

—— (1986b) "Introduction" to Nelson (1986a): ix–xvi.

Newman, Charles (1985) *The Post-Modern Aura: The Act of Fiction in an Age of Inflation*, Evanston, Ill.: Northwestern University Press.

Newton, Judith Lowder (1981) *Women, Power, and Subversion: Social Strategies in British Fiction 1778–1860*, Athens, Ga: University of Georgia Press.

Niesz, Anthony J. and Holland, Norman N. (1984) "Interactive Fiction," *Critical Inquiry* 11, 1: 110–29.

Nietzsche, Friedrich (1957) *The Use and Abuse of History*, trans. Adrian Collins, Indianapolis, Ind. and New York: Liberal Arts Press and Bobbs-Merrill.

Nochlin, Linda (1983) "The Imaginary Orient," *Art in America* 71, 5: 118–31; 187–9.

Norris, Christopher (1985) *The Contest of Faculties: Philosophy and Theory After Deconstruction*, London and New York: Methuen.

Nye, Russel B. (1966) "History and Literature: Branches of the Same Tree" in Bremner (1966): 123–59.

Oakeshott, Michael (1983) *On History and Other Essays*, Oxford: Oxford University Press.

Ohmann, Richard (1971) "Speech Acts and the Definition of Literature," *Philosophy and Rhetoric* 4, 1: 1–19.

Oliva, Achille Bonito (1984) "La trans-avanguardia," *Il Verri* n. 1–2, 7th series: 56–79.

Ondaatje, Michael (1976) *Coming Through Slaughter*, Toronto: Anansi.

—— (1982) *Running in the Family*, Toronto: McClelland & Stewart.

Orr, Linda (1986) "The Revenge of Literature: A History of History," *New Literary History* 18, 1: 1–22.

Ortega y Gasset, José (1963) *Meditations on Quixote*, trans. Evelyn Rugg and Diego Marín, New York: Norton.

Orvell, Miles (1980) "Reproduction and 'The Real Thing': The Anxiety of Realism in the Age of Photography" in de Lauretis, Huyssen, and Woodward (1980): 49–64.

Owens, Craig (1980a) "The Allegorical Impulse: Toward a Theory of Postmodernism. Part I," *October* 12: 67–86.

—— (1980b) "The Allegorical Impulse: Toward a Theory of Postmodernism. Part II," *October* 13: 59–80.

—— (1982) "Representation, Appropriation & Power," *Art in America* 70, 5: 9–21.

—— (1983) "The Discourse of Others: Feminists and Postmodernism" in Foster (1983): 57–82.

Palmer, Richard E. (1977) "Postmodernity and Hermeneutics," *Boundary 2* 5, 2: 363–93.

Parameswaran, Uma (1983) "Handcuffed to History: Salman Rushdie's Art," *Ariel* 14, 4: 34–45.

Parker, Andrew (1981) "'Taking Sides' (On History): Derrida Re-Marx," *Diacritics* 11, 2: 57–73.

Paterson, Janet (1986) "Le Roman 'postmoderne': mise au point et perspectives," *Canadian Review of Comparative Literature* 13, 2: 238–55.

Patteson, Richard (1974) "What Stencil Knew: Structure and Certitude in Pynchon's *V*," *Critique* 16, 2: 30–44.

Peckham, Morse (1965) *Man's Rage for Chaos: Biology, Behavior, and the Arts*, Philadelphia, Pa: Chilton Books.

Perloff, Marjorie (1985) *The Dance of the Intellect: Studies in the Poetry of the Pound Tradition*, Cambridge; Cambridge University Press.

Platts, Mark (ed.) (1980) *Reference, Truth and Reality*, London and Boston, Mass.: Routledge & Kegan Paul.

Pontbriand, Chantal (1983) "The Question in Performance," *Open Letter* 5th series, 5–6: 18–26.

Pops, Martin (1984) *Home Remedies*, Amherst: University of Massachusetts Press.

Portoghesi, Paolo (1974) *Le inibizioni dell'architettura moderna*, Bari: Laterza.

—— (1982) *After Modern Architecture*, trans. Meg Shore, New York: Rizzoli.

—— (1983) *Postmodern: The Architecture of the Postindustrial Society*, New York: Rizzoli.

—— (1985) "La forza della chiarezza," *Eupalino* 5: 7–17.

Puig, Manuel (1978, 1979) *Kiss of the Spider Woman*, trans. Thomas Colchie, New York: Random House.

Pullin, Faith (1980) "Landscapes of Reality: The Fiction of Contemporary Afro-American Women" in Lee (1980): 173–203.

Pütz, Manfred (1973) "The Struggle of the Postmodern: Books on a New Concept in Criticism," *Kritikon Litterarum* 2: 225–37.

Pynchon, Thomas (1961, 1963) *V*, New York: Bantam.

—— (1965) *The Crying of Lot 49*, New York: Bantam.

—— (1973) *Gravity's Rainbow*, New York: Viking.

Quarrington, Paul (1983) *Home Game*, Toronto and New York: Doubleday.

Rabinowitz, Peter J. (1981) "Assertion and Assumption: Fictional Patterns and the External World," *PMLA* 96, 3: 408–19.

Radhakrishnan, Rajagoplan (1983) "The Post-Modern Event and the End of Logocentrism," *Boundary 2* 12, 1: 33–60.

Rainwater, Catherine and Scheick, William J. (eds) (1985) *Contemporary American Women Writers: Narrative Strategies*, Lexington: University Press of Kentucky.

Rajchman, John (1985) *Michel Foucault: The Freedom of Philosophy*, New York: Columbia University Press.

Rawson, Claude (1986) "A Poet in the Postmodern Playground," *Times Literary Supplement* (London), 4 July: 723–4.

Reed, Ishmael (1967) *The Free-Lance Pallbearers*, Garden City, NY: Doubleday.

—— (1969) *Yellow Back Radio Broke-Down*, Garden City, NY: Doubleday.

—— (1972a) *Conjure: Selected Poems 1963–70*, Amhurst: University of Massachusetts Press.

—— (1972b) *Mumbo Jumbo*, Garden City, NY: Doubleday.

—— (1976) *Flight to Canada*, New York: Random House.

—— (1982) *The Terrible Twos*, New York: St Martin's/Marek.

Rees, A. L. and Borzello, Frances (eds) (1986) *The New Art History*, London: Camden Press.

Reiss, Timothy J. (1982) *The Discourse of Modernism*, Ithaca, NY: Cornell University Press.

—— (1983) "Critical Environments: Cultural Wilderness or Cultural History?" *Canadian Review of Comparative Literature* 10, 2: 192–209.

Renault, Mary (1973) "History in Fiction," *Times Literary Supplement* (London), 23 March: 315–16.

Richards, I. A. (1924) *Principles of Literary Criticism*, New York: Harcourt Brace Jovanovich.

Ricoeur, Paul (1976) *Interpretation Theory: Discourse and the Surplus of Meaning*, Fort Worth: Texas Christian University Press.

—— (1984a) *Time and Narrative: Volume I*, trans. Kathleen McLaughlin and David Pellauer, Chicago, Ill. and London: University of Chicago Press.

—— (1984b) *La Configuration dans le récit de fiction: Temps et récit II*, Paris: Seuil.

—— (1986) *Le Temps raconté: Temps et récit III*, Paris: Seuil.

Riffaterre, Michael (1984) "Intertextual Representation: On Mimesis as Interpretive Discourse," *Critical Inquiry* 11, 1: 141–62.

Robbins, Tom (1976) *Even Cowgirls Get the Blues*, New York: Houghton Mifflin.

Robertson, Mary F. (1984) "Hystery, Herstory, History: 'Imagining the Real' in Thomas's *The White Hotel*," *Contemporary Literature* 25, 4: 452–77.

Robinson, Lillian S. and Vogel, Lise (1971) "Modernism and History," *New Literary History* 3, 1: 177–99.

Rochberg, George (1984) "Can the Arts Survive Modernism? (A Discussion of the Characteristics, History, and Legacy of Modernism)," *Critical Inquiry* 11, 2: 317–40.

Rorty, Richard (1982) "Is There a Problem about Fictional Discourse?" in his *Consequences of Pragmatism (Essays: 1972–1980)*, Minneapolis: University of Minnesota Press: 110–38.

—— (1984a) "Habermas, Lyotard et la postmodernité," *Critique* 442: 181–97.

—— (1984b) "Deconstruction and Circumvention," *Critical Inquiry* 11, 1: 1–23.

—— (1985) "Texts and Lumps," *New Literary History* 17, 1: 1–16.

Rosenberg, Harold (1973) *Discovering the Present: Three Decades in Art, Culture and Politics*, Chicago, Ill.: University of Chicago Press.

Rosler, Martha (1981) *3 Works*, Halifax: Nova Scotia College of Art and Design.

—— (1984) "Lookers, Buyers, Dealers, and Makers: Thoughts on Audience" in Wallis (1984a): 310–39.

Rosso, Stefano (1983) "A Correspondence with Umberto Eco," trans. Carolyn Springer, *Boundary 2* 12, 1: 1–13.

Roth, Martin (1985) "Some Comments on Foucault's 'History of Madness,'" *Paragraph* 5: 103–7.

Rushdie, Salman (1981) *Midnight's Children*, London: Picador.

—— (1983) *Shame*, London: Picador.

Russell, Charles (1974) "The Vault of Language: Self-Reflective Artifice in Contemporary American Fiction," *Modern Fiction Studies* 20, 3: 349–59.

—— (1980a) "The Context of the Concept" in Garvin (1980): 181–93.

—— (1980b) "Individual Voice in the Collective Discourse: Literary Innovation in Postmodern American Fiction," *Sub-Stance* 27: 29–39.

—— (ed.) (1981) *The Avant-Garde Today: An International Anthology*, Urbana: University of Illinois Press.

—— (1985) *Poets, Prophets, and Revolutionaries: The Literary Avant-garde from Rimbaud through Postmodernism*, New York and Oxford: Oxford University Press.

Ruthven, K. K. (1984) *Feminist Literary Studies: An Introduction*, Cambridge: Cambridge University Press.

Ryan, Michael (1982) *Marxism and Deconstruction: A Critical Articulation*, Baltimore, Md and London: Johns Hopkins University Press.

Saad, Gabriel (1983) "L'Histoire et la révolution dans *Le Siècle des lumières*," in *Quinze Etudes autour de El Siglo de las luces de Alejo Carpentier*, Paris: L'Harmattan: 113–22.

Said, Edward W. (1975a) *Beginnings: Intention and Method*, New York: Basic.

—— (1975b) "Contemporary Fiction and Criticism," *TriQuarterly* 33: 231–56.

—— (1983) *The World, the Text, and the Critic*, Cambridge, Mass.: Harvard University Press.

—— (1985) "An Ideology of Difference," *Critical Inquiry* 12, 1: 38–58.

—— (1986) "Cultural and Imperialism," course at University of Toronto.

Sarduy, Severo (1974) "El barroco y el neobarroco" in Moreno (1974): 167–84.

Sayres, Sohnya, Stephanson, Anders, Aronowitz, Stanley, and Jameson, Fredric (eds) (1984) *The 60s Without Apology*, Minneapolis: *Social Text* and University of Minnesota Press.

Schafer, Roy (1980) "Narration in the Psychoanalytic Dialogue," *Critical Inquiry* 7, 1: 29–53.

Schaffer, E. S. (1985) "Editor's Introduction: Changing the Boundaries of Literature, Theory, and Criticism," *Comparative Criticism* 7: xi–xxiv.

Schmid, Herta (1986) "Postmodernism in Russian Drama: Vampilov, Amalrik, Aksënov" in Fokkema and Bertens (1986): 157–84.

Schmidt, S. J. (1984) "The Fiction Is that Reality Exists: A Constructivist Model of Reality, Fiction, and Literature," *Poetics Today* 5, 2: 253–74.

Scholes, Robert (1968) "Double Perspective on Hysteria," *Saturday Review* 24: 37.

—— (1980) "Language, Narrative, and Anti-Narrative," *Critical Inquiry* 7, 1: 204–12.

Schulz, Max (1973) *Black Humor Fiction of the Sixties: A Pluralistic Definition of Man and His World*, Athens, Ohio: Ohio University Press.

Scott, Chris (1982) *Antichthon*, Montreal: Quadrant.

Seamon, Roger G. (1983) "Narrative Practice and the Theoretical Distinction Between History and Fiction," *Genre* 16, 3: 197–218.

Searle, John R. (1975) "The Logical Status of Fictional Discourse," *New Literary History* 6, 2: 319–32.

Sebeok, Thomas (1960) *Style in Language*, Cambridge, Mass.: MIT Press.

Seelye, John (1976) "Doctorow's Dissertation," *New Republic* 10 April: 21–3.

Sekula, Allan (1978) "Dismantling Modernism, Reinventing Documentary (Notes on the Politics of Representation)," *Massachusetts Review* 19, 4: 859–83.

Shaw, Harry E. (1983) *The Forms of Historical Fiction: Sir Walter Scott and His Successors*, Ithaca, NY and London: Cornell University Press.

Showalter, Elaine (1977) *A Literature of Their Own: British Women Novelists from Brontë to Lessing*, Princeton, NJ: Princeton University Press.

—— (1979) "Towards a Feminist Poetics" in Jacobus (1979a): 22–41.

Silverman, Kaja (1983) *The Subject of Semiotics*, New York: Oxford University Press.

Sisk, John (1971) "Aquarius Rising," *Commentary* 51, 5: 83–4.

Siska, William C. (1979) "Metacinema: A Modern Necessity," *Literature/Film Quarterly* 7, 1: 285–9.

Skvorecky, Josef (1986) *Dvorak in Love: A Light-hearted Dream*, trans. Paul Wilson, Toronto: Lester & Orpen Dennys.

Smart, Robert Augustin (1985) *The Nonfiction Novel*, Lanham, New York and London: University Press of America.

Smith, Barbara (1979) "Toward a Black Feminist Criticism," *Women's Studies International Quarterly* 2: 193–4.

Smith, Barbara Herrnstein (1978) *On the Margins of Discourse: The Relation of Literature to Language*, Chicago, Ill.: University of Chicago Press.

—— (1980) "Narrative Versions, Narrative Theories," *Critical Inquiry* 7, 1: 213–36.

Smith, Paul (1985) "Difference in America," *Art in America* 73, 4: 190–9.

Snead, James A. (1984) "Repetition as a Figure of Black Culture" in Gates (1984a): 59–79.

Sollors, Werner (1986) *Beyond Ethnicity: Consent and Descent in American Culture*, New York and Oxford: Oxford University Press.

Solomon-Godeau, Abigail (1984) "Photography After Art Photography" in Wallis (1984a): 74–85.

Sontag, Susan (1967) *Against Interpretation and Other Essays*, New York: Dell.

Sosnoski, James J. (1985) "Literary Study as a Field for Inquiry," *Boundary 2* 13, 2–3: 91–104.

Spacks, Patricia Meyer (1976) *The Female Imagination: A Literary and Psychological Investigation of Women's Writing*, London: Allen & Unwin.

Spanos, William V. (1972) "The Detective and the Boundary: Some Notes on the Postmodern Literary Imagination," *Boundary 2* 1, 1: 147–68.

Spanos, William V., Bové, Paul A., and O'Hara, Daniel (eds) (1982) *The Question of Textuality: Strategies of Reading in Contemporary American Criticism*, Bloomington: Indiana University Press.

Sparshott, Francis E. (1967) "Truth in Fiction," *Journal of Aesthetics and Art Criticism* 26, 1: 3–7.

—— (1986) "The Case of the Unreliable Author," *Philosophy and Literature* 10, 2: 145–67.

Spivak, Gayatri (1978) "Feminism and Critical Theory," *Women's Studies International Quarterly* 1, 3: 241–6.

—— (1980) "Revolutions That As Yet Have No Model," *Diacritics* 10, 4: 29–49.

—— (1985) "Three Women's Texts and a Critique of Imperialism," *Critical Inquiry* 12, 1: 243–61.

Srivastava, Aruna (1986) "'The Empire Strikes Back': Salman Rushdie on Language, History and the Colonized in *Shame* and *Midnight's Children*," paper to Canadian Comparative Literature Association, Winnipeg.

Stark, John (1975) "Alienation and Analysis in Doctorow's *The Book of Daniel*," *Critique* 16, 3: 101–10.

Steinberg, Cobbett (1976) "History and the Novel: Doctorow's *Ragtime*," *Denver Quarterly* 10, 4: 125–30.

Steiner, Wendy (1985) "Intertextuality in Painting," *American Journal of Semiotics* 3, 4: 57–67.

Stern, Daniel (1971) "The Mysterious New Novel" in Hassan (1971a): 22–37.

Stevick, Philip (1981) *Alternative Pleasures: Postrealist Fiction and the Tradition*, Urbana: University of Illinois Press.

Strawson, P. F. (1963) "On Referring" in Caton (1963): 162–93.

Struever, Nancy S. (1985) "Historical Discourse" in van Dijk (1985a): 249–71.

Sukenick, Ronald (1985) *In Form: Digressions on the Act of Fiction*, Carbondale and Edwardsville: Southern Illinois University Press.

Suleiman, Susan Rubin (1983) *Authoritarian Fictions: The Ideological Novel as a Literary Genre*, New York: Columbia University Press.

—— (1986) "Naming a Difference: Reflections on 'Modernism versus Postmodernism' in Literature" in Fokkema and Bertens (1986): 255–70.

Sussman, Herbert L. (ed.) (1983, 1984) *At the Boundaries*, Boston, Mass.: Northeastern University Press.

Swan, Susan (1983) *The Biggest Modern Woman of the World*, Toronto: Lester & Orpen Dennys.

Swift, Graham (1983) *Waterland*, London: Heinemann.

Tafuri, Manfredo (1980) *Theories and History of Architecture*, London: Granada.

Tani, Stefano (1984) *The Doomed Detective: The Contribution of the Detective Novel to Postmodern American and Italian Fiction*, Carbondale and Edwardsville: Southern Illinois University Press.

Tanner, Tony (1971) *City of Words: American Fiction 1950–1970*, New York: Harper & Row.

Taylor, Ronald (ed.) (1977) *Aesthetics and Politics*, London: New Left Books.

Thiher, Allen (1984) *Words in Reflection: Modern Language Theory and Postmodern Fiction*, Chicago, Ill.: University of Chicago Press.

Thomas, Audrey (1984) *Intertidal Life*, Toronto: Stoddart.

Thomas, D. M. (1981) *The White Hotel*, Harmondsworth: Penguin.

Thompson, Hunter S. (1973) *Fear and Loathing: On the Campaign Trail '72*, San Francisco, Calif.: Straight Arrow Books.

Thompson, John O. (1981) "Real Pictures, Real Pleasures?" *Screen Education* 38: 89–94.

Thurley, Geoffrey (1983) *Counter-Modernism in Current Critical Theory*, London: Macmillan.

Todd, Richard (1986) "The Presence of Postmodernism in British Fiction: Aspects of Style and Selfhood" in Fokkema and Bertens (1986): 99–117.

Todorov, Tzvetan (1981a) *Introduction to Poetics*, trans. Richard Howard, Minneapolis: University of Minnesota Press.

—— (1981b) "The Last Barthes," trans. Richard Howard, *Critical Inquiry* 7, 3: 449–54.

Tompkins, Jane (ed.) (1980a) *Reader Response Criticism: From Formalism to Post-Structuralism*, Baltimore, Md: Johns Hopkins University Press.

—— (1980b) "The Reader in History: The Changing Shape of Literary Response" in Tompkins (1980a): 201–32.

Toulmin, Stephen (1972) *Human Understanding*, Princeton, NJ: Princeton University Press.

—— (1982) "The Construal of Reality: Criticism in Modern and Postmodern Science," *Critical Inquiry* 9, 1: 93–111.

Trenner, Richard (ed.) (1983) *E. L. Doctorow: Essays and Conversations*, Princeton, NJ: Ontario Review Press.

Turner, Joseph W. (1979) "The Kinds of Historical Fiction," *Genre* 12, 3: 333–55.

Ulmer, Gregory L. (1985) *Applied Grammatology: Post(e)-Pedagogy from Jacques Derrida to Joseph Beuys*, Baltimore, Md and London: Johns Hopkins University Press.

van Dijk, Teun A. (ed.) (1985a) *Handbook of Discourse Analysis: Vol. I: Disciplines of Discourse: Vol. IV: Discourse Analysis in Society*, London and New York: Academic Press.

van Dijk, Teun A. (1985b) "Introduction: The Role of Discourse Analysis in Society" in van Dijk (1985a): 1–8.

van Eyck, Aldo (1969) "The Interior of Time" in Jencks and Baird (1969): 171.

Vattimo, Gianni (1983) "Dialettica, differenza, pensiero debole" in Vattimo and Rovatti (1983): 12–28.

—— (1985) *La fine della modernità: Nichilismo ed ermeneutica nella cultura post-moderna*, Milano: Garzanti.

Vattimo, Gianni and Rovatti, Pier Aldo (eds) (1983) *Il Pensiero Debole*, Milano: Feltrinelli.

Veyne, Paul (1971) *Comment on écrit l'histoire*, Paris: Seuil.

Villemaire, Yolande (1980) *La Vie en prose*, Montréal: Les Herbes Rouges.

—— (1983) *La Constellation du cygne*, Montréal: Editions de la pleine lune.

Vonnegut, Kurt, Jr (1969) *Slaughterhouse-Five or The Children's Crusade: A Duty-Dance with Death*, New York: Delacorte.

Wagner, Linda W. (1985) "Toni Morrison: Mastery of Narrative" in Rainwater and Scheick (1985): 190–207.

Walker, Alice (1982) *The Color Purple*, New York: Harcourt Brace Jovanovich.

Wallis, Brian (ed.) (1984a) *Art After Modernism: Rethinking Representation*, New York: New Museum of Contemporary Art; Boston, Mass.: Godine.

Wallis, Brian (1984b) "What's Wrong With This Picture? An Introduction" to Wallis (1984a): xi–xviii.

Walton, Kendall L. (1978) "How Remote Are Fictional Worlds from the Real World?" *Journal of Aesthetics and Art Criticism* 37, 1: 11–23.

Wasson, Richard (1974) "From Priest to Prometheus: Culture and Criticism in the Post-Modernist Period," *Journal of Modern Literature* 3, 5: 1,188–1,202.

Watkins, Evan (1978) *The Critical Act: Criticism and Community*, New Haven, Conn. and London: Yale University Press.

Watson, Ian (1973) *The Embedding*, New York: Scribner.

—— (1983) *Chekhov's Journey*, London: Gollancz.

Watt, Ian (1957) *The Rise of the Novel*, Berkeley: University of California Press.

Waugh, Patricia (1984) *Metafiction: The Theory and Practice of Self-Conscious Fiction*, London and New York: Methuen.

Weber, Ronald (ed.) (1974) *The Reporter as Artist: A Look at the New Journalism Controversy*, New York: Hastings House.

Weber, Ronald (1980) *The Literature of Fact: Literary Nonfiction in American Writing*, Athens, Ohio: Ohio University Press.

Weinstein, Mark A. (1976) "The Creative Imagination in Fiction and History," *Genre* 9, 3: 263–77.

Weintraub, Stanley and Young, Philip (eds) (1973) *Directions in Literary Criticism*, University Park: Pennsylvania State University Press.

West, Cornel (1982–3) "Fredric Jameson's Marxist Hermeneutics," *Boundary 2* 11, 1 and 2: 177–200.

White, Hayden (1971) "The Culture of Criticism" in Hassan (1971a): 55–69.

—— (1973) *Metahistory: The Historical Imagination in Nineteenth-Century Europe*, Baltimore, Md: Johns Hopkins University Press.

—— (1976) "The Fictions of Factual Representation" in Fletcher (1976): 21–44.

—— (1978a) "The Historical Text as Literary Artifact" in Canary and Kozicki (1978): 41–62.

—— (1978b) *Tropics of Discourse: Essays in Cultural Criticism*, Baltimore, Md: Johns Hopkins University Press.

—— (1980) "The Value of Narrativity in the Representation of Reality," *Critical Inquiry* 7, 1: 5–27.

—— (1981) "The Narrativization of Real Events," *Critical Inquiry* 7, 4: 793–8.

—— (1984) "The Question of Narrative in Contemporary Historical Theory," *History and Theory* 23, 1: 1–33.

—— (1986) "Historical Pluralism," *Critical Inquiry* 12, 3: 480–93.

White, Morton (1963) "The Logic of Historical Narration" in Hook (1963): 3–31.

Widdowson, Peter (ed.) (1982) *Re-Reading English*, London: Methuen.

Wiebe, Rudy (1973) *The Temptations of Big Bear*, Toronto: McClelland & Stewart.

—— (1977) *The Scorched-Wood People*, Toronto: McClelland & Stewart.

Wilde, Alan (1981) *Horizons of Assent: Modernism, Postmodernism, and the Ironic Imagination*, Baltimore, Md: Johns Hopkins University Press.

—— (1985) "Shooting for Smallness: Limits and Values in Some Recent American Fiction," *Boundary 2* 13, 2–3: 343–69.

Williams, Brooke (1985) *History and Semiotic*, Toronto: Toronto Semiotic Circle Prepublications.

Williams, John (1973) "Fact in Fiction: Problems for the Historical Novelist," *Denver Quarterly* 7, 4: 1–12.

Williams, Nigel (1985) *Star Turn*, London and Boston, Mass.: Faber & Faber.

Williams, Raymond (1960) *Culture and Society 1780–1950*, Garden City, NY: Doubleday.

—— (1977) *Marxism and Literature*, Oxford: Oxford University Press.

—— (1983) *Keywords: A Vocabulary of Culture and Society*, rev. edn, London: Flamingo, Fontana.

Willis, Ellen (1984) "Radical Feminism and Feminist Radicalism" in Sayres *et al.* (1984): 91–118.

Willis, Susan (1984) "Eruptions of Funk: Historicizing Toni Morrison" in Gates (1984a): 263–83.

—— (1985) "Black Women Writers: Taking a Critical Perspective" in G. Greene and Kahn (1985): 211–37.

Wimsatt, W. K., Jr (1954) *The Verbal Icon*, Lexington: University of Kentucky Press.

Wolf, Christa (1982) *No Place on Earth*, trans. Jan Van Heurck, New York: Farrar, Straus, & Giroux.

—— (1984) *Cassandra: A Novel and Four Essays*, trans. Jan Van Heurck, London: Virago.

Wolfe, Tom (1968) *The Electric Kool-Aid Acid Test*, New York: Farrar, Straus, & Giroux.

—— (1970) *Radical Chic and Mau-Mauing the Flak Catchers*, New York: Farrar, Straus, & Giroux.

—— (1981) *From Bauhaus to Our House*, New York: Farrar, Straus, & Giroux.

Woolf, Virginia (1945) *A Room of One's Own*, Harmondsworth: Penguin.

Wylder, Delbert E. (1969) "Thomas Berger's *Little Big Man* as Literature," *Western American Literature* 3: 273–84.

Young, Robert (ed.) (1981a) *Untying the Text: A Post-Structuralist Reader*, Boston, Mass., London and Henley: Routledge & Kegan Paul.

Young, Robert (1981b) "Post-Structuralism: An Introduction" to Young (1981a): 1–28.

Zavarzadeh, Mas'ud (1976) *The Mythopoeic Reality: The Postwar American Nonfiction Novel*, Urbana: University of Illinois Press.

Zeidler, Eberhardt (1987) Panel on "Post-Modernism: From the Past into the

Future," at University College Symposium on "Our Postmodern Heritage", Toronto.

Zimmerman, Bonnie (1985) "What Has Never Been: An Overview of Lesbian Feminist Criticism" in G. Greene and Kahn (1985): 177–210.

Ziolkowski, Theodore (1969) "Toward a Post-Modern Aesthetics?" *Mosaic* 2, 4: 112–19.

Zurbrugg, Nicholas (1986) "Postmodernity, *Métaphore manquée*, and the Myth of the Trans-avant-garde," *SubStance* 48: 68–90.

INDEX

Absalom! Absalom!, 67, 88, 131
Ackroyd, Peter, 14–15, 139, 156
Adami, 54
Adler, Louise, 96, 192
Adorno, Theodor, 25–6, 182, 207, 208, 211, 217, 218
aestheticism, *see* modernism
Afro-American, *see* black
ahistorical, *see* history
Allen, Woody, 44
Alloula, Malek, 68
Alter, Robert, 41, 52
Althusser, Louis, 69, 85, 112, 138, 161, 167, 178, 188, 189, 211, 212
Altieri, Charles, 38, 51, 177
Amore, 10
analytic philosophy, 15, 53, 96, 144, 147–8, 226
analytico-referential discourse, 74–5, 78, 82, 86
Angenot, Marc, 127
Annales school, 95, 129
Antichthon, 16, 58, 114, 149
Antin, David, 38, 118, 226
Antiphonary, The, 192
Aquin, Hubert, 192
Arac, Jonathan, 212
Arakawa, Shosaku, 9, 54, 127
architecture, *see* modernism, in architecture; postmodernism, in architecture
Aristotle, 106, 108, 152, 210
Armies of the Night, The, 117, 202
Armitage, Karole, 228
Aron, Jean Paul, 95
Aronowitz, Stanley, 62
Arvon, Henri, 215
Ashbery, John, 121, 177
Asher, Michael, 9
Atwood, Margaret, 59, 139

authority/authenticity, xii, xiii, 11, 16, 35, 46, 50, 52, 57, 58, 60, 62, 66, 76, 77, 81, 84, 108, 109, 116, 121, 122, 129, 131, 138, 175, 176, 182, 184, 185, 190, 192, 202, 209, 210, 211, 220, 228
autobiography, 9, 60, 62, 70, 162–3, 164, 171, 172, 224
autonomy, ix, 43, 46, 51, 52, 53, 54, 56, 57, 60, 93, 94, 95, 108, 112, 124, 125, 127, 140, 141, 155, 158, 159, 167, 168, 169, 177, 225, 226, 228, 230
auto-representation, 41, 106, 119, 153, 155, 227
avant-garde, 18–19, 23–4, 32, 47, 177, 217, 218–19, 230

Baird, George, 28
Bakhtin, Mikhail, 54, 58, 80, 100–1, 126, 180, 183, 210
Banfield, Ann, 148
Banville, John, 9, 19, 43, 59, 60, 78, 93, 113, 142, 150, 184, 186, 190, 227
Barber, Bruce Alistair, 204, 218
Barilli, Renato, 225
Barnes, Julian, 77, 139
Barth, John, 4, 14, 17, 49, 50, 125, 126, 131, 132, 150
Barthes, Roland, xiii, 8, 10, 13, 21, 38, 53, 54, 60, 66, 76–7, 80–1, 100, 109, 126, 128, 144, 149, 153, 172, 203
Bataille, Georges, 223
Batsleer, Janet *et al.*, 40, 68, 202
Baudrillard, Jean, 6, 8, 13, 53, 189, 222, 223–4, 228, 229, 230
Bayley, John, 57
Becker, Carl, 122
Beckett, Samuel, 43
Beebe, Maurice, 50
Begnal, Michael, H., 50

Bellow, Saul, 131
Belsey, Catherine, 53, 54–5, 68, 70, 80, 99, 128, 165, 167, 169, 180, 182, 193, 220–1
Benjamin, Walter, 80, 181, 211, 227
Bennett, Susan, 130
Bennett, Tony, 79–80, 206, 224
Benveniste, Émile, 82, 85, 91, 151, 164, 168–70, 189
Berger, John, 76, 139, 180–1, 182, 183–4, 190, 213, 226
Berger, Thomas, 20, 132
Berio, Luciano, 93
Berkert, Heribert, 228
Bernstein, Charles, 222
Bertens, Hans, 8, 38, 40, 41, 52
Bertoff, Warner, 112
Bhabha, Homi K., 200
Bible, 113, 151; Book of Daniel, 137–8
Biggest Modern Woman of the World, The, 16–17
binary oppositions, 12, 18, 20, 42, 47, 49, 50, 61, 62, 65, 113, 154
biography, 9–10, 16, 60, 61, 70, 79, 118, 130, 172, 174, 224
Bird, Jon, 91
Biroli, Robert Pirzio, 30–1
black (theory and practice), xii, 16–17, 35, 44, 54, 61–5, 68, 71, 85, 89–90, 91, 131, 134–5, 137, 150, 151–2, 196–8, 199–200, 207, 217, 226, 230
Blackout, 160
Blake, Peter, 39
Block, 91
Bloom, Harold, 34
Boelhower, William, 71
Bofill, Ricardo, ix, 4, 27, 40
Bois, Yve-Alain, 61, 142
Book of Daniel, The, xii, 18, 23, 44, 56, 84, 114, 137–9, 185, 201–3, 215
Booth, Wayne C., 217
Borden, Lizzie, 55
Borges, Jorge Luis, 128
Bové, Paul, A., 215, 227
Bradbury, Malcolm, 14, 42, 50, 117, 130
Bradley, David, 200
Braudel, Fernand, 95, 129, 173
Braudy, Leo, 90, 95, 106
Brazil, 4–5
Brecht, Bertolt, 7, 8, 18, 35, 80, 86, 88, 156, 181, 201, 203, 206, 210, 211, 218–21
Broadbent, Geoffrey, 25
Brooke-Rose, Christine, 4
Brooks, Peter, 144
Buchloh, Benjamin H. D., 208, 218
Buck-Morss, Susan, 212
Buford, Bill, 203
Bürger, Peter, 213
Burgess, Anthony, 118, 139
Burgin, Victor, 12, 14, 38, 40, 191, 195, 226, 228
Burning Water, 114, 153

Butler, Christopher, 20, 52, 117
Byerman, Keith E., 68–9, 134, 151

Cage, John, 4
Calinescu, Matei, 6, 8, 49, 126, 205
Calvino, Italo, 127–8
capitalism, xiii, 3, 4, 6, 7, 12, 18, 23, 25, 31, 41, 47, 50, 61–2, 66–7, 76, 89, 129, 131, 134, 136, 137, 140, 188, 204, 207, 210, 212, 215–16, 217, 219, 222, 224, 230; *see also* Marx(ism); politics
Capote, Truman, 115
Caramello, Charles, 3, 37, 60, 144
Carmen, 51
Carney, 61
Carpentier, Alejo, 121–2, 216
Carrard, Philippe, 91
Carroll, Berenice A., 71
Carroll, David, 17, 92, 94, 97, 160, 170, 173–4
Carter, Angela, 61, 71–2, 101
Cassandra, xii, 23, 43, 85, 95, 194–5, 196
Caute, David, 36, 80, 221
center/centralized, 12, 16, 41, 42, 50, 57–73, 77, 85, 130, 159, 171, 180, 194, 198, 214
Chekhov's Journey, 15, 110–11
Chénetier, Marc, 14
China Men, 9, 16, 70, 73, 151, 198
Christensen, Inger, 52, 132
Christian, Barbara, 63, 68
Cixous, Hélène, 54
Clarke, Graham, 62
Clarke, T. J., 91
class, 12, 47, 58, 59, 61–3, 64, 69, 85, 89–90, 131, 134–6, 159, 179, 181, 183, 196–7, 198, 199, 207, 214, 215, 216–17; *see also* Marx(ism)
classical (architecture), 32, 34–5
closure, 23, 42, 45, 54, 57, 59, 94, 101, 121, 124, 127, 174, 176–7
Coetzee, J. M., 77–8, 107–8, 150, 198–9
Cohen, Marvin, 152–3
Cohen, Sande, 96
Collingwood, R. G., 190
Color Purple, The, 70, 134
Coming Through Slaughter, 9
Conrad, Joseph, 130, 135, 155
Conroy, Mark, 185
consciousness industry, 217
consumer culture, *see* mass culture
context(ualize), xi, 10, 12, 15, 18, 23, 25, 29, 32, 34, 35, 39, 40, 41, 44, 45, 46, 52–3, 54, 59, 64, 67, 70, 74–86, 88, 89, 90, 97, 100, 115, 144, 150, 159, 160, 185, 202, 213, 214, 217, 225, 227; *see also* enunciation
continuity, 11, 15, 45, 51, 57, 59, 74–5, 87, 94, 97, 98, 100, 162–3, 177, 192, 204
Coover, Robert, 18, 56, 112, 115, 126, 129, 133, 187, 193–4
Cornillon, Susan Koppelman, 67
Corregidora, 16, 72

Cortázar, Julio, 19, 181, 219
Coward, Rosalind, and Ellis, John, 65, 82, 160, 170, 178, 189, 213
Cox, Christoph, 14
Crimp, Douglas, 11, 159, 190, 191–2
Crosman, Inge, 154, 156
Crosse, Gordon, 51
Crossroads, 118
Crying of Lot 49, The, 130
Culler, Jonathan, 9, 17–18, 68, 70, 80, culture industry, 20–1, 41, 208, 211, 217
Cunningham, Merce, 119

Daiches, David, 43
Daitch, Susan, 63, 110, 139–40, 198, 216
dance, *see* postmodernism, in dance
Danto, Arthur C., 96
Davidson, Donald, 147, 151
Davies, Peter Maxwell, 51
Davis, Douglas, 7, 23, 38, 46, 86
Davis, Lennard, J., 106–7, 179–80
Davis, Natalie Zemon, 192
Death of Artemio Cruz, The, 9–10
decenter, 3, 12, 57–73, 85, 127, 130, 159, 163, 175, 180, 205, 214, 229
de Certeau, xii, 56, 90, 97, 121, 146
deconstruction, xiii, 59, 65, 68, 70, 95, 100, 144, 183, 188, 192, 211
Defoe, Daniel, 77–8, 107–8, 118, 198–9
de Lauretis, Teresa, 10, 16, 68, 70, 75, 85–6, 98, 160, 161, 165, 166–7, 169, 172–3, 174, 175, 200
Deleuze, Gilles, and Guattari, Félix, 59, 66
Derrida, Jacques, 6, 7, 10, 12–13, 14, 17, 38, 53, 54, 55, 58, 59, 60, 65, 66, 79, 81, 94, 96, 97, 98, 100, 127, 141, 145, 149, 150, 159, 189, 205, 214
Detienne, Marcel, 95
Dews, Peter, 150
D'Haen, Theo, 7, 10, 130, 181
dialectic, x, 21, 46, 58, 100, 106, 191, 209, 213, 215, 221
Dickens, Charles, 106, 130–1, 180
difference/different, 6, 12, 21, 38, 39, 42, 47, 57–73, 114, 131, 134, 159, 197, 198, 217
discourse, 14, 16, 54, 69–70, 74–5, 81, 82–3, 84, 89, 93, 98, 99, 111, 119, 125, 126, 128, 130, 134, 140, 142, 165, 169, 172, 177, 178–200, 213, 231
discourse analysis, xiii, 53, 54, 97, 168, 184–5, 226
discursive practices, *see* discourse
Ditsky, John, 136
Doctor Copernicus, 19, 59, 113, 114, 142, 150, 186, 190, 227
Doctorow, E. L., ix, xii, 18, 20, 23, 44, 56, 61–2, 84, 88–90, 93, 111–12, 114, 124, 125, 126, 130, 131, 133–4, 135–9, 145–6, 185, 200, 201–3, 207, 215, 223
document(ary), 10, 15, 16, 50, 56, 79, 92, 96,

100, 115, 118, 122–3, 133, 149, 156, 165, 171, 207
Doležel, Lubomir, 147, 156, 189
Donovan, Josephine, 70
Don Quixote, x, 41, 131, 181
Dos Passos, John, 88, 92, 136
Doyle, Nannie, 46
DuBois, Barbara, 70
DuBois, W. E. B., 44
Dvorak in Love, 88, 132

Eagleton, Terry, 3, 18–19, 23–4, 29, 30, 35, 37, 41, 43, 46, 49, 69–70, 75, 78, 80, 81–2, 86, 134, 159, 178, 184, 206, 207, 212, 214, 218
Earthly Powers, 118
Eco, Umberto, x, 10, 14, 24, 39, 42, 45, 59, 85, 86, 90, 100, 113, 126, 128, 210, 223
Egbert, Donald D., 6
Ehrmann, Jacques, 111
Eisenman, Peter, 26
Eisenstein, Hester, 68
ekphrasis, 121–2
Eliot, T. S., 6, 11, 24, 49, 78, 88, 97, 128, 134, 180, 218
Ellison, Ralph, 134
Ellman, Mary, 67
Embedding, The, 15, 184
enunciation (enunciative or discursive situation), 40, 44, 67, 70, 71, 74–86, 91–2, 115, 150–1, 160, 168, 184, 219–20, 229; *see also* context(ualize)
Enzensberger, Hans Magnus, 217
epic theater, *see* Brecht
ethnic(ity), xii, 12, 17, 32, 35, 59, 61, 62, 65, 71–3, 89–90, 91, 95, 130, 181, 183, 194, 226, 230
Even Cowgirls Get the Blues, 133
Even-Zohar, Itamar, 146
ex-centric, xi, 12, 16, 35, 41–2, 57–73, 85, 95, 114, 130, 134, 179, 194–5, 198, 200, 217, 226, 227, 230
Explosion in a Cathedral, 121–2, 216
extra-textual, 18, 81, 93, 120, 143, 149, 153, 154, 155–6

Falck, Robert, 182
Famous Last Words, ix, 5, 18, 84, 108, 109, 114, 120, 145, 147, 148, 152, 153, 155, 217
Faulkner, William, 67, 131, 134, 160
Federman, Raymond, 14, 52, 58, 202
Fekete, John, 226
feminism (theory and practice), xi–xii, xiii, 15, 16–17, 35, 44, 47, 53, 54, 55, 61–71, 72–3, 80, 85, 91, 95, 96, 97, 100, 110, 134, 139–40, 151, 159, 160, 161, 165, 166, 170, 172–3, 174, 175, 177, 179, 188, 194–5, 196, 198–200, 202, 205, 207, 214, 216, 217, 224, 226, 228, 230
Fetterley, Judith, 69, 80, 198
fiction, *see* historiographic metafiction; metafiction

Fiedler, Leslie, 20, 38, 44
film, *see* postmodernism, in film
Findley, Timothy, ix, 18, 84, 114, 120, 217
Finlay-Pelinski, Marike, 100
Fischer, David Hackett, 87, 96, 109
Fish, Stanley, 13, 45, 119
Fitzsimmons, Matthew A. *et al.*, 94
Flaubert's Parrot, 16, 44, 77, 109
Fleishman, Avrom, 113
Floating Opera, The, 132
Flynn, Elizabeth, A., and Schweickart,
    Patrocinio P., 68
Foe, 77–8, 107–8, 114, 150, 198–9
Fogel, Stanley, 206
Fokkema, Douwe, 21, 43, 44, 48, 51
Foley, Barbara, 88, 105–6, 112, 120, 123, 136,
    137, 191, 203
formalism, *see* modernism; closure;
    structuralism
Foster, Hal, 38, 46
Foucault, Michel, xi, 6–7, 8, 11, 13, 15, 20, 21,
    48, 55, 58, 61, 65, 66, 69, 74, 75, 81, 83, 84,
    86, 90, 96, 97, 98–9, 118, 120, 125, 127, 149,
    158, 159–60, 162–3, 165, 175, 185, 186, 189,
    196, 203, 205, 207, 214, 229
Fowler, Roger, 185, 186
Fowles, John, ix, 11, 20, 45, 47–8, 59, 64–5,
    88, 93, 118, 120, 126, 139, 196, 206, 223
Frampton, Kenneth, 24, 29, 39
Francken, Ruth, 54
Frankfurt School, 80, 204, 212
Frege, Gottlob, 147, 148
French, Philip, 133
French Lieutenant's Woman, The, 5, 20, 44, 45,
    46, 59, 88, 160, 189, 206
Freud, Sigmund, 6, 58, 165, 166–7, 169,
    171–2, 174–6, 225, 226; *see also* psycho-
    analysis
Fried, Albert, 116
Frye, Northrop, 109, 148
Fuentes, Carlos, 9–10, 88, 126, 155

G., 5, 76, 81, 180–1, 182, 183–4, 190, 213, 226
Gaillard, Françoise, 98
Gallop, Jane, 67, 165, 170
García Márquez, Gabriel, ix, 5, 129, 223
Gass, William H., 124, 149, 190
Gates, Henry Louis, Jr, 62, 65, 67, 134
gay/lesbian (theory and practice), xii, 35, 59,
    61–2, 65, 68, 69, 91, 95, 130, 159, 179, 194,
    198, 199, 200, 217, 230
Gay, Peter, 143
gender, 12, 16, 47, 61–71, 107–8, 130, 134,
    159, 160, 161, 165, 169, 172, 174, 175, 179,
    183, 194, 198–200, 216–17, 226; *see also*
    feminism
Genette, Gérard, 153
genius, *see* original(ity); individual(ity)
genre borders, 9–11, 53–4, 59, 60–1, 106–7,
    111, 113, 139, 224–5

Ghose, Zulfikar, 11
Giddens, Anthony, 8, 205
Gilbert, Sandra, and Gubar, Susan, 68,
    134
Gilliam, Terry, 4–5
Gilligan, Carol, 70
Goodman, Nelson, 145, 154
Gossman, Lionel, xii, 15–16, 90
Gottschalk, Louis, 92, 117
Graff, Gerald, 20, 38, 49, 50, 51, 88–9, 119,
    158, 179, 180, 205, 209–10
Graham, Joseph F., 6
Grass, Günther, ix, 93, 129, 197
Graves, Michael, 34, 88, 204
Gravity's Rainbow, 6, 58, 188
Green, Martin, 89
Greenaway, Peter, 23, 92
Greene, Thomas, M., 124
Greer, Colin, 71
Gropius, Walter, 27
Gross, David S., 134
Gruppo, 63, 141, 203
Gutman, Herbert G., 61
gynesis, 165

Haacke, Hans, 182, 211
Habermas, Jurgen, 6, 7, 8, 25, 46, 55, 191,
    205, 208–9, 214, 226, 229, 231
Haidu, Peter, 100
Hamburger, Käte, 148
Hamon, Philippe, 179
Handmaid's Tale, The, 59, 139
Harkness, James, 119, 141
Harrison, Bernard, 7, 83
Harshaw (Hrushovski), Benjamin, 144, 147,
    156
Hassan, Ihab, 3, 11, 15, 20, 38, 48, 49, 50, 59,
    93
Hawksmoor, 14–15, 156, 212
Hawthorne, Nathaniel, 131, 132, 139
Hayman, David, 51
Heath, Stephen, 71, 161
Heidegger, Martin, 6, 66, 141
Heller, Joseph, 126
Hellmann, John, 115, 116
Henderson, Harry B., 106
hermeneutic(s), 35, 125, 127, 147, 154, 156,
    162, 172, 174, 205
hermeticism, *see* modernism
Herzog, 131
heterogeneity, *see* difference
high art, 44, 51, 61, 208, 218, 228
Hill, Walter, 118
Hindess, Barry, 157
Hirst, Paul, 157
historical fiction, 5, 113–15, 120, 145, 212
historical knowledge, xii, 16, 20, 24, 46, 50,
    56, 87–9, 94, 98, 106, 114, 119, 122, 128,
    136, 144, 146, 183, 192, 209, 212, 218, 220,
    223, 225, 227, 230–1

historiographic metafiction, ix, xii, 5–6, 10, 20–1, 22–3, 26, 39, 40, 42, 44, 50, 55, 56, 73, 75, 76, 78, 81, 82, 83–5, 88, 92–4, 97, 98, 105–23, 124–40, 143, 144–57, 160, 164, 167, 168, 172, 177, 179, 180, 183–4, 185, 186–7, 188, 190, 192, 193–4, 198, 202–3, 207, 208, 211, 212, 213, 217, 219, 221, 223, 224, 225, 227, 228

history/historiography, x, xii, 4, 5, 9, 11, 12, 15–16, 17, 18, 19, 20, 21, 22, 24–5, 26, 28, 29, 30, 33, 34, 39, 40, 42, 43, 44, 46, 47, 51–61, 63–4, 67, 69–71, 75, 79–80, 82, 84–6, 87–101, 105–23, 124–40, 141, 143–57, 158–60, 162–4, 165–7, 172, 173–4, 175, 177–9, 181, 187, 189, 190–1, 192–8, 201–3, 205, 208, 209, 212–14, 216–18, 220, 221, 223–5, 227, 230–1; fact vs. event, x, xii, 89, 92–4, 122, 150–1, 153, 154, 225

Hoffmann, Gerhard, 58
Hoffmann, Gerhard *et al.*, 40
Hohendahl, Peter, 17
Holder, Alan, 132
Holloway, John, 106
Hollowell, John, 58, 115
Home Game, 61
Hough, Graham, 111
Hubbard, William, 26, 31
Hull, Gloria, 68
humanism, xi, xii, 4, 6, 8, 11, 13, 19, 43, 46, 51, 52, 56, 58, 68–9, 70, 75, 83, 99, 100, 126, 127, 129, 158–9, 163, 166, 167, 169, 172, 176–7, 178–200, 205, 207, 208, 211, 222, 224, 226, 227, 228, 229, 230; and positivism, xi, 6, 19, 58–9, 95, 106, 167, 186, 192, 193
Hurston, Zora Neale, 67, 134
Husserl, Edmund, 78
Hutcheon, Linda, x, 11, 41, 52, 66, 129
Huyssen, Andreas, 16, 25, 41, 43, 49, 65, 66, 71, 74, 159, 201, 205, 214, 217, 218, 227
hybrid, *see* difference

ideological/ideology, x, xii, xiii, 8, 13, 17, 18, 21, 23–6, 28, 33, 35, 36, 40, 50, 62, 64, 67–8, 76, 80, 81, 82, 85, 91, 94, 98, 106, 111, 112, 114, 115, 117, 120, 121, 129, 136, 141, 156, 159, 165, 166, 167, 169, 170, 177, 178–200, 201, 203, 205–7, 209, 211–12, 217–18, 219, 220–1, 222, 224–5, 227, 228, 230
individual(ity), xiii, 11, 26, 42, 46, 58, 59, 75, 76, 81, 82, 84, 95, 98, 99, 113, 129, 158, 166, 167, 173, 180, 188, 189, 191, 194, 197, 202, 205–6, 211, 218, 226
Infernal Desire Machines of Doctor Hoffman, The, 71–2, 101
institution(al), 9, 16, 21, 54, 60, 62, 68, 79, 84, 91, 95, 98, 122, 141, 142, 178, 184, 185, 190, 192, 202–3, 213, 218, 224–5, 226, 228
intertext(ual)(ity), x, xii, 15, 16, 40, 54, 67, 75, 79, 92, 105, 112, 116, 117, 118, 120, 121, 124–40, 142–3, 145, 150, 153, 154, 155–6, 162, 163, 167, 171–2, 181, 184, 190, 202, 225, 228
Intertidal life, 70, 139
intratextuality, 154–5
Invisible Cities, 127–8
Irigaray, Luce, 66, 159
irony, x, 4, 5, 11, 16, 19, 20, 23, 24, 26–7, 29, 30, 31, 34, 35, 39, 40, 41, 43, 44, 45, 47, 50, 51, 54, 56, 63, 64, 66–7, 71, 78, 80, 88, 89–90, 94, 109, 114, 118, 121, 124–40, 142, 150, 181, 188, 191, 199, 201, 203, 204, 214, 216, 225, 230

Jacobs, Jane, 30
Jacobus, Mary, 66
Jacques and his Master, 139
Jakobson, Roman, 75
James, Henry, 145, 161, 167
Jameson, Fredric, xii, 3, 6, 7, 11, 15, 18, 19, 23, 24–5, 26–7, 29, 30, 34, 35, 36, 37, 41, 46, 49, 50, 56, 82, 89, 93, 112, 121, 134, 143, 158, 206, 207–8, 211, 212, 213, 214, 215, 218, 226
Jardine, Alice, 66, 160, 165
Jauss, Hans Robert, 75
Jencks, Charles, ix, 16, 22, 28, 29, 31, 33–5, 36, 226
Johns, Jasper, 142, 177
Johnson, Barbara, 67
Johnson, Martin, 35
Johnson, Philip, 23, 33, 39
Jones, Ann Rosalind, 68
Jones, Gayl, 16, 72
Josipovici, Gabriel, 50, 51, 80, 107
Joyce, James, 6, 49, 50, 51, 78, 88, 111, 117, 128, 131, 135, 160, 180, 218

Kafka, Franz, 43
Kamuf, Penny, 16, 68
Kawin, Bruce F., 58
Kellman, Stephen G., 52
Kelly, Mary, 53
Keneally, Thomas, 116
Kennard, Jean E., 68
Kennedy, William, 61, 78–9, 83, 186
Kepler, 9, 19, 43, 60, 114, 142, 186, 227
Kermode, Frank, 43, 90–1, 111, 121, 178
Kern, Robert, 125
Kibbins, Gary, 9
Kingston, Maxine Hong, ix, 9, 16, 41, 70–1, 72–3, 151, 198
Kirby, Michael, 119
Kiremidjian, G. D., 128
Kiss of the Spider Woman, 19, 85, 168, 198
Klinkowitz, Jerome, 37, 44, 52
Kogawa, Joy, 72, 198
Köhler, Michael, 38
Kolbowski, Silvia, 66–7, 228
Kosinski, Jerzy, 10
Krafft, John, 120

Kramer, Jonathan D., 37, 93, 182
Krauss, Rosalind, 8, 11, 38, 54, 190
Kress, Gunther, 80, 179
Kress, Gunther and Hodge, Robert, 184
Krieger, Murray, 44, 92, 155
Kripke, Saul, 147, 152
Kristeva, Julie, 8, 66, 126, 177, 189, 194, 217
Kroetsch, Robert, 61, 139
Kroker, Arthur, and Cook, David, 4, 8–9,
    186, 213, 222, 223, 229
Kruger, Barbara, 66, 228
Krysinski, Wladimir, 50
Kuhn, Annette, 170
Kundera, Milan, 139
Kuwabara, Bruce, 31
Kuznetsov, Anatoli, 167, 171–2

Lacan, Jacques, 53, 65, 66, 159, 164, 169–70,
    189, 214; *see also* psychoanalysis
LaCapra, Dominick, xii, 15, 21, 41, 79, 96,
    97–8, 100, 106, 122, 129
Lacoue-Labarthe, Philippe, 20
Lange, Victor, 147
language, *see* linguistic(s)
Lasch, Christopher, 202
Lavis, Georges, 153
Lawrence, D. H., 135
Lawson, Thomas, 208
L.C., 63, 110, 139–40, 198, 216
Le Corbusier, 27, 28
Lefebvre, Henri, 6
Left, *see* politics; Marx(ism)
legitimation, *see* authority
Le Goff, Jacques, and Nora, Pierre, 95
Legs, 5, 78–9, 81, 83, 93, 114, 186
Leitch, Vincent B., 127, 186, 209
Lemaire, Gérard-Georges, 93
Lentricchia, Frank, x, 75, 90, 97, 98, 100
Leo, Vincent, 23
Lerner, Gerda, 71
Le Roy Ladurie, Emmanuel, 91, 92
lesbian, *see* gay/lesbian
Lethen, Helmut, 20
Letters, 131
Levine, George, 106
Levine, Paul, 58, 131, 134, 136, 203
Levine, Sherrie, 77, 119, 140, 190, 228
Lewis, David, 148
Lewis, Mark, 165, 182
Lewis, Philip, 54, 55
Lewis, Thomas E., 146
liberal humanism, *see* humanism
Lindenberger, Herbert, 91, 111
linguistic(s)/languages, 15, 17, 25, 53, 70, 75,
    82–3, 85, 105, 141, 144–57, 164, 168–9, 175,
    182–3, 184, 186, 187, 189, 191, 192, 194,
    197, 199, 207
Little Big Man, 20, 132, 133
Lives of Girls and Women, 9
Lives of the Poets, 31

local, 12, 51, 58, 61, 97, 99, 204
Lodge, David, 2, 14, 51, 60
Longenbach, James, 88
Loon Lake, ix, 61, 84, 135–6, 215–16
Lucas, John, 218
Lucente, Gregory L., 10, 142, 221
Lukács, Georg, 23, 113–15, 204, 212, 214, 218
Lyotard, Jean-François, x, xiii, 6, 7, 8, 13,
    14–15, 20, 25, 43, 46, 48, 50, 53, 54, 55, 56,
    58, 80, 83, 129, 145, 150–1, 152, 155, 205,
    208, 226, 229, 230

MacCabe, Colin, 184
McCaffery, Larry, 5–6, 8, 40, 50, 58, 194, 206
McCallum, Pamela, 122
MacCannell, Dean, and MacCannell, Juliet
    Flower, 54, 90
McCarthy, Mary, 145
McConnell, Frank, 134
McCormick, Carlo, 227
Macdonell, Diane, 184, 213, 214
McGinn, Colin, 147
McHale, Brian, 38, 50, 130
Macherey, Pierre, 211
MacKinnon, Catherine A., 68, 69
Macksey, Richard, and Donato, Eugenio,
    100, 159
McLuhan, Marshall, 12
Maggot, A., ix, 20, 40, 47–8, 59, 64–5, 106,
    109, 118, 120, 196
Mailer, Norman, 115, 117, 202
Major, Clarence, 206
Malmgren, Carl Darryl, 5, 154
Manganelli, Giorgio, 10, 142
Mann, Thomas, 50, 88, 128, 131
Manual for Manuel, A., 19, 181, 219
Marcuse, Herbert, 206
margin(al)(ize), 12, 16, 42, 49, 57–73, 96, 108,
    110, 114, 130, 179, 187, 194–5, 198, 199, 200
Margolis, Joseph, 148
Marks, Elaine, and de Courtivron, Isabelle,
    68
Martin, Richard, 93–4, 196
Martin, Wallace, 121
Marx(ism), xiii, 6, 7, 15, 21, 46, 53, 56, 66, 68,
    69, 70, 80, 87, 89, 91, 92, 93, 96, 97, 98, 100,
    134, 138, 139, 146, 178, 179, 184, 187, 188,
    199, 200, 206, 208, 210–17, 218, 223, 226,
    229, 230
Marxist-Feminist Literature Collective, 68
mass culture, 6, 7, 12, 21, 25–6, 41, 49, 61, 86,
    137, 210, 212, 218, 222, 225, 228, 230–1
Massumi, Brian, 66
master narrative/meta-narrative, x, 6, 7, 13,
    20, 46, 50, 56, 191, 229
Mazurek, Raymond A., 112, 133, 187, 193–4
Mazzaro, Jerome, 38, 182
Mellard, James M., 52
Menna, Filiberto, 120
metafiction, ix, 5–6, 17, 40, 41, 42, 44, 45, 52,

53, 56, 81, 94, 99, 108, 109, 110, 114, 115, 121, 124, 128, 132, 140, 142, 145, 149, 151, 153, 154, 155, 160, 161, 166, 170, 172, 179, 181, 183, 187, 206; *see also* historiographic metafiction
meta-narrative, *see* master narrative
Metscher, Thomas, 80
Michals, Duane, 177
Midnight's Children, xii, 5, 11, 18, 44, 59, 69, 72, 81, 92, 94, 114, 118, 129, 161–4, 168, 177, 180, 189, 190
Mies van der Rohe, 28
Miller, J. Hillis, 87
Miller, Nancy K., 68
Mink, Louis O., xii, 56, 90, 121, 193
Mitchell, Juliet, 67, 170
Mitchell, Juliet, and Rose, Jacqueline, 170
Mitchell-Kernan, Claudia, 67
Mitchell, W. J. T., 181
modernism, ix, xi, 4, 23–4, 37, 38, 42, 43, 56, 78, 81, 108, 112, 118, 119, 125, 140, 141–2, 144, 157, 179, 185, 204, 205, 207, 217–18, 225, 230, 231; in architecture, 23, 25, 26, 27–8, 39, 40, 60, 194, 204; in literature, xii, 11, 23–4, 38, 40, 59, 66, 78, 117, 160, 212; vs. postmodernism, xi, 7–8, 11, 18–19, 20, 23–4, 26–7, 28–32, 37–8, 40–1, 43, 48–53, 59, 60, 88, 90, 101, 112, 119, 125, 140, 141–2, 144, 146, 194, 204
Moi, Toril, 62, 68, 69, 73, 217
Moore, Charles, ix, 27, 31–3, 40, 231
Morante, Elsa, 221
Morgan, Robert P., 140
Morgan, Robin, 62
Morrison, Toni, 50, 63–4, 68–9, 85, 125, 131, 151–2, 186
Moser, Walter, 17
Mulvey, Laura, 69, 170
Mumbo Jumbo, 16, 196
Munich, Adrienne, 67
Munro, Alice, 9
Munz, Peter, 122
Musarra, Ulla, 128
music, *see* postmodernism, in music
myth, 16, 24, 26, 48, 50, 88, 101, 134

Nabokov, Vladimir, 51
Name of the Rose, The, x, 10, 14, 20, 44, 59, 100, 113, 128, 210
naming, 151–2, 183–4
narrative/narrativization, xii, 5, 11, 12, 17, 55, 56, 59, 61, 82, 84, 92, 93, 96–8, 106, 111, 112, 115, 117–18, 121–2, 128–9, 136–7, 143, 150–1, 160–1, 166, 171, 172, 183, 192–3, 227, 231
Nead, Lynda, 69
negative dialectics, 212, 218–19
Nelson, Cary, 185
neo-avant-garde, xii
neo-baroque, 4

neoconservative, xiii, 8, 46, 205, 207, 208–9, 222, 226
New Art History, 91, 195
New Historicism, xiii, 91, 100, 195
New Journalism, 93, 115–17
Newman, Charles, 3, 6, 13, 15, 37, 42, 49, 51, 57, 58, 125, 156, 194, 209, 213, 222
New Novel, New New Novel (*nouveau roman*), xii, 4, 14, 40, 52, 108, 160, 165, 202
Newton, Judith Lowder, 68
Niesz, Anthony J., and Holland, Norman N., 77
Nietzsche, Friedrich, 6, 28, 58, 66, 90, 98, 99, 162, 187, 223, 230
Nights at the Circus, 61, 114
Nochlin, Linda, 182
non-fictional novel, 5, 115–17, 119, 132, 202
No Place on Earth, 108–9
Norris, Christopher, 13, 53, 146, 148, 149, 157, 205
nostalgia, xii, xiii, 4, 19, 24, 30, 39, 45, 46, 89, 90, 93, 195, 201, 203, 204, 208, 209, 212, 218, 225, 230
nouveau roman, *see* New Novel
novel, *see* metafiction; historiographic metafiction
Nye, Russel, B., 105

Obasan, 72
Of a Fire on the Moon, 115
Ohmann, Richard, 148, 155
Old Gringo, The, 40, 88, 155
Oliva, Achille Bonito, 12
Ondaatje, Michael, 9, 60, 114
One Hundred Years of Solitude, ix, 5, 129, 197
origin(al)(ity), xii, 11, 23, 26, 46, 57, 58, 76, 81, 87, 110, 126, 129, 136, 172, 190, 191, 211, 220
Orr, Linda, 225
Ortega y Gasset, José, 38, 218
Orvell, Miles, 229
other(ness), 6, 12, 42, 61, 62, 65, 66, 130
Owens, Craig, 10, 59–60, 121, 165, 182, 189

painting, *see* postmodernism, in painting
Pale Fire, 51
Palmer, Richard, 6
paraliterary, 11, 38, 54
Parker, Andrew, 95
parody, x, 4, 5, 11, 16, 19, 20, 22–37, 39, 40, 44, 45, 50, 54, 59, 64, 66–7, 68, 77, 81, 82, 117, 118, 124–40, 175, 176, 182, 190, 192, 204, 207, 210–11, 220, 222, 224, 225
pastiche, 26, 211
Paterson, Janet, 3
Patteson, Richard, 130
Pavese, Cesare, 50
Peckham, Morse, 7
performance, *see* postmodernism, in performance and installations
Perloff, Marjorie, 4, 121

philosophy, *see* postmodernism, in philosophy

photography, *see* postmodernism, in photography

Pistoletto, Michelangelo, 140

politics, xii, xiii, 4, 18, 22–37, 46, 51, 52, 54, 60, 61–5, 69–70, 71, 75, 77, 80, 81, 82, 84, 85–6, 89, 94, 95, 100, 111, 115, 120–1, 141, 150, 158, 160, 163, 165, 170, 178, 179, 181, 182, 184–5, 186, 187, 188, 193–4, 197–200, 201–21, 224, 230; *see also* Marx(ism); neoconservative

Pop Art, 204, 228

Pops, Martin, 9

popular culture, 10, 20–1, 44–5, 132–3

Portoghesi, Paolo, ix, 4, 22, 24, 26, 28, 29, 30, 31, 32, 39, 60, 88, 93, 191, 226

possible worlds, 147, 152

postcolonial, 68, 72, 179, 200, 226, 230

postmodernism: in architecture, ix, xi, 3, 4, 16, 18, 22–37, 38, 39, 40, 41, 45, 52, 60, 61, 86, 88, 93, 101, 125, 128, 186, 194–5, 201, 204, 225, 228, 231; in dance, x, 3, 9, 22, 119, 182, 186, 228, 231; in drama, 38, 231; in fiction, *see* historiographic metafiction; in film, x, xi, 3, 4–5, 9, 19, 23, 26, 35, 41, 44, 51, 55, 61, 86, 88, 92, 118, 160, 165, 228, 231; and modernism, *see* modernism vs. postmodernism; in music, x, 3, 9, 22, 24, 26, 35, 51, 88, 93, 126, 182, 228, 231; in painting, x, 3, 9, 10, 20, 21, 22, 24, 26, 35, 38, 53, 61, 127, 128, 140, 165, 177, 182, 225, 227–8, 231; in performance and installations, 18, 60, 86; in philosophy, 3, 12, 15, 17, 19, 21, 50–1, 58, 151, 157, 159, 184, 191, 205, 229; in photography, x, 7, 10, 20, 23, 38, 53–4, 60, 77, 119, 159, 177, 190, 207, 228, 231; poetics of, ix, 3–21, 38, 48, 144, 158–9, 182, 186, 222, 224–5, 226, 231; in poetry, 9, 17, 38, 51, 61, 177, 182, 231; in sculpture, 3, 10, 20, 61; in television, 3; in theory, ix, xi, 10, 13, 14–21, 25, 38, 53–6, 60, 70, 71, 78–9, 81, 83–4, 85, 94, 99–100, 111, 144, 150, 157, 158–9, 165, 188–9, 222, 226, 228–9, 231; in video art, x, 3, 22, 23, 38, 46, 61, 86

poststructuralism, xii, xiii, 15, 53, 54, 55, 68, 70, 81, 96, 99, 149, 160, 165, 166, 167, 170, 177, 188, 194, 205, 226

Pound, Ezra, 78, 88, 145, 148, 149, 155, 183, 218

power, xi, 9, 16, 18, 45, 62, 69, 86, 96, 98, 101, 120, 176, 178–200, 203, 205, 207, 209, 214, 216, 224, 229

Prince, Richard, 190

problematize, xi, xiii, 21, 40, 46, 47, 52, 55, 70, 78, 84, 87–101, 106, 111, 112, 117, 121, 122, 141, 144, 145, 152, 160–1, 166, 169, 176, 183, 185, 192, 208, 209, 212, 218, 220, 221, 224–5, 227, 229, 231

psychoanalysis, 3, 15, 53, 58, 67–8, 130, 166–7, 170, 172, 174, 175, 189, 199, 230; *see also* Freud; Lacan

Public Burning, The, 18, 56, 93, 106, 112, 114, 115, 121, 128, 133, 187, 193–4, 212

Puig, Manuel, 19, 85, 168, 199

Pullin, Faith, 68

purism, *see* modernism, in architecture

Pütz, Manfred, 52

Pynchon, Thomas, 6, 47, 58, 120, 125, 130, 131, 133, 157, 192

Quarrington, Paul, 61

Rabinowitz, Peter J., 155

race, 12, 16, 59, 61–5, 70, 71, 72–3, 85, 98–90, 130, 134–5, 151–2, 159, 194, 196–9, 203, 216–17

Radhakrishnan, R., 13, 50

Ragtime, 5, 18, 40, 44, 61–2, 84, 89–90, 92, 114, 121, 130, 135, 136–7, 145–6, 147, 153, 203, 212

Rajchman, John, 58, 99

Rauschenberg, Robert, 9, 10, 11, 177

Rawson, Claude, 209

reader/reading/receiver, 5, 18, 36, 38, 45, 67, 68, 76–8, 79–80, 81, 83, 85, 86, 89, 91, 115, 117, 118, 120, 126, 156, 160, 161, 163, 167, 169, 172–3, 174, 198, 202–3, 206–7, 220–1, 223

realism, xii, 10, 15, 20, 43, 44, 45, 51, 59, 61, 75, 84, 91, 105, 109, 115, 117, 125, 129, 141, 147, 148, 149, 153, 161, 172, 173, 177, 180, 188, 210, 214, 219, 220, 225, 228, 229

Reed, Ishmael, ix, 16, 50, 70, 125, 126, 130–1, 134, 135, 196–8

Rees, A. L., and Borzello, Frances, 91

reference/referent(ial), xiii, 19, 20, 24, 40, 46, 52, 56, 57, 89, 93, 106, 117, 118–21, 127, 133, 141–57, 224, 225, 228, 229–30, 231

Reiss, Timothy J., 74–5, 83, 101

representation(s), xii, 7, 15, 17, 40, 41, 43, 52, 54, 69, 79, 82, 87, 92, 106, 108, 109, 110, 112, 117, 119, 120, 121–2, 125, 141, 142, 143, 144, 148, 156, 160, 161, 165, 172, 177, 180, 182, 183, 189, 192, 206, 207, 212, 228, 230

Return of Martin Guerre, The, 88, 192

revolutionary, ix, xiii, 63, 80, 86, 110, 129, 181, 182, 183, 198, 201, 206, 209, 210, 216, 218, 222, 230

Ricardou, Jean, 14

Richards, I. A., 109, 148

Ricoeur, Paul, 87, 92, 95–6, 100, 122, 147

Riffaterre, Michael, 126, 143

Rivers, Larry, 127

Robbe-Grillet, Alain, 14

Robbins, Tom, 133

Robertson, Mary F., 121

Robinson, Lillian S., and Vogel, Lise, 88

Rochberg, George, 11, 88, 93, 126, 182
romantic(ism), 24, 26, 42, 51, 52, 78, 108, 109, 179, 202, 205, 211, 217
Rorty, Richard, 13, 14, 25, 54, 55, 58, 145, 147, 148, 205
Rosenberg, Harold, 210, 211, 217
Rosler, Martha, viii, 14, 207, 228
Rossi, Aldo, ix
Rosso, Stefano, 39, 45, 86
Roth, Martin, 48
Running in the Family, 60, 114
Rushdie, Salman, ix xii, 9, 11, 47, 59, 60, 69, 72, 81, 92, 98, 108, 120, 126, 129, 161, 179, 187, 227
Russell, Charles, 6, 11, 13, 24, 25, 35, 36, 38, 41, 42, 47, 50, 51, 59, 84, 145, 181, 218, 219
Russian Formalism, 219, 227
Ruthven, K. K., 21, 66, 69
Ryan, Michael, 209, 224
Rzewski, Frederic, 182

Saad, Gabriel, 122
Said, Edward W., xii, 16, 24, 34, 54, 58, 61, 66, 69, 75, 81, 86, 98, 124, 129, 130, 158, 167, 189, 224
Sarduy, Severo, 4
Sauro, Carlos, 51
Saussure, Ferdinand de, 25, 55, 65, 70, 78, 141, 147, 148–9, 150
Sayres, Sohnya *et al.*, 57
Schafer, Roy, 174
Schaffer, E. S., 58
Schindler's Ark, 116
Schmid, Herta, 38
Schmidt, S. J., 146
Scholes, Robert, 58, 116, 183
Schulz, Max, 132
Scorched-Wood People, The, 16, 117, 147
Scott, Chris, 58
Scott, Walter, 106
sculpture, *see* postmodernism, in sculpture
Seamon, Roger, G., 105
Searle, John R., 119, 147, 148, 155
Seelye, John, 136
Segal, George, 93
Sekula, Allan, 207
(self-)reflexivity/self-consciousness, ix, x, xiii, 5, 12, 13, 14, 16, 17, 19, 22, 33, 35, 40, 41, 43–4, 45, 51, 52, 53, 56, 70, 75, 77, 79, 81, 82, 86, 114, 116, 117, 120, 128, 140, 142, 149, 153, 157, 160, 170, 181–3, 184, 205, 206, 211, 219, 220–1, 223, 224, 225, 227
semiotic(s), x, 21, 25, 33, 35, 39, 41, 53, 54, 82, 85, 90, 96, 99, 100, 122, 144, 146, 147, 156, 157, 161, 189, 218
sexual orientation, *see* gay/lesbian
Shakespeare, William, x, 68, 155, 179, 182, 208
Shame, ix, 9, 60, 72, 92, 106, 108, 120, 179, 187, 188, 206, 227

Shaw, Harry E., 113
Sherman, Cindy, 159, 228
Showalter, Elaine, 67
signifying practices (systems), 13, 21, 74–5, 82, 93, 98, 99, 112, 133, 140, 214, 230
Silverman, Kaja, 68, 159, 160, 165, 166, 168–70, 172, 176
simulacrum, xiii, 223, 228, 229
Siska, William C., 41
sixties, the, xi, 8, 57–8, 61–3, 93, 115–16, 201–3, 212
Skvorecky, Josef, 88, 132
Slaughterhouse-Five, 44, 92, 128, 194
Smart, Robert Augustin, 117
Smith, Barbara, 68
Smith, Barbara Herrnstein, 82, 109, 119
Smith, Paul, 54, 67, 211
Smith, Thomas Gordon, 34–5
Snead, James A., 67
Sollors, Werner, 71
Solomon-Godeau, Abigail, 207, 228
Song of Solomon, 63–4, 67, 131, 134–5, 151–2
Sontag, Susan, 8, 50
Sot-Weed Factor, The, 132, 133
Spacks, Patricia Meyer, 67
Spanos, William V., 38, 51, 52, 88
Sparshott, Francis E., 142, 148
speech-act theory, 76, 168
Spender, Stephen, 48
Spivak, Gayatri, 66, 68
Star Turn, 40, 92, 118, 147, 188, 212, 214
Stark, John, 137
Steinberg, Cobbett, 133
Steiner, Wendy, 140
Stern, Daniel, 6
Stern, Robert, ix, 33
Stockhausen, Karlheinz, 24, 93
Streep, Harry, 182
structuralism, 14, 52, 55, 82, 109, 147, 148–9, 169
Struever, Nancy S., 96, 115
Studhorse Man, The, 139
subject(ivity), xii, 8, 11, 12, 17, 19, 42, 55, 57, 58, 59, 65, 67–8, 70–1, 74–5, 81, 82, 83–6, 90, 98, 106, 117–18, 121, 126, 127, 158–77, 187, 188, 189, 191, 205, 218, 220, 226, 231
Sukenick, Ronald, 14, 40, 42, 71, 93, 94, 156, 186, 210, 211
Sula, 85
Suleiman, Susan Rubin, 4, 16, 38, 66, 180, 215
surfiction, xii, 14, 40, 52, 108, 111, 119, 141, 203
Swan, Susan, 16
Swift, Graham, xi, 15, 55, 61, 117, 123, 184

Tafuri, Manfredo, 101, 218, 226
Tani, Stefano, 20
Tansey, Mark, 140, 227–8
Tar Baby, 68–9, 186

teleology, *see* closure
television, *see* postmodernism, in television
Tel Quel, xii, 53, 126, 141, 203
Temptations of Big Bear, The, 15, 83, 144, 149
Terra Nostra, 212
Terrible Twos, The, 130–1, 196–7
text(ual)(ity), 13, 14, 16. 17, 18, 25, 66, 80–1,
    84, 93, 96, 98, 105, 106, 114, 118–19, 125,
    127, 128–9, 133, 136, 143, 153, 154, 155,
    156, 167, 190, 206, 213, 225, 231
theory, *see* postmodernism, in theory
Thiher, Allen, 17, 51, 125, 126, 128, 129, 141
Thomas, Audrey, 70, 139
Thomas, D. M., xii, 11, 59, 83, 117, 126, 165–7
Thompson, Hunter S., 115
Thompson, John O., 157
Thurley, Geoffrey, 226
Tigerman, Stanley, 4
Tin Drum, The, ix, 94, 121, 129, 197, 206
Todd, Richard, 44, 52
Todorov, Tzvetan, 14, 54, 109
Tompkins, Jane, 108
totalize, xi, 6, 10, 12, 15, 20, 25, 41, 46, 47, 51,
    55, 57, 58, 59, 60, 71, 75, 84, 87, 97, 98, 101,
    116, 133, 164, 166, 169, 175, 177, 186, 194,
    200, 205, 209, 214–15, 217, 224, 229, 231
Toulmin, Stephen, 6
trace, *see* Derrida; document(ary)
transparency, 75, 92, 105, 129, 166, 177, 212,
    219, 229
Trenner, Richard, 44, 93, 130, 136, 146, 200
Tristram Shandy, 41, 162, 181
Twombly, Cy, 9

universal, *see* humanism
USA, 136–7

V., 131
van Dijk, Teun A., 82
van Eyck, Aldo, 29–30
Vattimo, Gianni, 6, 7, 186, 191
Vattimo, Gianni, and Rovatii, Pier Aldo, 191
Venturi, Robert, 31
Veyne, Paul, xii, 56, 80, 90, 106, 111, 153
Vidal, Albert, 60
video art, *see* postmodernism, in video
Vie en Prose, La, 67
Villemaire, Yolande, 67
Volponi, Paolo, 150
Vonnegut, Kurt, Jr, 129, 194
Vreeland, Thomas, 33

Walker, Alice, 63, 70, 134, 200
Wallis, Brian, 230

Walton, Kendall L., 156
Wars, The, 114
Wasson, Richard, 8
Waterland, xi, 15, 55, 108, 117–18, 123, 180,
    214
Watkins, Evan, 17, 48
Watson, Ian, 15, 92, 110–11, 184
Watt, Ian, 162, 179
Waugh, Patricia, 128, 133, 180, 183, 197, 206
weak thought (*pensiero debole*), 7, 186, 191
Weber, Ronald, 116
Weinstein, Mark A., 113
Weiss, Peter, 217
Welcome to Hard Times, 20, 111–12, 133–4
Wesselman, Tom, 10, 127
West, Cornel, 214
Western genre, 20, 132, 133–4, 139
White, Hayden, xii, 14, 15, 56, 88, 90, 94, 96,
    98, 99, 100, 105, 106, 111, 120, 121, 123,
    128, 143–4, 146, 154, 192–3
White Hotel, The, xii, 11, 19, 59, 83, 92, 117,
    121, 160, 161, 165–7, 168–9, 170, 171–7, 189
White, Morton, 96
Wiebe, Rudy, 15, 83, 117, 144, 147, 198
Wilde, Alan, 2, 5, 7, 20, 48, 50, 52, 190
Wilde, Oscar, 96
Williams, Brooke, 122
Williams, John, 114
Williams, Nigel, 118, 147
Williams, Raymond, 8, 178, 213, 214
Willis, Ellen, 62–3
Willis, Susan, 63, 67, 68
Wimsatt, W. K., Jr, and Beardsley, Monroe,
    126
Wittgenstein, Ludwig, 113, 141, 150
Wolf, Christa, xii, 22–3, 43, 66, 85, 93, 95,
    108–9, 129, 194–5
Wolfe, Tom, 27, 31, 58, 115, 202
Wolff, Christian, 182
Woman Warrior, The, ix, 41, 70–1, 72–3
women/women's studies, *see* feminism
Woolf, Virginia, 49, 67, 88, 117, 139, 160
Wylder, Delbert E., 132

Yates, Marie, 53
Yellow Back Radio Broke-Down, 133

Zavarzadeh, Mas'ud, 42, 58, 116, 154, 188,
    192
Zeidler, Eberhardt, 31
Zimmerman, Bonnie, 68
Ziolkowski, Theodore, 9
Zurbrugg, Nicholas, 19, 50